A·N·N·U·A·L E·D·I·T·I·O·N·S

American History Volume I

17th Edition

Pre-Colonial Through Reconstruction

EDITOR

Robert James Maddox (Emeritus)

Pennsylvania State University
University Park

Robert James Maddox, distinguished historian and professor of American history at Pennsylvania State University, received a B.S. from Fairleigh Dickinson University in 1957, an M.S. from the University of Wisconsin in 1958, and a Ph.D. from Rutgers in 1964. He has written, reviewed, and lectured extensively, and is widely respected for his interpretations of presidential character and policy.

McGraw-Hill/Dushkin

530 Old Whitfield Street, Guilford, Connecticut 06437

Visit us on the Internet
http://www.dushkin.com

Credits

1. **The New Land**
   Unit photo—© 2002 by PhotoDisc, Inc.
2. **Revolutionary America**
   Unit photo—Courtesy of the Library of Congress.
3. **National Consolidation and Expansion**
   Unit photo—National Archives.
4. **The Civil War and Reconstruction**
   Unit photo—Courtesy of Library of Congress.

Copyright

Cataloging in Publication Data
Main entry under title: Annual Editions: American History Vol. One: Pre-Colonial Through Reconstruction. 17/E.
1. United States—History—Periodicals. 2. United States—Historiography—Periodicals. 3. United States—Civilization—
Periodicals. I. 1. Maddox, Robert James, comp. II Title: American History, Vol. One: Pre-Colonial Through Reconstruction.
ISBN 0–07–254823-1   973'.5   74-187540   ISSN 0733–3560

Seventeenth Edition

Cover image © 2003 PhotoDisc, Inc.
Printed in the United States of America   1234567890BAHBAH543   Printed on Recycled Paper

Editors/Advisory Board

Members of the Advisory Board are instrumental in the final selection of articles for each edition of ANNUAL EDITIONS. Their review of articles for content, level, currentness, and appropriateness provides critical direction to the editor and staff. We think that you will find their careful consideration well reflected in this volume.

To the Reader

In publishing ANNUAL EDITIONS we recognize the enormous role played by the magazines, newspapers, and journals of the public press in providing current, first-rate educational information in a broad spectrum of interest areas. Many of these articles are appropriate for students, researchers, and professionals seeking accurate, current material to help bridge the gap between principles and theories and the real world. These articles, however, become more useful for study when those of lasting value are carefully collected, organized, indexed, and reproduced in a low-cost format, which provides easy and permanent access when the material is needed. That is the role played by ANNUAL EDITIONS.

Traditional history was written mostly by white males about other white males. Presidents, captains of industry, generals, admirals, and other important figures were deemed the natural subjects for historical inquiry. This is understandable. These men were movers and shakers who influenced the world around them in various ways. Besides, they were the ones most likely to have left the materials conducive to research: diaries, manuscript collections, and the like. Only a few scholars wrote about prominent women, others about black or Indian leaders.

A dramatic change has taken place over the last 30 years. Although traditional history continues to be written and read—a biography of John Adams recently made the best-seller lists—an increasing amount of scholarly work has been devoted to individuals and groups that were previously ignored or mentioned only in passing. The roles of women, gays and lesbians, Native Americans, Hispanics, and Asians, to mention just some, now receive the attention formerly reserved for the white male elite. There also have been several changes in focus. Now scholars examine the lives of ordinary members of these groups as well as of their leaders. And these scholars try to learn not only what was done "to" these people, but how they organized their own lives and, at times, how they sought to change the status quo. In many cases, such inquiry has relied on nontraditional research methods such as oral history instead of concentrating exclusively on written documents.

These "new" histories have greatly enriched our understanding of the past. They have provided alternative viewpoints from which to view events and developments. Earlier books and articles, for instance, tended to view the settlement of the West as a triumphal process of "civilizing" the wilderness, with only a few setbacks along the way. When seen through the eyes of Native Americans, however, the westward movement looked quite different. Those who were not killed in battle or died of diseases spread by whites saw their cultures violently disrupted by forced migrations and, later, confinement to reservations. Unfortunately, much of the new scholarship that appears in books and in professional journals is written in academic jargon that is impenetrable to the lay reader. The seventeenth edition of *Annual Editions: American History, Volume I*, attempts to present a fair sampling both of traditional history and of the new approaches. A criterion for inclusion is that the essays be written in clear, if not always eloquent, prose.

Annual Editions: American History, Volume I, contains a number of features designed to aid students, researchers, and professionals. These include a *topic guide* for locating articles on specific subjects; the *table of contents* abstracts that summarize each essay, with key concepts in bold italics; and a comprehensive *index*. Again, in this edition, *World Wide Web* sites that can be used to further explore the topics are included.

Articles are organized into four units, each preceded by an overview that provides a background for informed reading of the articles, emphasizes critical issues, and presents *key points to consider*.

Every revision of *Annual Editions: American History, Volume I* replaces about 50 percent of the previous articles with new ones. We try to update and improve the quality of the sections, and we would like to consider alternatives that we may have missed. If you find an article that you think merits inclusion in the next edition, please send it to us (or at least send us the citation, so that the editor can track it down for consideration). We welcome your comments about the readings in this volume, and a postage-paid reader response card is included in the back of the book for your convenience. Your suggestions will be carefully considered and greatly appreciated.

Robert James Maddox

Robert James Maddox
Editor

Contents

UNIT 1
The New Land

Nine selections discuss the beginnings of America—the new land from pre-Columbian times, early life of the colonists, Indian revolts, Puritan wives, and the stirrings of liberty and independence.

The concepts in bold italics are developed in the article. For further expansion, please refer to the Topic Guide and the Index.

UNIT 2
Revolutionary America

Eight articles examine the start of the American Revolution. The new land offered opportunities for new ideas that led to the creation of an independent nation.

The concepts in bold italics are developed in the article. For further expansion, please refer to the Topic Guide and the Index.

UNIT 3
National Consolidation and Expansion

Ten selections examine the developing United States, the westward movement of people seeking a new life, the realities of living in early nineteenth-century America, and the first American terrorist.

Unit Overview   96

The concepts in bold italics are developed in the article. For further expansion, please refer to the Topic Guide and the Index.

UNIT 4
The Civil War and Reconstruction

Nine articles discuss the tremendous effects of the Civil War on America. With the abolishment of slavery, the United States had to reconstruct society.

The concepts in bold italics are developed in the article. For further expansion, please refer to the Topic Guide and the Index.

The concepts in bold italics are developed in the article. For further expansion, please refer to the Topic Guide and the Index.

Topic Guide

This topic guide suggests how the selections in this book relate to the subjects covered in your course. You may want to use the topics listed on these pages to search the Web more easily.

On the following pages a number of Web sites have been gathered specifically for this book. They are arranged to reflect the units of this *Annual Edition*. You can link to these sites by going to the DUSHKIN ONLINE support site at *http://www.dushkin.com/online/*.

ALL THE ARTICLES THAT RELATE TO EACH TOPIC ARE LISTED BELOW THE BOLD-FACED TERM.

Adams, John
19. 1796: The First Real Election

African Americans
8. The Right to Marry: *Loving v. Virginia*
11. Jefferson's Secret Life
25. The Lives of Slave Women
26. William W. Brown
28. "The Doom of Slavery": Ulysses S. Grant, War Aims, and Emancipation, 1861–1863
29. Coffee, Bibles & Wooden Legs: The YMCA Goes to War
30. A Gallant Rush for Glory
36. The New View of Reconstruction

Alien and Sedition Acts
7. Penning a Legacy

American Revolution
10. Flora MacDonald
12. Making Sense of the Fourth of July
13. George Washington, Spymaster
14. Founders Chic: Live From Philadelphia

Americas
2. A "Newfounde Lande"
11. Jefferson's Secret Life

Baseball
35. Bats, Balls, and Bullets

Blacks
25. The Lives of Slave Women
36. The New View of Reconstruction

Brown, John
27. The Father of American Terrorism

Brown, William W.
26. William W. Brown

Civil rights
36. The New View of Reconstruction

Civil War
28. "The Doom of Slavery": Ulysses S. Grant, War Aims, and Emancipation, 1861–1863
29. Coffee, Bibles & Wooden Legs: The YMCA Goes to War
30. A Gallant Rush for Glory
31. A Yankee Scarlett O'Hara in Atlanta
32. Between Honor and Glory
33. Jefferson Davis and the Jews
34. Lincoln Takes the Heat
35. Bats, Balls, and Bullets
36. The New View of Reconstruction

Clark, George Rogers
20. Lewis and Clark: Trailblazers Who Opened the Continent

Colonial America
3. Laboring in the Fields of the Lord
5. The Pueblo Revolt
6. Bearing the Burden? Puritan Wives
7. Penning a Legacy
8. The Right to Marry: *Loving v. Virginia*
9. Baptism of Fire

Columbus, Christopher
2. A "Newfounde Lande"

Constitution, U.S.
15. Founding Friendship: Washington, Madison and the Creation of the American Republic
16. Your Constitution Is Killing You
17. Do the People Rule?
21. Chief Justice Marshall Takes the Law in Hand

Culture
1. 1491
3. Laboring in the Fields of the Lord
4. Pocahontas
6. Bearing the Burden? Puritan Wives
8. The Right to Marry: *Loving v. Virginia*
11. Jefferson's Secret Life
24. "All Men & Women Are Created Equal"
35. Bats, Balls, and Bullets

Davis, Jefferson
33. Jefferson Davis and the Jews

Declaration of Independence
12. Making Sense of the Fourth of July

Environment
1. 1491
20. Lewis and Clark: Trailblazers Who Opened the Continent

Exploration
2. A "Newfounde Lande"
20. Lewis and Clark: Trailblazers Who Opened the Continent

Government
7. Penning a Legacy
12. Making Sense of the Fourth of July
14. Founders Chic: Live From Philadelphia
15. Founding Friendship: Washington, Madison and the Creation of the American Republic
16. Your Constitution Is Killing You
17. Do the People Rule?
18. The Whiskey Rebellion
19. 1796: The First Real Election
21. Chief Justice Marshall Takes the Law in Hand
23. Andrew Jackson Versus the Cherokee Nation

World Wide Web Sites

The following World Wide Web sites have been carefully researched and selected to support the articles found in this reader. The easiest way to access these selected sites is to go to our DUSHKIN ONLINE support site at *http://www.dushkin.com/online/*.

AE: American History, Volume 1

The following sites were available at the time of publication. Visit our Web site—we update DUSHKIN ONLINE regularly to reflect any changes.

General Sources

American Historical Association (AHA)
http://www.theaha.org
This site is an excellent source for data on just about any topic in American history. All affiliated societies and publications are noted, and AHA and its links provide material related to myriad fields of history.

American Studies Web
http://www.georgetown.edu/crossroads/asw/
Links to a wealth of Internet resources for research in American studies, from agriculture and rural development, to government, to race and ethnicity, are provided on this eclectic site.

Harvard's John F. Kennedy School of Government
http://www.ksg.harvard.edu
Starting from this home page, click on a huge variety of links to information about American history, politics, and government, including material related to debates of enduring issues.

History Net
http://www.thehistorynet.com/
Supported by the National Historical Society, this site provides information on a wide range of topics. The articles are of excellent quality, and the site has book reviews and even special interviews. It is also frequently updated.

Library of Congress
http://www.loc.gov
Examine this Web site to learn about the extensive resource tools, library services/resources, exhibitions, and databases available through the Library of Congress in many different subfields of government studies.

Smithsonian Institution
http://www.si.edu
This site provides access to the enormous resources of the Smithsonian, which holds some 140 million artifacts and specimens for "the increase and diffusion of knowledge." Learn about American social, cultural, economic, and political history from a variety of viewpoints here.

UNIT 1: The New Land

Early America
http://earlyamerica.com/earlyamerica/index.html
Explore the "amazing world of early America" through early media data at this site. Topics include Pages of the Past, Lives of Early Americans, Notable Women of Early America, Milestone Events, and many more.

1492: An Ongoing Voyage/Library of Congress
http://lcweb.loc.gov/exhibits/1492/
Displays examining the causes and effects of Columbus's voyages to the Americas can be accessed on this Web site. "An

Ongoing Voyage" explores the rich mixture of societies coexisting in five areas of this hemisphere before European arrival. It then surveys the polyglot Mediterranean world at a dynamic turning point in its development.

The Mayflower Web Page
http://members.aol.com/calebj/
The Mayflower Web Page represents thousands of hours of research, organization, and typing; it grows daily. Visitors include everyone from kindergarten students to history professors, from beginning genealogists to some of the most noted genealogists in the nation. The site is a merger of two fields: genealogy and history.

New Mexico's Pueblo Indians
http://members.aol.com/chloe5/pueblos.html
This Web site offers an overview of the history and culture of the Pueblo Indians.

UNIT 2: Revolutionary America

The Early America Review
http://www.earlyamerica.com/review/
Explore the Web site of *The Early America Review,* an electronic journal of fact and opinion on the people, issues, and events of eighteenth-century America. The quarterly is of excellent quality.

House of Representatives
http://www.house.gov
This home page of the House of Representatives will lead to information about current and past House members and agendas, the legislative process, and so on.

National Center for Policy Analysis
http://www.public-policy.org/web.public-policy.org/index.html
Through this site, click onto links to read discussions of an array of topics that are of major interest in the study of American history, from regulatory policy and privatization to economy and income.

Supreme Court/Legal Information Institute
http://supct.law.cornell.edu/supct/index.html
Open this site for current and historical information about the Supreme Court. The archive contains a collection of nearly 600 of the most historical decisions of the Court.

U.S. Founding Documents/Emory University
http://www.law.emory.edu/FEDERAL/
Through this site you can view scanned originals of the Declaration of Independence, the Constitution, and the Bill of Rights. The transcribed texts are also available, as are *The Federalist Papers.*

U.S. Senate
http://www.senate.gov
The U.S. Senate home page will lead to information about current and past Senate members and agendas, legislative activities, committees, and so on.

The White House
http://www.whitehouse.gov/
Visit the home page of the White House for direct access to information about commonly requested federal services, the

www.dushkin.com/online/

White House Briefing Room, and all of the presidents and vice presidents. The "Virtual Library" provides an opportunity to search White House documents, listen to speeches, and view photos.

The World of Benjamin Franklin
http://www.fi.edu/franklin/

Presented by the Franklin Institute Science Museum, "Benjamin Franklin: Glimpses of the Man" is an excellent multimedia site that lends insight into Revolutionary America.

UNIT 3: National Consolidation and Expansion

Consortium for Political and Social Research
http://www.icpsr.umich.edu

At this site, the inter-university Consortium for Political and Social Research offers materials in various categories of historical social, economic, and demographic data. Presented is a statistical overview of the United States beginning in the late eighteenth century.

Department of State
http://www.state.gov

View this site for an understanding into the workings of what has become a major U.S. executive branch department. Links explain what the Department does, what services it provides, what it says about U.S. interests around the world, and much more information.

The Mexican-American War Memorial Homepage
http://sunsite.unam.mx/revistas/1847/

For a change of pace and culture, visit this site from Mexico's Universidad Nacional Autonoma. It describes, from a Mexican perspective, the Mexican-American War.

Mystic Seaport
http://amistad.mysticseaport.org/main/welcome.html

The complex Amistad case is explored in a clear and informative manner on this online educational site. It places the event in the context of the issues of the 1830s and 1840s.

Social Influence Website
http://www.workingpsychology.com/intro.html

The nature of persuasion, compliance, and propaganda is the focus of this Web site, with many practical examples and applications. Students of such topics as the roles of public opinion and media influence in policy making should find these discussions of interest.

University of Virginia Library
http://www.lib.virginia.edu/exhibits/lewis_clark/

Created by the University of Virginia Library, this site examines the famous Lewis and Clark exploration of the trans-Mississippi west.

Women in America
http://xroads.virginia.edu/~HYPER/DETOC/FEM/

Providing the views of women travelers from the British Isles, France, and Germany on the lives of American women, this valuable site covers the years between 1820 and 1842 and is informative, stimulating, and highly original.

Women of the West
http://www.wowmuseum.org/

The home page of the Women of the West Museum offers several interesting links that include stories, poems, educational resources, and exhibits.

UNIT 4: The Civil War and Reconstruction

The American Civil War
http://sunsite.utk.edu/civil-war/warweb.html

This site provides a wide-ranging list of data on the Civil War. Some examples of the data that are available are: army life, the British connection, diaries/letters/memos, maps, movies, museums, music, people, photographs, and poetry.

Anacostia Museum/Smithsonian Institution
http://www.si.edu/archives/historic/anacost.htm

This is the home page of the Center for African American History and Culture of the Smithsonian Institution, which is expected to become a major repository of information. Explore its many avenues.

Abraham Lincoln Online
http://www.netins.net/showcase/creative/lincoln.html

This is a well-organized, high-quality site that will lead to substantial material about Abraham Lincoln and his era. Discussions among Lincoln scholars can be accessed in the Mailbag section.

Gilder Lehrman Institute of American History
http://vi.uh.edu/pages/mintz/gilder.htm

Click on the links to various articles presented through this Web site to read outstanding, first-hand accounts of slavery in America through the period of Reconstruction.

Secession Era Editorials Project
http://history.furman.edu/benson/docs/

Newspaper editorials of the 1800s regarding events leading up to secession are presented on this Furman University site. When complete, this distinctive project will offer additional features that include mapping, statistical tools, and text analysis.

We highly recommend that you review our Web site for expanded information and our other product lines. We are continually updating and adding links to our Web site in order to offer you the most usable and useful information that will support and expand the value of your Annual Editions. You can reach us at: *http://www.dushkin.com/annualeditions/*.

UNIT 1

The New Land

Unit Selections

1. **1491**, Charles C. Mann
2. **A "Newfounde Lande"**, Alan Williams
3. **Laboring in the Fields of the Lord**, Jerald T. Milanich
4. **Pocahontas**, William M. S. Rasmussen and Robert S. Tilton
5. **The Pueblo Revolt**, Jake Page
6. **Bearing the Burden? Puritan Wives**, Martha Saxton
7. **Penning a Legacy**, Patricia Hudson
8. **The Right to Marry:** *Loving v. Virginia*, Peter Wallenstein
9. **Baptism of Fire**, Paul A. Thomsen

Key Points to Consider

- It has been a commonly accepted view that the Americas in 1491 were only sparsely populated by native peoples who led a simple existence. How does new research challenge this view? What implications does it have on contemporary environmental issues?

- The essay on Pocahontas is an example of what is called "alternative history." Is it misleading to use an event that did not and could not have taken place to evaluate attitudes and ideas of a bygone era? Or, can such a device shed light on cultural contrasts? Explain.

- Discuss what led to the Pueblo Indian revolt in 1680? How did it affect the Spanish attitudes towards the Pueblo?

- In what ways did Puritan men justify the subordination of women? How could women achieve moral authority and influence under such circumstances?

- Discuss the constitution that William Penn framed for the colony he wished to establish. What aspects of it were "progressive" for the time?

- How did George Washington's first experiences in combat affect his reputation and career? Why was the French and Indian war a critical step towards American independence?

 **Links: www.dushkin.com/online/**
These sites are annotated in the World Wide Web pages.

What became known as the "New World" had stimulated interest in Europe for centuries. Drawings and paintings depicted lands inhabited by plants and animals the shapes and sizes of which were limited only by the artists' imaginations. Writers also told of wonderous, exotic places the likes of which Europeans had never seen. Humans who lived there were depicted as everything from ferocious, beastlike creatures to refined, noble peoples living in advanced civilizations. A constant thread in such creations was that there existed in the new world enormous quantities of jewels and precious metals. When there developed in Europe sufficient wealth to finance expeditions, and improvements in shipbuilding and navigation that made them feasible, the "age of exploration" began. It was led by the Spanish and Portugese, then followed by the French and English.

The motives for mounting these expeditions were mixed. One was to convert the heathens in the new world to Christianity. Another was to find new trade routes to tap the silks and spices of the Far East. And finally, there was the desire to obtain the riches some of the existing societies were thought to possess. Whatever the reasons, these forays had profound and often disastrous effects on indigenous peoples. Partly this was due to military operations conducted by the invaders, some of whom deliberately slaughtered anyone who stood in their way. Even if the explorers had come with the most peaceful intentions, however, they brought with them communicable diseases against which the native peoples had no immunity. Diseases killed many times more people than did muskets or swords.

Europeans "discovered" the new world only for Europe; the peoples who lived here had no need to be discovered by anyone. The first essay in this section, "1491," contends that the Western Hemisphere contained far larger and more sophisticated populations who had lived here a great deal longer than previously believed. The article also suggests that they had a profound effect on the environment. "Pocahontas" is the story of a woman about whom little is known but of whom much has been written. The essay describes the myths that grew about her, and how they were used to promote certain agendas over the years. In "A 'New-founde Lande,'" Alan Williams tells what is known of the Italian explorer, John Cabot, who headed the first European expedition known to have landed in North America. Next, "Laboring in the Fields of the Lord," by Jerald Milanich, examines the establishment of Spanish missions in what is now Georgia and Florida and the disastrous results that followed the highly motivated acts of many of the friars. "The Pueblo Revolt" provides and account of a little-known Indian uprising against the Spanish occupiers in New Mexico. The Spanish were forced to flee temporarily, and when they returned they showed greater respect for Pueblo religious practices.

The English came relatively late to the new world. Some of them were searching for gold, silver, and jewels, as had their predecessors. Others came to settle permanently, either to escape religious persecution or merely to build new lives for themselves. Women in the English colonies were subordinate to men legally and in a variety of other ways. The essay "Bearing the Burden? Puritan Wives" describes the changing roles of women in Puritan communities. It tells how they were able to attain moral and spiritual authority despite their unequal status.

William Penn's acquisition of a grant of land that would later become Pennsylvania is reviewed in the article "Penning a Legacy." Penn crafted a constitution that provided for religious freedom, voting rights, and penal reform. He also hoped that the Native Americans already in the area would permit the new settlers to live among them "with your love and consent." "The Right to Marry: *Loving v. Virginia*," describes efforts in Virginia to prevent racial mixing of whites and blacks. The last essay in this section, "Baptism of Fire," provides an account of a single battle in the almost constant war between the French and British for empire in North America. The encounter provided the young George Washington with his first combat experience.

1491

Before it became the New World, the Western Hemisphere was vastly more populous and sophisticated than has been thought—an altogether more salubrious place to live at the time than, say, Europe. New evidence of both the extent of the population and its agricultural advancement leads to a remarkable conjecture: the Amazon rain forest may be largely a human artifact

BY CHARLES C. MANN

The plane took off in weather that was surprisingly cool for north-central Bolivia and flew east, toward the Brazilian border. In a few minutes the roads and houses disappeared, and the only evidence of human settlement was the cattle scattered over the savannah like jimmies on ice cream. Then they, too, disappeared. By that time the archaeologists had their cameras out and were clicking away in delight.

Below us was the Beni, a Bolivian province about the size of Illinois and Indiana put together, and nearly as flat. For almost half the year rain and snowmelt from the mountains to the south and west cover the land with an irregular, slowly moving skin of water that eventually ends up in the province's northern rivers, which are sub-subtributaries of the Amazon. The rest of the year the water dries up and the bright-green vastness turns into something that resembles a desert. This peculiar, remote, watery plain was what had drawn the researchers' attention, and not just because it was one of the few places on earth inhabited by people who might never have seen Westerners with cameras.

Clark Erickson and William Balée, the archaeologists, sat up front. Erickson is based at the University of Pennsylvania; he works in concert with a Bolivian archaeologist, whose seat in the plane I

usurped that day. Balée is at Tulane University, in New Orleans. He is actually an anthropologist, but as native peoples have vanished, the distinction between anthropologists and archaeologists has blurred. The two men differ in build, temperament, and scholarly proclivity, but they pressed their faces to the windows with identical enthusiasm.

Indians were here in greater numbers than previously thought, and they imposed their will on the landscape. Columbus set foot in a hemisphere thoroughly dominated by humankind.

Dappled across the grasslands below was an archipelago of forest islands, many of them startlingly round and hundreds of acres across. Each island rose ten or thirty or sixty feet above the floodplain, allowing trees to grow that would otherwise never survive the water. The forests were linked by raised berms, as straight as a rifle shot and up to three miles long. It is Erickson's belief that this entire landscape—30,000 square miles of forest mounds surrounded by

raised fields and linked by causeways—was constructed by a complex, populous society more than 2,000 years ago. Balée, newer to the Beni, leaned toward this view but was not yet ready to commit himself.

Erickson and Balée belong to a cohort of scholars that has radically challenged conventional notions of what the Western Hemisphere was like before Columbus. When I went to high school, in the 1970s, I was taught that Indians came to the Americas across the Bering Strait about 12,000 years ago, that they lived for the most part in small, isolated groups, and that they had so little impact on their environment that even after millennia of habitation it remained mostly wilderness. My son picked up the same ideas at his schools. One way to summarize the views of people like Erickson and Balée would be to say that in their opinion this picture of Indian life is wrong in almost every aspect. Indians were here far longer than previously thought, these researchers believe, and in much greater numbers. And they were so successful at imposing their will on the landscape that in 1492 Columbus set foot in a hemisphere thoroughly dominated by humankind.

Given the charged relations between white societies and native peoples, inquiry into Indian culture and history is inevitably contentious. But the recent scholarship is especially controversial. To begin with, some researchers—many but not all from an older generation—deride the new theories as fantasies arising from an almost willful misinterpretation of data and a perverse kind of political correctness. "I have seen no evidence that large numbers of people ever lived in the Beni," says Betty J. Meggers, of the Smithsonian Institution. "Claiming otherwise is just wishful thinking." Similar criticisms apply to many of the new scholarly claims about Indians, according to Dean R. Snow, an anthropologist at Pennsylvania State University. The problem is that "you can make the meager evidence from the ethnohistorical record tell you anything you want," he says. "It's really easy to kid yourself."

More important are the implications of the new theories for today's ecological battles. Much of the environmental movements is animated, consciously or not, by what William Denevan, a geographer at the University of Wisconsin, calls, polemically, "the pristine myth"—the belief that the Americas in 1491 were an almost unmarked, even Edenic land, "untrammeled by man," in the words of the Wilderness Act of 1964, one of the nation's first and most important environmental laws. As the University of Wisconsin historian William Cronon has written, restoring this long-ago, putatively natural state is, in the view of environmentalists, a task that society is morally bound to undertake. Yet if the new view is correct and the work of humankind was pervasive, where does that leave efforts to restore nature?

The Beni is a case in point. In addition to building up the Beni mounds for houses and gardens, Erickson says, the Indians trapped fish in the seasonally flooded grassland. Indeed, he says, they fashioned dense zigzagging networks of earthen fish weirs between the causeways. To keep the habitat clear of unwanted trees and undergrowth, they regularly set huge areas on fire. Over the centuries the burning created an intricate ecosystem of fire-adapted plant species dependent on native pyrophilia. The current inhabitants of the Beni still burn, although now it is to maintain the savannah for cattle. When we flew over the ar-

eas, the dry season had just begun, but mile-long lines of flame were already on the march. In the charred areas behind the fires were the blackened spikes of trees—many of them one assumes, of the varieties that activists fight to save in other parts of Amazonia.

After we landed, I asked Balée, Should we let people keep burning the Beni? Or should we let the trees invade and create a verdant tropical forest in the grasslands, even if one had not existed here for millennia?

Balée laughed. "You're trying to trap me, aren't you?" he said.

LIKE A CLUB BETWEEN THE EYES

According to family lore, my great-grandmother's great-grandmother's great-grandfather was the first white person hanged in America. His name was John Billington. He came on the *Mayflower*, which anchored off the coast of Massachusetts on November 9, 1620. Billington was not a Puritan; within six months of arrival he also became the first white person in America to be tried for complaining about the police. "He is a knave," William Bradford, the colony's governor, wrote to Billington, "and so will live and die." What one historian called Billington's "troublesome career" ended in 1630, when he was hanged for murder. My family has always said the he was framed—but we *would* say that, wouldn't we?

A few years ago it occurred to me that my ancestor and everyone else in the colony had voluntarily enlisted in a venture that brought them to New England without food or shelter six weeks before winter. Half the 102 people on the *Mayflower* made it through to spring, which to me was amazing. How, I wondered, did they survive?

In his history of Plymouth Colony, Bradford provided the answer: by robbing Indian houses and graves. The *Mayflower* first hove to at Cape Cod. An armed company staggered out. Eventually it found a recently deserted Indian settlement. The newcomers—hungry, cold, sick—dug up graves and ransacked houses, looking for underground stashes of corn. "And sure it was God's good

providence that we found this corn," Bradford wrote, "for else we know not how we should have done." (He felt uneasy about the thievery, though.) When the colonists came to Plymouth, a month later, they set up shop in another deserted Indian village. All through the coastal forest the Indians had "died on heapes, as they lay in their houses," the English trader Thomas Morton noted. "And the bones and skulls upon the several places of their habitations made such a spectacle" that to Morton the Massachusetts woods seemed to be "a new found Golgotha"—the hill of executions in Roman Jerusalem.

To the Pilgrims' astonishment, one of the corpses they exhumed on Cape Cod had blond hair. A French ship had been wrecked there several years earlier. The Patuxet Indians imprisoned a few survivors. One of them supposedly learned enough of the local language to inform his captors that God would destroy them for their misdeeds. The Patuxet scoffed at the threat. But the Europeans carried a disease, and they bequeathed it to their jailers. The epidemic (probably of viral hepatitis, according to a study by Arthur E. Spiess, an archaeologist at the Maine Historic Preservation Commission, and Bruce D. Spiess, the director of clinical research at the Medical College of Virginia) took years to exhaust itself and may have killed 90 percent of the people in coastal New England. It made huge differences to American history. "The good hand of God favored our beginnings," Bradford mused, by "sweeping away great multitudes of the natives... that he might make room for us."

By the time my ancestor set sail on the *Mayflower*, Europeans had been visiting New England for more than a hundred years. English, French, Italian, Spanish, and Portuguese mariners regularly plied the coastline, trading what they could, occasionally kidnapping the inhabitants for slaves. New England, the Europeans saw, was thickly settled and well defended. In 1605 and 1606 Samuel de Champlain visited Cape Cod, hoping to establish a French base. He abandoned the idea. Too many people already lived there. A year later Sir Ferdinando Gorges—British despite his name—tried to establish an English community in southern Maine. It had more founders than Plymouth and seems to have been better organized. Confronted by numerous well-armed local Indians, the settlers abandoned the project within months. The Indians at Plymouth would surely have been an equal obstacle to my ancestor and his ramshackle expedition had disease not intervened.

Faced with such stories, historians have long wondered how many people lived in the Americas at the time of contact. "Debated since Columbus attempted a partial census on Hispaniola in 1496," William Denevan has written, this "remains one of the great inquiries of history." (In 1976 Denevan assembled and edited an entire book on the subject, *The Native Population of the Americas in 1492*.) The first scholarly estimate of the indigenous population was made in 1910 by James Mooney, a distinguished ethnographer at the Smithsonian Institution. Combing through old documents, he concluded that in 1491 North America had 1.15 million inhabitants. Mooney's glittering reputation ensured that most subsequent researchers accepted his figure uncritically.

That changed in 1966, when Henry F. Dobyns published "Estimating Aboriginal American Population: An Appraisal of Techniques With a New Hemispheric Estimate," in the journal *Current Anthropology*. Despite the carefully neutral title, his argument was thunderous, its impact long-lasting. In the view of James Wilson, the author of *The Earth Shall Weep* (1998), a history of indigenous Americans, Dobyns's colleagues "are still struggling to get out of the crater that paper left in anthropology." Not only anthropologists were affected. Dobyns's estimate proved to be one of the opening rounds in today's culture wars.

Dobyns began his exploration of pre-Columbian Indian demography in the early 1950s, when he was a graduate student. At the invitation of a friend, he spent a few months in northern Mexico, which is full of Spanish-era missions. there he poked through the crumbling leather-bound ledgers in which Jesuits recorded local births and deaths. Right

away he noticed how many more deaths there were. The Spaniards arrived, and then Indians died—in huge numbers at incredible rates. It hit him, Dobyns told me recently, "like a club right between the eyes."

It took Dobyns eleven years to obtain his Ph.D. Along the way he joined a rural-development project in Peru, which until colonial times was the seat of the Incan empire. Remembering what he had seen at the northern fringe of the Spanish conquest, Dobyns decided to compare it with figures for the south. He burrowed into the papers of the Lima cathedral and read apologetic Spanish histories. The Indians in Peru, Dobyns concluded, had faced plagues from the day the conquistadors showed up—in fact, before then: smallpox arrived around 1525, seven years ahead of the Spanish. Brought to Mexico apparently by a single sick Spaniard, it swept south and eliminated more than half the population of the Incan empire. Smallpox claimed the Incan dictator Huayna Capac and much of his family, setting off a calamitous war of succession. So complete was the chaos that Francisco Pizarro was able to seize an empire the size of Spain and Italy combined with a force of 168 men.

Smallpox was only the first epidemic. Typhus (probably) in 1546, influenza and smallpox together in 1558, smallpox again in 1589, diphtheria in 1614, measles in 1618—all ravaged the remains of Incan culture. Dobyns was the first social scientist to piece together this awful picture, and he naturally rushed his findings into print. Hardly anyone paid attention. But Dobyns was already working on a second, related question: If all those people died, how many had been living there to begin with? Before Columbus, Dobyns calculated, the Western Hemisphere held ninety to 112 million people. Another way of saying this is that in 1491 more people lived in the Americas than in Europe.

His argument was simple but horrific. It is well known that Native Americans had no experience with many European diseases and were therefore immunologically unprepared—"virgin soil," in the metaphor of epidemiologists. What Dobyns realized was that such diseases could have swept from the coastlines ini-

tially visited by Europeans to inland areas controlled by Indians who had never seen a white person. The first whites to explore many parts of the Americas may therefore have encountered places that were already depopulated. Indeed, Dobyns argued, they must have done so.

Peru was one example, the Pacific Northwest another. In 1792 the British navigator George Vancouver led the first European expedition to survey Puget Sound. He found a vast charnel house: human remains "promiscuously scattered about the beach, in great numbers." Smallpox, Vancouver's crew discovered, had preceded them. Its few survivors, second lieutenant Peter Puget noted, were "most terribly pitted... indeed many have lost their Eyes." In *Pox Americana* (2001), Elizabeth Fenn, a historian at George Washington University, contends that the disaster on the northwest coast was but a small part of a continental pandemic that erupted near Boston in 1774 and cut down Indians from Mexico to Alaska.

Because smallpox was not endemic in the Americas, colonials, too, had not acquired any immunity. The virus, an equal-opportunity killer, swept through the Continental Army and stopped the drive into Quebec. The American Revolution would be lost, Washington and other rebel leaders feared, if the contagion did to the colonists what it had done to the Indians. "The small Pox! The small Pox!" John Adams wrote to his wife, Abigail. "What shall We do with it?" In retrospect, Fenn says, "One of George Washington's most brilliant moves was to inoculate the army against smallpox during the Valley Forge winter of '78." Without inoculation smallpox could easily have given the United States back to the British.

So many epidemics occurred in the Americas, Dobyns argued, that the old data used by Mooney and his successors represented population nadirs. From the few cases in which before-and-after totals are known with relative certainty, Dobyns estimated that in the first 130 years of contact about 95 percent of the people in the Americas died—the worst demographic calamity in recorded history.

Dobyns's ideas were quickly attacked as politically motivated, a push from the hate-America crowd to inflate the toll of imperialism. The attacks continue to this day. "No question about it, some people want those higher numbers," says Shepard Krech III, a Brown University anthropologist who is the author of *The Ecological Indian* (1999). These people, he says, were thrilled when Dobyns revisited the subject in a book, *Their Numbers Become Thinned* (1983)—and revised his own estimates upward. Perhaps Dobyns's most vehement critic is David Henige, a bibliographer of Africana at the University of Wisconsin, whose *Numbers from Nowhere* (1998) is a landmark in the literature of demographic fulmination. "Suspect in 1966, it is no less suspect nowadays," Henige wrote of Dobyns's work. "If anything, it is worse."

When Henige wrote *Numbers From Nowhere,* the fight about pre-Columbian populations had already consumed forests' worth of trees; his bibliography is ninety pages long. And the dispute shows no sign of abating. More and more people have jumped in. This is partly because the subject is inherently fascinating. But more likely the increased interest in the debate is due to the growing realization of the high political and ecological stakes.

INVENTING BY THE MILLIONS

On May 30, 1539, Hernando de Soto landed his private army near Tampa Bay, in Florida. Soto, as he was called, was a novel figure: half warrior, half venture capitalist. He had grown very rich very young by becoming a market leader in the nascent trade for Indian slaves. The profits had helped to fund Pizarro's seizure of the Incan empire, which had made Soto wealthier still. Looking quite literally for new worlds to conquer, he persuaded the Spanish Crown to let him loose in North America. He spent one fortune to make another. He came to Florida with 200 horses, 600 soldiers, and 300 pigs.

From today's perspective, it is difficult to imagine the ethical system that would justify Soto's actions. For four years his force, looking for gold, wandered through what is now Florida,

Georgia, North and South Carolina, Tennessee, Alabama, Mississippi, Arkansas, and Texas, wrecking almost everything it touched. The inhabitants often fought back vigorously, but they had never before encountered an army with horses and guns. Soto died of fever with his expedition in ruins; along the way his men had managed to rape, torture, enslave, and kill countless Indians. But the worst thing the Spaniards did, some researchers say, was entirely without malice—bring the pigs.

According to Charles Hudson, an anthropologist at the University of Georgia who spent fifteen years reconstructing the path of the expedition, Soto crossed the Mississippi a few miles downstream from the present site of Memphis. It was a nervous passage: the Spaniards were watched by several thousand Indian warriors. Utterly without fear, Soto brushed past the Indian force into what is now eastern Arkansas, through thickly settled land—"very well peopled with large towns," one of his men later recalled, "two or three of which were to be seen from one town." Eventually the Spaniards approached a cluster of small cities, each protected by earthen walls, sizeable moats, and deadeye archers. In his usual fashion, Soto brazenly marched in, stole food, and marched out.

After Soto left, no Europeans visited this part of the Mississippi Valley for more than a century. Early in 1682 whites appeared again, this time Frenchmen in canoes. One of them was Réné-Robert Cavelier, Sieur de la Salle. The French passed through the area where Soto had found cities cheek by jowl. It was deserted—La Salle didn't see an Indian village for 200 miles. About fifty settlements existed in this strip of the Mississippi when Soto showed up, according to Anne Ramenofsky, an anthropologist at the University of New Mexico. By La Salle's time the number had shrunk to perhaps ten, some probably inhabited by recent immigrants. Soto "had a privileged glimpse" of an Indian world, Hudson says. "The window opened and slammed shut. When the French came in and the record opened up again, it was a transformed reality. A civilization crumbled. The question is, how did this happen?"

> *Swine alone can disseminate anthrax, brucellosis, leptospirosis, trichinosis, and tuberculosis. Only a few of Hernando de Soto's pigs would have had to wander off to infect the forest.*

The question is even more complex than it may seem. Disaster of this magnitude suggests epidemic disease. In the view of Ramenofsky and Patricia Galloway, an anthropologist at the University of Texas, the source of the contagion was very likely not Soto's army but its ambulatory meat locker: his 300 pigs. Soto's force itself was too small to be an effective biological weapon. Sicknesses like measles and smallpox would have burned through his 600 soldiers long before they reached the Mississippi. But the same would not have held true for the pigs, which multiplied rapidly and were able to transmit their diseases to wildlife in the surrounding forest. When human beings and domesticated animals live close together, they trade microbes with abandon. Over time mutation spawns new diseases: Avian influenza becomes human influenza, bovine rinderpest becomes measles. Unlike Europeans, Indians did not live in close quarters with animals—they domesticated only the dog, the llama, the alpaca, the guinea pig, and here and there, the turkey and the Muscovy duck. In some ways this is not surprising: the New World had fewer animal candidates for taming than the Old. Moreover, few Indians carry the gene that permits adults to digest lactose, a form of sugar abundant in milk. Non-milk-drinkers, one imagines, would be less likely to work at domesticating milk-giving animals. But this is guesswork. The fact is that what scientists call zoonotic disease was little known in the Americas. Swine alone can disseminate anthrax, brucellosis, leptospirosis, taeniasis, trichinosis, and tuberculosis. Pigs breed exuberantly and can transmit diseases to deer and turkeys. Only a few of

Soto's pigs would have had to wander off to infect the forest.

Indeed, the calamity wrought by Soto apparently extended across the whole Southeast. The Coosa city-states, in western Georgia, and the Caddoan-speaking civilization, centered on the Texas-Arkansas border, disintegrated soon after Soto appeared. The Caddo had had a taste for monumental architecture: public plazas, ceremonial platforms, mausoleums. After Soto's army left, notes Timothy K. Perttula, an archaeological consultant in Austin, Texas, the Caddo stopped building community centers and began digging community cemeteries. Between Soto's and La Salle's visits, Perttula believes, the Caddoan population fell from about 200,000 to about 8,500—a drop of nearly 96 percent. In the eighteenth century the tally shrank further, to 1,400. An equivalent loss today in the population of New York City would reduce it to 56,000—not enough to fill Yankee Stadium. "That's one reason whites think of Indians as nomadic hunters," says Russell Thornton, an anthropologist at the University of California at Los Angeles. "Everything else—all the heavily populated urbanized societies—was wiped out."

Could a few pigs truly wreak this much destruction? Such apocalyptic scenarios invite skepticism. As a rule, viruses, microbes, and parasites are rarely lethal on so wide a scale—a pest that wipes out its host species does not have a bright evolutionary future. In its worst outbreak, from 1347 to 1351, the European Black Death claimed only a third of its victims. (The rest survived, though they were often disfigured or crippled by its effects.) The Indians in Soto's path, if Dobyns, Ramenofsky, and Perttula are correct, endured losses that were incomprehensibly greater.

One reason is that Indians were fresh territory for many plagues, not just one. Smallpox, typhoid, bubonic plague, influenza, mumps, measles, whooping cough—all rained down on the Americas in the century after Columbus. (Cholera, malaria, and scarlet fever came later.) Having little experience with epidemic diseases, Indians had no knowledge of how to combat them. In contrast, Europeans were well versed in the brutal logic

of quarantine. They boarded up houses in which plague appeared and fled to the countryside. In Indian New England, Neal Salisbury, a historian at Smith college, wrote in *Manitou and Providence* (1982), family and friends gathered with the shaman at the sufferer's bedside to wait out the illness—a practice that "could only have served to spread the disease more rapidly."

Indigenous biochemistry may also have played a role. The immune system constantly scans the body for molecules that it can recognize as foreign—molecules belonging to an invading virus, for instance. No one's immune system can identify all foreign presences. Roughly speaking, an individual's set of defensive tools is known as his MHC type. Because many bacteria and viruses mutate easily, they usually attack in the form of several slightly different strains. Pathogens win when MHC types miss some of the strains and the immune system is not stimulated to act. Most human groups contain many MHC types; a strain that slips by one person's defenses will be nailed by the defenses of the next. But, according to Francis L. Black, an epidemiologist at Yale University, Indians are characterized by unusually homogeneous MHC types. One out of three South American Indians have similar MHC types; among Africans the corresponding figure is one in 200. The cause is a matter for Darwinian speculation, the effects less so.

In 1966 Dobyns's insistence on the role of disease was a shock to his colleagues. Today the impact of European pathogens on the New World is almost undisputed. Nonetheless, the fight over Indian numbers continues with undiminished fervor. Estimates of the population of North America in 1491 disagree by an order of magnitude—from 18 million, Dobyns's revised figure, to 1.8 million, calculated by Douglas H. Ubelaker, an anthropologist at the Smithsonian. To some "high counters," as David Henige calls them, the low counters' refusal to relinquish the vision of an empty continent is irrational or worse. "Non-Indian 'experts' always want to minimize the size of aboriginal populations," says Lenore Stiffarm, a Native American-education specialist at the University of

Saskatchewan. The smaller the numbers of Indians, she believes, the easier it is to regard the continent as having been up for grabs. "It's perfectly acceptable to move into unoccupied land," Stiffarm says. "And land with only a few 'savages' is the next best thing."

"Most of the arguments for the very large numbers have been theoretical," Ubelaker says in defense of low counters. "When you try to marry the theoretical arguments to the data that are available on individual groups in different regions, it's hard to find support for those numbers." Archaeologists, he says, keep searching for the settlements in which those millions of people supposedly lived, with little success. "As more and more excavation is done, one would expect to see more evidence for dense populations than has thus far emerged." Dean Snow, the Pennsylvania State anthropologist, examined Colonial-era Mohawk Iroquois sites and found "no support for the notion that ubiquitous pandemics swept the region." In his view, asserting that the continent was filled with people who left no trace is like looking at an empty bank account and claiming that it must once have held millions of dollars.

The low counters are also troubled by the Dobynsian procedure for recovering original population numbers: applying an assumed death rate, usually 95 percent, to the observed population nadir. Ubelaker believes that the lowest point for Indians in North America was around 1900, when their numbers fell to about half a million. Assuming a 95 percent death rate, the pre-contact population would have been 10 million. Go up one percent, to a 96 percent death rate, and the figure jumps to 12.5 million—arithmetically creating more than two million people from a tiny increase in mortality rates. At 98 percent the number bounds to 25 million. Minute changes in baseline assumptions produce wildly different results.

"It's an absolutely unanswerable question on which tens of thousands of words have been spent to no purpose," Henige says. In 1976 he sat in on a seminar by William Denevan, the Wisconsin geographer. An "epiphanic moment" occurred when he read shortly afterward that scholars had "uncovered" the existence of eight million people in Hispaniola. *Can you just invent millions of people?* he wondered. "We can make of the historical record that there was depopulation and movement of people from internecine warfare and diseases," he says. "But as for how much, who knows? When we start putting numbers to something like that—applying large figures like ninety-five percent—we're saying things we shouldn't say. The number implies a level of knowledge that's impossible."

Nonetheless, one must try—or so Denevan believes. In his estimation the high counters (though not the highest counters) seem to be winning the argument, at least for now. No definitive data exist, he says, but the majority of the extant evidentiary scraps support their side. Even Henige is no low counter. When I asked him what he thought the population of the Americas was before Columbus, he insisted that any answer would be speculation and made me promise not to print what he was going to say next. Then he named a figure that forty years ago would have caused a commotion.

To Elizabeth Fenn, the smallpox historian, the squabble over numbers obscures a central fact. Whether one million or 10 million or 100 million died, she believes, the pall of sorrow that engulfed the hemisphere was immeasurable. Languages, prayers, hopes, habits, and dreams—entire ways of life hissed away like steam. The Spanish and the Portuguese lacked the germ theory of disease and could not explain what was happening (let alone stop it). Nor can we explain it; the ruin was too long ago and too all-encompassing. In the long run, Fenn says, the consequential finding is not that many people died but that many people once lived. The Americas were filled with a stunningly diverse assortment of peoples who had knocked about the continents for millennia. "You have to wonder," Fenn says. "What were all those people *up* to in all that time?"

BUFFALO FARM

In 1810 Henry Brackenridge came to Cahokia, in what is now southwest Illinois, just across the Mississippi from St. Louis. Born close to the frontier, Brack-

enridge was a budding adventure writer; his *Views of Louisiana,* published three years later, was a kind of nineteenth-century *Into Thin Air,* with terrific adventure but without tragedy. Brackenridge had an eye for archaeology, and he had heard that Cahokia was worth a visit. When he got there, trudging along the desolate Cahokia River, he was "struck with a degree of astonishment." Rising from the muddy bottomland was a "stupendous pile of earth," vaster than the Great Pyramid at Giza. Around it were more than a hundred smaller mounds, covering an area of five square miles. At the time, the area was almost uninhabited. One can only imagine what passed through Brackenridge's mind as he walked alone to the ruins of the biggest Indian city north of the Rio Grande.

To Brackenridge, it seemed clear that Cahokia and the many other ruins in the Midwest had been constructed by Indians. It was not so clear to everyone else. Nineteenth-century writers attributed them to, among others, the Vikings, the Chinese, the "Hindoos," the ancient Greeks, the ancient Egyptians, lost tribes of Israelites, and even straying bands of Welsh. (This last claim was surprisingly widespread; when Lewis and Clark surveyed the Missouri, Jefferson told them to keep an eye out for errant bands of Welsh-speaking white Indians.) The historian George Bancroft, dean of his profession, was a dissenter: the earthworks, he wrote in 1840, were purely natural formations.

Bancroft changed his mind about Cahokia, but not about Indians. To the end of his days he regarded them as "feeble barbarians, destitute of commerce and of political connection." His characterization lasted, largely unchanged, for more than a century. Samuel Eliot Morison, the winner of two Pulitzer Prizes, closed his monumental *European Discovery of America* (1974) with the observation that Native Americans expected only 'short and brutish lives, void of hope for any future." As late as 1987 *American History: A Survey,* a standard high school textbook by three well-known historians, described the Americas before Columbus as "empty of mankind and its works." The story of Europeans in the New World, the book explained, "is the story

of the creation of a civilization where none existed."

Alfred Crosby, a historian at the University of Texas, came to other conclusions. Crosby's *The Columbian Exchange: Biological Consequences of 1492* caused almost as much of a stir when it was published, in 1972, as Henry Dobyns's calculation of Indian numbers six years earlier, though in different circles. Crosby was a standard names-and-battles historian who became frustrated by the random contingency of political events. "Some trivial thing happens and you have this guy winning the presidency instead of that guy," he says. He decided to go deeper. After he finished his manuscript, it sat on his shelf—he couldn't find a publisher willing to be associated with his new ideas. It took him three years to persuade a small editorial house to put it out. *The Columbian Exchange* has been in print ever since; a companion, *Ecological Imperialism: The Biological Expansion of Europe, 900–1900,* appeared in 1986.

Human history, in Crosby's interpretation, is marked by two world-altering centers of invention: the Middle East and central Mexico, where Indian groups independently created nearly all of the Neolithic innovations, writing included. The Neolithic Revolution began in the Middle East about 10,000 years ago. In the next few millennia humankind invented the wheel, the metal tool, and agriculture. The Sumerians eventually put these inventions together, added writing, and became the world's first civilization. Afterward Sumeria's heirs in Europe and Asia frantically copied one another's happiest discoveries; innovations ricocheted from one corner of Eurasia to another, stimulating technological progress. Native Americans, who had crossed to Alaska before Sumeria, missed out on the bounty. "They had to do everything on their own," Crosby says. Remarkably, they succeeded.

When Columbus appeared in the Caribbean, the descendants of the world's two Neolithic civilizations collided, with overwhelming consequences for both. American Neolithic development occurred later than that of the Middle East, possibly because the Indians needed more time to build up the requisite population density. Without beasts of burden they could not capitalize on the wheel (for individual workers on uneven terrain skids are nearly as effective as carts for hauling), and they never developed steel. But in agriculture they handily outstripped the children of Sumeria. Every tomato in Italy, every potato in Ireland, and every hot pepper in Thailand came from this hemisphere. Worldwide, more than half the crops grown today were initially developed in the Americas.

Maize, as corn is called in the rest of the world, was a triumph with global implications. Indians developed an extraordinary number of maize varieties for different growing conditions, which meant that the crop could and did spread throughout the planet. Central and Southern Europeans became particularly dependent on it; maize was the staple of Serbia, Romania, and Moldavai by the nineteenth century. Indian crops dramatically reduced hunger, Crosby says, which led to an Old World population boom.

In the Aztec capital Tenochtitlán the Spaniards gawped like hayseeds at the side streets, ornately carved buildings, and markets bright with goods from hundreds of miles away.

Along with peanuts and manioc, maize came to Africa and transformed agriculture there, too. "The probability is that the population of Africa was greatly increased because of maize and other American Indian crops," Crosby says. "Those extra people helped make the slave trade possible." Maize conquered Africa at the time when introduced diseases were leveling Indian societies. The Spanish, the Portuguese, and the British were alarmed by the death rate among Indians, because they wanted to exploit them as workers. Faced with a labor shortage, the Europeans turned their eyes to Africa. The continent's quarrelsome

societies helped slave traders to siphon off millions of people. The maize-fed population boom, Crosby believes, let the awful trade continue without pumping the well dry.

Back home in the Americas, Indian agriculture long sustained some of the world's largest cities. The Aztec capital of Tenochtitlán dazzled Hernán Cortés in 1519; it was bigger than Paris, Europe's greatest metropolis. The Spaniards gawped like hayseeds at the wide streets, ornately carved buildings, and markets bright with goods from hundreds of miles away. They had never before seen a city with botanical gardens, for the excellent reason that none existed in Europe. The same novelty attended the force of a thousand men that kept the crowded streets immaculate. (Streets that weren't ankle-deep in sewage! The conquistadors had never heard of such a thing.) Central America was not the only locus of prosperity. Thousands of miles north, John Smith, of Pocahontas fame, visited Massachusetts in 1614, before it was emptied by disease, and declared that the land was "so planted with Gardens and Corne fields, and so well inhabited with a goodly, strong and well proportioned people... [that] I would rather live here than any where."

Smith was promoting colonization, and so had reason to exaggerate. But he also knew the hunger, sickness, and oppression of European life. France—"by any standards a privileged country," according to its great historian, Fernand Braudel—experienced seven nationwide famines in the fifteenth century and thirteen in the sixteenth. Disease was hunger's constant companion. During epidemics in London the dead were heaped onto carts "like common dung" (the simile is Daniel Defoe's) and trundled through the streets. The infant death rate in London orphanages, according to one contemporary source, was 88 percent. Governments were harsh, the rule of law arbitrary. The gibbets poking up in the background of so many old paintings were, Braudel observed, "merely a realistic detail."

The Earth Shall Weep, James Wilson's history of Indian America, puts the comparison bluntly: "the western hemisphere was larger, richer, and more populous than Europe." Much of it was freer, too. Europeans, accustomed to the serfdom that thrived from Naples to the Baltic Sea, were puzzled and alarmed by the democratic spirit and respect for human rights in many Indian societies, especially those in North America. In theory, the sachems of New England Indian groups were absolute monarchs. In practice, the colonial leader Roger Williams wrote, "they will not conclude of ought... unto which the people are averse."

Pre-1492 America wasn't a disease-free paradise, Dobyns says, although in his "exuberance as a writer," he told me recently, he once made that claim. Indians had ailments of their own, notably parasites, tuberculosis, and anemia. The daily grind was wearing; life-spans in America were only as long as or a little longer than those in Europe, if the evidence of indigenous graveyards is to be believed. Nor was it a political utopia—the Inca, for instance, invented refinements to totalitarian rule that would have intrigued Stalin. Inveterate practitioners of what the historian Francis Jennings described as "state terrorism practiced horrifically on a huge scale," the Inca ruled so cruelly that one can speculate that their surviving subjects might actually have been better off under Spanish rule.

I asked seven anthropologists, archaeologists, and historians if they would rather have been a typical Indian or a typical European in 1491. Every one chose to be an Indian.

I asked seven anthropologists, archaeologists, and historians if they would rather have been a typical Indian or a typical European in 1491. None was delighted by the question, because it required judging the past by the standards of today—a fallacy disparaged as "presentism" by social scientists. But every one chose to be an Indian. Some early colonists gave the same answer. Horrifying the leaders of Jamestown and Plymouth, scores of English ran off to live with the Indians. My ancestor shared their desire, which is what led to the trumped-up murder charges against him—or that's what my grandfather told me, anyway.

As for the Indians, evidence suggests that they often viewed Europeans with disdain. The Hurons, a chagrined missionary reported, thought the French possessed "little intelligence in comparison to themselves." Europeans, Indians said, were physically weak, sexually untrustworthy, atrociously ugly, and just plain dirty. (Spaniards, who seldom if ever bathed, were amazed by the Aztec desire for personal cleanliness.) A Jesuit reported that the "Savages" were disgusted by handkerchiefs: "They say, we place what is unclean in a fine white piece of linen, and put it away in our pockets as something very precious, while they throw it upon the ground." The Micmac scoffed at the notion of French superiority. If Christian civilization was so wonderful, why were its inhabitants leaving?

Like people everywhere, Indians survived by cleverly exploiting their environment. Europeans tended to manage land by breaking it into fragments for farmers and herders. Indians often worked on such a grand scale that the scope of their ambition can be hard to grasp. They created small plots, as Europeans did (about 1.5 million acres of terraces still exist in the Peruvian Andes), but they also reshaped entire landscapes to suit their purposes. A principal tool was fire, used to keep down underbrush and create the open, grassy conditions favorable for game. Rather than domesticating animals for meat, Indians retooled whole ecosystems to grow bumper crops of elk, deer, and bison. The first white settlers in Ohio found forests as open as English parks—they could drive carriages through the woods. Along the Hudson River the annual fall burning lit up the banks for miles on end; so flashy was the show that the Dutch in New Amsterdam boated upriver to goggle at the blaze like children at fireworks. In North America, Indian torches had their biggest impact on the Midwestern prairie,

much or most of which was created and maintained by fire. Millennia of exuberant burning shaped the plains into vast buffalo farms. When Indian societies disintegrated, forest invaded savannah in Wisconsin, Illinois, Kansas, Nebraska, and the Texas Hill Country. Is it possible that the Indians changed the Americas more than the invading Europeans did? "The answer is probably yes for most regions for the next 250 years or so" after Columbus. William Denevan wrote, "and for some regions right up to the present time."

Amazonia has become the *emblem of vanishing wilderness—an admonitory image of untouched Nature. But the rain forest itself may be a cultural artifact—that is, an artificial object.*

When scholars first began increasing their estimates of the ecological impact of Indian civilization, they met with considerable resistance from anthropologists and archaeologists. Over time the consensus in the human sciences changed. Under Denevan's direction, Oxford University Press has just issued the third volume of a huge catalogue of the "cultivated landscapes" of the Americas. This sort of phrase still provokes vehement objection—but the main dissenters are now ecologists and environmentalists. The disagreement is encapsulated by Amazonia, which has become *the* emblem of vanishing wilderness—an admonitory image of untouched Nature. Yet recently a growing number of researchers have come to believe that Indian societies had an enormous environmental impact on the jungle. Indeed, some anthropologists have called the Amazon forest itself a cultural artifact—that is, an artificial object.

GREEN PRISONS

Northern visitors' first reaction to the storied Amazon rain forest is often

disappointment. Ecotourist brochures evoke the immensity of Amazonia but rarely dwell on its extreme flatness. In the river's first 2,900 miles the vertical drop is only 500 feet. The river oozes like a huge runnel of dirty metal through a landscape utterly devoid of the romantic crags, arroyos, and heights that signify wilderness and natural spectacle to most North Americans. Even the animals are invisible, although sometimes one can hear the bellow of monkey choruses. To the untutored eye—mine, for instance—the forest seems to stretch out in a monstrous green tangle as flat and incomprehensible as a printed circuit board.

The area east of the lower-Amazon town of Santarém is an exception. A series of sandstone ridges several hundred feet high reach down from the north, halting almost at the water's edge. Their tops stand drunkenly above the jungle like old tombstones. Many of the caves in the buttes are splattered with ancient petroglyphs—renditions of hands, stars, frogs, and human figures, all reminiscent of Miró, in overlapping red and yellow and brown. In recent years one of these caves, La Caverna da Pedra Pintada (Painted Rock Cave), has drawn attention in archaeological circles.

Wide and shallow and well lit, Painted Rock Cave is less thronged with bats than some of the other caves. The arched entrance is twenty feet high and lined with rock paintings. Out front is a sunny natural patio suitable for picnicking, edged by a few big rocks. People lived in this cave more than 11,000 years ago. They had no agriculture yet, and instead ate fish and fruit and built fires. During a recent visit I ate a sandwich atop a particularly inviting rock and looked over the forest below. The first Amazonians, thought, must have done more or less the same thing.

In college I took an introductory anthropology class in which I read *Amazonia: Man and Culture in a Counterfeit Paradise* (1971), perhaps the most influential book ever written about the Amazon, and one that deeply impressed me at the time. Written by Betty J. Meggers, the Smithsonian archaeologist, *Amazonia* says that the apparent lushness of the rain forest is a sham. The soils are poor and can't hold nutrients—the jungle flora exists only because it snatches up everything worthwhile before it leaches away in the rain. Agriculture, which depends on extracting the wealth of the soil, therefore faces inherent ecological limitations in the wet desert of Amazonia.

As a result, Meggers argued, Indian villages were forced to remain small—any report of "more than a few hundred" people in permanent settlements, she told me recently, "makes my alarm bells go off." Bigger, more complex societies would inevitably overtax the forest soils, laying waste to their own foundations. Beginning in 1948 Meggers and her late husband, Clifford Evans, excavated a chiefdom on Marajó, an island twice the size of New Jersey that sits like a gigantic stopper in the mouth of the Amazon. The Marajóara, they concluded, were failed offshoots of a sophisticated culture in the Andes. Transplanted to the lush trap of the Amazon, the culture choked and died.

Green activists saw the implication: development in tropical forests destroys both the forests and their developers. Meggers's account had enormous public impact—Amazonia is one of the wellsprings of the campaign to save rain forests.

Then Anna C. Roosevelt, the curator of archaeology at Chicago's Field Museum of Natural History, re-excavated Marajó. Her complete report, Mound-builders of the Amazon (1991), was like the anti-matter version of Amazonia. Marajó, she argued, was "one of the outstanding indigenous cultural achievements of the New World," a powerhouse that lasted for more than a thousand years, had "possibly well over 100,000" inhabitants, and covered thousands of square miles. Rather than damaging the forest, Marajó's "earth construction" and "large, dense populations" had improved it: the most luxuriant and diverse growth was on the mounds formerly occupied by the Marajóara. "If you listened to Meggers's theory, these places should have been ruined," Roosevelt says.

Meggers scoffed at Roosevelt's "extravagant claims," "polemical tone," and "defamatory remarks." Roosevelt, Meggers argued, had committed the beginner's error of mistaking a site that had been occupied many times by small, unstable groups for a single, long-lasting society. "[Archaeological remains] build up on areas of half a kilometer or so," she told me, "because [shifting Indian groups] don't land exactly on the same spot. The decorated types of pottery don't change much over time, so you can pick up a bunch of chips and say, 'Oh, look, it was all one big site!' Unless you know what you're doing, of course." Centuries after the conquistadors, "the myth of El Dorado is being revived by archaeologists," Meggers wrote last fall in the journal Latin American Antiquity, referring to the persistent Spanish delusion that cities of gold existed in the jungle.

The dispute grew bitter and personal; inevitable in a contemporary academic context, it has featured vituperative references to colonialism, elitism, and employment by the CIA. Meanwhile, Roosevelt's team investigated Painted Rock Cave. On the floor of the cave what looked to me like nothing in particular turned out to be an ancient midden: a refuse heap. The archaeologists slowly scraped away sediment, traveling backward in time with every inch. When the traces of human occupation vanished, they kept digging. ("You always go a meter past sterile," Roosevelt says.) A few inches below they struck the charcoal-rich dirt that signifies human habitation—a culture, Roosevelt said later, that wasn't supposed to be there.

For many millennia the cave's inhabitants hunted and gathered for food. But by about 4000 years ago they were growing crops—perhaps as many as 140 of them, according to Charles R. Clement, an anthropological botanist at the Brazilian National Institute for Amazonian Research. Unlike Europeans, who planted mainly annual crops, the Indians, he says, centered their agriculture on the Amazon's unbelievably diverse assortment of trees: fruits, nuts, and palms. "It's tremendously difficult to clear fields with stone tools," Clement says. "If you can plant trees, you get twenty years of productivity out of your work instead of two or three."

Planting their orchards, the first Amazonians transformed large swaths of the river basin into something more pleasing to human beings. In a widely cited article from 1989, William Balée, the Tulane anthropologist, cautiously estimated that about 12 percent of the nonflooded Amazon forest was of anthropogenic origin—directly or indirectly created by human beings. In some circles this is now seen as a conservative position. "I basically think it's all human-created," Clement told me in Brazil. He argues that Indians changed the assortment and density of species throughout the region. So does Clark Erickson, the University of Pennsylvania archaeologist, who told me in Bolivia that the lowland tropical forests of South America are among the finest works of art on the planet. "Some of my colleagues would say that's pretty radical," he said, smiling mischievously. According to Peter Stahl, an anthropologist at the State University of New York at Binghamton, "lots" of botanists believe that "what the eco-imagery would like to picture as a pristine, untouched Urwelt [primeval world] in fact has been managed by people for millennia." The phrase "built environment," Erickson says, "applies to most, if not all, Neotropical landscapes."

"Landscape" in this case is meant exactly—Amazonian Indians literally created the ground beneath their feet. According to William I. Woods, a soil geographer at Southern Illinois University, ecologists' claims about terrible Amazonian land were based on very little data. In the late 1990s Woods and others began careful measurements in the lower Amazon. They indeed found lots of inhospitable terrain. But they also discovered swaths of terra preta—rich, fertile "black earth" that anthropologists increasingly believe was created by human beings.

Terra preta, Woods guesses, covers at least 10 percent of Amazonia, an area the size of France. It has amazing properties, he says. Tropical rain doesn't leach nutrients from terra preta fields; instead the soil, so to speak, fights back. Not far from Painted Rock Cave is a 300-acre area with a two-foot layer of terra preta quarried by locals for potting soil. The bottom third of the layer is never removed, workers there explain, because over time it will re-create the original soil layer in its initial thickness. The reason, scientists suspect, is that terra preta is generated by a special suite of micro-organisms that resists depletion. "Apparently," Woods and the Wisconsin geographer Joseph M. McCann argued in a presentation last summer, "at some threshold level… dark earth attains the capacity to perpetuate—even *regenerate* itself—thus behaving more like a living 'super'-organism than an inert material."

In as yet unpublished research the archaeologists Eduardo Neves, of the University of São Paulo; Michael Heckenberger, of the University of Florida; and other colleagues examined *terra preta* in the upper Xingu, a huge southern tributary of the Amazon. Not all Xingu cultures left behind this living earth, they discovered. But the ones that did generated it rapidly—suggesting to Woods that *terra preta* was created deliberately. In a process reminiscent of dropping microorganism-rich starter into plain dough to create sourdough bread, Amazonian peoples, he believes, inoculated bad soil with a transforming bacterial charge. Not every group of Indians there did this, but quite a few did, and over an extended period of time.

When Woods told me this, I was so amazed that I almost dropped the phone. I ceased to be articulate for a moment and said things like "wow" and "gosh." Woods chuckled at my reaction, probably because he understood what was passing through my mind. Faced with an ecological problem, I was thinking, the Indians *fixed* it. They were in the process of terraforming the Amazon when Columbus showed up and ruined everything.

Scientists should study the microorganisms in *terra preta,* Woods told me, to find out how they work. If that could be learned, maybe some version of Amazonian dark earth could be used to improve the vast expanses of bad soil that cripple agriculture in Africa—a final gift from the people who brought us tomatoes, corn, and the immense grasslands of the Great Plains.

"Betty Meggers would just die if she heard me saying this," Woods told me. "Deep down her fear is that this data will be misused." Indeed, Meggers's recent *Latin American Antiquity* article charged that archaeologists who say the Amazon can support agriculture are effectively

telling "developers [that they] are entitled to operate without restraint." Resuscitating the myth of El Dorado, in her view, "makes us accomplices in the accelerating pace of environmental degradation." Doubtless there is something to this—although, as some of her critics responded in the same issue of the journal, it is difficult to imagine greedy plutocrats "perusing the pages of *Latin American Antiquity* before deciding to rev up the chain saws." But the new picture doesn't automatically legitimize paving the forest. Instead it suggests that for a long time big chunks of Amazonia were used nondestructively by clever people who knew tricks we have yet to learn.

Environmentalists want to preserve as much of the world's land as possible in a putatively intact state. But "intact" may turn out to mean "run by human beings for human purposes."

I visited Painted Rock Cave during the river's annual flood, when it wells up over its banks and creeps inland for miles. Farmers in the floodplain build houses and barns on stilts and watch pink dolphins sport from their doorsteps. Ecotourists take shortcuts by driving motorboats through the drowned forests. Guys in dories chase after them, trying to sell sacks of incredibly good fruit.

All of this is described as "wilderness" in the tourist brochures. It's not, if researchers like Roosevelt are correct. Indeed, they believe that fewer people may be living there now than in 1491. Yet when my boat glided into the trees, the forest shut out the sky like the closing of an umbrella. Within a few hundred years the human presence seemed to vanish. I felt alone and small, but in a way that was curiously like feeling exalted. If that place was not wilderness, how should I think of it? Since the fate of the forest is in our hands, what should be our goal for its future?

NOVEL SHORES

Hernando de Soto's expedition stomped through the Southeast for four years and apparently never saw bison. More than a century later, when French explorers came down the Mississippi, they saw "a solitude unrelieved by the faintest trace of man," the nineteenth-century historian Francis Parkman wrote. Instead the French encountered bison, "grazing in herds on the great prairies which then bordered the river."

To Charles Kay, the reason for the buffalo's sudden emergence is obvious. Kay is a wildlife ecologist in the political-science department at Utah State University. In ecological terms, he says, the Indians were the "keystone species" of American ecosystems. A keystone species, according to the Harvard biologist Edward O. Wilson, is a species "that affects the survival and abundance of many other species." Keystone species have a disproportionate impact on their ecosystems. Removing them, Wilson adds, "results in a relatively significant shift in the composition of the [ecological] community."

When disease swept Indians from the land, Kay says, what happened was exactly that. The ecological ancien régime collapsed, and strange new phenomena emerged. In a way this is unsurprising; for better or worse, humankind is a keystone species everywhere. Among these phenomena was a population explosion in the species that the Indians had kept down by hunting. After disease killed off the Indians, Kay believes, buffalo vastly extended their range. Their numbers more than sextupled. The same occurred with elk and mule deer. "If the elk were here in great numbers all this time, the archaeological sites should be chock-full of elk bones," Kay says. "But the archaeologists will tell you the elk weren't there." On the evidence of middens the number of elk jumped about 500 years ago.

Passenger pigeons may be another example. The epitome of natural American abundance, they flew in such great masses that the first colonists were stupefied by the sight. As a boy, the explorer Henry Brackenridge saw flocks "ten miles in width, by one hundred and twenty in length." For hours the birds darkened the sky from horizon to horizon. According to Thomas Neumann, a consulting archaeologist to Lilburn, Georgia, passenger pigeons "were incredibly dumb and always roosted in vast hordes, so they were very easy to harvest." Because they were readily caught and good to eat, Neumann says, archaeological digs should find many pigeon bones in the pre-Columbian strata of Indian middens. But they aren't there. The mobs of birds in the history books, he says, were "outbreak populations—always a symptom of an extraordinarily disrupted ecological system."

Throughout eastern North America the open landscape seen by the first Europeans quickly filled in with forest. According to William Cronon, of the University of Wisconsin, later colonists began complaining about how hard it was to get around. (Eventually, of course, they stripped New England almost bare of trees.) When Europeans moved west, they were preceded by two waves: one of disease, the other of ecological disturbance. The former crested with fearsome rapidity; the later sometimes took more than a century to quiet down. Far from destroying pristine wilderness, European settlers bloodily *cre-ated* it. By 1800 the hemisphere was chockablock with new wilderness. If "forest primeval" means a woodland unsullied by the human presence, William Denevan has written, there was much more of it in the late eighteenth century than in the early sixteenth.

Cronon's *Changes in the Land: Indians, Colonists, and the Ecology of New England* (1983) belongs on the same shelf as works by Crosby and Dobyns. But it was not until one of his articles was excerpted in *The New York Times* in 1995 that people outside the social sciences began to understand the implications of this view of Indian history. Environmentalists and ecologists vigorously attacked the anti-wilderness scenario, which they described as infected by postmodern philosophy. A small academic brouhaha ensued, complete with hundreds of footnotes. It precipitated *Reinventing Nature?* (1995), one of the few academic critiques of postmodernist philosophy written largely by biologists. *The Great New Wilderness Debate* (1998), another lengthy book on the subject, was edited by two philosophers who earnestly identified themselves as "Euro-American men [whose] cultural legacy is patriarchal Western civiliza-tion in its current postcolonial, globally hegemonic form."

It is easy to tweak academics for opaque, self-protective language like this. Nonetheless, their concerns were quite justified. Crediting Indians with the role of keystone species has implications for the way the current Euro-American members of that keystone species manage the forests, watersheds, and endangered species of America. Because a third of the United States is owned by the federal government, the issue inevitably has political ramifications. In Amazonia, fabled storehouse of biodiversity, the stakes are global.

Guided by the pristine myth, mainstream environmentalists want to preserve as much of the world's land as possible in a putatively intact state. But "intact," if the new research is correct, means "run by human beings for human purposes." Environmentalists dislike this, because it seems to mean that anything goes. In a sense they are correct. Native Americans managed the continent as they saw fit. Modern nations must do the same. If they want to return as much of the landscape as possible to its 1491 state, they will have to find it within themselves to create the world's largest garden.

From *The Atlantic Monthly*, March 2002, pp. 41-53. © 2002 by Charles C. Mann. Reprinted by permission.

A "Newfounde Lande"

Five hundred years after John Cabot's 1497 voyage brought word of the North American continent to Europe, scholars still hotly debate the exact location of his landfall.

BY ALAN WILLIAMS

In 1992, THE AMERICAS marked the five-hundredth anniversary of the European discovery of the lands of the Western Hemisphere by Christopher Columbus, a Genoese navigator sailing in the service of Spain's King Ferdinand and Queen Isabella. Considerable controversy surrounded the commemoration of that event, as some disputed the notion that lands already occupied could be "discovered" and others pointed to earlier claims by Europeans of having crossed the Atlantic and visited the Americas long before the arrival of Columbus.

This year the world marks another important quincentennial, and again there is controversy, especially surrounding the exact landfall of the explorer, John Cabot. While the precise location of Columbus's initial landfall has been questioned, it is generally conceded that his discoveries involved first the islands of the Caribbean and later, the mainland of South America. Cabot is honored, especially in England and in Atlantic Canada, as the man who forged the way from Europe to the North American continent, but where in North America remains at issue.

Legends about Atlantic crossings by Carthaginians, Jews, Chinese, and the Welsh place visitors from the Old World in the Western Hemisphere as early as the fifth century B.C. The Irish tell of St. Brendan island-hopping the northern North Atlantic a thousand years later.

And the exploits of the Vikings in North America between A.D. 800–1400 are not only recorded in oral Norse sagas, but have been substantiated through modern archaeological investigations in northern Newfoundland, particularly at the Norse settlement uncovered at L'Anse aux Meadows, now recognized as a World Heritage site.

Columbus's four voyages to the New World are well documented. His initial visit to the Caribbean region in 1492–93 was followed the next year by his exploration of the southern coast of Cuba, which he was convinced was the territory of the Grand Khan of China, and Haiti, which he named Hispaniola because it resembled Spain. In 1498, Columbus cruised the Venezuelan coast, believing it to be the coast of Asia. And on his fourth and final voyage to the New World in 1502, Columbus touched what is now known as Central America.

While the "Admiral of the Ocean Sea" was so engaged, John Cabot set sail in 1497 to test his own theories on an all-water route to the Indies and returned to England with the first certain news of the coast of North America. Unlike Columbus, however, Cabot left little documentary information about himself or his voyages to help today's scholars reconstruct his achievements.

It is generally believed that Cabot was really Giovanni Caboto, a native of Gaeta, near Naples, in Italy. Born in or before 1455, he grew up in Genoa and is thus of the same generation and city as Columbus. Cabot later moved to Venice and became a citizen of that city in 1476. He married a Venetian named Mattea, with whom he had three sons, Ludovico, Sancio, and the most famous, Sebestiano.

Cabot made his living as a merchant, trading with Alexandria, in North Africa, from where he acquired Asian spices, dyes, and silks for markets in Europe. Like other seafaring European merchants, Cabot wished for a way to avoid dealing with the Arab "middlemen" who controlled practically all of the land that surrounded the Mediterranean Sea.

An experienced mapmaker and navigator, Cabot believed that it was possible to sail west in order to reach Asia. Hoping to win financial backing that would enable him to prove his theories, Cabot moved to Spain in 1490 and soon after approached officials in Seville with plans for a westward voyage to Cathay (China). When word reached him of the triumph of Christopher Columbus, Cabot knew that there would be little chance of his gaining the patronage of Spain's royalty for his own scheme.

By now obsessed with the idea of finding a western route to Asia, Cabot turned to England for help in his quest. He counted on King Henry VII's desire to outdo his Spanish rival, King Ferdinand II, in the possible acquisition of

Originally intending to seek Spanish backing to test his theory on an all-water route to Asia, Cabot realized the futility of that course when Christopher Columbus returned from his first voyage to the New World in 1493 (right). The Italian-born explorer then moved his family from Spain to England, where he proposed his plan—to sail west as Columbus had, but at more northerly latitudes—to the merchants of Bristol and to King Henry VII (above, left).

new territories and the opportunity to tap the wealth that would presumably come to the first nation to reach the shores of Cathay.

In England, Cabot settled with his family in the western port of Bristol, one of the nation's wealthiest cities. The Bristol merchants were a cosmopolitan group, fond of civic pomp, whose city, adorned with fine churches, mimicked London. Their trade in wool, cloth, hides, wine, and fish took their vessels to Iceland, Norway, Iberia, and the Mediterranean. The merchants, like the Norse before them, also sent seamen westward in search of fish and wood. Now Cabot approached them with a new and tantalizing objective.

Confidently asserting that he could reach the East by sailing west, as Columbus had done, Cabot promised to bring back the riches of Asia directly by sea, by-passing the Moslem traders of the eastern Mediterranean. He knew how far Columbus had sailed in southern latitudes without reaching Cathay and he cogently argued that, starting from England's more northerly latitude, he could reach the northeastern part of Cathay by

traveling half the distance, just as German cartographer Martin Behaim had indicated on his globe in 1492.[1] Once they reached land, all that was necessary, Cabot told the Englishmen, was to sail southwestward to the warmer, populated regions of the East, such as Cipango (Japan) and India.

Probably on the basis of his skill as an advanced navigator, Cabot persuaded the merchants of his capability to captain such an expedition. Some of the instruments and charts that he carried were by far the most modern that the merchants had seen. Most of the instruments measured the angle between the stars or the sun and the horizon, so that the ship's position could be calculated. The cross-staff measured the angle of a star in relation to the horizon; the nocturnal figured the position of Ursa Major or Minor in relation to the Pole star; and the indispensable astrolabe determined latitude, the distance north or south of the equator.

After successfully securing the financial backing of the merchants of Bristol, Cabot petitioned the king for permission to sail. He realized that he would not be able to claim any discoveries for En-

gland without royal assent, leaving his finds free for the taking by any European country. On March 5, 1496, Cabot and his sons, who do not seem to have accompanied him on his voyage, received letters patent (royal grants of right) from Henry VII authorizing them "to seek out, discover, and find whatsoever isles, countries, regions, or provinces of the heathen and infidels, whatsoever they be, and in what part of the world soever they be...."

A letter written by John Day, an English merchant—"rather a slippery character with many irons in the fire"—who was reporting to Christopher Columbus on John Cabot's voyage, does not indicate exactly when or from where Cabot made his first attempt to cross the ocean, but it appears to have been in 1496, soon after he won his first letters patent from the English king. Day simply noted that Cabot "went with one ship, had a disagreement with his crew, he was short of supplies and ran into weather, and he decided to turn back."

Trying again in 1497, Cabot left Bristol, probably early in May in the *Matthew,* most likely named after his wife,

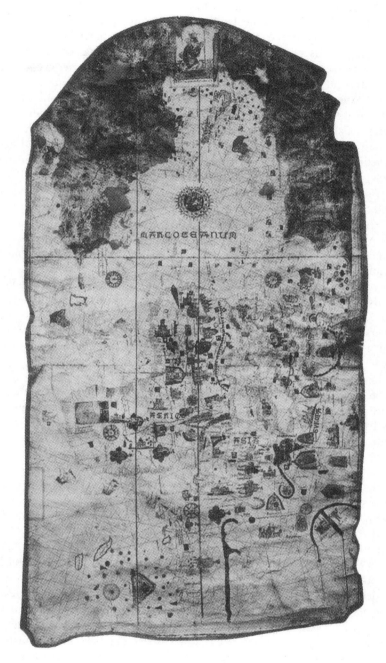

Dating from around 1500, the planisphere of the whole known world drawn by Juan de la Cosa, is the earliest cartographic representation of any part of the North American continent. La Cosa depicted that section of the map (top) on a larger scale than the Old World and included references to both Columbus's and Cabot's New World discoveries. Five English flags, thought by some to represent places claimed by Cabot for King Henry VII of England, appear along the northwest Atlantic coast. Because there exists scant documentary information about Cabot's voyage, scholars have for centuries debated exactly what route his ship, the Matthew, followed and where in North America he landed. One suggested route takes Cabot directly to the coast of the island of Newfoundland, while the other has him missing Newfoundland on his outbound journey, landing instead on the northern tip of Cape Breton Island (bottom).

MUSEO NAVAL, MADRID

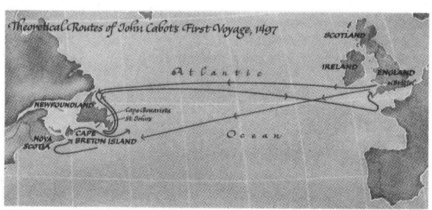

MAP BY JOAN PENNINGTON

Mattea. He struck out westwards for Cathay somewhere off the Atlantic coast of Ireland. Fifty-three days later, the *Matthew* reached land.

Cabot and his crew went ashore, the first Englishmen, although led by an Italian, to set foot on North American soil. They erected a cross and the banners of England and Venice, claiming all the country for the king. His party being small—Day wrote in a letter soon after Cabot returned home—Cabot "did not dare advance inland beyond the shooting distance of a crossbow and after taking fresh water he returned to his ship." Although they met no inhabitants, Cabot was certain that he had reached the northeastern extremity of Asia. Like Columbus when he coasted Cuba, Cabot expected that populous cities with roofs of gold and sources of silk and spices could not be too far off.

The exact point of Cabot's landing has been the subject of weighty argument. Scholars have so differently reconstructed Cabot's voyage, his known coasting, and his return journey that his North American landfall could have been anywhere between Labrador and Maine, perhaps even the Carolinas, with at least one historian taking him as far south as Florida.

Since no journal kept by Cabot or his crew has survived to indicate precisely where they went, historians have had to rely for documentation on a handful of letters sent from England to Spain and Italy by foreign diplomats. Even the fragmentary information contained in existing chronicles and maps made in the succeeding years, allegedly from Cabot's own globe and charts, may not be reliable.

The problem is further complicated by the fact that Cabot lost his life in 1498, either at sea or in the New World. The great Cabot scholar J. A. Williamson explained the reason why so little of Cabot's discovery is known, saying that while "Columbus had a faithful friend, the Bishop Las Casas [his biographer], and a son who revered his father's memory and saved it from being forgotten, John Cabot… had a son Sebastian, who seems to have been jealous of his father's fame and to have done his best to destroy the memory of his achievements."

Nineteenth-century American historiographer Henry Harrisse declared that Sebastian was one of the greatest liars in the history of discovery who, despite his long and generally successful career as a navigator and mapmaker in England and Spain, nevertheless wanted credit for his father's 1497 discovery. Thanks to the younger Cabot's efforts at distortion, the earliest chroniclers referred only to "a Venetian," and if they mentioned a name, it was that of Sebastian, not John.

The "Sebastian supremacy" lasted until the records were carefully searched by a Bristol librarian named Nicholls and an American Cabot scholar, Richard Biddle, in the first half of the nineteenth century. The investigations led historians on both sides of the Atlantic to eventually restore John Cabot to his rightful place in time for the four-hundredth anniversary of the landing in 1897, which saw a flurry of writing on the subject of his voyages.

Discussions concerning Cabot's right to be known as the "first discoverer of North America" and renewed debate on his likely route received added impetus with the uncovering of early cartographic evidence. The earliest find was a world map, made about the year 1500 by Juan de la Cosa, a skilled Biscayan navigator who had sailed with Columbus. Found in 1832, this was the first map to represent any part of the North American continent[2] and indicates both Columbus's "Indies" and Cabot's "northeastern part of Asia," which forms the western border of the Atlantic Ocean. La Cosa lined these lands with five English flags, possibly indicating spots at which Cabot claimed territory for the Crown. La Cosa also identifies "Cauo de ynglaterra" (Cape of England) and "mar de descubierta por inglese" (sea discovered by the English).

William Ganong, a great cartographic scholar from New Brunswick, Canada, performed an analysis of the La Cosa map, which has been called "one of the most brilliant 'old map' expositions ever written." Ganong concluded that the La Cosa map could be a simplification of Cabot's own map, the result of successive re-drawings. He further theorized that Cabot missed Newfoundland on the outward voyage, landed on

Cape Breton Island, off Nova Scotia, and returned along the southern coast of Newfoundland.

The case can be made that the land below the English flags, heading southward, represents the *whole* coast of North America, from Labrador to the Gulf of Mexico, but with part of the latter hidden by a depiction of St. Christopher. The distinguished historical cartographer R. A. Skelton considered the Cosa map "the only map which unambiguously illustrates John Cabot's voyage of 1497 and—with less certainty—his voyage of 1498."

Ganong's contention that Cabot could have missed Newfoundland on the outward voyage and reached Cape Breton is, naturally enough, disputed by Newfoundlanders, who maintain that it is highly unlikely he would not have sighted the coast of that large island, which is in such close proximity to the eastern shores of Cape Breton Island. However, given the fog-shrouded conditions often existing in that part of the North Atlantic, it is entirely possible that Cabot and his men could have missed observing Newfoundland as they sailed west.

The so-called "Sebastian Cabot" map of 1544, discovered in Germany in 1856, backs Cape Breton as the likely landfall. The words "Prima Tierra Vista" (land first seen) against a promontory obviously meant for Cape North, at the northernmost tip of Cape Breton Island, would seem to indicate that this was the point of land that first met the eyes of Cabot's crew as they looked from the sea.

The notion that Cabot landed on Newfoundland's Bonavista Peninsula seems to go back only to the 1620s, when Captain John Mason's map of the island included the words "Bona Vista Caboto primum reperta." Many believe that Mason, a governor of the London and Bristol Company who resided in Newfoundland for three years, had either privileged information from an older chart now lost or knew fishermen whose fathers or grandfathers had sailed with Cabot.

But if Sebastian Cabot's claim for Cape Breton was personal, perhaps Mason's was political. Newfoundland author W. A. Munn suggested that Mason printed the Cabot discovery claim over Cape Bonavista in Latin because he wanted every mapmaker in Spain, Portugal, France, and Italy to interpret the meaning clearly: the English "got here first in 1497."

During the quatrocentennial celebrations of Cabot's voyages in 1897, a great rivalry developed between Newfoundlanders and residents of Canada's Maritime provinces, particularly in view of the fact that Newfoundland was not yet a part of Canada.[3] Both groups celebrated discovery with representatives from Bristol joining the Canadians in Halifax, Nova Scotia, while the Newfoundlanders laid the foundation stone of Cabot Tower, which now sits brooding over The Narrows, at the entrance to the harbor at its capital of St. John's.

The debate continued into the twentieth century. In 1936, Munn scathingly dismissed the "Cape Breton theorists," complaining that the efforts made by L. J. Burpee, editor of the *Canadian Geographical Journal,* and subsequent celebrations in Cape Breton and mainland Nova Scotia in 1934 "created a resentment from Newfoundlanders that Canadians have over-stepped the bounds of courtesy by asserting what they cannot prove."

Great mystery surrounds John Cabot's third and last voyage, undertaken in 1498. Henry VII authorized six ships for Cabot's new venture, but the mariner departed England with five, well-victualed and stocked with trade goods. The expedition encountered a fierce storm that forced one of the ships to seek shelter in an Irish port, but "the Genoese kept on his way."

Although one contemporary wrote that it was believed that Cabot "found the new lands nowhere but on the very bottom of the sea," it is generally assumed that Cabot or at least some of his captains reached distant shores, or how else can the unflagged coasts on the La Cosa map be explained? "[W]e know what they found," Williamson commented, "primeval tracts and Indian tribes, no great state or government, no cities, no seaports, ships of trade, no spices and silks for barter—in a word, no Asia. Did any of them come back to tell this? The change in English outlook suggests that they did."

But Cabot was never seen again. Explorer Gaspar Côrte-Real's new world expedition of 1501 obtained a broken gilt sword of Italian manufacture and a pair of silver earrings of Venetian type from Indians somewhere in North America, which could suggest Cabot's fate. But while one story sinks Cabot at Grates Cove on Newfoundland's Avalon Peninsula, another suggests that some of his ships sailed southwestward to Florida and into the Caribbean, where Spaniards, resentful of the encroachment on lands and seas reserved for them by the Treaty of Tordesillas,[4] overcame and killed him.

While Christopher Columbus must be given credit for paving Europe's way to the New World, it does seem safe to say that John Cabot, the uncertainty surrounding his landfall notwithstanding, was the European "discoverer" of North America. The controversy is likely to remain unsettled, at least for the time being, and both Newfoundland and Cape Breton can commemorate this significant anniversary in the history of the "Age of Explorers" without fear of concrete contradiction.

NOTES

1. Behaim, using the academic geography available at the end of the fifteenth century, produced a terrestrial globe that showed only islands separating Europe from Asia. He grossly underestimated the actual circumference of the earth as well as the distance between Europe and Asia when sailing west.

2. In 1965, Yale University Press published a privately owned medieval map of the world that included Vinland, a Norse or Viking settlement on the east coast of North America, as detailed by Icelandic navigator Leif Ericson, who visited and named the site in the early eleventh century. However, the authenticity of the New World sections of the Yale map have been sharply disputed.

3. The Canadian province of Newfoundland and Labrador was admitted to confederation in March 1949.

4. The Treaty of Tordesillas, signed on July 7, 1494, settled differences between Spain and Portugal that were brought about after Columbus's first voyage. The treaty divided the lands of the New World between the two Iberian nations.

Alan Williams has headed the Department of American and Canadian Studies in the School of History at England's University of Birmingham since 1987.

Laboring in the Fields of the Lord

The Franciscan missions of seventeenth-century Florida enabled Spain to harness the energies of tens of thousands of native people.

Jerald T. Milanich

Beginning in the 1590s Franciscan friars established dozens of missions in what is today southern Georgia and northern Florida, but by the time Spain relinquished its Florida colony to Great Britain in 1763 only two missions remained. Spain regained control of the colony in 1783, only to cede it to the United-ed States 38 years later. With the Spaniards gone, memories of their missions faded. Their wood-and-thatch buildings, like the native peoples they had served, simply disappeared from the landscape.

In the late 1940s archaeologists began searching for the north Florida missions. By the end of the 1970s fieldwork and historical research had, it was thought, closed the book on the history of the settlements. My own research and that of my colleagues has reopened that book, adding new chapters to the history of the Spanish colony.

The missions of La Florida were an integral part of Pedro Menéndez de Avilés' master plan for his colony, whose first town, St. Augustine, was established in 1565. By converting the native peoples to Catholicism, as required by contract between him and his sovereign, Philip II, Menéndez hoped to insure loyal, obedient subjects. He initially arranged for Jesuit friars to establish a handful of missions along the Atlantic and Gulf coasts. The Jesuits, however, failed to build support among the native peoples and returned to Spain in 1572. They were replaced by Franciscans subsidized by the Spanish Crown. At first the hardships of mission work—the rigors of travel, climate, and lack of supplies—sent them packing as well. By 1592 only two friars and one lay brother remained, but three years later 12 new friars arrived, and missionary efforts began in earnest. The friars were assigned to *doctrinas*, missions with churches where native people were instructed in religious doctrine.

This quartz pendant, nearly three inches long, was found at San Luis, a late seventeenth-century Apalachee mission

The first Franciscan missions were established along the Atlantic coast, from St. Augustine north to Santa Elena on Parris Island, South Carolina. In 1587, however, raids by unfriendly Indians forced the abandonment of Santa Elena, and the chain of coastal missions serving the Timucuas and their northern neighbors, the Guale, stopped just short of present-day South

J. T. Milanich

This Guale Indian grasping a cross was interred in a shallow grave on the floor of the church at mission Santa Catalina on Amelia Island, Florida. The piety of the Christian Indians was, in the eyes of the mission friars, extraordinary.

Carolina. During the next 35 years a second chain of missions was established on the *camino real*, or royal road, that led westward about 350 miles from St. Augustine through the provinces of Timucua and Apalachee in northwestern Florida. Over time, these missions were moved or abandoned and new ones founded. Historian John Hann of the Florida Bureau of Archaeological Research estimates that as many as 140 existed at one time or another.

After the British settled Charleston in 1670—in territory that had once been under Spanish control—they began to challenge Spain's hold on La Florida. Through its Carolinian colonists, the British began to chip away at the Spanish presence. One effective way was to destroy the Franciscan missions. In the 1680s Carolinian militia and their native allies raided several missions in north Florida and the Georgia coast. Timucuas and Guale were captured and taken to Charleston where they were sold into slavery to work plantations in the Carolinas and the West Indies. The raids on the Georgia coastal missions grew so intense that by the late 1680s all of the missions north of Amelia Island were abandoned.

In 1702 and 1704 Carolinian raids on the Apalachee and Timucuan missions in northern Florida effectively destroyed the mission system west of the St. Johns River. Churches were burned and their contents smashed. Villagers were scattered, tortured, and killed. Nearly 5,000 Indians were sold into slavery, while others fled west to the Gulf of Mexico. Of some 12,000 original mission Indians fewer than 1,000 remained, and they fled to refugee villages that grew up around St. Augustine. When Spain turned La Florida over to Britain in 1763, only 63 Christian Indians remained, and the retreating Spanish took them to Cuba.

By the early 1980s archaeologists had found the remains of perhaps a dozen missions. In doing so, they had relied on an important document written by a seventeenth-century bishop of Cuba, Gabriel Díaz Vara Calderón. The bishop had visited La Florida from 1674 to 1675 to witness firsthand what the Franciscan friars had accomplished. His report lists 24 missions along the camino real and provides the distances between them:

ten leagues [1 league = 3.5 miles] from the city of Saint Augustine, on the bank of the river Corrientes [the St. Johns], is the village and mission of San Diego de Salamototo. It [the river] is very turbulent and almost a league and a half in width. From there to the village and mission of Santa Fe there are some 20 uninhabited leagues. Santa Fe is the principal mission of this province. Off to the side [from Santa Fe] toward the southern border, at a distance of 3 leagues, is the deserted mission and village of San Francisco. Twelve leagues from Santa Fe is the mission of Santa Catalina, with Ajohica 3 leagues away and Santa Cruz de Tarihica 2. Seven leagues away, on the bank of the large river Guacara [the Suwannee], is the mission of San Juan of the same name. Ten [further on] is that of San Pedro de Potohiriba, 2 that of Santa Helena de Machaba, 4, that of San Matheo, 2, that of San Miguel de Asyle, last in this… province.

What made this guide especially valuable was the discovery and publication in 1938 of a map of the camino real drawn by a British surveyor in 1778, when the road was still a major route across northern Florida. Some names of Spanish missions appear on the map. It seemed that it would only be a matter of time until we had discovered all of the sites.

The first clue that the accepted history of the missions needed a major overhaul came in 1976. Excavating a seventeenth-century Spanish-Indian site in north Florida, I had uncovered the burnt remains of a small wooden church and an earth-floored friars' quarters, both adjacent to a Timucuan village. The evidence suggested that the site was one of the missions along the camino real. But which mission was it? Its position on the road did not match any of the locations mentioned in Bishop Calderón's account. It was too far east to be mission San Juan and too far west to be Santa Cruz.

More questions about the geography of the missions surfaced in the late 1980s when I was looking for archaeological traces of the Spanish conquistador Hernando de Soto's 1539 march across northern Florida (see ARCHAEOLOGY, May/June 1989). My field crews did indeed find de Soto-era native villages, but they also discovered two seventeenth-century Spanish missions, both north of the camino real. Again, neither was listed by Bishop Calderón. The good news was that we had an excellent idea of de Soto's route; the bad news was that something was terribly wrong with our understanding of the history and geography of the missions.

I needed dates for the three mysterious sites. One way to get them was to study Spanish majolica pottery, a tin-glazed tableware that is common at Spanish colonial sites in the Americas

Florida Division of Historical Resources

In this pencil drawing by Edward Jonas, the mission church at San Luis, in modern Tallahasse, Florida, faces the central plaza. Size and construction details—the walls, the thatched roof, position of the front door, and presence of two bells—are based on data from excavations by Bonnie McEwan, an archaeologist with the San Luis project, Florida Division of Historical Resources.

and abundant at all three missions. Majolicas can be divided into types based on differences in vessel shapes, colors of glazes, and glazed designs. Because some types were popular mainly before ca. 1650 and others mainly after that date, we can date collections to the early or late seventeenth century. Analysis of majolicas from the mystery missions showed that all three were occupied only before 1650. Had something occurred in the mid-seventeenth century that led to their abandonment two decades before Bishop Calderón's visit?

Since the 1930s historians have known of Spanish accounts documenting a 1656 Indian rebellion at the Timucuan missions. The governor of Spanish Florida, Diego de Rebolledo, sent troops to put down the rebellion. Ten native leaders were rounded up and hanged. The governor was subsequently charged with having displayed great cruelty and was slated to answer for his actions, but he died before a hearing could be held.

What was not known until the early 1990s was that an investigation took place after Rebolledo's death. In the Archivo General de Indias in Seville, Spain, John Worth, then a doctoral student at the University of Florida, found lengthy testimony taken at the hearing and related documents that described the re-

bellion and its aftermath. They also rewrote what we had known about mission geography.

The documents recount how the rebellion began in the spring of 1656, when Lúcas Menéndez, one of the major chiefs in Timucua, and other chiefs defied Governor Rebolledo's orders. Hearing a report that the British were planning a raid on St. Augustine, the governor had commanded the chiefs of Apalachee and Timucua to assemble 500 men and march to St. Augustine. The Indians were ordered to carry food for a stay of at least a month. Because construction of fortifications was still under way and the number of soldiers stationed in the colony was well below its full complement, the town was poorly prepared to withstand an attack. The governor wanted to reinforce its defenses with Indian warriors.

But the chiefs of Timucua refused to go, a decision that grew out of dissatisfaction with treatment they had received from the governor on previous visits to St. Augustine. Rebolledo had not properly feasted the chiefs, nor had he given them gifts, as was customary. The chiefs also refused to carry their own food and supplies or to provide warriors to defend the town without compensation. The power of native leaders in Timucua had already

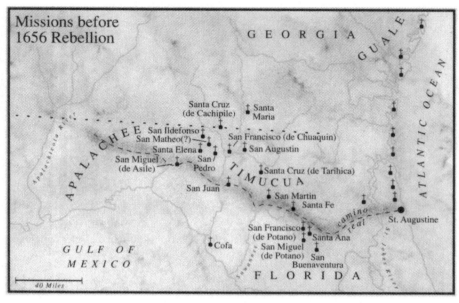

Missions before 1656 Rebellion

GEORGIA
GUALE
ATLANTIC OCEAN

Santa Cruz (de Cachipile)
Santa Maria
San Ildefonso
San Matheo(?)
San Francisco (de Chuaquin)
Santa Elena
San Augustin
San Miguel (de Asile)
San Pedro
Santa Cruz (de Tarihica)
San Juan
San Martin
Santa Fe
camino real
San Francisco (de Potano)
St. Augustine
Cofa
San Miguel (de Potano)
Santa Ana
San Buenaventura

APALACHEE
TIMUCUA

GULF OF MEXICO
FLORIDA

40 Miles

Bette Duke

Beginning in 1595 Franciscan missions were built along the Atlantic coast from St. Augustine to just short of present-day South Carolina. In 1606 a second chain of missions was started north and south of the camino real, or royal road, that led westward about 350 miles from St. Augustine through the provinces of Timucua and Apalachee in Northwestern Florida.

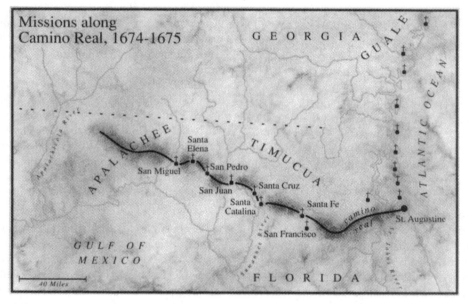

Missions along Camino Real, 1674-1675

GEORGIA
GUALE
ATLANTIC OCEAN

APALACHEE
Santa Elena
San Miguel
San Pedro
San Juan
Santa Cruz
Santa Catalina
Santa Fe
camino real
San Francisco
St. Augustine

TIMUCUA

GULF OF MEXICO
FLORIDA

40 Miles

Bette Duke

After the Timucuan rebellion of 1656, Governor Robolledo relocated the Timucuan missions along the camino real, roughly a day's travel apart, where they functioned as way stations between Apalachee province and St. Augustine. The relocation also reflected the demographic devastation caused by epidemics, especially smallpox and measles.

been threatened by nearly a century of Spanish colonization, and Rebolledo's 1656 order was seen by the Timucuan chiefs as demeaning and an attempt to undercut their authority.

Chief Lúcas Menéndez told his followers and the other chiefs to kill Spaniards, though not the mission friars. The first deaths occurred at San Miguel and San Pedro in western Ti-

mucua. At each site a Spanish soldier, part of the small military presence in the province, was slain. A Spanish servant and a Mexican Indian who by chance had camped in Timucua while traveling the camino real were the next to die. Warriors led by Lúcas Menéndez then raided a Spanish cattle ranch near modern Gainesville, killing a third Spanish soldier and two Af-

Florida Division of Historical Resources

Painting by John LoCastro depicts the Apalachee Indian council house at San Luis. The 120-foot diameter building was at one end of a central plaza which served as a field for a game in which teams tried to kick a ball into an eagle-nest target atop a pole.

rican workers. All across northern Florida Timucuas abandoned their missions.

Knowing the Spanish would retaliate, some of the rebellious Timucuas gathered at mission Santa Elena, which they converted into a palisaded fort. Rebolledo sent 60 Spanish infantry and several hundred Apalachee Indians to capture the rebels. After extended negotiations the Timucuas came out. Their leaders were seized along with several Timucuas who had participated in the murders. One man confessed almost immediately and was executed, probably by hanging. Other prisoners were taken to Apalachee and held while word was sent to the governor.

In late November Rebolledo and a small entourage marched from St. Augustine, capturing several chiefs along the way. A trial was held in Apalachee. Ten of the prisoners were sentenced to forced labor in St. Augustine, while ten others, most of whom were chiefs, were sentenced to death. Rebolledo ordered the men hanged at various places along the camino real as grim reminders of the power of the Spaniards and the fate that awaited those who rebelled against the Crown.

Rebolledo also seized the opportunity to reorganize the province and its missions so they would better serve the needs of the colony and its Spanish overlords. Missions were relocated roughly a day's travel apart so they could function as way stations between Apalachee province and St. Augustine. This arrangement of missions was what Bishop Calderón had observed in 1674 and 1675. That explained two of our three mystery sites. One of the northern two was the pre-1656 mission of Santa Cruz, which was moved south to the camino real after the rebellion. The site we had excavated in 1976 was the mission of San Juan which, after the rebellion, was moved six miles west to a point on the camino real that intersected the Suwannee River. The identity of our third mission remains a mystery, although it seems certain it too was abandoned after the rebellion.

Worth's research led us to believe there were two mission systems in Timucua, one before and one after 1656. What made it necessary for the governor to reorganize the missions? To answer that question we began to reexamine other Spanish docu-

ments discovered by Hann and Worth. They indicated that by 1656 epidemics had devastated the population of Timucua province. Although the occurrence of epidemics—especially smallpox and measles—had long been recognized by scholars, we had no inkling that demographic devastation had occurred so quickly in Timucua. The Spanish sources indicate that by the 1620s Timucuan mission villages had been hard hit, some so reduced in population that their chiefs could not send men to St. Augustine to provide labor for the Spaniards. The documents also indicate that epidemics struck soon after the first missions were founded. In 1595 an unknown epidemic hit the coastal missions. Between 1612 and late 1616 epidemics killed as many as 10,000 mission Indians. Another epidemic struck in 1649–1650, and in 1655 smallpox ravaged Timucua and Guale. In 1657, following the rebellion, Governor Rebolledo wrote that the Indians of Guale and Timucua were few in number "because they have been wiped out with the sickness of the plague [*peste*] and smallpox which have overtaken them in the past years." Two years later a new governor, Francisco de Corcoles y Martínez, reported that 10,000 mission Indians had died in a measles epidemic.

The decimation of mission Indians is grimly reflected in the archaeological record. The remains of hundreds of native villagers have been found in shallow graves under the floors of more than ten mission churches excavated in Apalachee, Guale, and Timucua. At some churches bodies were found stacked in layers three deep. Many older burials had been pushed aside to make room for new ones. The depopulation of Timucua is what apparently led Rebolledo to convert the missions into way stations on the camino real. With its larger native population, Apalachee province would be the focus of Spanish farming and ranching efforts, the colony's breadbasket, and the main source of labor.

The severity of the epidemics and the geographical reorganization of the Timucuan missions has provided a basis for reinterpreting the role of the missions in Spanish Florida. Now more than ever we see that missions and colonization were integrally related. Christianized Indians enabled the colony to function. In

J. T. Milanich

Remains of 59 villagers buried in a corner of Amelia Island's Santa Catalina church attest to the decimation of native people. A 1659 report states that 10,000 people died in one measles epidemic.

return for providing religious education for native people, the Spanish could harness them as workers in support of colonial interests. Religious instruction converted villagers to Catholicism and made them obedient, productive members of Spain's empire. One should not underestimate the hold the new beliefs and customs had on these people. The piety of converted Indians was, even in the eyes of the friars, extraordinary. In 1614 Father Francisco Pareja, a Franciscan friar at mission San Juan (north of modern-day Jacksonville), described the intensity of that devotion:

Among them are Indian men who have sufficient knowledge to give instructions while there are Indian women who catechize other Indian women, preparing them for the reception of Christianity. They assist at Masses of obligation on Sundays and feastdays in which they take part and sing; in some districts that have their confraternities and the procession of Holy Thursday, and from the mission stations they come to the principal mission to hear the Salve [the Salve Regina] which is sung on Saturdays.... They take holy water and recite their prayers in the morning and evening. They come together in the community house to teach one another singing and reading.... Do they confess as Christians? I answer yes.... Many persons are found, men and women, who confess and who receive [Holy Communion] with tears, and who show up advantageously with many Spaniards. And I shall make bold and say and sustain my contention by what I have learned by experience that with regard to the mysteries of the faith, many of them answer better than the Spaniards.

Father Pareja also noted the effectiveness of conversion, writing that Catholicism had vanquished many of the native superstitions so effectively that the mission Indians "do not even remember them... so much so that the younger generation which has been nourished by the milk of the Gospel derides and laughs at some old men and women...."

Faith was an efficient tool for organizing native people who, now laboring in the fields of the Lord, performed a variety of tasks for the Spaniards. Adult males carried corn from Apalachee and Timucua to the Gulf Coast, where it was shipped to St. Augustine or exported to Cuba or other nearby Spanish colonies. Villagers also drove cattle over the camino real to St. Augustine. Supplies for the missions—lamp and cooking oil for the friars and construction hardware for repairing buildings—were shouldered from St. Augustine back to the missions. Indians tended fields and harvested crops for the soldiers stationed at St. Augustine. They helped build forts and other fortifications; they cut and transported logs used for lumber; and they quarried coquina stone on Anastasia Island to build the town gates and the massive castillo that still dominates St. Augustine's waterfront. As many as 300 Christian Indians were involved in the construction of the castillo when it was begun in the 1670s.

Native laborers were paid in hawks' bells, knives, colorful glass beads, pieces of sheet brass, razors, cloth, and scissors. Some of these items were then traded to non-mission Indians to the north who did not have access to the much sought-after European imports. Mission Indians received deer hides and, perhaps, furs in exchange. These could be traded back to the Spaniards for more trinkets. The Spaniards, in turn, exported these hides, which were far more valuable than the trinkets they handed out.

Conde De Revilla Gigedo and University Press of Florida
Pedro Menendez de Aviles, founder of La Florida, believed converting natives to Catholicism would ensure loyal subjects.

Native people also labored for the Spaniards in the mission provinces. They maintained the camino real, clearing brush, repairing creek crossings, and even building bridges. Where roads crossed rivers too deep to ford, they operated ferries, probably little more than rafts or canoes lashed together. At the missions men, women, and children labored in support of the friars. They cooked, tended gardens, looked after farm animals, did household chores, hunted and fished, collected firewood, made charcoal, carried burdens, and paddled canoes when the friars traveled. Cornfields were planted, hoed, and harvested; the corn husked, shelled, ground into meal, and stored. Any surplus was sold by the friars to St. Augustine when times were hard in town, a clever way to generate credit against which Franciscans, who had taken vows of poverty, could charge items needed to maintain the missions. In Spanish Florida corn was money, whether it was taken to St. Augustine for use there or shipped out of the colony. Mission Indians were encouraged to increase production, aided by iron tools such as the hoes found at several missions. Increased production of corn for export resulted in huge numbers of ears being shelled, producing an equally large number of cobs

that were used as fuel. Hundreds of charred corncobs have been found at every Spanish mission excavated thus far.

Lifetimes of labor in support of the Spaniards are reflected in bioanthropological analyses of the mission Indians themselves. The native workers enjoyed better living conditions than did their Precolumbian ancestors, but the stresses of labor resulted in more broken bones and injuries. Was this a benign system that improved the lot of the native people of Apalachee, Guale, and Timucua? Hardly. Although individual friars went to La Florida to bring a better life to the native people, in reality the missions provided the means for compelling the Indians to serve the Spanish Empire. In the end the process proved catastrophic. Tens of thousands of Apalachee, Guale, and Timucuas were destroyed by disease and war. By the time the British took over the territory, they had ceased to exist. Archaeology and history are now giving voice to that forgotten past.

Florida Division of Historical Resources
Spanish ceramics, made throughout the seventeenth century, are useful in dating mission sites across northern Florida.

Jerald T. Milanich is curator of archaeology in the department of anthropology at the Florida Museum of Natural History, Gainesville.

Reprinted with permission from *Archaeology* magazine, Vol. 49, No. 1, January/February 1996, pp. 60-67. © 1996 by the Archaeological Institute of America.

Pocahontas

Four hundred years after her birth, this Native American girl is defined more by myth than reality. What is the truth about Pocahontas?

By William M.S. Rasmussen and Robert S. Tilton

FEW FIGURES from America's early history are better known than the Powhatan girl who has come to us as "Pocahontas." Called America's Joan of Arc by some for her virtue and her courage to risk death for a noble cause, Pocahontas has even been revered as the "mother" of the nation, a female counterpart to George Washington. Her 1607 rescue of Captain John Smith is one of the most appealing episodes in colonial history.

A number of the original chroniclers of the Jamestown colony mention Pocahontas by name and note her interactions with the English settlers. By the early 1700s her reputation was well established, but it was during the nineteenth century, when the brief history of America was recognized as containing elements useful in the construction of romantic visual and literary narratives, that saw the greatest dissemination of the Pocahontas legend. Her story was wrested from the exclusive purview of historians by novelists, dramatists, and artists, who, noting the potential in the great events of her life for stirring fictional portrayals, re-created and glamorized her accomplishments.

During the centuries since its creation, therefore, the Pocahontas narrative has so often been retold and embellished and so frequently adapted to contemporary issues that the actual, flesh-and-blood woman has become almost totally obscured by the burgeoning mythology.

This young woman, who was known among her own people as "Matoaka" and whose nickname was "Pocahontas" ("little wanton" or "little plaything"), apparently possessed a number of extraordinary qualities, including a spirited and engaging personality, but only scattered references to her appearance and character have survived. William Strachey, in his rendition of the early days of the Virginia colony (for which he was the first secretary), provided the shocking depiction of her as a naked young girl cavorting with the boys of the settlement, as well as the report that she had been married to an Indian named Kocoum. The chief architect of the Pocahontas legend, however, is Captain John Smith, who wrote of her in his *Generall Historie* published in 1624.

The trustworthiness of all the early accounts can be called into question, but the scarcity of verifiable "facts" proved in a way to be a boon to the literary and visual artists who wished to tell her story; they were therefore free to depict its events in whatever form they wished. By the end of the nineteenth century, although their historical veracity was still at times debated, their truth as sources had grown beyond the power of those who would attempt to demythologize the heroine of Jamestown.

In his *Generall Historie,* Smith recorded that after being taken prisoner by Indians in December 1607, his life was endangered by the men of the village to which he was taken. As they prepared to "beate out [my] braines," he wrote, Pocahontas—the adolescent daughter of Chief Powhatan—"got his head in her armes, and laid her owne upon his to save him from death."

Through much of the late 1800s, New England historians, intent on discrediting the South's efforts to formulate an impressive history of its own, concluded that debunking the legend of Pocahontas would cause the "Virginia aristocracy" to be "utterly gravelled." These historians ultimately succeeded in casting serious doubt on whether a rescue had ever taken place.

Ethnologists are inclined to dismiss the rescue as highly problematical because Smith did not mention it in his earliest accounts of his capture, and the behavior described does not conform to what is known of Indians of the Powhatan Confederacy.

Sharing the ethnologists' suspicion that Smith's life was never in danger, some historians have suggested that the rescue was a ritual the Englishman simply did not understand. According to that theory, Pocahontas served as a sponsor for Smith as he was adopted into Powhatan's tribe. Smith's death was only ceremonial, a prelude to his rebirth into Indian society. Ethnologists, however, have no evidence that the Indians practiced such a ritual.

A final possibility is that the incident was a test of Smith's manliness and that the outcome was left unresolved when Pocahontas intervened. Throughout their lives, the courage of

Powhatan men was under scrutiny. Because they were repeatedly tested, they often similarly tested opponents through physical torture or the threat of it.

Smith's account of the rescue was apparently accepted by his contemporaries. In 1623, when Smith testified to a commission conducting an in-depth investigation of the Virginia Company, he credited the "King's daughter as the means to returne me safe to James towne." He would hardly have lied to an investigative committee that had access to multiple witnesses with firsthand knowledge.

Did Pocahontas really rescue Smith? The question may never be answered conclusively. Although there are disturbing anthropological questions, the historical evidence is persuasive. Until proven otherwise, Pocahontas should probably be awarded credit for saving Smith, if only from a test of his composure under duress.

In the spring of 1613, Captain Samuel Argall, a navigator and administrator who had arrived in the colony in 1612, learned that Pocahontas was visiting the Patowomeck Indians of what is now northern Virginia. He arranged for her abduction in order to exchange her for several English prisoners held by Powhatan and for arms, tools, and corn.

Powhatan was "much grieved" to learn of the capture of Pocahontas. He immediately sent instructions that the Englishman should "use his Daughter well, and bring my [Argall's] ship into his River, and there he would give mee my demands." Within a "few dayes" Powhatan returned seven English hostages and three tools. This was not enough to satisfy the English, however, and a year went by before another attempt was made to resolve the impasse.

In March 1614, colonial administrator Sir Thomas Dale set out toward Powhatan's residence with Pocahontas and 150 men, determined "either to move [the Indians] to fight for her... or to restore the residue of our demands."

When the two sides met, a battle seemed imminent until "[t]wo of Powhatans sonnes being very desirous to see their sister... came unto us, at the sight of whom, and her well fare... they much rejoyced, and promised that they would undoubtedly persuade their father to redeeme her, and to conclude a firme peace forever with us."

At this point, however, colonist John Rolfe, a twenty-eight-year-old widower, announced to Dale by letter his love for Pocahontas and his interest in marrying her. Dale readily approved the pairing and thereby ended any chance for the "redemption" of Pocahontas, who had already been baptized, or who was in the process of becoming well versed enough in the religion of her captors to contemplate conversion.

There is no written account of the details surrounding Pocahontas's baptism in 1613 or early in 1614, at which she was given the name Rebecca. John Smith recorded, however, that by Rolfe's "diligent care" she was taught to speak English "as might well bee understood," and was "well instructed in Christianitie."

During Pocahontas's captivity, "John Rolfe had bin in love with [her] and she with him." Although is "hartie and best thoughts [had] a long time bin so intangled," Rolfe agonized over what he perceived to be a moral dilemma. He attempted to convince himself that he was not motivated by "the unbridled desire of carnall affection" but was acting "for the good of this plantation, for the honour of our countrie, for the glory of God, for my owne saluation, and for the converting to the true knowledge of God and Jesus Christ, an unbeleeving creature...." Finally, Rolfe concluded that marriage to Pocahontas would be morally correct, even a "holy... worke."

Powhatan found the proposed marriage of his daughter "acceptable" and gave his consent. He sent "an olde uncle of hirs, named Opachisco, to give her as his deputy in the Church, and two of his sonnes to see the marriage solemnized."

Two years later, Pocahontas traveled to England with her husband and young son, Thomas. Her journey was an arrangement of the Virginia Company, the organization that sponsored the Jamestown settlement. The company was continually in search of investors and colonists and eager for the potential financial reward of colonization, but its leadership also had a genuine concern that Virginia's Indians be Christianized. Pocahontas, the converted daughter of a chief, was impressive evidence of the attractiveness of Virginia as an investment and of the founding's success as a missionary endeavor.

Pocahontas, Rolfe, and Thomas left Virginia in the spring of 1616 with Dale and his party. The Virginia Company provided Pocahontas with a small living allowance while in England and saw to it that she was presented to society. The reception given "Rebecca Rolfe" was warm, and her visit generated a great deal of attention and excitement. She "did not onely accustome her selfe to civilitie, but still carried her selfe as the Daughter of a King, and was accordingly respected, not onely by the company... but of divers particular persons of Honor, in their hopefull zeale by her to advance Christianitie."

The Rolfes began the return trip to Virginia in the spring of 1617 but got no further than Gravesend. There Pocahontas died at the age of twenty-two, the victim of an illness that had "unexpectedly" developed. Her Christian faith remained constant; those who witnessed her death were "joy[ous]... to heare and see her make so religious and godly an end."

Dr. William M. S. Rasmussen is Virginius C. Hall Curator of Art at the Virginia Historical Society. Dr. Robert S. Tilton is professor of American Literature at Queens College in New York.

The Pueblo Revolt

The Pueblo Indians in the province of New Mexico had long chafed
under Spanish rule. In 1680 all their grievances flared into a violent rebellion
that surprised the Europeans with its ferocity.

by Jake Page

THERE WAS A CHILL in the air in the pre-dawn hours of August 10, 1680, as Brother Juan Batista Pío settled himself on his horse. The Franciscan priest had heard rumors that the Pueblo Indians were planning to revolt against the Spanish who lived in New Mexico, the most remote and least productive colony in all of New Spain. Indians had murdered a Spanish settler the night before at the pueblo of Tesuque, situated among the low hills some 10 miles from Santa Fe, and Brother Pío set off for the village in the belief that he could calm its people and turn them from rebellion to join in the fellowship of Holy Mass.

Pedro Hidalgo made a mad dash for his life after he realized that Pueblo Indians had murdered Brother Juan Batista Pío. The Franciscan's death marked the beginning of a resistance movement that drove the Spanish from New Mexico.

Brother Pío and his soldier escort, Pedro Hidalgo, proceeded through the dark green piñon pines and desert junipers that dotted the rolling, reddish-brown landscape. Finding Tesuque deserted, they continued on into the surrounding countryside in search of the Indians. As they descended into a shallow ravine the two men saw the villagers, carrying weapons and with their faces painted red, headed for the mountains. "What is this, children?" the Franciscan cried out. "Are you mad? Do not disturb yourselves. I will die a thousand deaths for you."

As Hidalgo rode along, he watched Brother Pío move deeper into the ravine and disappear around a corner. A short time later one of the Indians suddenly burst from the ravine, carrying the friar's shield. Close behind him came another Indian, spattered with blood. More Indians swarmed out of the ravine to attack Hidalgo, but the soldier spurred his horse into a gallop and escaped. He saw no sign of the priest. Hidalgo rode back to Santa Fe to alert the Spanish governor of New Mexico, Antonio de Otermín, that the uprising was no longer a rumor.

BROTHER PÍO'S MURDER that morning was among the first actions of the Pueblo Indian revolt, an uprising that profoundly and permanently altered the history of the American Southwest. The violence had been a long time coming. The Indian's resentment against the Spanish had begun to smolder with Francisco Vásquez de Coronado's trek through their country in 1540–42. The Spaniard had demanded food and supplies from the Indians and had attacked any pueblos that refused him. The resentment intensified with the arrival of settlers, soldiers, and friars in 1598. The colonists found communities of trim multi-storied houses built of dried mud and surrounded by green fields all along the river the Europeans called the Rio Del Norte. They called the Indian towns *pueblos,* after the Spanish word for village. The settlers moved in between the pueblos, the friars moved into the villages, and the secular authorities established a capital in one of the northern pueblos, which they called San Juan. The Spaniards later moved the capital to Santa Fe, establishing what is today the oldest continuing capital in the United States.

The Franciscan cried out. "Are you mad? Do not disturb yourselves. I will die a thousand deaths for you."

It wasn't long before these developments had thrown the traditional world of the peaceful and agricultural Pueblo Indians into chaos. The Spanish governors demanded food tributes and labor, and they responded to Indian resistance with beatings, mutilations, or death. European diseases, such as smallpox and measles, devastated the native population, claiming more than one-third of the estimated 25,000 Indians that inhabited the Southwest.

*The Pueblo Indians'
decades of resentment
finally erupted as they
burned the Spaniards'
missions, murdered
priests, and defiled altars.
"Now God and Santa
Maria were dead," the
Indians said.*

Some cultural exchanges, however, proved beneficial. European irrigation techniques helped the Pueblo farmers, and the Spanish absorbed local Indian lore about herbal remedies. The colonists brought livestock and useful crops, such as peaches, to add to the Indian staples of corn, melons, and beans. But even these advantages brought difficulties, as the bounty made the Pueblo villages all the more attractive to raids by nomadic bands of Apaches. Traditionalists among the Pueblo Indians complained that the new God of the Spanish and His representatives were not taking care of the people.

Of all the Native Americans' grievances, however, the greatest was the Franciscans' determination to stamp out all vestiges of the Indians' religion. The priests found the elaborate performances by masked dancers representing the manifold spirits of nature, called *kachinas,* particularly offensive. The Indians performed the dances in underground chambers called *kivas,* which the Spanish ridiculed as *estufas,* or stoves, for the smoke that issued forth from their roof entrances. The Spanish clergy saw such rites as works of the devil and witchcraft.

As the years passed, circumstances and Spanish intolerance worked to feed the Pueblos' resentment. Prior to the Spaniards' arrival, the Indians withstood the Southwest's periodic droughts by storing reserves and bartering with other pueblos. But the Spanish took all surplus as tribute, monopolized the Indian labor force, and prohibited trade between pueblos, so the Indians had nothing to sustain them when a four-year drought struck in 1666. According to Brother Juan Bernal, "For three years now no

crops have been harvested. In the past year, 1668, a great many Indians perished of hunger, lying dead along the roads, in ravines, and in their huts. There were pueblos where more than 450 died of hunger." Then in 1671 a new epidemic broke out, possibly anthrax, killing thousands of Indians and creating the psychological havoc that only a totally mysterious catastrophe can cause. Thus weakened, the province became even easier prey for marauding tribes. The resentments smoldered.

In addition to roughly 100 celestial and temporal officials and soldiery, by the 1670s the Spanish population included more than 1,000 settlers who lived among 17,000 Pueblo Indians. Although drastically outnumbered, the Spanish colonial government continued to crack down on native resistance, even stepping up its programs against native religion by outlawing it altogether and destroying many *kivas.* When Governor Juan Francisco de Treviño heard rumors in 1675 of Pueblo Indians practicing witchcraft, he rounded up 47 of their religious leaders, hauled them to the provincial capital of Santa Fe, and had them publicly whipped. The governor sentenced four to hang. In response, 70 warriors stormed Treviño's private rooms and threatened to kill him and lead a revolt unless he released the remaining 43 prisoners. Treviño relented.

Among those released was a man named Popé, from the northern pueblo of San Juan. Popé was said to have remarkable powers, including the ability to communicate directly with a revered deity called Po-Se-Ye-Mo. Fleeing further Spanish harassment, Popé retreated to a *kiva* in the northernmost Pueblo of Taos and communicated with Po-Se-Ye-Mo, who demanded nothing less than total eradication of the Spanish invaders. Various pueblos began to set aside some of their traditional isolation from each other and listen to this prophet's talk of rebellion.

Since the arrival of the Spanish colonists, the Pueblo Indians had attempted several revolts. Typically they had involved only a few pueblos, which were ultimately betrayed by Indians loyal to the Holy Church and the Europeans. The Spanish publicly hanged rebellion

leaders, so Popé became a fanatic about secrecy. He supposedly executed his own son-in-law when the man fell under suspicion.

Popé found a growing number of pueblos who were willing to work together against their mutual enemy. Achieving such unity among the Indian villages—historically independent, spread out over hundreds of miles, and speaking different languages and dialects—was one of Popé's most astonishing feats. Planning took place over several years, and in 1680 the auspices appeared good. Snowfall in the mountains along the Rio Grande had been heavy and the spring especially cool, delaying snowmelt. Popé knew that the snow would melt quickly in the summer heat, and the rivers would run unusually high. As a result, the triennial pack train—would be unable to ford the waterways. With their stores and ammunition running low, the Spanish in the province would be vulnerable.

The plotters chose August 12, 1680, for the day of the uprising and dispatched runners to spread the word. The messengers delivered a knotted string to all the rebel Pueblo leaders. They were to untie one knot each day. On the day they untied the last knot, it was time to strike. But rumors of the revolt reached the new governor, Antonio de Otermín, in Santa Fe on August 9. He immediately sent troops to search out and capture the Indian runners. Two youths were brought to the capital and tortured until they revealed that August 12 was the date of the uprising. They were then executed. The province of New Mexico was rife with intrigue and hidden allegiances, so Popé and the other leaders learned almost immediately that their plans had been discovered. They sent word around the pueblos that the date of the revolt had been changed to August 10, the very next day. With surprise on their side, the Indians of Tesuque killed Brother Pío, while other Pueblos overran haciendas from Taos to Santa Fe, killing European men, women and children. Taking horses and whatever weapons they could find, the attackers moved on. At missions Indian bands killed the priests, vandalized icons, befouled altars, and set the churches on fire in ferocious retribution for the stolen *kachina* masks and the other depredations the friars had wrought on their ceremonial ways for more than 80 years.

The Spanish finally submitted to the inevitable and left New Mexico after more than 80 years of colonization. However, the Pueblo alliances that made the Spanish defeat possible soon fell apart.

A handful of Spanish settlers escaped to Santa Fe with word of the uprising's progress. Otermín ordered all settlers in and around Santa Fe to congregate in the governor's palace for safety. By noon, the palace's plaza was jammed with settlers, soldiers, and livestock. Messengers brought word of Indian claims that "God and Santa Maria were dead," and that their own god had never died.

To the south, Indians sympathetic to the Europeans gathered together with the settlers under the command of Lieutenant Governor Alonso García in the Isleta Pueblo. A few rebellion Indians brought "news" to García that all the Spanish to the north—including Governor Otermín—were dead. A standing Spanish order forbade anyone, even the lieutenant governor, from leaving the province without the governor's permission. But believing Otermín dead and his own position untenable, García ordered those assembled to head south in the hope of meeting up with the triennial pack train and reinforcements.

Thanks to this disinformation campaign, Otermín remained isolated in Santa Fe for three more days as reports of death and destruction poured in. On August 13, the governor received word that many pueblos that had professed loyalty to the Spanish government were now joining the rebellion. According to Brother Francisco Gómez, Otermín, "foreseeing that all the nations [of the province] will join together and destroy this villa," ordered Gómez to "consume the most holy sacrament, and take the

images, sacred vessels, and things appertaining to divine worship, close the church and convent, and bring everything to the palace."

Two days later, as small armies of Indians assembled outside the capital to lay siege, Otermín was astonished to see his former manservant, an Indian he called Juan, arrive on horseback for a parley at the governor's palace. Juan wore as a sash one of the cloth bookmarks from the altar of a nearby convent and carried two crosses, one red, the other white. He offered Otermín a choice—take the white cross and the Spanish could leave the province without further harm. If the Spanish governor chose the red cross, more blood would flow.

Otermín chose neither, but instead offered amnesty to the Indians if they would go home after swearing fealty to Spain and the Holy Church. The Indians simply jeered at this and began setting fire to Santa Fe's outlying buildings. Otermín ordered all his soldiers—who numbered less than 100—into battle formation outside the government buildings. According to Spanish records, in a day of fighting "many of the enemy were killed and they wounded many of our men, because they came with the harquebuses and the arms which they had taken from the religious and Spaniards, and were well provided with powder and shot." Despite their losses, the Indians held fast until more warriors arrived and forced the Spanish back into the plaza of the governor's palace. During the next three days, the Indians' ranks swelled to some 2,500, and they rained arrows into the plaza, adding to the panic that was rapidly growing as food supplies ran out and sanitary conditions grew desperate in the heat.

Then August 18 the Indians cut off Santa Fe's water supply by damming the river that ran through the plaza. Two days later, deciding that "it would be a better and safer step to die fighting than of hunger and thirst," Otermín and his remaining soldiers charged the Pueblo Indians. In the melee, the Spanish claimed to have killed some 300 Indians and captured another 47. They herded their captives into the plaza for interrogation and execution. The remaining warriors temporarily withdrew, but every Spanish

soldier bore at least one wound, including Otermín, who had three.

By August 21, Otermín recognized that the situation in the plaza was hopeless. He believed that from north to south "all the people, religious, and Spaniards have perished…. For which reasons, and finding ourselves out of provisions, with very few horses, weary, and threatened by the enemy, and not being assured of water, or of defense" Otermín decided to "withdraw, marching [south] from this villa in full military formation until reaching the Pueblo of La Isleta." There he expected to find Lieutenant Governor García. The Spanish said Mass, then Otermín and approximately 1,000 others filed out of the plaza. Most were on foot.

The Pueblo warriors simply watched as the hated invaders finally left.

They feared the Indians would attack once they left the shelter of the plaza, but no assault occurred. Instead, the Pueblo warriors simply watched as the hated invaders finally left. All along the dreary road south the Spanish saw the burned buildings and grisly remains of the revolt's victims, while the Indians monitored their progress from the surrounding high ground. On August 26, just a day away from Isleta and the much-needed provisions they expected to find there, Otermín learned from a captured rebel Indian that García had taken his people away to the south.

Otermín sent scouts to overtake the lieutenant governor, and García immediately rode north to meet the governor. Otermín arrested his lieutenant governor for desertion and began court proceedings. In his defense, García argued that all intelligence from the north reported everyone there dead, and he claimed never to have received Otermín's orders to send aid to Santa Fe. Otermín acquitted García, and together they resumed their journey south.

They reached El Paso del Norte in early October. There, in what are today the slums of Ciudad Juarez, a few Indians and the Spanish refugees settled uncomfortably, some for good. Otermín estimated that 380 settlers had died in the uprising, and of that number only 73 had been adult males. Twenty-one out of 40 Franciscans had been martyred.

Although their victory proved temporary, in the history of Indian-white relations in North America the Pueblo Indians were the only Native Americans to successfully oust European invaders from their territory. A few years earlier in New England, eastern woodlands tribes had battled against colonists in King Philip's War, but they were defeated and driven to near extinction. Other great Indian leaders such as Pontiac and Tecumseh later organized their people into rebellions against encroaching Europeans, but they too were beaten. The Sioux would win the Battle of the Little Bighorn in 1876, but they ultimately lost the war for the Plains. Apart from the Pueblos, only the Seminoles were able to retain some of their homeland for any length of time, by waging war from the swamps of the Florida Everglades (see "The Florida Quagmire," October 1999).

For the Pueblo Indians, victory was short-lived. Popé demanded complete eradication of all things Spanish, including the valuable crops, such as peaches, they had introduced. He became something of a dictator, and the Pueblo alliance began to unravel soon after the Spanish exodus. Leadership changed hands, old feuds resurfaced, and the pueblos reverted to their normal quarreling. Popé apparently died in disgrace.

The lesson of the revolt was clear—the Pueblo people would rather die than relinquish their religious practices.

In January 1681 the Spanish government issued an order that the New Mexican province was to be reestablished as soon as possible. But it wasn't until 1693 that the Spanish staged a successful return under a new governor, Diego de Vargas. As before, the Europeans met resistance with force, literally obliterating some pueblos. Not for another three years would an uneasy peace again reign in New Mexico. The success of the Pueblo revolt continued to affect the regions beyond New Mexico, however, for years afterward. Word spread south into the tribes of Mexico and encouraged rebellions and resistance that plagued the colonists for decades. Plains Indians gained access to Spanish horses and began to breed them, transforming tribes such as the Cheyenne, Sioux, Apache, and Comanche into some of the finest light cavalry the world has ever seen.

There was lasting change in New Mexico too, as demonstrated by the returning Spanish, in particular the Franciscan friars. They now had an odd respect for the natives. The lesson of the revolt was clear—the Pueblo people would rather die than relinquish their religious practices. The friars, thus chastened, made no further attempt to stamp out the pagan religions of the Pueblos, but instead allowed them and the Catholic rites to co-exist. Pueblo people today attribute the persistence of their cultures to the 1680 uprising.

On a given Pueblo Indian feast day, the people assembled at night in the mission church for Mass and at dawn they carry the patron saint's statue from the church to the plaza. Enshrined there, the saint watches the new day unfold as hundreds of Pueblos dance through the day in a performance that both celebrates and reinforces their own unique heritage and culture.

Jake Page and his photographer wife, Susanne, have produced two books on the Hopi and Navajo Indians, along with numerous other books and articles on Indian affairs. Page is currently writing a popular history of the Pueblo rebellion.

Bearing the Burden?
Puritan Wives

Obedience, modesty, taciturnity—all hallmarks of the archetypal 'good woman' in colonial New England. But did suffering in silence invert tradition and give the weaker sex a new moral authority in the community? Martha Saxton investigates, in the first piece from a mini series examining women's social experience in the New World.

Martha Saxton

Seventeenth-century American Puritans subordinated female to male, wife to husband, and mother to father, insisting on obedience, modesty, and taciturnity for women. They justified this arrangement by emphasising woman's descent from Eve and her innate irrationality, both of which made her more vulnerable to error and corruption than man. Because of this she was to view her husband as God's representative in the family. He would mediate her religious existence and direct her temporal one. She would produce children and care for them, but he would have the ultimate authority over them.

At the same time, the experience of Puritans of both sexes in the second half of the seventeenth century undermined this clearly defined system of authority in which the allocation of secular power flowed from a presumed moral and spiritual hierarchy. After 1660, women began outnumbering men in the churches, and by the end of the century the numerical difference was sufficient to prompt Cotton Mather to attempt to account for the demonstrated female proclivity for spirituality. Mather ascribed enhanced female religiosity precisely to that subordination that Puritan men insisted upon

as well as mothers' suffering during childbirth.

Long before Mather published his conclusions at the end of the seventeenth century, other Puritan men anticipated his thinking about female virtue, and many identified its sources in female suffering. Men praised the patient endurance of wives with abusive husbands. Others granted to childbirth pain the power to enhance goodness. Some saw the sacrifices of mothering, rather than childbirth per se, as a source of virtue and testified to the moral significance of their mothers in the conduct of their lives. And still others simply acknowledged their mothers, wives, or other female relatives as inspirational or spiritually influential to them.

In the Puritan world then, women could and did earn respect for their moral stature in the family, and this was meaningful to women deprived of public recognition in a society run by men. It would be an important heritage to women of a later era. Pious women would pass on the idea that their principled expressions of conscience could shape morally, both family and society.

Before looking at the way women achieved moral authority, let us look at how Puritan men elaborated beliefs

about the propriety of subordinating women to men. John Winthrop, Governor of Massachusetts, who was happily married to three submissive women, writing in the mid-seventeenth century put the ideal case:

A true wife accounts her subjection her honor and freedom and would not think her condition safe and free but in her subjection to her husband's authority. Such is the liberty of the church under the authority of Christ, her king and husband; his yoke is so easy and sweet to her as a bride's ornaments; and if through forwardness or wantonness, etc., she shakes it off at any time, she is at no rest in her spirit until she take it up again; and whether her lord smiles upon her and embraceth her in his arms, or whether he frowns and rebukes her, or smites her, she comprehends the sweetness of his love in all, and is refreshed, and instructed by every such dispensation of his authority over her.

While not all American Puritans saw female obedience in such a cheerful light as Winthrop did, all agreed that it was essential to marital satisfaction and should exist regardless of the husband's comportment. John Cotton compared wifely obedience to the excellence and inevitability of the universe, the air we breathe, and the clouds that shower rain upon the earth. Benjamin Wadsworth, in a book published in 1712, wrote that a woman should 'reverence' her husband, as the Bible commanded. He was God's representative in the family, and even if he should 'pass the bounds of wisdom and kindness; yet must not she shake off the bond of submission but must bear patiently the burden, which God hath laid upon the daughters of Eve'. And Cotton Mather, writing before his final, tempestuous marriage to Lydia Lee George would give these words a wistful ring, insisted that though the husband be 'ever so much a Churl, yet she treats him considerately'.

An important facet of this unanimous male insistence on female submission was the envy and fascination Puritan men felt for womanly meekness and obedience. Salvation demanded that men, as well as women, submit to God's will in all things. For women, submission to God's will and the will of the men around them made their lives, ideally, a continuum of obedience.

Men, however, enjoyed considerable social power during their lifetime as husbands and, depending upon their status, as community leaders. Submission and the self-suppression that it required, was, therefore, a more prickly and intractable issue for men than for women. Furthermore, as husbands, men determined how heavily or lightly the yoke of marriage would rest on their wives' shoulders. Men's direct responsibility for the suffering that their domination might cause women was likely to make them particularly alive to the issue.

Cotton Mather, who had openly linked woman's tendency to spiritual excellence with her subordination and suffering, wrote 'But if thou hast an Husband that will do so, [beat his wife] bear it patiently; and know thou shalt have—Rewards—hereafter for it, as well as *Praises* here...'. And Puritan men since the settlement of Plymouth had praised women for remaining uncomplainingly with husbands who were

violent and/or unfaithful. Mrs Lyford, of Plymouth endured—and sometimes witnessed—her husband's sexual escapades for years in silence. Eventually, she testified against him. But, wrote the governor of the colony, William Bradford, approvingly, 'being a grave matron, and of good carriage... spoake of those things out of the sorrow of her harte, sparingly'.

The wife of Jared Davis submitted to years of her husband's cruelty, drunkenness, lies, scandalous behaviour, and indolence. He had, according to John Winthrop, neither compassion nor humanity toward his wife, insisted on sex with her when she was pregnant (which Puritans regarded as dangerous) and did not provide for her. The governor admired Mrs Davis who, under all these provocations, continued to try to help her husband. As Winthrop had written elsewhere, Mrs Davis was able to find in her husband's blows, God's love and correction. Winthrop and Bradford believed that the Christlike acceptance of lengthy, undeserved abuse endowed women with a unique moral vantage point from which they might even venture to criticise their victimisers.

Men were also fascinated by—and implicated in—the crisis of child labour and delivery, which combined submission to physical suffering as well as the more difficult task: resignation to the possibility of death. Husbands were awed by their wives' apparent conquest of mortal fear. Puritans believed that pregnancy rendered women more fearful than usual. The Reverend Peter Thacher wrote in his diary in February 1680, that his wife had fallen on a chair, and was 'soe frighted with it that shee had like to have fainted away' because she feared she had hurt the child in her womb. When normally timid women, rendered even more so by pregnancy, triumphed over the terror of death, they reassured the whole community of its ability to conquer its fear of the hereafter through submission to God. As Mather said at the funeral of seventeen-year-old Mrs Rebeckah Burnel in 1724:

But when it pleases Him, to take *children,* and those of that *Sex* which *Fear* is most incident and

enslaving to; and make such *Babes and Sucklings* to triumph over the *Enemy,*—Oh! The *Wondrous Power* of our God!...

Thirteen years earlier, Cotton Mather's sister, Jerusha, decided when she was five months pregnant that it was time to get herself ready for death. She acknowledged that she was a fearful creature, and especially so because of her pregnancy, and wished to give herself up completely to God. She vowed that if God gave her an easy and short labour that she would dedicate herself to bringing up her child in fear of Him. She petitioned for a 'resigned will' and to be made fit for whatever God demanded for her. When her labour approached she prayed to be delivered from the sin of fear. As it happened, her labour was easy, but she and her baby died a short time later.

Mather, in recording his sister's death, assured his readers that Jerusha, while exceptionally joyous, said 'nothing that look'd at all Delirious', lest they discount the God-given courage with which she had faced her end. He quoted her as saying that when she was healthy 'Death was a Terror to me. But now I know, I shall Dy, I am not at *all afraid of it. This* is a Wonderful *Work of God!* I know *that I am* going to Christ... *I see things that are Unutterable!'*. Her father, Increase Mather, asked her if she were not afraid of death. 'She replied with great Earnestness; "Not in the least! Not in the least! Not in the least!"' Mather ended his memoir with what he said were her last words, 'Eye has not seen, Ear has not heard, neither entered into the Heart of Man, the things which God has prepared for them that Love Him!' Mather's text pointed out in many ways that if a frail, sickly and frightened (i.e. womanly) woman lived as a Puritan woman should, she would die blissfully; hence, ran the implicit parallel, how much easier would it be for a strong man to do the same.

Similarly, Barbara Ruggles, an inhabitant of Roxburg, was able, according to the Roxburg Church records, to 'shine in her life & death' because of the way she dealt with her afflictions, including a fatal delivery. She had a 'stone chollik in which sicknesse she manifested much patiens, and faith; she dyed in childbed... & left a godly savor behind her'.

When a woman lost the mortal battle of birth graciously, she acquired unhesitating male praise. When she won, her husband's admiration might be muted by feelings of competition or guilty ambivalence about the pleasure in which such suffering originated. In journal accounts, husbands often expropriated the religious significance of their wives' brushes with death to themselves. They mingled their admiration with a vision of their *own* sins as the origin of their wives' agonies.

When, in the late 1660s, God visited upon the wife of the Reverend Joseph Thompson of Billerica such a weakness as made the couple fear her pregnancy might end badly, Thompson took a lesson in submission to the Lord's will from his wife's peril. He acknowledged that nothing could happen without God's intervention. The Lord further let him see that he had not been sufficiently grateful for the health, companionship, and work of his wife. He therefore feared that God might punish him by taking her away—although one can imagine that Mrs Thompson probably saw the punishment as hers. He prayed that the Lord would restore his wife's health and vowed perpetual gratitude for her. When his wife recovered, he charged himself with a return to indifference toward his blessings in her and a 'vile hart'. Mrs Thompson's near-death underlined to Thompson the sinful contrast between his unthankful acceptance of his spouse and his brief, divinely-inspired awareness of her value. And uncertainty and fear gave Thompson an all-too-brief reminder of the level of active, spiritual struggle on which he should be conducting more of his life.

The Reverend Thomas Shepard, in ruminating about the imminent birth of his child in the 1640s, wondered what would happen if the labour did not go well 'and her pains be long and [the] Lord remember my sin? And I began to trouble my heart with fear of the worst'. When he learned that his wife had delivered a baby safely, '... I saw the Lord's mercy and my own folly, to disquiet my heart with fear of what never shall be nor will be, and not rather to submit unto the Lord's will, and, come what can come, to be quiet there'. Like Thompson, Shepard's wife's mortal risk made him acutely conscious of his own sins. When his fears went unrealised he attempted to learn the lesson of peaceful resignation to God's will. He could not avoid seeing that his wife, in giving herself up to the miseries and uncertain outcome of travail, embodied this lesson.

In the same period the Reverend Michael Wigglesworth described his intimate involvement in his wife's labour. When she had pain, he:

> lay sighing, sweating, praying, almost fainting through weakness before morning. The next day, the spleen much enfeebled me, and setting in with grief took away my strength, my heart was smitten within me, and as sleep departed from myne eyes my stomach abhored meat, I was brought very low and knew not how to pass away another night.

He then described feeling hasty and impatient', presumably with the excessive duration of their labour, and he prayed that the Lord make him want to 'stoop to his will'. His wife's endurance taunted him with the patience and submission he lacked. And although he portrayed his wife's labour as his own, it was she who demonstrated uncomplaining fortitude in the face of pains which he likened to 'the pangs of eternal death'.

If women who were courageous in childbirth accrued complicated, competitive admiration from men, energetically religious mothering produced more straightforward praise. Sons whose mothers had toiled over their salvation knew from their own deep experience of maternal force what such efforts entailed. Unlike husbands who had impregnated their wives but been excluded from the redemptive suffering of labour, sons had been the object of mothers' strenuous efforts and sacrifices. Cotton Mather described a good mother 'travail[ing] for her children more than once' to save them from the abominable sinfulness with which human birth had infected them. She was to work as hard as she could, instilling the principles of religion in her babies and catechising them as soon as they could speak.

Perhaps the most fearsome aspect of a righteous mother was that she would rather see her children dead than living outside the grace of God. In Michael Wigglesworth's famous epic, *The Day of Doom,* (1662) 'The tender mother will own no other/of all her numerous brood/ But such as stand at Christ's right hand/ acquitted through his blood'. Mothers with this unique spiritual ferocity, who gave more importance to their children's salvation than to their physical lives, were exhibiting the highest form of human love a Puritan could imagine. And yet, it could engender the starkest fear.

Of all imagery pertaining to females, Puritans had the most positive associations with the lactating breast. In sermons, ministers used metaphors giving God, the father, the capacity to nurse his children. This potent symbol of security, warmth and joy—the union of loving mother and nursing infant stood in stark contrast to the mother who would repudiate her unsaved offspring. In the eyes of a small child, the mother's immense power to give peace and happiness was paired with her ability to destroy forever the ease and hope of the unrepentant child.

These contrasting childhood images of perfect love and total terror persisted in the imaginations of children of such fervent mothers. In childbirth husbands saw wives resigned to God's will to sacrifice their own lives to create life. But the sons of deeply pious women remembered their mothers' seeming willingness to sacrifice *them* if their wickedness demanded it. Such fearsome, Janus-faced mothers undoubtedly contributed to men's admiration for female virtue at the same time that they implanted an abiding fear of powerful women.

Thomas Shepard recalled admiringly that his second wife cried and prayed in secret for her son, requesting that 'if the Lord did not intend to glorify himself by thee, that he would cut thee off by death rather than to live to dishonour him by sin'. His first wife, on the other hand, displayed the other ultimate motherly virtue. In explaining to his son his mother's death, Shepard said that she 'died in the Lord, departing out of this world to another, who did lose her life by being careful to preserve thine, for in the ship thou wert so feeble and froward both in the day and night that hereby she lost her strength and at last her life'. The first Mrs Shepard had sacrificed her life so that her child could live, and the second Mrs Shepard was willing to sacrifice her *son* if his soul became corrupt. A mighty Puritan mother elicited both veneration and terror.

The sons of other spiritually influential women came up with more tranquil memories, formed from less terrifying maternal images. These men recalled prayerful women to whom love meant hawklike watchfulness for their sons' salvation. Thomas Shepard remembered that his own mother, who died when he was still young, bore 'exceeding great love to me and made many prayers for me'. In Increase Mather's *Autobiography* he called his mother, Cotton's grandmother, 'a very Holy, praying woman. She desired two things for him, he remembered: grace and learning. As a boy he learned to read from his mother. His father taught him to write, 'who also instructed me in grammar learning' in Latin and Greek. But, as Cotton later remembered, Increase's mother taught her son, his father, 'all that was Good... among her Instructions... she mightily Inculcated the lesson of *Diligence*'.

Mather had often heard about his grandmother's potent combination of love and exhortation. He proudly recounted family lore: when Increase was very little his mother told him, that he was 'very much her *Darling*', and that all she wished for him was to be a good Christian and a good scholar. She pleaded successfully on her deathbed that her fifteen-year-old son go into the ministry. She had been most 'honourable... for her *Vertue*,... that for which a *Woman* is most of all *to be Praised*'. She was Mather's model for his twice-travailing mother. He wrote, 'She was a Woman of Uncommon Devotion, and in her Importunate Prayers for this her son, she... became *Twice a Mother* to him'. Mather's own mother had similar moral structure, challenging the family to live up to her example. Mather remembered

her as 'a Godly, an Humble, and a Praying Woman, and one that often set apart *Whole Days* for prayer and Secret Interviews with Heaven'.

Frances Boland arrived in America from Scotland in 1682. In his journal he gave special thanks for the 'pious nurture and example of my godly mother.... She was a praying woman and prayed much for her children'. He went on to say what a blessing it was for the young to have parents such as his.

John Dane, a surgeon in Ipswich, Massachusetts, remembered with respect that his mother had been a 'serious woman'. He recalled that she had once had a dream in which she heard a certain minister deliver a sermon; according to Dane's account she accurately foresaw the date, the place, and the text of that preacher's talk. Dane prudently did not praise his mother as a seer and mystic, which would have unsettled New World Puritans. Instead, he portrayed her as a sober student, indifferent to her gift of prophecy and desirous only to make 'good improvement of that sermon', which, thanks to her vision, she was able to enjoy twice.

The zealous mother was an exacting conscience to her children and, by extension, to the community. Embedded in the Puritan notion of community was mutual moral responsibility and the notion that the sin of one member stained the whole society. Boys and girls both grew up cultivating the ability to spot a sin in themselves and others. Cotton Mather wrote approvingly that his sister, Jerusha, recorded in her journal judgments on the activities and behaviour of people in the community. He wrote that in her journal:

She Remarks on the Dealings of God with Others; Especially if anything either Good or Bad were observable in the condition of the Town; But most of all what occur'd Joyful or Grievous, unto her nearest *Relatives,* and their Families; and she employes agreeable *Meditations* and *Supplications* there-upon.

Wives, in particular, were supposed to watch their husbands' spiritual state. Benjamin Wadsworth had written that

'If Husbands that call themselves Christian, are vain, wicked, ungodly; their pious Wives (if such they have) should by a meek winning Conversation, indeavour their spiritual & eternal Good'. Christopher Lawson sued his wife for divorce in 1669, accusing her of failing in her duty as a converted Puritan to attend to the spiritual needs of her unconverted husband. 'The unbelieving husband', he wrote, 'should be wonn by the good conversation of the believing wife...'.

The Reverend John Ward praised his wife for being an 'accusing conscience' and letting him know when he was acting in an ungodly manner. Mather extolled Ward's wife who had lived happily with her husband for forty years:

Although she would so faithfully tell him of everything that might seem amendable in him... yet she ever pleased him wonderfully. And she would oft put him upon the duties of secret fasts, and when she met with anything in reading that she counted singularly agreeable, she would still impart it unto him.

The marriage of the Wards was an active spiritual partnership in which Mrs Ward not infrequently gave her husband direction.

Women often achieved the role of conscience by becoming shadow ministers, absorbing, sometimes writing down (as Jerusha Mather did), and acting upon the weekly sermons of their husbands and/or pastors. Thomas Shepard commended his wife for her 'excellency to reprove for sin and discern the evils of men'. He went on to say that she loved the words of the Lord exceedingly and was, therefore, glad to read his notes for his sermons every week and ponder the thoughts therein.

Cotton Mather memorialised the second Mrs Whiting for her 'singular piety and gravity', who prayed in her closet every day to God. He commended her for writing down the sermons that she heard 'on the Lord's days with much dexterity', while living by their messages all week.

Although Puritan traditions cast doubt on women's capacity for goodness and prohibited them from exercising concrete authority, Puritan women did achieve moral stature from quietly enduring suffering, intense dedication to the salvation of their children, and gentle correction of the behaviour of their spouses and neighbours. The blessing Puritan men bestowed on notably virtuous women registered the conflict in which it was born. Women had to criticise, suggest, and direct others—particularly men—with extreme caution as Puritan men were deeply alarmed when women presumed to judge them. Nonetheless, Puritan women, inclined to religious depth, would find respect and deference in their communities, no small treasures in a male-dominated world.

And they would bequeath to later generations of women a tradition of moral criticism and the conviction that zealous effort on behalf of the salvation of others was part of their human responsibility. This belief would empower women to turn their moral energies upon their husbands, families, and, in time, the world around them.

FOR FURTHER READING

Laurel Thacher Ulrich, *Goodwives: Image and Reality in the Lives of Women of Northern New England, 1650–1750* (Knopt, 1982); Carol Karlsen, *The Devil in the Shape of a Woman* (Norton, 1987; David Leverenz, *The Language of Puri-tan Feeling* (Rutgers University Press, 1980); Perry Miller, *The American Puritan* (Doubleday/Anchor, 1956); Lyle Koehler, *A Search for Power, The "Weaker Sex" in Seventeenth Century New England* (University of Illinois Press, 1980); Kenneth Silverman, *The Life and Times of Cotton Mather* (Harper & Row, 1970).

Martha Saxton teaches Colonial History at Columbia University. She is author of Louisa May Alcott *(Andre Deutsch, 1977) and is currently working on a study of American women's moral standards—those prescribed for them and those they fashioned for themselves.*

Penning a Legacy

Imprisoned and vilified for his religious views, William Penn, a member of the Society of Friends, sought to establish a colony in the New World where people of all faiths could live in mutual harmony.

By Patricia Hudson

On A CHILL WINTER DAY in 1668, 24-year-old William Penn paced back and forth in a cramped chamber in the Tower of London. Arrested for blasphemy after publishing a pamphlet that questioned the doctrine of the Trinity, Penn was being held in close confinement. The Bishop of London had decreed that if Penn didn't recant publicly he would remain imprisoned for the rest of his life. Penn's reply was unequivocal: "My prison shall be my grave before I will budge a jot, for I owe my conscience to no mortal man."

WILLIAM PENN WAS born on October 14, 1644, just a stone's throw from the Tower where he would one day be a prisoner. His father, William, Sr., was an ambitious naval officer who rose to the rank of admiral. Knighted by King Charles II, the elder Penn formed a friendship with the royal family that would play a major role in his son's future.

The Penn family's next-door neighbor on Tower Hill was the diarist Samuel Pepys, who noted in his journal that Admiral Penn was "a merry fellow and pretty good-natured and sings very bawdy songs." Pepys also recorded instances of William, Jr., playing cards with his father, going to the theater, and carelessly leaving his sword in a hired coach and then racing across London to retrieve it.

One incident from Penn's youth foreshadowed his later preoccupation with religious matters—at 17 William was expelled from Oxford University for daring to criticize certain Church of England rituals. Appalled, Admiral Penn packed his overly serious son off to France, hoping that he would grow more worldly amid the glitter of Paris.

When William returned to England after two years abroad, Pepys described him as "a most modish person, grown a fine gentlemen, but [having] a great deal, if not too much, of the vanity of the French garb and affected manner of speech and gait." The admiral, well-pleased with his fashionable son, sent William to Ireland to attend to family business, but it was there, in 1667, that the younger Penn embraced the Quaker faith.

The Society of Friends—dubbed Quakers by their enemies because they admonished listeners to "tremble at the word of the Lord"—had been founded in 1647 by George Fox, a weaver's son-turned-preacher who spoke of the Inner Light and believed that there was "that of God in every man." According to Fox, all people, regardless of their status here on earth, are equal in God's eyes. It was a challenge directed at the very heart of England's class-conscious society, and though all religious dissenters were subject to fines and imprisonments, the establishment singled out Quakers with particular ferocity.

When Penn again returned to London, his family was aghast at the change in him. Not only did young William insist on attending the outlawed Quaker meetings, he also ignored common courtesy by refusing to take off his hat in the presence of his "betters," just one of several methods Friends used to illustrate their belief in equality. In the eyes of acquaintances and family, William had betrayed not only the religious principles of the Church of England but also his social class. Noted Pepys in his diary: "Mr. Will Penn, who is lately come over from Ireland, is a Quaker... or some very melancholy thing."

Better educated than most of the early Friends, Penn quickly became one of their most outspoken advocates, taking part in public debates and writing pamphlets that he published at his own expense. One respected London minister, enraged by the conversion of two female members of his congregation to Quakerism, stated that he would "rather lose them to a bawdy house than a Quaker meeting" and then went on to denounce the group's theology.

When Penn responded to the attack in print, the pamphlet became the talk of the city and led to his imprisonment in the Tower. "Hath got me W. Pen's book against the Trinity," Pepys wrote. "I find it so well writ, as I think it too good for him ever to have writ it—and it is a serious sort of book, and not fit for everybody to read."

Despite the threat of life imprisonment, the cold confines of the Tower failed to dampen Penn's crusading spirit. He spent his time there writing a rough draft of *No Cross, No Crown*, one of his most enduring works. After nine months in custody, William was released, perhaps in part as a favor to Admiral Penn, who had loaned the cash-hungry King Charles II a great deal of money over the years.

In 1672, William married Gulielma Maria Springett. During their more than 21 years of marriage, the couple became the parents of seven children. Family responsibilities, however, did not keep Penn from again risking imprisonment by speaking at Friends' meetings, writing political and religious pamphlets, and refusing to take an oath of allegiance.

By the late 1670s, after more than a decade of clashes with the nation's authorities, Penn had grown pessimistic about the likelihood of religious and civil reforms in

England and so turned his thoughts to the New World. Although the colonies were heavily populated with dissenters from England, many colonial authorities exercised no more tolerance for Quakers than their English counterparts. In Puritan-controlled Boston, for example, two Quaker women were hanged when they refused to stop preaching in public.

Having experienced firsthand the horrors of forced religious conformity, Penn dreamed of showing the world that peaceful coexistence among diverse religious groups was possible and that a single, state-supported religion was not only unnecessary but undesirable. "There can be no reason to persecute any man in this world about anything that belongs to the next," he wrote.

When Admiral Penn died without collecting the money owed to him by the king, William saw a way to make his dream a reality. In 1680, he petitioned King Charles for a grant of land in America to retire the debt. Acceding to his request, the king conferred upon Penn an enormous tract of land, the largest that had ever been granted to an individual. William proposed calling the colony New Wales, it being "a pretty hilly country," but King Charles insisted on calling it "Pennsylvania"—Penn's Woods—in honor of his old friend, the admiral.

At the age of 36, Penn suddenly faced the enormous task of designing a government from scratch. The constitution he created, with its provisions for religious freedom, extensive voting rights, and penal reform, was remarkably enlightened by seventeenth-century standards. Despite the vast power it conferred on him as proprietor, Penn had been careful to leave "to myself and successors no power of doing mischief, that the will of one man may not hinder the good of an whole country...."

Before he set sail for Pennsylvania himself, Penn appointed three commissioners and charged them with establishing the new colony. While William saw nothing wrong with Europeans settling in the New World, he was among the few colonizers of his time who recognized the

prior claims of the indigenous people. Thus, he gave the commissioners a letter, dated October 18, 1681, addressed to the people of the Lenni Lenape tribe who inhabited his proprietorship. The letter stated that King Charles had granted him "a great province; but I desire to enjoy it with your love and consent, that we may always live together as neighbours and friends, else what would the great God say to us, who hath made us not to devour and destroy one another but to live soberly and kindly together in the world?"

When he finally arrived in the colony in October 1682, Penn made a treaty with the Indians, in effect purchasing the land he had already been given by the king. Truly wishing to live in peace, he tried to be fair in his dealings with the Lenni Lenape, unmindful that they—like their Delaware kinsmen who "sold" Manhattan Island to Peter Minuit—did not understand the concept of exclusive ownership of the land and believed that the white men simply sought to share its use.

Penn had intended to settle permanently in Pennsylvania, but within two years a boundary dispute with neighboring Maryland required him to return to London, where a web of troubles awaited him. As a result, nearly 16 years passed before he again set foot in his colony. During his long absence, the colonists had grown resentful of his authority, and in 1701, less than two years after his second voyage to Pennsylvania, a disillusioned Penn sailed back to England, never to return. All told, he spent less than five years in America.

From his return to England until his death 16 years later, Penn continually struggled to stave off financial disaster. Never an astute businessman, he discovered, to his horror, that his trusted business manager had defrauded him, leaving him deeply i5n debt. At the age of 63, Penn was sent to a debtor's prison. Marveled one friend, "The more he is pressed, the more he rises. He seems of a spirit to bear and rub through difficulties." Before long, concerned friends raised enough money to satisfy his creditors.

Prior to his death in 1718 at the age of 73, Penn attempted to sell Pennsylvania back to the Crown, hoping to forge at least a modicum of financial security for his six surviving children. In making the offer, Penn sought to extract a promise from the English Crown that the colony's laws and civil rights would be preserved. But while the negotiations were still in progress, Penn suffered a debilitating stroke, and the transaction was never completed. Penn's descendants thus retained control of the colony until the American Revolution.

Despite imprisonment, vilification, and financial ruin, Penn had labored unceasingly to establish the principle of religious freedom in both his homeland and in America. He espoused such "modern" concepts as civil rights, participatory government, interracial brotherhood, and international peace.

Yet, despite the rich legacy that the founder of the colony of Pennsylvania left to Americans, William Penn remains a shadowy figure in our popular consciousness. For most people, his name conjures up little more than a vague picture that is remarkably similar to the bland, beaming face that adorns boxes of Quaker Oats cereal. The reality, however, was quite different; Penn was an extremely complex individual, whose life was filled with triumph and tragedy and was marked by startling contrasts.

In 1984, more than 300 years after the founding of Pennsylvania, the United States Congress posthumously granted Penn U.S. citizenship. "In the history of this Nation," the proclamation read, "there has been a small number of men and women whose contributions to its traditions of freedom, justice, and individual rights have accorded them a special place of honor... and to whom all Americans owe a lasting debt." The man who pursued his "Holy Experiment" on the shores of the New World was, indeed, one of those men.

Patricia Hudson is a freelance writer from Tennessee and a former contributing editor of Americana *magazine.*

The Right to Marry:
Loving v. Virginia

Peter Wallenstein

In June 1958, Mildred Jeter and Richard Loving left their native Caroline County, Virginia, for a visit to Washington, D.C., where they got married. They then returned to Virginia and took up residence in the home of the bride's parents. Early in the morning a few weeks later, everyone in the house was asleep—Mr. and Mrs. Loving downstairs, Mr. and Mrs. Jeter upstairs—when the Lovings awoke to find three policemen in their bedroom with flashlights. The intruders arrested and jailed the Lovings. The charge? Their marriage violated state law. He was white, and she was black. By marrying in D.C. to avoid a Virginia law prohibiting interracial marriage, they had committed a serious crime.

In January 1959, Judge Leon M. Bazile sentenced the couple to a year in jail. He suspended the sentences on the condition that "both accused leave Caroline County and the state of Virginia at once and do not return together or at the same time to said county and state for a period of twenty-five years." They moved to Washington, D.C., where they lived with Mrs. Loving's cousin Alex Byrd and his wife Laura. They continued to live in their home away from home, and this is where they raised their three children, Sidney, Donald, and Peggy.

In 1963 they determined to take a stand against the injustice that had forced them into exile. They wrote United States Attorney General Robert F. Kennedy asking for help. He directed their letter to the National Capitol Area Civil Liberties Union, and the ACLU assigned the case to Bernard S. Cohen, a young lawyer practicing in Alexandria, Virginia. Some months later another young lawyer, Philip A. Hirschkop, who had been working in Mississippi assisting civil rights workers, joined Cohen on the case.

The law that the Lovings broke originated in 1691, when the House of Burgesses sought to reduce the number of mixed-race children born in the Virginia colony, particularly mixed-race children whose mothers were white. The Burgesses enacted a measure designed "for prevention of that abominable mixture and spurious issue which hereafter may encrease in this dominion, as well by negroes, mulattoes, and Indians intermarrying with English, or other white woman, as by their unlawfull accompanying with one another." It outlawed interracial marriage for white men and white women alike. While it did not ban the marriage *per se*, it did mandate the banishment of the white partner in any interracial marriage that occurred, at least if that person was not an indentured servant and, thus, did not owe labor to any planter: "Whatsoever English or other white man or women being free shall intermarry with a negroe, mulatto, or Indian man or woman bond or free, shall within three months after such marriage be banished and removed from this dominion forever."

> *The law that the Lovings broke originated in 1691 when the House of Burgesses sought to reduce the number of mixed-race children born in the Virginia colony, particularly mixed-race children whose mothers were white.*

Thus, the white wife of a nonwhite man was forced to have mixed-race children outside of Virginia. If she tried to evade banishment from the colony by skipping the marriage ceremony but then had a mixed-race child in Virginia out of wedlock, she would have to pay a heavy fine. If unable to pay the fine, she would be sold as a servant for five years. Either way, the child would be sold into servitude until he or she reached the age of thirty.

Only the specifics of the law changed in the years that followed. Through the American Revolution and the Civil War, Virginia law placed a severe penalty on any white person who married a nonwhite. The law was amended in 1705 to eliminate banishment; the new penalty was a fine and six months in prison. In 1848, the legislature changed the term of imprisonment for the white partner in an interracial marriage to a maximum of twelve months. The Code of 1849 declared interracial marriages "absolutely void."

In 1865, slavery came to an end in Virginia. Interracial marriages remained "absolutely void," but the laws began to take on the more specific shape of those that the Lovings encountered nearly a hundred years later. Both partners in an interracial relationship—the black Virginian and the white—became subject to prosecution. Andrew Kinney, a black man, and Mahala Miller, a white woman, wished to live as husband and wife but could not marry under Virginia law. In 1874, after living together nearly eight years and having three children, they went to Washington, D.C., to get married. When they returned home to Augusta County, authorities brought charges against them for "lewdly associating and cohabiting" together without being married. At his trial, Mr. Kinney urged the judge to instruct the jury that the marriage was "valid and a bar to this prosecution." Instead, the judge instructed the jury that the marriage was "but a vain and futile attempt to evade the laws of Virginia." The question, simply put, was: Did the defendant have a valid marriage that gave him an effective defense against the charge he faced? Or, was his living as though he were married precisely the basis for that charge? Was he married? Or was he guilty?

After being convicted and sentenced to pay the heaviest fine the law allowed, $500, Mr. Kinney appealed to the Virginia Supreme Court. That court upheld the conviction. As to whether the law of Washington, D.C., or that of Virginia governed the case, Judge Joseph Christian, speaking for a unanimous court, declared, "There can be no doubt as to the power of every country to make laws regulating the marriage of its own subjects; to declare who may marry, how they may marry, and what shall be the legal consequences of their marrying." The judge went on to say that "purity of public morals, the moral and physical development of both races, and the highest advancement of our cherished southern civilization, under which two distinct races are to work out and accomplish the destiny to which the Almighty has assigned them on this continent—all require that they should be kept distinct and separate, and that connections and alliances so unnatural that God and nature seem to forbid them, should be prohibited by positive law, and be subject to no evasion." What "God and nature" had sundered, let no man seek to bring together. The law would not allow the marriage of Andrew Kinney and Mahala Miller to persist, at least in Virginia. "If the parties desire to maintain the relations of man and wife, they must change their domicile and go to some state or country where the laws recognize the validity of such marriages." Despite their loss in the courts, the couple made their own stand. Five years later, they were still living together and had had five sons. They remained subject to additional prosecution, but local authorities seem to have been content with winning the one case against them.

In 1878, the Virginia General Assembly made two changes—the most significant since the 1691 law. Not only would both partners in an interracial marriage be subject to prosecution but, if convicted, they would also both be sentenced to the state penitentiary for a term of two to five years. And if,

like the Kinneys, they sought to evade the law by marrying outside of Virginia, "they shall be as guilty, and be punished as if the marriage had been in this state. The fact of their cohabitation here as man and wife shall be evidence of their marriage." By the time of the Lovings, the legislature had changed the minimum sentence from two years to one year.

> *"Mr. Cohen, tell the Court I love my wife, and it is just unfair that I can't live with her in Virginia."*

But what about the Fourteenth Amendment? Approved in 1868, its first section declared, in part, that no state could "deny to any person within its jurisdiction the equal protection of the laws." Indeed, in 1872 the Alabama Supreme Court ruled Alabama's law against interracial marriages unconstitutional. The court said that the Civil Rights Act of 1866 had conferred "the right to make and enforce contracts, amongst which is that of marriage with any citizen capable of entering into that relation," and that the Fourteenth Amendment had placed the Civil Rights Act's "cardinal principle" in the United States Constitution. Yet, the Alabama Supreme Court itself soon overruled that decision, and no other court adopted its position for many years.

Thus, the Fourteenth Amendment failed to help couples like the Lovings, as a black man in Alabama, Tony Pace, and a white woman, Mary Jane Cox, found out. Convicted of carrying on an interracial relationship, each was sentenced to two years in the Alabama penitentiary, the minimum term the law permitted. They appealed their convictions, but the Alabama Supreme Court ruled against them. Each defendant's punishment, "white and black," was "precisely the same." They appealed again to the nation's highest court, but the United States Supreme Court ruled in 1883 as had the Alabama court. Tony Pace served his sentence in the Alabama penitentiary.

Gradually, laws like Virginia's and Alabama's came under successful attack. In 1948, in *Perez v. Sharp,* the California Supreme Court ruled that a California law against interracial marriage was unconstitutional—the first such ruling since Alabama's short-lived effort in 1872. In the years that followed, states outside the South repealed their laws and left the question of marriage up to individuals regardless of their race. When the Lovings returned to court in the 1960s, however, all southern states retained such laws. As late as 1966, Oklahoma plus every state that had had slavery as late as the Civil War—Texas, Arkansas, Louisiana, Mississippi, Alabama, Tennessee, Georgia, Florida, the Carolinas, Virginia and West Virginia, Maryland, Delaware, Kentucky, and Missouri—still had such laws on the books.

At about the same time, the United States Supreme Court breathed new life into the Fourteenth Amendment's equal protection clause. For example, in 1948 the court ruled in *Shelley v. Kraemer* that state courts could not enforce restrictive covenants in housing documents that prevented nonwhite families from moving into white communities. Several rulings declared

UPI/Bettman

Mildred and Richard Loving at their news conference on 12 June 1967, the day the U.S. Supreme Court ruled unanimously in their favor.

against states' banning black students from enrolling in state law schools. And in 1954, the nation's highest court ruled in *Brown v. Board of Education,* on Fourteenth Amendment grounds, that "in the field of public education the doctrine of 'separate but equal' has no place."

The Supreme Court ruled on various cases in the area of privacy at about the same time. How much control should people have over their lives, and how much power should state governments have to restrict people's freedom? What fundamental rights did people have—even if those rights are not explicit in the United States Constitution? The Court declared that people had the right to teach their children a foreign language *(Meyer v. Nebraska,* 1923) and the right to send their children to private schools *(Pierce v. Society of Sisters, 1925).* Married people had the right to have children; the Court voided a law that mandated that people convicted of certain types of crime be sterilized *(Skinner v. Oklahoma,* 1942). In the leading privacy case up to the time of the Loving case, the Court ruled that married people also had the right to decide whether to use birth control information and devices to prevent pregnancy *(Griswold v. Connecticut,* 1965). In 1973, in *Roe v. Wade,* the Court extended its rulings on matters of privacy when it struck down statutes that prohibited women from obtaining abortions, especially in the

first three months of pregnancy. Thus, across a fifty-year period between 1923 and 1973, the Court determined that people had a zone of privacy—the right, at least under certain circumstances, to go about their lives without having authorities intervene and tell them what they must and must not do.

These various developments in twentieth-century American constitutional history came together in the case of the Lovings. There was no reason to assume that the Lovings would be successful. They had not even tried to contest their exile in 1959 but had waited more than four years before contacting the Attorney General's office. Only a few years before their marriage, convictions, and exile, other couples had tried unsuccessfully to get the United States Supreme Court to rule laws like Virginia's unconstitutional. In 1955, a black woman named Linnie Jackson, who had been sentenced to the Alabama penitentiary for an interracial relationship, appealed her conviction to the United States Supreme Court. The Court refused to hear her case. At about the same time, a Chinese man in Virginia, Ham Say Naim, tried to take a case to the United States Supreme Court to have his marriage to a white woman recognized, but the Court turned a deaf ear to him too. That left intact a ruling by the Virginia Supreme Court which had insisted that "regulation of the marriage relation" is "distinctly one of the rights guaranteed to the States and safeguarded by that bastion of States' rights, somewhat battered perhaps but still a sturdy fortress in our fundamental law, the tenth section of the Bill of Rights."

In 1963, despite the obstacles, the Lovings renewed their quest to live together as husband and wife and to raise their three children in Caroline County, Virginia. Their lawyers, Bernard Cohen and Philip Hirschkop, consulted with various ACLU lawyers in preparing the case. They began where the Lovings had finished previously, in Judge Bazile's courtroom. The judge saw no reason to change his mind about anything. The Lovings' marriage, he said, was "absolutely void in Virginia," and they could not "cohabit" there "without incurring repeated prosecutions" for doing so. He declared his convictions on the law in dispute: "Almighty God created the races white, black, yellow, malay and red, and he placed them on separate continents. And but for the interference with his arrangement there would be no cause for such marriages. The fact that he separated the races shows that he did not intend for the races to mix."

"Under our Constitution, the freedom to marry, or not to marry, a person of another race resides with the individual and cannot be infringed by the State."

The Lovings appealed their case to the Virginia Supreme Court, but that court saw nothing that required change since its ruling in the Naim case ten years earlier. Richard and Mildred Loving then went to the United States Supreme Court to challenge their convictions for having violated Virginia's laws against racial intermarriage. In the months ahead, the nation's high court faced squarely, for the first time, the question of whether such laws as Virginia's violated the Fourteenth Amendment. Cohen and Hirschkop quoted one judge in the 1948 California decision on interracial marriage: "If the right to marry is a fundamental right, then it must be conceded that an infringement of that right by means of a racial restriction is an unlawful infringement of one's liberty." They also asserted that "caprice of the politicians cannot be substituted for the minds of the individual in what is man's most personal and intimate decision. The error of such legislation must immediately be apparent to those in favor of miscegenation statutes, if they stopped to consider their abhorrence to a statute which commanded that 'all marriages must be between persons of different racial backgrounds.'" Such a statute, they contended, would be no more "repugnant to the constitution"—and no less so—than the law under consideration. Something "so personal as the choice of a mate must be left to the individuals involved," they argued; "race limitations are too unreasonable and arbitrary a basis for the State to interfere." They reviewed the history of

Virginia's anti-miscegenation statutes—going all the way back to the seventeenth century—to characterize them as "relics of slavery" and, at the same time, "expressions of modern day racism." And, finally, in oral argument, Bernard Cohen conveyed Richard Loving's own words. "Mr. Cohen, tell the Court I love my wife, and it is just unfair that I can't live with her in Virginia."

Speaking for a unanimous Court on 12 June 1967, Chief Justice Earl Warren declared that states' rights had to defer to the Fourteenth Amendment when it came to the claim of "exclusive state control" over the "regulation of marriage." The argument that Virginia's "miscegenation statutes punish equally both the white and the Negro participants in an interracial marriage" could not pass constitutional muster in the 1960s. The burden of proof rested on the state, for "the fact of equal application does not immunize the statute from the heavy burden of justification" required by the Fourteenth Amendment, particularly when racial classifications appeared in criminal statutes. "The fact that Virginia prohibits only interracial marriages involving white persons demonstrates" that those laws were "designed to maintain White Supremacy." Indeed, the statute's original purpose held no interest for the Court; the Chief Justice declared the racial classifications "repugnant to the Fourteenth Amendment, even assuming an even-handed state purpose to protect the 'integrity' of all races." According to Warren the Fourteenth Amendment's clear and central purpose was to "eliminate all official state sources of invidious racial discrimination."

The Chief Justice was sure of the Court's recent history in civil rights cases. He wrote: "We have consistently denied the constitutionality of measures which restrict the rights of citizens on account of race. There can be no doubt that restricting the freedom to marry solely because of racial classifications violates the central meaning of the Equal Protection Clause." As for the Due Process Clause, the Chief Justice noted that "the freedom to marry has long been recognized as one of the vital personal rights essential to the orderly pursuit of happiness by free men.... To deny this fundamental freedom on so unsupportable a basis as the racial classifications embodied in these statutes, classifications so directly subversive of the principle of equality at the heart of the Fourteenth Amendment, is surely to deprive all the State's citizens of liberty without due process of law. The Fourteenth Amendment requires that the freedom of choice to marry not be restricted by invidious racial discriminations. Under our Constitution, the freedom to marry, or not marry, a person of another race resides with the individual and cannot be infringed by the State." Chief Justice Warren's final sentence put an end to the Lovings' odyssey through the courts: "These convictions must be reversed."

Richard and Mildred Loving finally won the case ten days after their ninth wedding anniversary. From their temporary farm home in Bowling Green, near Fredericksburg, Mr. and Mrs. Loving drove north to Alexandria for a news conference at their lawyers' office. There Mr. Loving said, "We're just really overjoyed," and Mrs. Loving said, "I feel free now." A photographer snapped a picture, law books in the background, of two happy people sitting close together, his arm around her neck. "My wife and I plan to go ahead and build a new house now," said Richard Loving the construction worker about the permanent new home in Virginia that Richard Loving the husband and father wanted his family to live in. And they did so.

Reporting on the decision, the *New York Times* noted its larger significance. "In writing the opinion that struck down the last group of segregation laws to remain standing—those requiring separation of the races in marriage—Chief Justice Warren completed the process that he set in motion with his opinion in 1954 that declared segregation in public schools to be unconstitutional." Bernard S. Cohen, the Lovings' lawyer, offered a similar benediction on the proceedings. At his clients' press conference, he said: "We hope we have put to rest the last vestiges of racial discrimination that were supported by the law in Virginia and all over the country."

The black-owned newspaper in Virginia's largest city, the *Norfolk Journal and Guide,* led off its front page with the headline "Top Court Junks Marriage Bars" and printed an editorial on "Freedom of Choice at the Altar." It predicted "no noticeable increase in the number of mixed marriages in Virginia." As it explained, "prospective grooms" would continue to enjoy "the privileges of withholding their requests for the bride's hand," and brides would retain "the privilege and authority to prevent mixed marriages simply by saying 'no.'" Nonetheless, the *Journal and Guide* insisted on the importance of the Court's ruling: "What makes this Supreme Court decision so desirable is that it lifts an onerous and brutalizing stigma from Negro Virginians by knocking down that psychological barrier which, in effect, told them and the world that no Negro is good enough to be the husband or wife of a white Virginian." Furthermore, it saluted the Lovings for having taken a stand. "They have done an incalculably great service for their community, their state, and their nation. Had they been less persevering, the legal battle to end Virginia's oppression on the marital front might have been forfeited long ago."

BIBLIOGRAPHY

Garrow, David J. *Liberty and Sexuality: The Right to Privacy and the Making of Roe v. Wade.* New York: Macmillan, 1994.

Grossberg, Michael. *Governing the Hearth: Law and the Family in Nineteenth-Century America.* Chapel Hill: University of North Carolina Press, 1985.

Ross, William G. *Forging New Freedoms: Nativism, Education, and the Constitution, 1917–1927.* Lincoln: University of Nebraska Press, 1994.

Schwartz, Bernard. *Super Chief: Earl Warren and His Supreme Court—A Judicial Biography.* New York: New York University Press, 1983.

Sickels, Robert J. *Race, Marriage, and the Law.* Albuquerque: University of New Mexico Press, 1972.

Wallenstein, Peter. "Race, Marriage, and the Law of Freedom: Alabama and Virginia, 1860s–1960s." *Chicago-Kent Law Review* 70 (1995).

Peter Wallenstein is Associate Professor of History at Virginia Polytechnic Institute and State University.

From OAH Magazine of History, Winter 1995, pp. 37-41. © 1995 by the Organization of American Historians. Reprinted by permission.

baptism of *FIRE*

A flotilla of bateaux and canoes carrying a French fighting force of some 500 men made its way down the Allegheny River to the Three Forks area on the morning of April 17, 1754. The troops disembarked on the site of modern day Pittsburgh, where the Ohio, Monongahela, and Allegheny Rivers converge. There they quickly routed an encampment of Virginians, demolished the colonials' half-built fort, and erected their own. They named it Fort Duquesne, in honor of the Marquis Duquesne, Canada's governor general.

by Paul A. Thomsen

Young George Washington first tasted combat when he fought for the British during the French and Indian War. On the battlefield he experienced both the exhilaration of victory, and the humiliation of defeat.

Great Britain had been watching with growing concern as France extended and strengthened its power in North America, and was greatly displeased by this latest incursion. The French already occupied areas of Nova Scotia, the St. Lawrence River valley, and the Great Lakes, and they had a line of trading posts down the Mississippi valley to the Gulf of Mexico. By early 1754 it was evident that France saw the Ohio Valley as an essential link with its western fur trade and Louisiana, and intended to take possession of it.

Early in April 1754 a young lieutenant colonel of the Virginia militia took an expeditionary force north to face the French. The officer's name was George Washington. Virginia's lieutenant governor, Robert Dinwiddie, had ordered the 22-year-old militiaman to secure the fort the Virginia colonials had erected and to "capture, kill, or repel all who interrupted the progress of the English settlements in that country."

Washington had dealt with the French in the region before, when Dinwiddie dispatched him to the Ohio Valley the previous year to deliver a demand that the French leave British territory. The French refused. Now Washington was prepared to take more decisive measures. When his Virginians encountered a French party on May 28, the colonials opened fire and left 10 Frenchmen dead, including the commander. They were the first fatalities in what would later be called the French and Indian War.

Washington's troops suffered only one man wounded, and their commander was exhilarated by his first taste of battle. "I can with truth assure you," he wrote to his younger brother John Augustine, "I heard the bullets whistle; and believe me, there is something charming in the sound."

The situation went rapidly downhill from there. Washington and his men fell back to an area called Great Meadows and hastily threw up a makeshift fortification, which they named Fort Necessity. More French soldiers soon arrived to seek vengeance for their dead comrades, and after a nine-hour siege on July 3, they captured the outnumbered force and its fort. The French permitted Washington and his troops to march back to Williamsburg, but Washington's ignorance of the French language prevented him from understanding that the surrender articles he had signed included a confession that the death of the French commander on May 28 had been an act of assassination.

The future Revolutionary War hero returned home to Virginia in disgrace and resigned his commission. Yet when he heard that Britain had sent Major General Edward Braddock to America to take command of all regular and colonial forces there, Washington wrote to him. On March 14, 1755, Washington received a letter from Robert Orme, Braddock's principal aide-de-camp, offering him a place in the general's elite red-clad army.

Primedia Enthusiast Pub. Inc.

As a boy, George had been determined to follow the example of his half-brother, Lawrence, who had fought pirates at sea before his death in July 1752. His mother, Mary Ball Washington, successfully blocked any such ambitions, but she did give the 16-year-old George permission to travel with a surveying party to the remote south branch of the Potomac River in 1748. The expedition launched him on a career as a surveyor and gave him a taste for adventure that he craved. As tensions increased between France and Britain in North America, Washington saw an opportunity to follow in his father's footsteps as a militiaman. He became a military envoy and later a full militia commander, but his disgrace at Fort Necessity temporarily put his military career on hold.

" I heard the bullets whistle; and believe me, there is something charming in the sound," Washington wrote.

In England the news of Washington's defeat prompted King George II to dispatch Braddock and two regiments of British Regulars to Virginia. At the age of 60, Braddock had 45 years of experience in His Majesty's Service on the Continent of Europe, but he had no experience in wilderness fighting. Once he reached Virginia he perceived the value of Washington's wilderness knowledge and offered him a captain's commission by brevet. Washington had recently taken over management of

Mount Vernon and considered himself "unprepared...at present to quit a family and estate scarcely settled and in the utmost confusion." He wanted permission to leave the general's service during any inactive periods so that he could return to his plantation. Braddock agreed to the request. Although that meant serving as a volunteer with no pay, Washington dutifully took up his responsibilities as the British general's aide-de-camp.

Washington earnestly studied military logistics under Braddock. Each evening he would scrutinize the general's written orders. During the day he served as Braddock's emissary to the growing numbers of militiamen who hoped to expel the French once and for all from the land beyond the Allegheny Mountains. By late June 1755 the Virginia "Blues," so called for the color of their militia uniforms, had augmented Braddock's two previously understrength regiments of redcoats. The mixed Virginian and British expedition, now totaling 2,200 men, should have been more than a match for the French. The humorless Braddock, however, had a low opinion of colonial forces. The general grew attached to Washington, but he thought little of Virginia militiamen in general, expressing his view that their "slothful and languid disposition renders them very unfit for military service."

While the troops prepared for the long march into the Ohio Valley, young George Washington dealt with his nervous mothers. "I am very happy in the General's Family," he replied to one letter with calm resolution, "and I'm treated with the complaisant Freedom which is quite agreeable; so that I have no occasion to doubt the satisfaction I proposed in making the Campaigne." Even during the war, Mary Ball Washington regularly pestered her son with unsolicited correspondence asking him to furnish certain necessities. George Washington took each letter in stride. "I am sorry," he replied to one, "it is not in my power to provide you with either a Dutch man, or the butter as you desire, for we are quite out of that part of the Country where either are to be had, as there are few or no Inhabitants were we now lie encamp'd, and butter cannot be had here to supply the wants of the Camp...." He signed it as "Yr. Most Affect. and Dutiful Son."

While Washington was careful to paint things in the best possible light for his mother, he knew that the army faced serious problems. His recent experience had taught him that traveling into the enemy-controlled Ohio Valley would be a dangerous proposition under the best of circumstances. Few native scouts had joined the expedition, and moving a large contingent of men, supplies, and munitions across the Allegheny Mountains without adequate intelligence made a difficult task all the more daunting.

Braddock's army set out for the contested western border in early June, "thro' an uninhabited wilderness over steep rocky mountains and almost impassable morasses," cutting down trees and moving aside rocks along the way. The rough terrain slowed progress to an average of a mile or two a day, and the troops labored continuously to construct a roadway for their siege cannons. The heavy weapons were an unwieldy burden in the American wilderness, but the army needed them to smash Fort Duquesne's wooden ramparts. Braddock hoped the mere sight of the formidable guns would encourage the French to sur-

Fort Necessity National Battlefield

The landscape of the Allegheny Mountains, where the French and Indians defeated Colonel George Washington at Fort Necessity and where General Edward Braddock's army marched to confront them, changed dramatically in the late 1800s when logging altered the face of the heavily forested land. But the National Park Service is now striving to cultivate a sense of wilderness at the Fort Necessity National Battlefield site in southwestern Pennsylvania.

When Colonel Washington and his troops arrived in the grassland area known as Great Meadows on July 1, 1754, they erected Fort Necessity in just three days to defend themselves against the approaching French troops. But when the French defeated the Virginians on July 3, they burned Fort Necessity to the ground. Archaeologists determined the location of the fort's site in 1932, and visitors today see the reconstruction built there the following year.

The reconstructed Fort Necessity sits in the center of Great Meadows, "a charming field for an encounter" said Washington. The National Park Service is working to restore the meadow's original tree line, while much of the land beyond its boundaries is slowly reforesting naturally. The fort itself is an accurate replica of the meager structure Washington erected. The palisades are in the exact location of the original stockade posts, and entrenchments Washington's troops reinforced in the days before the battle still surround the structure. The fort is only 53 feet in diameter, with a small store-house in the center. That's hardly large enough to have held some 200 of Washington's troops, much less 200 men firing muskets and jockeying for position to shoot out of the few notches in the wooden walls.

A mile northwest of the fort, an elaborate monument at the side of US Route 40 marks the grave of General Braddock, who led the army of British and colonial troops to attack the French at Fort Duquesne. The general was shot during the battle, and he lingered for three days before succumbing to his wounds. Washington officiated at the funeral the next day. He later wrote, "thus died a man, whose good and bad qualities were intimately blended.... His attachments were warm, his enmities were strong, and having no disguise about him, both appeared in full forces." Obviously, the French did not hold the British general in such high regard, so Braddock's men buried him in their recently constructed road and marched with their equipment over the site to prevent the grave's detection and desecration.

The military road Braddock opened on his way to Fort Duquesne remained a main thoroughfare in the area even after the French and Indian War. Laborers working on the road in 1804 discovered human remains near the place where Braddock was reportedly buried. The bones were re-interred nearby, and a 12-foot granite monument was erected over the grave in 1913. Adjacent to the grave, a few hundred yards of the painstakingly constructed Braddock road still remain.

During the summer, National Park rangers present talks at Fort Necessity about the importance of the campaign, while re-enactors stage living history programs on weekends. The Park Service plans to replace the existing visitor center, which sits on the edge of the battlefield and mars the view from the fort. The new center will be on the edge of the area, out of sight. If all goes as planned, it will open on July 3, 2004, 250 years to the day after the French defeated Washington at Fort Necessity.
—Fran Severn-Levy

Visitor Information

Fort Necessity National Battlefield is 11 miles southeast of Uniontown, Pennsylvania, on U. S. 40. There is an admission charge for the battlefield, but none at Braddock's grave or Braddock's road. The park is open from 9:00 to 5:00 daily, except for federal holidays between November and February. Call (724) 329-5512 or see www.nps.gov/parks.html for further information.

render quickly. The general had planned strategy for many European campaigns, but throughout his career he had grown accustomed to being far behind the battle lines, and he was a reluctant initiate to combat, wilderness or otherwise.

Braddock's men crossed into the French-occupied region without incident. Enemy scouts observed their passage, but Washington knew little of the enemy's strength or number. Braddock knew even less. A year earlier the French army's superior numbers had overwhelmed Washington's command. Now the British worried that the French might have increased their forces with large numbers from the Native-American tribes who were already predisposed to stop Britain's expanding settlements.

Once Braddock moved within sight of Fort Duquesne's great wooden ramparts, he ordered the siege cannons brought up from the rear and put in place to bombard the French stronghold. With the cannons within range, the British contingent knew the day would soon be theirs. Just then, shots echoed in the distance. The French were firing upon an advance party of scouts that Braddock had sent ahead under the command of Lieutenant Colonel Thomas Gage.

Native-American scouts had apprised Fort Duquesne's commander, Claude Pierre Pécaude de Contrecoeur, of the British advance almost before the army had begun to march. Contrecoeur knew he was outnumbered—he had only 1,600 men, 800 of whom were Native Americans—and that his fort stood little chance of enduring a siege of any length. He had even less chance of driving off his enemies with conventional means. So, instead of planning a frontal attack, the French commander opted to use a strategy better suited for the wilderness—an ambush. On the morning of July 9, 1755, a contingent of 600 Native Americans and more than 200 French soldiers slipped out of the fort and moved to engage the British and colonials.

So, instead of planning a frontal attack, the French commander opted to use a strategy better suited for the wilderness —an ambush.

Shortly after noon, about a half-mile beyond the place where Braddock and his troops had crossed the Monongahela River, Colonel Gage's advance scouting party watched in terror as the forest suddenly came alive with French soldiers and Native Americans screaming war whoops and firing from behind the trees. As Braddock's men brought their siege cannons to bear on their attackers, the enemy's ranks began to disintegrate, but the French officers rallied their men, turned them round, and, with the battle cry *Vive le Roi,* suddenly fell upon the thin British advance. They simultaneously enveloped the head and both flanks of the British column. Braddock's advance party and the main column behind them fell into disorder. The French riddled the huddled mass of redcoats with a devastating fire from the dense woods, until the panicked British broke and ran.

Washington had been stricken with a severe case of dysentery for more time than he cared to contemplate, and Braddock had ordered him to remain in the column's rear to recuperate. But when the young Virginian heard the fighting, he tied a pillow to his horse's saddle and rode into the melee just as Gage's retreating scouting party fell headlong into nearly 1,000 red-clad Regulars charging to join the battle. Chaos ensued.

When a rumor swept through the ranks that the French were attacking the rear guard and baggage, the Regulars believed they were completely surrounded. They abandoned the cannon on which they had pinned their hopes and retreated. Washington arrived on the battlefield in time to witness "about thirteen hundred well-armed men, chiefly Regulars, who were immediately struck with such an inconceivable panic that nothing but confusion and disobedience of orders prevailed among them." By contrast, Washington later recounted that the officers "behaved with incomparable bravery, for which they greatly suffered...."

In the melee Washington had two horses shot out from under him, and four more shots ripped through his coat. Realizing the futility of fighting with conventional tactics against an enemy sheltered behind trees and rocks, he offered to take command of the provincials "before it was too late," and "engage the enemy in their own way," but a British officer immediately rebuffed him.

The British troops could see nothing of the foe attacking them on three sides, except for an occasional Native American who would run out of the woods to scalp a dead or wounded soldier. As the Regulars "broke and ran as sheep pursued by hounds, "Washington recounted, the blue-coated Virginia pro-

vincials pulled together and covered the retreat. Braddock, who had several horses shot from beneath him during the three-hour battle, attempted to shore up his faltering army by riding into their midst and striking out with the flat of his sword. Then shots ripped through the general's chest and shoulder, knocking him to the ground and leaving him mortally wounded.

When the battle ended, more than 900 of Braddock's men were dead or wounded. Of the three companies of 30 Virginia Blues, which had valiantly covered the flight of Britain's elite troops, scarcely 30 militiamen survived. In their fear the Regulars had abandoned "artillery, ammunition, provisions, baggage, and, in short, everything a prey to the enemy."

Washington was one of only a handful of 60 officers who survived the battle unscathed. He followed the shattered army southeast to Fort Cumberland at Wills Creek, Maryland. "We have been scandalously beaten by a trifling body of men..." he wrote his brother John.

Washington knew he would soon hear from his mother, so he penned a second, more telling letter to her. "Honour'd Mad'm," he wrote, "As I doubt not but you have heard of our defeat, and perhaps have it represented in a worse light (if possible) than it deserves; I have taken this earliest opportunity to give you some acct. of the Engagement, as it happen'd...."

This time George Washington did not have to bear the personal responsibility for a retreat, and he returned to Virginia a hero.

"We March'd on to that place with't any considerable loss, having only now and then a stragler pick'd up by the French Scoutg. Ind'nd. When we came there, we were attack'd by a Body of French and Indns. Whose number (I am certain) did not exceed 300 men; ours consisted of abt. 1,300 well arm'd Troops; chiefly of the English Soldiers, who were struck with such a panick, that they behav'd with more cowardice than it is possible to conceive....In short the dastardly behaviour of those they call regular's expos'd all others that were inclin'd to do their duty to almost certain death....I am, Hon'd Madam Yr. Most dutiful Son."

This time George Washington did not have to bear the personal responsibility for a retreat, and he returned to Virginia a hero. The British Regulars had attempted to pin blame on the Virginians, but the facts eventually won out. As one man later recalled, Braddock himself, who had earlier been so contemptuous of the colonial troops, now "could not bare the sight of a red coat. [Seeing one] he raved immoderately, but when one of the blues [appeared], he said he hop'd to live to reward em." For the colony's Blues, at least, it was a noble defeat.

Mary Ball Washington later wrote to her son and asked him not to go back to the Ohio. On August 14, 1755, he sent a letter to her from Mount Vernon. "If it is in my power to avoid going to the Ohio again, I shall, but if the Command is press'd upon me by the genl voice of the Country, and offerd upon such terms as can't be objected against," he wrote, "it would reflect eternal dishonour upon me to refuse it."

In 1758, Washington, now a general and commander in chief of Virginia's entire military force, returned to the site of Braddock's defeat with British Brigadier General John Forbes and his army of 5,000 provincials and 1,400 Scottish Highlanders. On November 25, Forbes's army routed the heavily outnumbered French troops and seized Fort Duquesne after the defenders had set it alight. The French retreat from the fort's ruins effectively symbolized the end of France's dream of controlling the Ohio Valley.

Braddock was not around to see this reversal of fortune. He had died three days after being wounded. His soldiers buried the body in an unmarked grave in the middle of the road so that the retreating army would eradicate all traces and prevent the French and Native Americans from desecrating it. But Braddock's last words had proved prophetic, "We shall better know how to deal with them another time."

Paul A. Thomsen is a freelance writer and researcher from New York.

UNIT 2

Revolutionary America

Unit Selections

Key Points to Consider

- Thomas Jefferson remains one of the most popular of the Founders. Discuss the significance of the new evidence about about his relationship with Sally Hemmings. Does it mean that he was a hypocrite with regard to slavery? Defend your answer.

- What purposes was the Declaration of Independence supposed to serve? How have perceptions of this document changed over the years?

- Discuss why the debate over the Second Amendment is so hotly contested? Examine each side of the argument. Should Americans retain the right to bear arms?

- Why were the Founders considered extreme radicals for their day? How did their beliefs make the American Revolution possible?

 **Links: www.dushkin.com/online/**
These sites are annotated in the World Wide Web pages.

The Early America Review
http://www.earlyamerica.com/review/
House of Representatives
http://www.house.gov
National Center for Policy Analysis
http://www.public-policy.org/web.public-policy.org/index.html
Supreme Court/Legal Information Institute
http://supct.law.cornell.edu/supct/index.html
U.S. Founding Documents/Emory University
http://www.law.emory.edu/FEDERAL/
U.S. Senate
http://www.senate.gov
The White House
http://www.whitehouse.gov/
The World of Benjamin Franklin
http://www.fi.edu/franklin/

During the first half of the 18th century, relations between the American colonies and Great Britain were stable and, for the most part, friendly. There were squabbles between one or another colony and the government in London, of course, but these were family affairs. The British had a worldwide empire to administer, of which the American possessions were only a part. Given the great length of time it took for messages to cross the Atlantic, Britain was content to rule largely through its colonial governors. In return for submitting to certain economic restrictions that will be discussed below, the colonists received protection of the British navy and army.

The prevailing economic theory at the time was known as "mercantilism." It held that the mother country should regulate commercial activity for the benefit of the entire empire. Generally, this meant that the colonies should provide raw materials unavailable in the British Isles in return for manufactured goods. The goal was to ensure a favorable balance of trade between the empire and other nations, and to attain self-sufficiency with regard to strategic materials such as lumber for shipbuilding. The British did not want to rely on other countries for such materials because the supply might be cut off in time of war. Whatever made the empire as a whole richer and more powerful, in theory, benefited all its component parts.

Mercantilism had mixed effects on the American colonies. Southern producers of rice and corn, for instance, had the advantage of selling in a protected market and of purchasing manufactured goods on British credit. New Englanders gained from selling lumber and from building ships—one of the few industries the British government encouraged for economic and strategic reasons. Others fared less well. People in the middle colonies, especially, often chafed at regulations that prevented them from buying cheaper goods from other countries and from manufacturing products that competed with British companies. Such problems as there were diminished when London often failed to enforce its own regulations. And, as the colonists of all sections well knew, they needed the protection of the British army and navy against the French and Spanish.

Decades of benign neglect, the passage of time, and the distance from England brought changes in colonists' attitudes. Although still regarding themselves as British subjects, they came to assume the autonomy they enjoyed as the natural state of affairs. Few of them had ever visited the mother country, some spent their lives without seeing any visible trappings of the government to which they owed their loyalty. In short, many colonists regarded themselves as "American" as well as subjects of the crown.

The end of what the colonists called the French and Indian War in 1763 brought dramatic changes in the relationship. The war had virtually bankrupted England, and extremely heavy taxes were levied on the British people. The government understandably concluded that colonists should pay their share for a conflict in which they had been involved. After all, one result of

the war had been removal of the French from North America, which meant they no longer presented a threat to the colonists.

The new taxes and regulations, along with the much more vigorous efforts to enforce the latter, were perceived by the colonists as an unwarranted intrusion on the rights and privileges that they had come to take for granted. These burdens were imposed, moreover, at a time when removal of the French threat made the colonists less dependent upon the crown's protection. Economic disputes quickly spilled over into other areas such as religion and politics. What seemed to the colonists as outrageous behavior by the British government caused more and more of them to conclude that the colonies would be best off if they cut ties with the empire and struck out alone. The British, of course, were determined to hold on to their possessions. Efforts by the government to enforce its will led to armed clashes and then to the Revolutionary War.

The first unit essay, "Flora MacDonald," tells the story of a woman who had become a Scottish heroine in 1746 when she had helped "Bonnie Prince Charlie" escape British authorities. She was received with some fanfare when she moved to North Carolina in 1774, but, when she began recruiting men of Scottish descent to fight for the crown during the revolution, her popularity vanished.

In "Jefferson's Secret Life," the authors discuss new evidence that seems to confirm the old allegation that Thomas Jefferson had sired a number of children with his slave mistress, Sally Hemmings. The article assesses the likely effect of this revelation on the reputation of the author of the Declaration of Independence. Next, the Declaration itself is analyzed in "Making Sense of the Fourth of July." Author Pauline Maier discusses how the meaning and function of the Declaration has changed over the course of time.

Then, "George Washington, Spymaster" reviews a less well known aspect of Washington's military leadership during the Revolutionary War. In "Founders Chic: Live From Philadelphia," Evan Thomas argues that those who led the American Revolution and helped consolidate the new government were truly radical at the time despite their knee breeches and powdered wigs. "Founding Friendship: Washington, Madison and the Creation of the American Republic" analyzes the extremely fruitful relationship between these two men before they parted ways.

The last two articles in this section treat aspects of the Constitution. "Your Constitution is Killing You" analyzes changing interpretations of the Second Amendment. This issue continues to be hotly debated between those who adamantly believe they have a constitutional right to own guns and those who just as adamantly believe they do not. Finally, politicians across the political spectrum are apt to toss off a statement to the effect that the "the people rule" without explaining whether they mean the people of the 50 states or the people of the entire nation. "Do the People Rule?" tries to discover what the founders meant during the Constitutional Convention and the ratification process that followed.

Flora MacDonald

By a twist of fate, the Scottish heroine who helped Bonnie Prince Charlie escape the British in 1746 immigrated to North Carolina in 1774, only to find herself allied with the Crown during the American Revolution.

By Jean Creznic

"… FLORA MACDONALD, a name that will be mentioned in history, and if courage and fidelity be virtues, mentioned with honour," wrote Doctor Samuel Johnson in *Journey to the Western Isles* after he and his friend James Boswell visited her in Scotland in September 1773. As Johnson predicted, her name is honored among her fellow Scots, and her life has become legend, a story that took this eighteenth-century heroine from the islands of Scotland to the colony of North Carolina, on the eve of America's Revolutionary War.

Flora MacDonald gained renown and the affection of her Scottish Highland countrymen when she helped Prince Charles Edward, the Stuart pretender to the British throne, escape capture in 1746. Her later association with America, though brief, placed her in the thick of the Revolutionary War.

Flora was born in 1722 in Milton, South Uist, one of the Hebrides Islands that lie off the western coast of Scotland.

Her father died when she was a child, and her mother remarried in 1728 and moved to the Hebridean Isle of Skye. Ever the independent thinker, six-year-old Flora declared that she would stay in Milton with her older brother, Angus, rather than go to her mother's new home. She said that she would be happier with him there than in a house that was strange to her. Later, an aunt and uncle took charge and sent her to school in Edinburgh, after which, she lived as a member of a privileged family, spending her time in ladylike pursuits, frequently traveling to visit relatives and friends.

The adventure that brought Flora fame began as she was staying with relatives at Ormaclade, on South Uist. The talk in Scotland was all about Prince Charles Edward Stuart, known by the Scots as Bonnie Prince Charlie, and how he might reestablish the Catholic Stuarts as Great Britain's rightful rulers. The prince was the grandson of the Stuart King James II, who had reigned in Britain during 1685–88. English sentiment against Catholicism ran high during his reign, and James, whose sympathies leaned more and more toward Rome, fled to France in 1688 when the overthrow of the throne appeared imminent. His son, also named James, spent his life in France and Italy, plotting to regain his father's throne.

During the first half of the eighteenth century, the pressure on James's son, Charles Edward, to succeed to the throne

was enormous, but England under Protestant King George II had no intention of allowing the Catholic Stuarts to wear the crown. Despite the fact there was no encouragement for Prince Charles Edward from that quarter, agents of the exiled Stuarts traveled the Scottish Highlands, striving to enlist the support of the Highland clans. They succeeded in rallying a small band of Jacobites (supporters of the House of Stuart), most of them MacDonalds, to the cause.

Arriving in Scotland in August 1745, the prince and his followers launched their long awaited campaign. Although well begun, the effort was nevertheless doomed to failure and ended the next year on April 16, 1746, at the Battle of Culloden, where the prince and his five thousand Highland supporters were crushed by some nine thousand infantrymen led by George II's son, William, the Duke of Cumberland.

The English showed the weakened Scots no mercy, and this defeat sealed the fate of the prince and of the resurgence of the House of Stuart. Charles Edward fled for his life after the battle, hiding from the Duke of Cumberland's soldiers wherever he could, finally making his way to the western isles, and Flora MacDonald.

Some say that Flora's stepfather, Hugh MacDonald—a sympathizer of Prince Charles Edward despite his position as the commander of the government militia in South Uist—suggested her participation in the escape. Others credit the scheme to the prince's comrade and fellow soldier, Captain Felix O'Neill, who was acquainted with Flora and knew her to be a young woman of admirable common sense. Still other accounts say that her actions were entirely spontaneous. Whichever version of the events is accurate, the facts surrounding the plan that Flora devised and carried out have never been disputed.

With a bounty of £30,000 offered for his capture, the Bonnie Prince was hunted by British troops as well as local militia. Every traveler was suspect, and a passport was required of anyone wishing to leave the island or to come ashore. Careful planning would be required to effect the escape of such a notorious fugitive.

Flora, who already had her passport, built a scheme around her intended trip to see her sick mother at Armadale on the Isle of Skye. Once she succeeded in getting the prince to Skye, he would make his way to mainland Scotland and be picked up by a French naval vessel, which would transport him to safety in Europe.

Hugh MacDonald supplied the passports that Flora needed for the several boatmen, a manservant, and an Irish spinning maid who would help care for his ailing wife. According to the plan, Betty Burke, the Irish maid, would make the crossing bundled up against the wind and sea in a bonnet, cloak, and shawl, making it difficult for anyone to have a close look at her face—all for the best since "Betty," an ignorant and ungainly looking servant girl, would indeed be the Bonnie Prince.

Daylight lingers in June in the Hebrides, which increased the risk of the travelers being discovered by government scouts. The prince's party decided to hide themselves on shore until dark, when there would be less chance of being intercepted by British patrol vessels. In spite of high winds and stormy seas, they set out for the Isle of Skye on the night of June 28. En route, they narrowly avoided at least one British boat that passed so close they could hear the sailors' voices.

Landing on Skye the following morning, they made their way to Portree,

where friends hid the prince until he could exchange his female attire for kilt and plaid, then sail to the mainland, and on to France. At Portree, Prince Charles Edward and Flora parted, never to meet again.[1]

Flora spent a few days with her mother, then went to visit her brother at Milton. But word of the adventure got out. The authorities quickly apprehended Flora, and after questioning her, imprisoned her aboard a British sloop-of-war. In July, the ship made for Leith, just beside Edinburgh on the Firth of Forth, where it lay for several weeks.

By this time, all of Scotland seemed to have learned of Flora's part in the prince's escape, and many people, proclaiming her a heroine, came to visit her on the prison ship. November found her in the Tower of London, but she was soon paroled to the house of a Mr. Dick, an official Messenger at Arms in whose home prisoners of war who could pay for their keep were permitted to stay. Virtually free, Flora was allowed to visit friends, albeit always accompanied by Mr. Dick's daughters. She became something of a celebrity in London, and wealthy benefactors soon appeared with funds for her support at Mr. Dick's home.

Freed once and for all in July 1747, Flora headed straight for Scotland and home. She went to stay with her mother at Armadale, but her adventures had brought her such renown that she was a coveted visitor about Skye.

On November 6, 1750, Flora—reportedly dressed in a gown of Stuart tartan—married Allen MacDonald. But living happily ever after was not to be the lot of Flora and Allen. Hard times for the Highlanders increased after the shortlived campaign that had ended at Culloden, and those who had sided with Prince Charles Edward, especially the few who had given him shelter as he fled, seemed to face the most difficulties.

Over the years, the financial situation of Flora and Allen and their seven children steadily worsened. Feeling they had nothing to look forward to in Scotland but more oppression, the couple decided to leave for America. In 1774, they followed a growing number of their neighbors on Skye, including their married

daughter, Anne, to North Carolina.[2] Leaving their youngest son and daughter with friends in Scotland who would see to the youngsters' education, they took two of their older boys with them.

Flora and Allen were met in North Carolina with great fanfare and ceremony; friends held a ball in her honor at Wilmington. When the festivities subsided after several days, the new immigrants moved on to Cross Creek (now Fayetteville), where Flora stayed while Allen searched for a site on which to establish their new home. Near Rockingham, he found a place that would suit them and named it "Killiegrey." The property already had a dwelling and several outbuildings, so Flora, in her fifties by now, settled in, perhaps thinking she had found peace and security at last.

Their neighbors treated the famous Flora and her husband with great respect, and they came to occupy a prominent position in the community. Aside from one claim that Allen built and operated a grist mill on their land, almost nothing is known of their everyday life. J. P. MacLean's *Flora MacDonald in America*, published in 1909, does say, however, that "their influence was everywhere felt and acknowledged."

The peace that Flora was enjoying proved to be momentary; the American War for Independence erupted, and even remote Killiegrey soon became entangled in the troubles. At first it seemed that the North Carolina Scots would take up the American cause, urged on by a committee of patriots who conferred "with the gentlemen who have lately arrived from the Highlands in Scotland to settle in this province… to explain to them the nature of our unhappy controversy with Great Britain, and to advise and urge them to unite with the other inhabitants of America in defense of their rights.…"

But Josiah Martin, royal governor of North Carolina, did everything in his power to persuade the Highlanders to remain loyal to the Crown. In view of the treatment they had suffered at home at the hands of the British, it seemed unlikely they would ally themselves with the British cause in America. But threats, propaganda, and coercion from Governor Martin and his agents prevailed, and the

Scots, many of them MacDonalds, were won over. They organized a sizable army of volunteers, with Allen as a colonel.

In February 1776, events rushed toward a climax for the Highlanders. Word came that they were to meet a British fleet scheduled to land at Cape Fear and then nip the revolution in North Carolina in the bud. Although they were as secretive as possible, the difficulty inherent in concealing the movements of groups of armed men soon led to the patriots learning what was taking place.

An estimated 1,500 to 3,000 Highlanders assembled for the march, and Flora came out to cheer them on their way. Mounted on a white horse, she reviewed the troops, and then rode along for a short distance with Allen and their son-in-law, Alexander MacLeod, a captain in the regiment. With all attempts at maintaining secrecy apparently forgotten, the marching column made a dramatic departure, "drums beating, pipes playing, flags flying."

The Highlanders headed east to the coast, marching at night and criss-crossing creeks along the way in an attempt to evade opposing forces. They eluded Colonel James Moore, who, with about 650 troops from the First North Carolina Continentals, had been sent to head them off at Corbett's Ferry on the Black River.

When he realized that he had been outmaneuvered, Moore ordered Colonel Richard Caswell, commanding some eight hundred Parisan Rangers from New Bern, to cut the Scots off at Moore's Creek Bridge. Caswell and his men, along with 150 other troops commanded by Colonel Alexander Lillington, reached the bridge and quickly constructed earthworks on the west side of the creek. Deciding to abandon these works and meet the loyalist troops on the other side of the creek, they crossed the bridge, removing a section of flooring behind them as they went. After digging new entrenchments, they waited for the Scots to arrive.

Seeing the abandoned earthworks, the Highlanders assumed that their crossing of the bridge would be unopposed. Nonetheless, Colonel Donald McLeod, the Scots' senior officer, led a charge, shouting "King George and Broadswords" as he ran toward the bridge. Shielded by breastworks, the Americans, who had two cannon to assist them, opened fire, almost immediately shattering the attack.

The first battle of the Revolution fought in North Carolina, "the Insurrection of the MacDonalds" left many Highlanders dead or wounded; a number of the loyalist troops drowned after losing their footing while trying to cross the section of the bridge where the flooring had been removed.[3] Many of the Highlanders were taken prisoner, among them Allen MacDonald and his son Alexander, a lieutenant in the loyalist regiment, who were jailed in the town of Halifax.

Things went badly for Flora after the Battle of Moore's Creek Bridge. Recognizing the part she had played in recruiting Highlanders and her influential role in the Scottish settlements, the revolutionaries were not about to allow her to escape punishment. She was viewed with suspicion by those who took the patriot side and deeply resented by the families who had lost men in the battle at Moore's Creek. Summoned to appear before the local Committee of Safety, Flora answered the charges against her with dignity and courage, defending her activities among her Scottish countrymen. Although the committee permitted her to return to Killiegrey, her property was confiscated a year later.

In August 1777, after having been moved several times by his captors, Allen was permitted to go to New York City to negotiate an exchange for himself and his son, Alexander. He was on his honor "not to convey to the enemy or bring back any intelligence whatever of a political nature, and to return [to Reading, Pennsylvania] in a certain time to be fixed by his parole or when called for, on behalf of the United States."

By November, he had succeeded in his mission and soon joined his battalion in Nova Scotia, where he was stationed at Fort Edward, in Windsor. Flora, having first made her way to British-held New York City with her daughter and grandsons, arrived there the next year. Her health had suffered from her ordeal, and in late 1779, Flora, her daughter, and the children sailed for Scotland.

Home at last, Flora went to stay in a cottage on her brother's property in Milton. In 1784, the war over and his regiment disbanded, Allen returned home to Flora. The couple went back to Kingsburgh House on Skye, where they had started their marriage. Less than six years later, on March 5, 1790, Flora died. One of the bed sheets on which Prince Charles Edward had slept so many years before served as her shroud. She had kept the sheet with her during her North American sojourn and carried it back again to Skye, requesting that she be buried in it when the time came.

By all accounts, Flora's funeral was the grandest ever seen on the Isle of Skye. The procession to the cemetery stretched for more than a mile. People had traveled from all the islands and from the mainland to pay their last respects to the patriotic lady in whose heart Scotland was always first.

NOTES

1. Charles Edward Stuart spent the next twenty years in Europe, devising futile plots to establish his claim to the British throne. He returned to Rome, the city of his birth, at the time of his father's death in 1766. He remained there until he died in 1788. His remains are entombed in the vaults of St. Peter's Basilica in Rome.
2. More than 23,000 Highland Scots left their homeland for the American colonies between 1764 and '76.
3. The surviving loyalist troops claimed that the Americans had greased the wooden girders of the bridge with soft soap and tallow after removing the flooring, causing the attackers to slip while trying to cross.

Jean Creznic is senior editor of Early American Homes *magazine and a student of Scottish lore.*

Jefferson's Secret Life

Did the author of the Declaration of Independence take a slave for his mistress?
DNA tests say yes.

By Barbra Murray and Brian Duffy

It begins in 1802 as an attack on America's high-minded president, the man who declared that all men are created equal. James Callender, a vengeful drunk and disappointed job seeker, accuses Thomas Jefferson of fathering illegitimate children by one of his slaves, Sally Hemings. Jefferson declines even to respond to the charge. But it becomes an unblottable stain. Political opponents and the Federalist press gleefully trumpet the alleged affair.

Decades pass and more evidence surfaces. A young man, descended from the beautiful slave woman in question, tells a newspaper in 1873 that Jefferson was his father. But a year later comes a refutation: A Jefferson biographer suggests that the woman's light-skinned children were sired not by the president but by two nephews. A hundred years on, another bombshell: A national bestseller asserts the Jefferson-Hemings liaison as fact and infers that they were genuinely in love. Defenders ridicule the allegation.

But it was not so easily dismissed. Schoolchildren with only the most casual acquaintance of history can usually be trusted to know only two things about Jefferson: That he authored the Declaration of Independence and that he was alleged to have had a long-running affair with Sally Hemings, the quadroon half-sister of his late wife, Martha.

Popular perceptions aside, the circumstantial case has grown more persuasive in recent years: Jefferson, who traveled widely and often, was found to have been present at Monticello nine months before the birth of each of Hemings's children (except for the first, a son who apparently was conceived in Paris when Jefferson was the minister to France and Sally, at 16, was his daughter's servant). Coincidence? So skeptics would have us believe.

But new evidence appears to set the stage for the final episode of the Jefferson-Hemings epic. This week's issue of the British journal *Nature* presents the results of scientific tests that show a conclusive DNA match between a male descendant of Sally Hemings and another man who can trace his lineage to Thomas Jefferson's paternal uncle. Advances in the mapping of the so-called Y chromosome, which confers maleness on embryos, allow scientists now to consider DNA matches of the type reported by *Nature* as virtual proof positive of genetic linkage. The evidence here, in other words, removes any shadow of a doubt that Thomas Jefferson sired at least one son by Sally Heming (*see* box, "The history that lies in men's genes."

It would be naive to assume the new evidence will settle the old debate over Jefferson and his legacy. But the confirmation of the Jefferson-Hemings affair could provoke a fresh examination of the American experience of slavery, and of relations between the races. Moreover, it may help reconcile the disparate perceptions of blacks and whites of their common heritage. "America lives in denial," says Clarence Walker, an African-

American history professor at the University of California—Davis. "This story has been part of black historical consciousness since the late 18th century." Walker recalls that when the story of Sally and Tom came up in a graduate-school discussion, his white peer dismissed it because Jefferson was a "man of the enlightenment."

The confirmation of the Hemings-Jefferson relationship will also play a pivotal role in dispelling the myth of separation between blacks and whites. "Jefferson's literal embrace of Sally, producing children, becomes almost symbolic of what the South was," notes Orlando Patterson, a professor of sociology at Harvard University and author of the forthcoming book on slavery, *Rituals of Blood*. "What we have now is a powerful, symbolic blurring of the lines, with the most famous of the founding fathers intimately, biologically involved [with his black slave]."

Ultimately it was word of mouth among Hemings family members that kept the story alive. Nearly 50 years after Jefferson's death, Sally Hemings's penultimate child, Madison Hemings, confides in an obscure Ohio newspaper that Jefferson was his father and, in fact, sired all of his mother's other offspring. Another ex-slave from Monticello, Israel Jefferson, backs up the tale in a later account to the same newspaper. But Jefferson defenders will have none of it. Known among critics as an overly protective "Monticello mafia," they seek other explanations for the several children Hemings had that were obviously fathered by white men, some of whom bore a striking resemblance to Jefferson. A year after Madison Hemings's Ohio interview, James Parton's *Life of Thomas Jefferson* purported to solve the Hemings mystery by laying the paternity of her white offspring off on Jefferson's philandering nephew, Peter Carr, son of Jefferson's sister. Others blamed another notorious Carr, Samuel.

'Jefferson's embrace of Sally is almost symbolic of what the South was'

The parentage question. Thus it was that there were two parallel universes of thought on the Jefferson-Hemings question. Among the Jefferson specialists, the question of his parentage of *any* Hemings offspring was answered, almost universally, in the negative. Among the multifarious Hemings heirs and in the wider black community, meanwhile, there was no doubt but that the man from Monticello had fathered children with Hemings. "Those of us who are descendants have 100 percent certainty—you cannot modify 100 percent certainty," says Hemings descendant Michele Cooley-Quille, who comes from the Thomas Woodson branch of the family.

After the 1974 publication of *Thomas Jefferson: An Intimate History* by historian Fawn Brodie, mainstream white America began to buy into the story's veracity. But among the academic elite, the 1974 bestseller ignited a furious debate. Brodie's arguments, while highly persuasive, were not conclusive, and many Jefferson scholars refused to embrace them.

That's pretty much where matters stood. Until now. In fact, had it not been for Gene Foster, that's probably where matters might have stood, period. Dr. Eugene A. Foster, technically retired after a distinguished career as a pathology professor at the Tufts University School of Medicine and the University of Virginia, is a genial bear of a man, 6 foot 4, the strong, silent type. Foster jokes that he is only "technically" retired because he keeps himself busy with a constant stream of "projects of interest." One of those, as it happened, was Thomas Jefferson. Which is not altogether surprising, since Jefferson's presence is felt everywhere in Charlottesville, where Foster lives with his wife, Jane, a retired instructor of French. But Foster got onto Jefferson in a roundabout way. At dinner one evening back in 1996 with a family friend, the conversation turned to the subject of Anastasia, the daughter of the last Romanov czar, Nicholas. Specifically, the talk centered on how DNA had been used to determine whether a deceased Charlottesville woman, Anna Anderson, was the Romanov daughter Anastasia, as she claimed. Winifred Bennett, the Fosters' friend, proposed that the same methodology might be used to resolve the Jefferson-Hemings mystery. The reverberations from Fawn Brodie's book were still echoing in Charlottesville. Gene Foster was intrigued.

'There arose two parallel universes of thought, one white, the other black'

He started poking around. A biology professor at the university passed along word of recent advances in mapping techniques for the Y chromosome. That was fine, but where to get samples to test? Foster would have to find male-line Jefferson descendants. But Jefferson's only legitimate son died in infancy. (Jefferson's wife, Martha, gave birth to six children, but only two lived to adulthood.) That left Foster with only two Jefferson male lines to research: that of the president's brother, Randolph, and of their paternal uncle, Field Jefferson. The Randolph line looked promising at first. But it turned out that the line of direct male descendants had expired sometime in either the 1920s or 1930s.

Foster turned to the Field line. First he sought out Herbert Barger, a respected Jefferson family genealogist. Barger agreed to help. By early 1997, Foster had the names and phone numbers of seven living descendants of Field Jefferson. He fired off letters to all of them. Only one wrote back. So Barger intervened on Foster's behalf, and five of Field's descendants agreed to cooperate, allowing Foster to draw blood samples.

That was one part of the equation. But if he were to obtain a definitive Y chromosome match, Foster would need DNA from a male who had good reason to believe he was a descendant of Jefferson and Hemings. There was one obvious place to look: among the 1,400 members of the Thomas Woodson Family Association, an organization of African-Americans scattered across the country. The group is named for Hemings's first son, Tom, the child apparently conceived in Paris. Byron Woodson agreed to cooperate with Foster. But then his father, Col. John Woodson, put a stop to it. He didn't want to be messing around with subjects like illegitimacy, he said.

The Woodsons had maintained for nearly two centuries that they were descendants of Jefferson, but other branches of the family pooh-poohed the claim. Foster pressed. If they were to come up without any evidence linking the Woodson line to Jefferson, he told the colonel, "they'll say you knew that all along. But if we come up with evidence that, in fact, Jefferson was the father...." Foster let the sentence drop. The colonel relented. The Woodsons, he said, would cooperate with Foster's study. Five Woodsons eventually gave blood.

Closing loopholes. But there was more to be done. The philandering Carr boys could not be dismissed out of hand. Jefferson's distinguished defenders would dismiss any paternity evidence that didn't address that question. Foster tracked down three male descendants of the Carrs. They, too, gave blood. There remained one other line of male descendants to track down, and here Foster got lucky. Eston Hemings was Sally Hemings seventh and last child and Foster identified a lone male descendant. The man readily agreed to participate. Next Foster wanted some "control" samples. These were drawn from male descendants of several old-line Virginia families. The idea was to eliminate potential similarities in the Y chromosome tests due to geographic proximity. Foster was amazed by the cooperation. These were people, he said, "who had nothing to gain." And yet they welcomed him into

Tracking the Jefferson Y chromosome

Only males carry the Y chromosome. All direct descendants in a line share the same or nearly the same Y chromosome. Here's how the match was made.

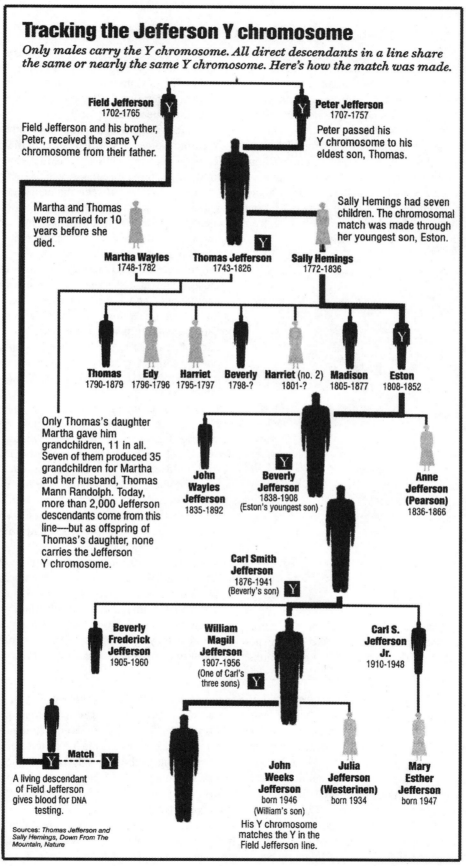

Field Jefferson
1702-1765

Field Jefferson and his brother, Peter, received the same Y chromosome from their father.

Peter Jefferson
1707-1757

Peter passed his Y chromosome to his eldest son, Thomas.

Martha and Thomas were married for 10 years before she died.

Martha Wayles
1748-1782

Thomas Jefferson
1743-1826

Sally Hemings
1772-1836

Sally Hemings had seven children. The chromosomal match was made through her youngest son, Eston.

Thomas
1790-1879

Edy
1796-1796

Harriet
1795-1797

Beverly
1798-?

Harriet (no. 2)
1801-?

Madison
1805-1877

Eston
1808-1852

Only Thomas's daughter Martha gave him grandchildren, 11 in all. Seven of them produced 35 grandchildren for Martha and her husband, Thomas Mann Randolph. Today, more than 2,000 Jefferson descendants come from this line----but as offspring of Thomas's daughter, none carries the Jefferson Y chromosome.

John Wayles Jefferson
1835-1892

Beverly Jefferson
1838-1908
(Eston's youngest son)

Anne Jefferson (Pearson)
1836-1866

Carl Smith Jefferson
1876-1941
(Beverly's son)

Beverly Frederick Jefferson
1905-1960

William Magill Jefferson
1907-1956
(One of Carl's three sons)

Carl S. Jefferson Jr.
1910-1948

A living descendant of Field Jefferson gives blood for DNA testing.

Match

John Weeks Jefferson
born 1946
(William's son)

His Y chromosome matches the Y in the Field Jefferson line.

Julia Jefferson (Westerinen)
born 1934

Mary Esther Jefferson
born 1947

Sources: *Thomas Jefferson and Sally Hemings, Down From The Mountain, Nature*

USN&WR

A FATHER'S GIFT

The History That Lies in Men's Genes

The use of Y chromosome testing to verify the long-debated assertion that Thomas Jefferson fathered at least one slave child is among the more dramatic consequences of a scientific discovery early in this century, one that helped gain a 1933 Nobel Prize for American geneticist Thomas Hunt Morgan. By studying fruit flies, Morgan found that recognizably different bundles of genes, which he called X and Y chromosomes, determine whether the insects are male or female. He soon recognized that the pattern holds in higher organisms, including humans. Inheritance of two X's, one from each parent, confers femaleness, while an X from mother and a Y from father produce a male.

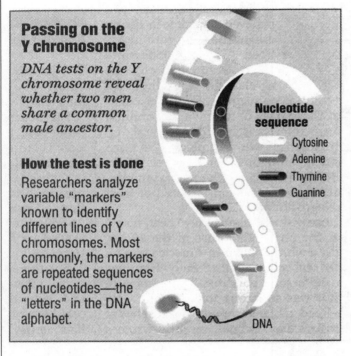

Passing on the Y chromosome

DNA tests on the Y chromosome reveal whether two men share a common male ancestor.

How the test is done

Researchers analyze variable "markers" known to identify different lines of Y chromosomes. Most commonly, the markers are repeated sequences of nucleotides—the "letters" in the DNA alphabet.

Nucleotide sequence

Cytosine
Adenine
Thymine
Guanine

DNA

In people, the sex chromosomes are but one pair among 23 pairs of chromosomes in all, each packed with genes. Most chromosomes get shuffled in succeeding generations.

By contrast, Y chromosomes carry a unique set of genes and, except for rare, random mutations, pass down unchanged through generations. They thus provide a deep view into the string of males in any man's ancestry.

Perfect match. The methods used to identify individual Y chromosomes have arisen only in the past 10 years or so. The key is identification of distinct genetic markers, sometimes called polymorphisms, which are typically stretches of "nonsense" DNA between the actual genes. They can vary widely from one man to the next. One or two markers can be identical purely by coincidence, but if many (scores are known) are identical, chances mount that two men have a recent, common ancestor. The British labs that performed the Jefferson tests compared 19 markers, all matched exactly those found in a descendant of Field Jefferson, the president's uncle, and a descendant of Eston Hemings Jefferson, Sally Hemings's youngest son. The researchers, who published their results in *Nature [see Nov. 1998 issue],* put the odds of a non-Jefferson match at less than 0.1 percent, based on their failure to find any Y chromosome that came close to matching the Jefferson pattern in 1,200 samples from unrelated men.

Even if no match were found among living men in the Hemings and Jefferson lines, or between some but not all subbranches of those lines, that would not exclude unions between Thomas Jefferson and Sally Hemings. The genetic trail could have been broken in subsequent generations if any of the mothers in the presumed chain actually had her son by a man outside the Jefferson line. Similarly, while people linked to Jefferson via a maternal link would probably carry some of his genes on other chromosomes, the Y chromosome test cannot show that.

Study of Y chromosomes has brought other big payoffs for genealogists and geneticists. Members of a Jewish priesthood, the Cohanim, who by tradition must be sons of a priest and who date their ancestry back 3,300 years to Aaron, older brother of Moses, found their Y chromosomes to be so similar that they must indeed share a common ancestor from about that long ago.—*Charles W. Petit*

their homes. One even had fresh-baked brownies waiting for him when he turned up to draw blood.

Now it was time to test. Foster had 19 samples in all. A fellow pathologist at the University of Virginia extracted the DNA from the blood samples. Foster numbered and coded them, then stowed them in a bubble-wrapped envelope. Researchers at Oxford had agreed to test the samples. Foster flew to London, the samples secure in his carry-on. A bus from Heathrow air-

port deposited him at the ancient university town, and Foster delivered the samples to researcher Chris Tyler-Smith, whom Foster describes as his "main collaborator." First the two men placed the materials in a refrigerator. Then they toddled off to a pub for lunch.

The rest, as the saying goes, is history, albeit of a peculiar sort. According to Hemings's heirs, Jefferson fathered seven children by her, four boys and three girls. Foster's meticulously collected samples

were tested by three different Oxford labs using different procedures. The results fail to match the Field Jefferson line with the Woodson line, Hemings, or, interestingly, with the heirs of the Carr brothers. But the tests did establish a definite Y chromosome match on Eston Hemings, who was born in the second term of Jefferson's presidency.

What does that mean? That one can say with certainty that Sally Hemings bore Thomas Jefferson at least one son.

Holding out for an Icon

Character counts, the historians insisted

By Lewis Lord

For the black Americans who 44 years ago read and believed an article in *Ebony* magazine—the one headlined "Thomas Jefferson's Negro Grandchildren"—the revelations from the DNA labs come as no surprise. *Ebony,* circulated in those days to nearly a half-million African-Americans, profiled several "elderly Negroes" who had placed a third president atop their family tree. "Many reputable historians," the magazine said, "concede that Jefferson fathered at least five Negro children."

Those historians must have been black. Until the civil rights days of the 1960s, hardly a white scholar in America was on record as believing that Sally Hemings bore Jefferson's children. The pattern of denials was so strong that Annette Gordon-Reed, a black woman who teaches at New York Law School, recently wrote a much-acclaimed book—*Thomas Jefferson and Sally Hemings: An American Controversy*—meticulously dissecting the historians' conclusions and the ways in which they were reached and articulated. The DNA results, she says, barely concern her. "It's the historiography that's offensive. You can't use arguments that are dehumanizing to blacks to turn around a story."

Foremost among the historical naysayers was Dumas Malone, a Mississippi-born and Georgia-raised Pulitzer winner who dismissed "the miscegenation legend" as "filth." Malone placed Jefferson with Washington and Lincoln in "our Trinity of immortals." The possibility of a "vulgar liaison," he wrote, was "virtually unthinkable in a man of Jefferson's moral standards."

For nearly a century, the prime evidence of an affair was an account by Madison Hemings, Sally's next-to-last child, who settled in Ohio. In an 1873 interview in Ohio's *Pike County Republican,* Hemings reported that his mother told him that Jefferson fathered all of her children. Another former Monticello slave, interviewed by the same paper, agreed with Heming's richly detailed account.

But the ex-slaves' memoirs hardly got outside Pike County. What kept the Tom-and-Sally story alive was a tradition of oral history in a scattering of black families across America, as one generation quietly and, in many instances, secretly told the next what had happened. Occasionally, as in the 1954 *Ebony* article, the story would emerge, then recede into the closet.

'Amalgamation,' Jefferson said, 'produces a degradation'

The few historians who addressed the subject seemed determined to keep it there. In 1960, Merrill Peterson, in *The Jefferson Image in the American Mind,* found the Sally story sustained in part by the "Negroes' pathetic wish for a little pride and their subtle ways of confounding the white folks." Dumas Malone cautioned, "There is material here for the tragedian, but the historian must recognize that oral tradition is not established fact."

Black vs. white. Malone, while discounting oral accounts by blacks, welcomed the testimony of Jefferson's aristocratic white kin. He even embraced a pair of stories that conflicted with each other. Explaining why the Hemings children looked like Jefferson, the historian recalled that a grandson of the president once told an interviewer that their father was Peter Carr, a Jefferson nephew. A granddaughter, Malone also noted, identified Sally's lover as Peter's brother Samuel. (DNA tests... indicate that neither nephew was involved.)

For their chief argument, Jefferson's defenders invariably turned to his character. Sex with a slave would be an abuse of power, one historian contended, and Jefferson was not an "abusive" person. To show that sex with a black was unlikely, scholars trotted out Jefferson's pseudo-scientific views on race, among them: "Amalgamation produces a degradation to which no one... can innocently consent." Still others concluded that the Sage of Monticello, once he was widowed at 39, had no interest in sex and was content to devote his remaining 44 years to architecture, laws, and literature.

The first white historian to suggest that a Hemings-Jefferson affair just might have happened was Winthrop Jordan, now at the University of Mississippi, whose 1968 book *White Over Black* made a relevant biological point. Taking a fresh look at Malone's Monticello data, Jordan reported that "Jefferson was at home nine months prior to each birth."

That helped clear the way for an event that transformed how millions of Americans viewed Jefferson. In a 1974 bestseller, UCLA historian Fawn Brodie used a blend of history and psychoanalysis to shape an argument that Jefferson and Hemings had a long and caring sexual relationship. Jefferson's "slave family," she suggested, represented "not a flaw in the hero but a flaw in society."

Five years later, Brodie's book, *Thomas Jefferson: An Intimate History,* inspired a piece of Barbara Chase-Riboud fiction, *Sally Hemings: A Novel,* which, in turn, prompted programmers at CBS to envision a Tom-and-Sally television miniseries. Several Virginia historians, led by Malone, were outraged. The basis for such a miniseries, Malone wrote CBS, was a "tawdry and unverifiable story." The network scrapped the project after Jefferson's Virginia descendants joined the campaign to protect his name.

But the notion that Jefferson had a slave mistress no longer could be brushed aside. Even Malone, who had worked 43 years on a six-volume biography of the president, seemed to sense where the story was going. In 1984, two years before he died at age 94, the historian told the *New York Times* that what struck him as most speculative about Brodie's account was not that Jefferson might have slept with Hemings but rather that he had carried on a love affair with her in Paris and later as president for years on end. A sexual encounter, on the other hand, Malone said, could be neither proved nor disproved: "It might have happened once or twice."

When a Saint Becomes a Sinner

Public affection for Jefferson is so strong that his legacy seems secure

By Joseph J. Ellis

Well, now we know. More fastidious minds may linger over scientific details and statistical probabilities, and a few die-hard Jefferson worshipers will surely mount a spirited assault on the reliability of DNA evidence. The fact that there is not a match with the first of Sally Hemings's children, Thomas, may deflect some attention from the match with her last child, Eston.

But the Eston match is really all that matters because, in conjunction with the circumstantial evidence that already existed, it proves beyond any reasonable doubt that Jefferson had a long-term sexual relationship with his mulatto slave. As one of those students of Jefferson who had previously questioned that possibility, I think it is important that this near certain conclusion be announced to what Jefferson called "a candid world." Over its long history, the story of "Tom and Sally" has achieved the status of America's most enduring soap opera. We have now reached the final episode.

The salient question now seems to be: What difference does it make? For the several hundred Hemings descendants who have maintained that their oral tradition was more reliable than the oral tradition of the white members of the Jefferson family, and also more historically accurate than a substantial group of Jefferson scholars was prepared to acknowledge, this news is deliverance. It confirms the stories they have been passing along from generation to generation. Robert Cooley, one of the most outspoken Hemings descendants, once said he looked forward to a long talk with Mr. Jefferson in the hereafter. Cooley, who died last July, must be enjoying that conversation now.

'Tom and Sally,' America's most enduring soap opera, has reached its finale

---

President William Jefferson Clinton also has a vested interest in this revelation. He launched his first-term inaugural parade at Monticello and hosted at the White House a special screening of the Ken Burns documentary on Jefferson. I happened to be present at the reception afterward when Clinton asked the assembled historical consultants: "Do you think the story of a sexual liaison with Sally Hemings is true?" When one of the historians responded in the negative, a look of disappointment streaked across the president's face. He was, we now know, at that very time involved in his own sexual liaison with Monica Lewinsky.

And he is now, of course, under scrutiny by the House Judiciary Committee for this dalliance and the subsequent coverup, and DNA evidence (i.e., the famous blue dress) also played a clinching role. The Foster study seems impeccably timed to arrive like a comet that has been winging through space for 200 years before landing squarely in the middle of the Clinton impeachment inquiry.

Witness for Clinton. Jefferson has always been Clinton's favorite Founding Father. Now, a sexually active, all-too-human Jefferson appears alongside his embattled protégé. It is as if Clinton had called one of the most respected character witnesses in all of U.S. history to testify that the primal urge has a most distinguished presidential pedigree. The dominant effect of this news will be to make Clinton's sins seem less aberrant and more palatable. If a vote against Clinton is also a vote against Jefferson, the prospects for impeachment become even more remote.

Within the scholarly world, the acceptance of a Jefferson-Hemings liaison had been gaining ground over recent years. Now that it is proven beyond any reasonable doubt, the net effect is to reinforce the critical picture of Jefferson as an inherently elusive and deeply duplicitous character. We already knew that he lived the great paradox of American history. Which is to say he could walk past the slave quarters at Monticello thinking grand thoughts about human equality and never notice the disjunction. Now it would seem that his oft-stated belief in black inferiority and his palpable fear of racial amalgamation somehow coexisted alongside his intimate relationship with an attractive black woman. His public announcements and his private behavior apparently occupied wholly different and mutually exclusive compartments in his soul. The man who wrote "A Dialogue Between My Head and My Heart" in a letter to Maria Cosway, with whom he was intensely infatuated during his Paris years, apparently did not permit those different parts of his own personality to speak to one another.

If the scholarly portrait of Jefferson had already begun to depict him as inherently hypocritical, the popular perception has remained resolutely reverential. If the scholarly Jefferson has become a more controversial and problematic icon, the vast majority of ordinary Americans continue to regard him as the most potent symbol of American values in the entire gallery of national greats. He is on Mount Rushmore, the Tidal Basin, the nickel, and the $2 bill. He is somehow central to our national sense of self. Lincoln said that America was founded on a proposition. Well, Jefferson wrote the proposition in 1776, in 35 magical words: *We hold these Truths to be self-evident, that all Men are created equal, that they are endowed by their Creator with certain unalienable Rights, that among these are Life, Liberty, and the pursuit of Happiness.*

As one of his earnest biographers put it: "If America is right, Jefferson was right." Since his enshrinement in the Jefferson Memorial in 1943, he has levitated out of the historical muck and into a midair location that hovers over the political landscape like a dirigible at the Super Bowl, flashing inspirational messages to both teams. Not just an essential ingredient in the American political tradition, he has become the essence itself.

American symbol. This mythological Jefferson has also become the one American hero who is also at home abroad. The values Jefferson has come to embody were the values of Polish dissidents in the Gdansk shipyards; the Chinese youths in Tiananmen Square; the Buddhist monks in Tibet. Wherever there is a struggle between the forces of light and the forces of darkness, Jefferson is America's most accessible and effective ambassador. He translates more resonantly than any other American symbol.

Will these new revelations about his sexual connection to Sally Hemings undermine this apparently bottomless affection? Will Jefferson be knocked off the elevated pedestal on which we have placed him? My best guess is that he will survive this trial even more successfully than Clinton survives his. Jefferson's reputation, to be sure, has had its ups and downs. But his legacy, or what we

(continued)

When a Saint Becomes a Sinner *continued*

take to be his legacy, has so thoroughly infiltrated the national ethos, has so fully insinuated itself into the creedal convictions of America's promise to itself and the world, that a diminution of Jefferson will be regarded, as he put it, as "treason against the hopes of mankind." If the American past were a gambling casino, everyone who has bet against Jefferson has eventually lost. There is no reason to believe it will be different this time.

Inherently elusive, Jefferson, we now know, lived the great paradox of American history

---

Indeed, Jefferson's legacy might appear more lustrous than ever before. For he is now thoroughly human, the American demigod made flesh who dwelt among us, the saint who sinned, the great man with ordinary weaknesses. As we approach the end of the "American Century," he has metamorphosed into the new role model for our postmodern temperament, if you will, a '90s kind of guy.

This new chapter in the Jefferson saga of renewed relevance can also develop quite naturally by spinning the Sally and Tom story as a tragic romance between two besmitten lovers prohibited from declaring their mutual affection by the racial strictures of the day. There is no historical evidence to support such an interpretation. But then there is no historical evidence to refute it, either. Several biographers, most famously Fawn Brodie, along with a larger group of novelists and poets, have already introduced this imaginative version of the story into the mainstream American culture, with

considerable success. Given the strong pro-Jefferson currents that run relentlessly beneath the surface of our national mythology, the urge to make Jefferson and Hemings America's premier biracial couple could prove irresistible.

Finally, some of Jefferson's most severe critics in recent years—Michael Lind and Conor Cruise O'Brien come to mind—have argued that the man from Monticello is an inappropriate icon for our more racially diverse and multicultural American society. From a strictly logical point of view, this makes eminent sense, since Jefferson's writings clearly reveal a prevailing presumption that America must remain a white man's country.

Now, however, Jefferson's life and his most intimate personal choices just as clearly reveal an interracial commitment that probably endured for 38 years. The Hemings descendants have sustained the story of their lineage for many generations because they are proud of their biological connection to Jefferson. While it will require a rather large stretch to transform Jefferson from a thinking man's racist to a multi-cultural hero, some commentators are sure to make the leap.

Perhaps a more historically responsible way to make a similar if slightly different case is to suggest that advancing technology has at least allowed us to open a window onto the covert and concealed interracial intimacies that have always been there but that many white Americans have preferred to deny. So now Jefferson surfaces again, not only offering aid and comfort to an embattled President Clinton but also making himself useful as a most potent guide into a fresh round of more candid conversations about the way we truly were and are one people.

Joseph J. Ellis, a professor of history at Mount Holyoke College, won a 1997 National Book Award for American Sphinx: The Character of Thomas Jefferson.

But the tests do not preclude the possibility that there were other offspring. Indeed, abundant historical evidence suggests that this is so.

Beverly and Harriet Hemings very likely had Jefferson blood. After being allowed to run away—a privilege granted only to Hemings's children—the two blended into white society in the Washington, D.C., area. Today, they may have hundreds of descendants who have never suspected that their ancestry is either African or presidential.

Madison Hemings cannot be ruled out. Freed by Jefferson's will, he settled among blacks in Ohio, where he told an interviewer that his mother was Jefferson's "concubine" and he and his siblings were the president's children. But Madison's Y chromosome line cannot be tested; one of his three sons vanished into white society and the other two had no children. (But one daughter had a son who became California's first black state legislator.)

Tom, the boy conceived in Paris, still may have been Jefferson's son, even though there was no DNA match in his family line. The negative may have resulted from an unknown male—an illegitimate father—breaking the Y chromosome chain.

The link with Eston Hemings could easily have been missed. Freed with his

brother Madison, he moved to Wisconsin, changed his name to Eston Jefferson, and gave everyone the impression he was white. One of his sons, John Jefferson—redheaded like the third president—was wounded at Vicksburg while serving as a lieutenant colonel in the Union Army. A century later, descendants working on the family tree kept hitting a dead end, running up against the name "Hemings." Not until they read Fawn Brodie's book did they sense they were kin to a slave and a president.

With Gerald Parshall and Lewis Lord

Making Sense of the Fourth of July

The DECLARATION OF INDEPENDENCE is not what Thomas Jefferson thought it was when he wrote it—and that is why we celebrate it

By Pauline Maier

JOHN ADAMS THOUGHT AMERICANS would commemorate their Independence Day on the second of July. Future generations, he confidently predicted, would remember July 2, 1776, as "the most memorable Epocha, in the History of America" and celebrate it as their "Day of Deliverance by solemn Acts of Devotion to God Almighty. It ought to be solemnized with Pomp and Parade, with Shews, Games, Sports, Guns, Bells, Bonfires and Illuminations from one End of this Continent to the other from this Time forward forever more."

His proposal, however odd it seems today, was perfectly reasonable when he made it in a letter to his wife, Abigail. On the previous day, July 2, 1776, the Second Continental Congress had finally resolved "That these United Colonies are, and of right ought to be, free and independent States, that they are absolved from all allegiance to the British Crown, and that all political connection between them and the State of Great Britain is, and ought to be, totally dissolved." The thought that Americans might instead commemorate July 4, the day Congress adopted a "Declaration on Independency" that he had helped prepare, did not apparently occur to Adams in 1776. The Declaration of Independence was

one of those congressional statements that he later described as "dress and ornament rather than Body, Soul, or Substance," a way of announcing to the world the fact of American independence, which was for Adams the thing worth celebrating.

In fact, holding our great national festival on the Fourth makes no sense at all—unless we are actually celebrating not just independence but the Declaration of Independence. And the declaration we celebrate, what Abraham Lincoln called "the charter of our liberties," is a document whose meaning and function today are different from what they were in 1776. In short, during the nineteenth century the Declaration of Independence became not just a way of announcing and justifying the end of Britain's power over the Thirteen Colonies and the emergence of the United States as an independent nation but a statement of principles to guide stable, established governments. Indeed, it came to usurp in fact if not in law a role that Americans normally delegated to bills of rights. How did that happen? And why?

According to notes kept by Thomas Jefferson, the Second Continental Congress did not discuss the resolution on in-

dependence when it was first proposed by Virginia's Richard Henry Lee, on Friday, June 7, 1776, because it was "obliged to attend at that time to some other business." However, on the eighth, Congress resolved itself into a Committee of the Whole and "passed that day & Monday the 10th in debating on the subject." By then all contenders admitted that it had become impossible for the colonies ever again to be united with Britain. The issue was one of timing.

John and Samuel Adams, along with others such as Virginia's George Wythe, wanted Congress to declare independence right away and start negotiating foreign alliances and forming a more lasting confederation (which Lee also proposed). Others, including Pennsylvania's James Wilson, Edward Rutledge of South Carolina, and Robert R. Livingston of New York, argued for delay. They noted that the delegates of several colonies, including Maryland, Pennsylvania, Delaware, New Jersey, and New York, had not been "impowered" by their home governments to vote for independence. If a vote was taken immediately, those delegates would have to "retire" from Congress, and their states might secede from the union, which would seriously weaken the Americans' chance of realizing their independence. In the past, they said, members of Congress had followed the "wise & proper" policy of putting off major decisions "till the voice of the people drove us into it," since "they were our power, & without them our declarations could not be carried into effect." Moreover, opinion on independence in the critical middle colonies was "fast ripening & in a short time," they predicted, the people there would "join in the general voice of America."

CONGRESS DECIDED TO GIVE THE laggard colonies time and so delayed its decision for three weeks. But it also appointed a Committee of Five to draft a declaration of independence so that such a document could be issued quickly once Lee's motion passed. The committee's members included Jefferson, Livingston, John Adams, Roger Sherman of Connecticut, and Pennsylvania's Benjamin Franklin. The drafting committee met, decided what the declaration should say and how it would be organized, then asked Jefferson to prepare a draft.

Meanwhile, Adams—who did more to win Congress's consent to independence than any other delegate—worked feverishly to bring popular pressure on the governments of recalcitrant colonies so they would change the instructions issued to their congressional delegates. By June 28, when the Committee of Five submitted to Congress a draft declaration, only Maryland and New York had failed to allow their delegates to vote for independence. That night Maryland fell into line.

Even so, when the Committee of the Whole again took up Lee's resolution, on July 1, only nine colonies voted in favor (the four New England states, New Jersey, Maryland, Virginia, North Carolina, and Georgia). South Carolina and Pennsylvania opposed the proposition, Delaware's two delegates split, and New York's abstained because their twelve-month-old instructions precluded them from approving anything that impeded reconciliation with the mother country. Edward Rutledge now asked that Congress put off its decision until the next day, since he thought that the South

Carolina delegation would then vote in favor "for the sake of unanimity." When Congress took its final tally on July 2, the nine affirmative votes of the day before had grown to twelve: Not only South Carolina voted in favor, but so did Delaware—the arrival of Caesar Rodney broke the tie in that delegation's vote—and Pennsylvania. Only New York held out. Then on July 9 it, too, allowed its delegates to add their approval to that of delegates from the other twelve colonies, lamenting still the "cruel necessity" that made independence "unavoidable."

Once independence had been adopted, Congress again formed itself into a Committee of the Whole. It then spent the better part of two days editing the draft declaration submitted by its Committee of Five, rewriting or chopping off large sections of text. Finally, on July 4, Congress approved the revised Declaration and ordered it to be printed and sent to the several states and to the commanding officers of the Continental Army. By formally announcing and justifying the end of British rule, that document, as letters from Congress's president, John Hancock, explained, laid "the Ground & Foundation" of American self-government. As a result, it had to be proclaimed not only before American troops in the hope that it would inspire them to fight more ardently for what was now the cause of both liberty and national independence but throughout the country, and "in such a Manner, that the People may be universally informed of it."

Not until four days later did a committee of Congress—not Congress itself—get around to sending a copy of the Declaration to its emissary in Paris, Silas Deane, with orders to present it to the court of France and send copies to "the other Courts of Europe." Unfortunately the original letter was lost, and the next failed to reach Deane until November, when news of American independence had circulated for months. To make matters worse, it arrived with only a brief note from the committee and in an envelope that lacked a seal, an unfortunately slipshod way, complained Deane, to announce the arrival of the United States among the powers of the earth to "old and powerfull states." Despite the Decla-

ration's reference to the "opinions of mankind," it was obviously meant first and foremost for a home audience.

As copies of the Declaration spread through the states and were publicly read at town meetings, religious services, court days, or wherever else people assembled, Americans marked the occasion with appropriate rituals. They lit great bonfires, "illuminated" their windows with candles, fired guns, rang bells, tore down and destroyed the symbols of monarchy on public buildings, churches, or tavern signs, and "fixed up" on the walls of their homes broadside or newspaper copies of the Declaration of Independence.

BUT WHAT EXACTLY WERE THEY celebrating? The news, not the vehicle that brought it; independence and the assumption of self-government, not the document that announced Congress's decision to break with Britain. Considering how revered a position the Declaration of Independence later won in the minds and hearts of the people, Americans' disregard for it in the first years of the new nation verges on the unbelievable. One colonial newspaper dismissed the Declaration's extensive charges against the king as just another "recapitulation of injuries," one, it seems, in a series, and not particularly remarkable compared with earlier "catalogues of grievances." Citations of the Declaration were usually drawn from its final paragraph, which said that the united colonies "are and of Right ought to be Free and Independent states" and were "Absolved of all Allegiance to the British Crown"—words from the Lee resolution that Congress had inserted into the committee draft. Independence was new; the rest of the Declaration seemed all too familiar to Americans, a restatement of what they and their representatives had already said time and again.

The adoption of independence was, however, from the beginning confused with its declaration. Differences in the meaning of the word *declare* contributed to the confusion. Before the Declaration of Independence was issued—while, in fact, Congress was still editing Jefferson's draft—Pennsylvania newspapers announced that on July 2 the Continental Congress had "declared the United Colonies Free and Independent States," by which it meant simply that it had officially accepted that status. Newspapers in other colonies repeated the story. In later years the "Anniversary of the United States of America" came to be celebrated on the date Congress had approved the Declaration of Independence. That began, it seems, by accident. In 1777 no member of Congress thought of marking the anniversary of independence at all until July 3, when it was too late to honor July 2. As a result, the celebration took place on the Fourth, and that became the tradition. At least one delegate spoke of "celebrating the Anniversary of the Declaration of Independence," but over the next few years references to the anniversary of independence and of the Declaration seem to have been virtually interchangeable.

The Fourth of July was rarely celebrated during the Revolution and seems actually to have declined in popularity once the war was over.

Accounts of the events at Philadelphia on July 4, 1777, say quite a bit about the music played by a band of Hessian soldiers who had been captured at the Battle of Trenton the previous December, and the "splendid illumination" of houses, but little about the Declaration. Thereafter, in the late 1770s and 1780s, the Fourth of July was not regularly celebrated; indeed, the holiday seems to have declined in popularity once the Revolutionary War ended. When it was remembered, however, festivities seldom, if ever—to judge by newspaper accounts—involved a public reading of the Declaration of Independence. It was as if that document had done its work in carrying news of independence to the people, and it neither needed nor deserved further commemoration. No mention was made of Thomas Jefferson's role in composing the document, since that was not yet public knowledge, and no sug-

gestion appeared that the Declaration itself was, as posterity would have it, unusually eloquent or powerful.

In fact, one of the very few public comments on the document's literary qualities came in a Virginia newspaper's account of a 1777 speech by John Wilkes, an English radical and a long-time supporter of the Americans, in the House of Commons. Wilkes set out to answer a fellow member of Parliament who had attacked the Declaration of Independence as "a wretched composition, very ill written, drawn up with a view to captivate the people." Curiously, Wilkes seemed to agree with that description. The purpose of the document, he said, was indeed to captivate the American people, who were not much impressed by "the polished periods, the harmonious, happy expressions, with all the grace, ease, and elegance of a beautiful diction" that Englishmen valued. What they liked was "manly, nervous sense… even in the most awkward and uncouth dress of language."

All that began to change in the 1790s, when, in the midst of bitter partisan conflict, the modern understanding and reputation of the Declaration of Independence first emerged. Until that time celebrations of the Fourth were controlled by nationalists who found a home in the Federalist party, and their earlier inattention to the Declaration hardened into a rigid hostility after 1790. The document's anti-British character was an embarrassment to Federalists who sought economic and diplomatic rapprochement with Britain. The language of equality and rights in the Declaration was different from that of the Declaration of the Rights of Man issued by the French National Assembly in 1789, but it still seemed too "French" for the comfort of Federalists, who, after the execution of Louis XVI and the onset of the Terror, lost whatever sympathy for the French Revolution they had once felt. Moreover, they understandably found it best to say as little as possible about a fundamental American text that had been

drafted by a leader of the opposing Republican party.

It was, then, the Republicans who began to celebrate the Declaration of Independence as a "deathless instrument" written by "the immortal Jefferson." The Republicans saw themselves as the defenders of the American Republic of 1776 against subversion by pro-British "monarchists," and they hoped that by recalling the causes of independence, they would make their countrymen wary of further dealings with Great Britain. They were also delighted to identify the founding principles of the American Revolution with those of America's sister republic in France. At their Fourth of July celebrations, Republicans read the Declaration of Independence, and their newspapers reprinted it. Moreover, in their hands the attention that had at first focused on the last part of the Declaration shifted toward its opening paragraphs and the "self-evident truths" they stated. The Declaration, as a Republican newspaper said on July 7, 1792, was not to be celebrated merely "as affecting the separation of one country from the jurisdiction of another"; it had an enduring significance for established governments because it provided a "definition of the rights of man, and the end of civil government."

The Federalists responded that Jefferson had not written the Declaration alone. The drafting committee—including John Adams, a Federalist—had also contributed to its creation. And Jefferson's role as "the scribe who penned the declaration" had not been so distinguished as his followers suggested. Federalists rediscovered similarities between the Declaration and Locke's *Second Treatise of Government* that Richard Henry Lee had noticed long before and used them to argue that even the "small part of that memorable instrument" that could be attributed to Jefferson "he stole from *Locke's Essays.*" But after the War of 1812, the Federalist party slipped from sight, and with it, efforts to disparage the Declaration of Independence.

When a new party system formed in the late 1820s and 1830s, both Whigs and Jacksonians claimed descent from Jefferson and his party and so accepted the old Republican position on the Declaration and Jefferson's glorious role in its creation. By then, too, a new generation of Americans had come of age and made preservation of the nation's revolutionary history its particular mission. Its efforts, and its reverential attitude toward the revolutionaries and their works, also helped establish the Declaration of Independence as an important icon of American identity.

THE CHANGE CAME SUDDENLY. As late as January 1817 John Adams said that his country had no interest in its past. "I see no disposition to celebrate or remember, or even Curiosity to enquire into the Characters, Actions, or Events of the Revolution," he wrote the artist John Trumbull. But a little more than a month later Congress commissioned Trumbull to produce four large paintings commemorating the Revolution, which were to hang in the rotunda of the new American Capitol. For Trumbull, the most important of the series, and the one to which he first turned, was the Declaration of Independence. He based that work on a smaller painting he had done between 1786 and 1793 that showed the drafting committee presenting its work to Congress. When the new twelve-by-eighteen-foot canvas was completed in 1818, Trumbull exhibited it to large crowds in Boston, Philadelphia, and Baltimore before delivering it to Washington; indeed, *The Declaration of Independence* was the most popular of all the paintings Trumbull did for the Capitol.

Soon copies of the document were being published and sold briskly, which perhaps was what inspired Secretary of State John Quincy Adams to have an exact facsimile of the Declaration, the only one ever produced, made in 1823. Congress had it distributed throughout the country. Books also started to appear: the collected biographies of those who signed the Declaration in nine volumes by Joseph M. Sanderson (1823–27) or one volume by Charles A. Goodrich (1831), full biographies of individual revolutionaries that were often written by descendants who used family papers, and collections of revolutionary docu-

ments edited by such notable figures as Hezekiah Niles, Jared Sparks, and Peter Force.

Postwar efforts to preserve the memories and records of the Revolution were undertaken in a mood of near panic. Many documents remained in private hands, where they were gradually separated from one another and lost. Even worse, many revolutionaries had died, taking with them precious memories that were gone forever. The presence of living remnants of the revolutionary generation seemed so important in preserving its tradition that Americans watched anxiously as their numbers declined. These attitudes first appeared in the decade before 1826, the fiftieth anniversary of independence, but they persisted on into the Civil War. In 1864 the Reverend Elias Brewster Hillard noted that only seven of those who had fought in the Revolutionary War still survived, and he hurried to interview and photograph those "venerable and now sacred men" for the benefit of posterity. "The present is the last generation that will be connected by living link with the great period in which our national independence was achieved," he wrote in the introduction to his book *The Last Men of the Revolution*. "Our own are the last eyes that will look on men who looked on Washington; our ears the last that will hear the living voices of those who heard his words. Henceforth the American Revolution will be known among men by the silent record of history alone."

Most of the men Hillard interviewed had played modest roles in the Revolution. In the early 1820s, however, John Adams and Thomas Jefferson were still alive, and as the only surviving members of the committee that had drafted the Declaration of Independence, they attracted an extraordinary outpouring of attention. Pilgrims, invited and uninvited, flocked particularly to Monticello, hoping to catch a glimpse of the author of the Declaration and making nuisances of themselves. One woman, it is said, even smashed a window to get a better view of the old man. As a eulogist noted after the deaths of both Adams and Jefferson on, miraculously, July 4, 1826, the world had not waited for death to "sanctify" their names. Even while they

remained alive, their homes became "shrines" to which lovers of liberty and admirers of genius flocked "from every land."

ADAMS, IN TRUTH, WAS MIFFED BY Jefferson's celebrity as the penman of Independence. The drafting of the Declaration of Independence, he thought, had assumed an exaggerated importance. Jefferson perhaps agreed; he, too, cautioned a correspondent against giving too much emphasis to "mere composition." The Declaration, he said, had not and had not been meant to be an original or novel creation; his assignment had been to produce "an expression of the American mind, and to give that expression the proper tone and spirit called for by the occasion."

Jefferson, however, played an important role in rescuing the Declaration from obscurity and making it a defining event of the revolutionary "heroic age." It was he who first suggested that the young John Trumbull paint *The Declaration of Independence*. And Trumbull's first sketch of his famous painting shares a piece of drawing paper with a sketch by Jefferson, executed in Paris sometime in 1786, of the assembly room in the Old Pennsylvania State House, now known as Independence Hall. Trumbull's painting of the scene carefully followed Jefferson's sketch, which unfortunately included architectural inaccuracies, as Trumbull later learned to his dismay.

Jefferson forgot, as the years went by, how substantial a role other members of the committee had played in framing the Declaration's text.

Jefferson also spent hour after hour answering, in longhand, letters that he said numbered 1,267 in 1820, many of which asked questions about the Declaration and its creation. Unfortunately, his responses, like the sketch he made for Trumbull, were inaccurate in many details. Even his account of the drafting process, retold in an important letter to James Madison of 1823 that has been accepted by one authority after another, conflicts with a note he sent Benjamin Franklin in June 1776. Jefferson forgot, in short, how substantial a role other members of the drafting committee had played in framing the Declaration and adjusting its text before it was submitted to Congress.

INDEED, IN OLD AGE JEFFERSON FOUND enormous consolation in the fact that he was, as he ordered inscribed on his tomb, "Author of the Declaration of American Independence." More than anything else he had done, that role came to justify his life. It saved him from a despair that he suffered at the time of the Missouri crisis, when everything the Revolution had accomplished seemed to him in jeopardy, and that was later fed by problems at the University of Virginia, his own deteriorating health, and personal financial troubles so severe that he feared the loss of his beloved home, Monticello (those troubles, incidentally, virtually precluded him from freeing more than a handful of slaves at his death). The Declaration, as he told Madison, was "the fundamental act of union of these States," a document that should be recalled "to cherish the principles of the instrument in the bosoms of our own citizens." Again in 1824 he interpreted the government's re-publication of the Declaration as "a pledge of adhesion to its principles and of a sacred determination to maintain and perpetuate them," which he described as a "holy purpose."

But just which principles did he mean? Those in the Declaration's second paragraph, which he understood exactly as they had been understood in 1776—as an assertion primarily of the right of revolution. Jefferson composed the long sentence beginning "We hold these truths to be self-evident" in a well-known eighteenth-century rhetorical style by which one phrase was piled on another and the meaning of the whole became clear only at the end. The sequence ended with an assertion of the "Right of the People to alter or to abolish" any government that failed to secure their inalienable rights and to institute a new

form of government more likely "to effect their Safety and Happiness." That was the right Americans were exercising in July 1776, and it seemed no less relevant in the 1820s, when revolutionary movements were sweeping through Europe and Latin America. The American example would be, as Jefferson said in the last letter of his life, a "signal arousing men to burst the chains under which monkish ignorance and superstition had persuaded them to bind themselves, and to assume the blessings and security of self-government."

Others, however, emphasized the opening phrases of the sentence that began the Declaration's second paragraph, particularly "the memorable assertion, that 'all men are created equal, that they are endowed by their Creator with certain unalienable rights, and that to secure these rights, governments are instituted among men, deriving their just powers from the consent of the governed.'" That passage, the eulogist John Sergeant said at Philadelphia in July 1826, was the "text of the revolution," the "ruling vital principle" that had inspired the men of the 1770s, who "looked forward through succeeding generations, and saw stamped upon all their institutions, the great principles set forth in the Declaration of Independence." In Hallowell, Maine, another eulogist, Peleg Sprague, similarly described the Declaration of Independence as an assertion *by a whole people, of... the native equality of the human race,* as the true foundation of all political, of all human institutions."

AND SO AN INTERPRETATION OF THE declaration that had emerged in the 1790s became ever more widely repeated. The equality that Sergeant and Sprague emphasized was not, however, asserted for the first time in the Declaration of Independence. Even before Congress published its Declaration, one revolutionary document after another had associated equality with a new American republic and suggested enough different meanings of that term—equal rights, equal access to office, equal voting power—to keep Americans busy sorting them out and fighting over inegalitarian practices far

into the future. Jefferson, in fact, adapted those most remembered opening lines of the Declaration's second paragraph from a draft Declaration of Rights for Virginia, written by George Mason and revised by a committee of the Virginia convention, which appeared in the *Pennsylvania Gazette* on June 12, 1776, the day after the Committee of Five was appointed and perhaps the day it first met. Whether on his own inspiration or under instructions from the committee, Jefferson began with the Mason draft, which he gradually tightened into a more compressed and eloquent statement. He took, for example, Mason's statement that "all men are born equally free and independent," rewrote it to say they were "created equal & independent," and then cut out the "& independent."

Jefferson was not alone in adapting the Mason text for his purposes. The Virginia convention revised the Mason draft before enacting Virginia's Declaration of Rights, which said that all men were "by nature" equally free and independent. Several other states—including Pennsylvania (1776), Vermont (1777), Massachusetts (1780), and New Hampshire (1784)—remained closer to Mason's wording, including in their state bill of rights the assertions that men were "born free and equal" or "born equally free and independent." Unlike the Declaration of Independence, moreover, the state bills or "declarations" of rights became (after an initial period of confusion) legally binding. Americans' first efforts to work out the meaning of the equality written into their founding documents therefore occurred on the state level.

IN MASSACHUSETTS, FOR EXAMPLE, several slaves won their freedom in the 1780s by arguing before the state's Supreme Judicial Court that the provision in the state's bill of rights that all men were born free and equal made slavery unlawful. Later, in the famous case of *Commonwealth* v. *Aves* (1836), Justice Lemuel Shaw ruled that those words were sufficient to end slavery in Massachusetts, indeed that it would be difficult to find others "more precisely adapted to the abolition of negro slavery." White Americans also found the equality provisions in their state bills of rights useful. In the Virginia constitutional convention of 1829–30, for example, a delegate from the trans-Appalachian West, John R. Cooke, cited that "sacred instrument" the Virginia Declaration of Rights against the state's system of representing all counties equally in the legislature regardless of their populations and its imposition of a property qualification for the vote, both of which gave disproportional power to men in the eastern part of the state. The framers of Virginia's 1776 constitution allowed those practices to persist despite their violation of the equality affirmed in the Declaration of Rights, Cooke said, because there were limits on how much they dared change "in the midst of war." They therefore left it for posterity to resolve the inconsistency "as soon as leisure should be afforded them." In the hands of men like Cooke, the Virginia Declaration of Rights became a practical program of reform to be realized over time, as the Declaration of Independence would later be for Abraham Lincoln.

But why, if the states had legally binding statements of men's equality, should anyone turn to the Declaration of Independence? Because not all states had bills of rights, and not all the bills of rights that did exist included statements on equality. Moreover, neither the federal Constitution nor the federal Bill of Rights asserted men's natural equality or their possession of inalienable rights or the right of the people to reject or change their government. As a result, contenders in national politics who found those old revolutionary principles useful had to cite the Declaration of Independence. It was all they had.

THE SACRED STATURE GIVEN THE Declaration after 1815 made it extremely useful for causes attempting to seize the moral high ground in public debate. Beginning about 1820, workers, farmers, women's rights advocates, and other groups persistently used the Declaration of Independence to justify their quest for equality and their opposition to the "tyranny" of factory owners or railroads or great corporations or the male power structure. It remained, however, especially easy for the opponents of slavery to cite the Declaration on behalf of their cause. Eighteenth-century statements of equality referred to men in a state of nature, before governments were created, and asserted that no persons acquired legitimate authority over others without their consent. If so, a system of slavery in which men were born the subjects and indeed the property of others was profoundly wrong. In short, the same principle that denied kings a right to rule by inheritance alone undercut the right of masters to own slaves whose status was determined by birth, not consent. The kinship of the Declaration of Independence with the cause of antislavery was understood from the beginning—which explains why gradual emancipation acts, such as those in New York and New Jersey, took effect on July 4 in 1799 and 1804 and why Nat Turner's rebellion was originally planned for July 4, 1831.

Even in the eighteenth century, however, assertions of men's equal birth provoked dissent. As slavery became an increasingly divisive issue, denials that men were naturally equal multiplied. Men were not created equal in Virginia, John Tyler insisted during the Missouri debates of 1820: "No, sir, the principle, although lovely and beautiful, cannot obliterate those distinctions in society which society itself engenders and gives birth to." Six years later the acerbic, self-styled Virginia aristocrat John Randolph called the notion of man's equal creation "a falsehood, and a most pernicious falsehood, even though I find it in the Declaration of Independence." Man was born in a state of "perfect helplessness and ignorance" and so was from the start dependent on others. There was "not a word of truth" in the notion that men were created equal, repeated South Carolina's John C. Calhoun in 1848. Men could not survive, much less develop their talents, alone; the political state, in which some exercised authority and others obeyed, was in fact man's "natural state," that in which he "is born, lives and dies." For a long time the "false and dangerous" doctrine that men were created equal had lain "dormant," but by the late 1840s Americans had begun "to experience the danger of admitting so great an error… in the Declaration of Independence," where it had been inserted needlessly, Calhoun said, since separation from Britain could have been justified without it.

FIVE YEARS LATER, IN SENATE DEBATES over the Kansas-Nebraska Act, Indiana's John Pettit pronounced his widely quoted statement that the supposed "self-evident truth" of man's equal creation was in fact "a self-evident lie." Ohio's senator Benjamin Franklin Wade, an outspoken opponent of slavery known for his vituperative style and intense patriotism, rose to reply. Perhaps Wade's first and middle names gave him a special bond with the Declaration and its creators. The "great declaration cost our forefathers too dear," he said, to be so "lightly thrown away by their children." Without its inspiring principles the Americans could not have won their independence; for the revolutionary generation the "great truths" in that "immortal instrument," the Declaration of Independence, were "worth the sacrifice of all else on earth, even life itself." How, then, were men equal? Not, surely, in physical power or intellect. The "good old Declaration" said "that all men are equal, and have inalienable rights; that is, [they are] equal in point of right; that no man has a right to trample on another." Where those rights were wrested from men through force or fraud, justice demanded that they be "restored without delay."

Abraham Lincoln, a little-known forty-four-year-old lawyer in Springfield, Illinois, who had served one term in Congress before being turned out of office, read these debates, was aroused as by nothing before, and began to pick up the dropped threads of his political career. Like Wade, Lincoln idealized the men of the American Revolution, who were for him "a forest of giant oaks," "a fortress of strength," "iron men." He also shared the deep concern of his contemporaries as the "silent artillery of time" removed them and the *living history* they embodied from this world. Before the 1850s, however, Lincoln seems to have had relatively little interest in the Declaration of Independence. Then, suddenly, that document and its assertion that all men were created equal became his "ancient faith," the "father of all moral principles," an "axiom" of free society. He was provoked by the attacks of men such as Pettit and Calhoun. And he made the arguments of those who defended the Declaration his own, much as Jefferson had done with Mason's text, reworking the ideas from speech to speech, pushing their logic, and eventually, at Gettysburg in 1863, arriving at a simple statement of profound eloquence. In time his understanding of the Declaration of Independence would become that of the nation.

Lincoln's position emerged fully and powerfully during his debates with Illinois's senator Stephen Douglas, a Democrat who had proposed the Kansas-Nebraska Act and whose seat Lincoln sought in 1858. They were an odd couple, Douglas and Lincoln, as different physically—at full height Douglas came only to Lincoln's shoulders—as they were in style. Douglas wore well-tailored clothes; Lincoln's barely covered his limbs. Douglas was in general the more polished speaker; Lincoln sometimes rambled on, losing his point and his audience, although he could also, especially with a prepared text, be a powerful orator. The greatest difference between them was, however, in the positions they took on the future of slavery and the meaning of the Declaration of Independence.

Douglas defended the Kansas-Nebraska Act, which allowed the people of those states to permit slavery within their borders, as consistent with the revolutionary heritage. After all, in instructing their delegates to vote for independence, one state after another had explicitly retained the exclusive right of defining its domestic institutions. Moreover, the Declaration of Independence carried no implications for slavery, since its statement on equality referred to white men only. In fact, Douglas said, it simply meant that American colonists of European descent had equal rights with the King's subjects in Great Britain. The signers were not thinking of "the negro or… savage Indians, or the Feejee, or the Malay, or any other inferior or degraded race." Otherwise they would

have been honor bound to free their own slaves, which not even Thomas Jefferson did. The Declaration had only one purpose: to explain and justify American independence.

Lincoln believed the Declaration "contemplated the progressive improvement in the condition of all men everywhere." Otherwise, it was "mere rubbish."

To LINCOLN, DOUGLAS'S ARGUMENT left only a "mangled ruin" of the Declaration of Independence, whose "plain, unmistakable language" said *"all* men" were created equal. In affirming that government derived its "just powers from the consent of the governed," the Declaration also said that no man could rightly govern others without their consent. If, then, "the negro is a man," was it not a "total destruction of self-government, to say that he too shall not govern *himself?"* To govern a man without his consent was "despotism." Moreover, to confine the Declaration's significance to the British peoples of 1776 denied its meaning, Lincoln charged, not only for Douglas's "inferior races" but for the French, Irish, German, Scandinavian, and other immigrants who had come to America after the Revolution. For them the promise of equality linked new Americans with the founding generation; it was an "electric cord" that bound them into the nation "as though they were blood of the blood, and flesh of the flesh of the men who wrote that Declaration," and so made one people out of many. Lincoln believed that the Declaration "contemplated the progressive improvement in the condition of all men everywhere." If instead it was only a justification of independence "without the *germ,* or even the *suggestion* of the individual rights of man in it," the document was "of no practical use now— mere rubbish—old wadding left to rot on the battlefield after the victory is won,"

an "interesting memorial of the dead past… shorn of its vitality, and practical value."

LIKE WADE, LINCOLN DENIED THAT the signers meant that men were equal in *"all respects,"* including "color, size, intellect, moral developments, or social capacity." He, too, made sense of the Declaration's assertion of man's equal creation by eliding it with the next, separate statement on rights. The signers, he insisted, said men were equal in having "'certain inalienable rights….' This they said, and this they meant." Like John Cooke in Virginia three decades before, Lincoln thought the Founders allowed the persistence of practices at odds with their principles for reasons of necessity: to establish the Constitution demanded that slavery continue in those original states that chose to keep it. "We could not secure the good we did if we grasped for more," but that did not "destroy the principle that is the charter of our liberties." Nor did it mean that slavery had to be allowed in states not yet organized in 1776, such as Kansas and Nebraska.

Again like Cooke, Lincoln claimed that the authors of the Declaration understood its second paragraph as setting a standard for free men whose principles should be realized "as fast as circumstances… permit." They wanted that standard to be "familiar to all, and revered by all; constantly looked to, and constantly labored for, and even though never perfectly attained, constantly approximated and thereby constantly spreading and deepening its influence, and augmenting the happiness and value of life to all people of all colors everywhere." And if, as Calhoun said, American independence could have been declared without any assertion of human equality and inalienable rights, that made its inclusion all the more wonderful. "All honor to Jefferson," Lincoln said in a letter of 1859, "to the man who… had the coolness, forecast, and capacity to introduce into a merely revolutionary document, an abstract truth, applicable to all men and all times, and to embalm it there," where it would remain "a rebuke and a stumbling-block to the very harbingers of re-appearing tyranny and oppression."

JEFFERSON AND THE MEMBERS OF THE second contInental Congress did not understand what they were doing in quite that way on July 4, 1776. For them, it was enough for the Declaration to be "merely revolutionary." But if Douglas's history was more accurate, Lincoln's reading of the Declaration was better suited to the needs of the Republic in the mid-nineteenth century, when the standard of revolution had passed to Southern secessionists and to radical abolitionists who also called for disunion. In his hands the Declaration became first and foremost a living document for an established society, a set of goals to be realized over time, the dream of "something better, than a mere change of masters" that explained why "our fathers" fought and endured until they won the Revolutionary War. In the Civil War, too, Lincoln told Congress on July 4, 1861, the North fought not only to save the Union but to preserve a form of government "whose leading object is to elevate the condition of men—to lift artificial weights from all shoulders—to clear the paths of laudable pursuit for all." The rebellion it opposed was at base an effort "to overthrow the principle that all men were created equal." And so the Union victory at Gettysburg in 1863 became for him a vindication of that proposition, to which the nation's fathers had committed it in 1776, and a challenge to complete the "unfinished work" of the Union dead and bring to "this nation, under God, a new birth of freedom."

The Declaration Lincoln left was not Jefferson's Declaration, although Jefferson and other revolutionaries shared the values Lincoln stressed.

Lincoln's Gettysburg Address stated briefly and eloquently convictions he had developed over the previous decade, convictions that on point after point echoed earlier Americans: Republicans of the 1790s, the eulogists Peleg Sprague and John Sergeant in 1826, John Cooke in the Virginia convention a few years later, Benjamin Wade in 1853. Some of those men he knew; others were unfamiliar to him, but they had also struggled to understand the practical implications of their revolutionary heritage and followed the same logic to the same conclusions. The Declaration of Independence Lincoln left was not Jefferson's Declaration, although Jefferson and other revolutionaries shared the values Lincoln and others stressed: equality, human rights, government by consent. Nor was Lincoln's Declaration of Independence solely his creation. It remained an "expression of the American mind," not, of course, what all Americans thought but what many had come to accept. And its implications continued to evolve after Lincoln's death. In 1858 he had written a correspondent that the language of the Declaration of Independence was at odds with slavery but did not require political and social equality for free black Americans. Few disagreed then. How many would agree today?

The Declaration of Independence is in fact a curious document. After the Civil War members of Lincoln's party tried to write its principles into the Constitution by enacting the Thirteenth, Fourteenth, and Fifteenth Amendments, which is why issues of racial or age or gender equality are now so often fought out in the courts. But the Declaration of Independence itself is not and has never been legally binding. Its power comes from its capacity to inspire and move the hearts of living Americans, and its meaning lies in what they choose to make of it. It has been at once a cause of controversy, pushing as it does against established habits and conventions, and a unifying national icon, a legacy and a new creation that binds the revolutionaries to descendants who confronted and continue to confront issues the Founders did not know or failed to resolve. On Independence Day, then, Americans celebrate not simply the birth of their nation or the legacy of a few great men. They also commemorate a Declaration of Independence that is their own collective work now and through time. And that, finally, makes sense of the Fourth of July.

Pauline Maier is William Rand Kenan, Jr., Professor of American History at the Massachusetts Institute of Technology.

This article originally appeared in *American Heritage*, July/August 1997, pp. 54-65. Adapted from *American Scripture: Making the Declaration of Independence*, by Pauline Maier. © 1998 by Alfred A. Knopf, Inc. Reprinted by permission.

George Washington, Spymaster

Without his brilliance at espionage the Revolution could not have been won

By Thomas Fleming

GEORGE WASHINGTON A MASTER OF espionage? It is commonly understood that without the Commander in Chief's quick mind and cool judgment the American Revolution would have almost certainly expired in 1776. It is less well known that his brilliance extended to overseeing, directly and indirectly, extensive and very sophisticated intelligence activities against the British.

Washington had wanted to be a soldier almost from the cradle and seems to have acquired the ability to think in military terms virtually by instinct. In the chaos of mid-1776, with half his army deserting and the other half in a funk and all his generals rattled, he kept his head and reversed his strategy. The Americans had started with the idea that a general action, as an all-out battle was called, could end the conflict overnight, trusting that their superior numbers would overwhelm the presumably small army the British could afford to send to our shores. But the British sent a very big, well-trained army, which routed the Americans in the first several battles in New York. Washington sat down in his tent on Harlem Heights and informed the Continental Congress that he was going to fight an entirely different war. From now on, he wrote, he would "avoid a general action." Instead he would "protract the war."

HE WAS involved in figuring out how to burn down New York City despite orders not to.

In his 1975 study of Washington's generalship, *The Way of the Fox,* Lt. Col. Dave Richard Palmer has called this reversal "a masterpiece of strategic thought, a brilliant blueprint permitting a weak force to combat a powerful opponent." It soon became apparent that for the blueprint to be followed, Washington would have to know what the British were planning to do, and he would have to be able to prevent them from finding out what he was doing. In short, espionage was built into the system.

Washington had been acquainted with British colonial officials and generals and colonels since his early youth, and he knew how intricately espionage was woven into the entire British military and political enterprise. Any Englishman's mail could be opened and read if a secretary of state requested it. Throughout Europe every British embassy had its intelligence network.

Thus Washington was not entirely surprised to discover, shortly after he took command of the American army in

1775, that his surgeon general, Dr. Benjamin Church, was telling the British everything that went on in the American camp at Cambridge, Massachusetts. He *was* surprised to find out, not long after he had transferred his operations to New York in the spring of 1776, that one of his Life Guard, a soldier named Thomas Hickey, was rumored to be involved in a plot to kill him.

By that time Washington had pulled off his own opening gambit in a form of intelligence at which he soon displayed something close to genius: disinformation. Shortly after he took command in Cambridge, he asked someone how much powder the embryo American army had in reserve. Everyone thought it had three hundred barrels, but a check of the Cambridge magazine revealed most of that had been fired away at Bunker Hill. There were only thirty-six barrels—fewer than nine rounds per man. For half an hour, according to one witness, Washington was too stunned to speak. But he recovered and sent people into British-held Boston to spread the story that he had eighteen hundred barrels, and he spread the same rumor throughout the American camp.

In chaotic New York, grappling with a large and aggressive British army, deserting militia, and an inapplicable strategy, Washington temporarily lost control of the intelligence situation. That explains the dolorous failure of Capt. Nathan Hale's mission in September 1776. Hale, sent to gather information behind British lines, was doomed almost from the moment he volunteered. He had little or no contact with the American high command, no training as a spy, no disguise worthy of the name, and an amorphous mission: to find out whatever he could wherever he went.

HONEYMAN TOLD Rall about his narrow "escape" and assured him the Americans were half-naked and freezing.

There is little evidence that Washington was even aware of Hale's existence. He was involved in something far more serious: figuring out how to burn down New York City in order to deprive the British of their winter quarters, despite orders from the Continental Congress strictly forbidding him to harm the place. He looked the other way while members of Hale's regiment slipped into the city; they were experts at starting conflagrations thanks to a tour of duty on fire ships—vessels carrying explosives to burn enemy craft—on the Hudson.

O N SEPTEMBER 21 A THIRD OF NEW York went up in flames. The timing was disastrous for Hale, who was captured the very same day. Anyone with a Connecticut accent became highly suspect, and the British caught several incendiaries and hanged them on the spot. They gave Hale the same treatment: no trial, just a swift, humiliating death. Hale's friends were so mortified by his fate, which they considered shameful, that no one mentioned his now-famous farewell speech for another fifty years. Then an old man told his daughter about it, and Yale College, seeking Revolutionary War heroes among its graduates, quickly immortalized him.

Washington never said a word about Hale. His only intelligence comment at the time concerned New York. The fire had destroyed Trinity Church and about six hundred houses, causing no little discomfort for the British and the thousands of Loyalist refugees who had crowded into the city. In a letter, Washington remarked that "Providence, or some good honest fellow, has done more for us than we were disposed to do for ourselves."

One of Hale's best friends, Maj. Benjamin Tallmadge, never got over his death. He probably talked about it to Washington, who assured him that once they got the protracted war under control, all espionage would be handled from Army headquarters, and no spy's life would be wasted the way Hale's had been.

Surviving long enough to fight an extended conflict was no small matter. In the weeks after Hale's death, disaster after disaster befell the American army. Washington was forced to abandon first New York and then New Jersey. On the other side of the Delaware, with only the shadow of an army left to him, he issued orders in December 1776 to all his generals to find "some person who can be engaged to cross the river as a spy" and added that "expense must not be spared" in securing a volunteer.

He also rushed a letter to Robert Morris, the financier of the Revolution, asking for hard money to "pay a certain set of people who are of particular use to us." He meant spies, and he had no illusion that any spy would risk hanging for the paper money the Continental Congress was printing. Morris sent from Philadelphia two canvas bags filled with what hard cash he could scrape together on an hour's notice: 410 Spanish dollars, 2 English crowns, 10 shillings, and 2 sixpence.

The search soon turned up a former British soldier named John Honeyman, who was living in nearby Griggstown, New Jersey. On Washington's orders Honeyman rediscovered his loyalty to the king and began selling cattle to several British garrisons along the Delaware. He had no trouble gaining the confidence of Col. Johann Rall, who was in command of three German regiments in Trenton. Honeyman listened admiringly as Rall described his heroic role in the fighting around New York and agreed with him that the Americans were hopeless soldiers.

On December 22, 1776, having spent about a week in Trenton, Honeyman wandered into the countryside, supposedly in search of cattle, and got himself captured by an American patrol and hustled to Washington's headquarters. There he was publicly denounced by the Commander in Chief as a "notorious" turncoat. Washington insisted on interrogating him personally and said he would give the traitor a chance to save his skin if he recanted his loyalty to the Crown.

A half-hour later the general ordered his aides to throw Honeyman into the guardhouse. Tomorrow morning, he stated, the Tory would be hanged. That night Honeyman escaped from the guardhouse with a key supplied by Washington and dashed past American sentries, who fired on him. Sometime on December 24 he turned up in Trenton and told Colonel Rall the story of his narrow escape.

The German naturally wanted to know what Honeyman had seen in Washington's camp, and the spy assured him that the Americans were falling apart. They were half-naked and freezing, and they lacked the food and basic equipment, such as shoes, to make a winter march. Colonel Rall, delighted, prepared to celebrate Christmas with no military worries to interrupt the feasting and drinking that were traditional in his country. He never dreamed that Honeyman had given Washington a professional soldier's detailed description of the routine of the Trenton garrison, the location of the picket guards, and everything else an assaulting force would need to know.

A T DAWN ON DECEMBER 26 Washington's ragged Continentals charged through swirling snow and sleet to kill the besotted Colonel Rall and capture most of his troops. New Jersey had been on the brink of surrender; now local patriots began shooting up British patrols, and the rest of the country, in the words of a Briton in Virginia, "went liberty mad again."

Washington set up a winter camp in Morristown and went to work organizing

American intelligence. He made Tallmadge his second-in-command, though he was ostensibly still a major in the 2d Continental Dragoons. That regiment was stationed in outposts all around the perimeter of British-held New York, and Tallmadge visited these units regularly, supposedly to make sure that all was in order but actually working as a patient spider setting up spy networks inside the British lines. His methods, thanks to Washington's tutelage, could not have been more sophisticated. He equipped his spies with cipher codes, invisible ink, and aliases that concealed their real identities. The invisible ink, which the Americans called "the stain," had been invented by Dr. James Jay, a brother of the prominent patriot John Jay, living in England. It was always in short supply.

Two of the most important American agents operating inside British-held New York were Robert Townsend, a Quaker merchant, and Abraham Woodhull, a Setauket, Long Island, farmer. Their code names were Culper Jr. and Culper Sr. As a cover, Townsend wrote violently Loyalist articles for the New York *Royal Gazette;* this enabled him to pick up information from British officers and their mistresses, and he sent it on to Woodhull via a courier named Austin Roe.

Woodhull would then have a coded signal hung on a Setauket clothesline that was visible through a spyglass to Americans on the Connecticut shore. A crew of oarsmen would row across Long Island Sound by night, collect Townsend's letters, and carry them to Tallmadge's dragoons, who would hurry them to Washington. The general applied a "sympathetic fluid" to reveal the secret messages written in Dr. Jay's "stain."

When the British occupied Philadelphia, in 1777, Washington salted the city with spies. His chief assistant there was Maj. John Clark, a cavalryman who became expert at passing false information about American strength at Valley Forge to a spy for the British commander General Howe. Washington laboriously wrote out muster reports of the Continental Army, making it four or five times its actual size; the British, recognizing

the handwriting, accepted the information as fact and gave the spy who had obtained it a bonus. Washington must have enjoyed this disinformation game; at one point, describing a particularly successful deception, Clark wrote, "This will give you a laugh."

WASHINGTON had Tallmadge equip all his spies with cipher codes, invisible ink, and aliases.

The most effective American spy in Philadelphia was Lydia Darragh, an Irish-born Quaker midwife and undertaker. The British requisitioned a room in her house to serve as a "council chamber" and discussed their war plans there. By lying with her ear to a crack in the floor in the room above, Mrs. Darragh could hear much of what they said. Her husband wrote the information in minute shorthand on scraps of paper that she hid in large cloth-covered buttons. Wearing these, her fourteen-year-old son would walk into the countryside to meet his brother, a lieutenant in the American army. He snipped off the buttons, and the intelligence was soon in Washington's hands.

Mrs. Darragh's biggest coup was getting word to Washington that the British were about to make a surprise attack on his ragged army as it marched to Valley Forge in early December 1777. When the attack came, the Continentals were waiting with loaded muskets and cannon, and the king's forces withdrew.

THE BRITISH RETURNED TO PHILAdelphia determined to find whoever had leaked their plan. Staff officers went to Mrs. Darragh's house and demanded to know exactly when everyone had gone to bed the previous night—except one person. "I won't ask you, Mrs. Darragh, because I know you retire each night exactly at nine," the chief interrogator said. Lydia Darragh smiled and said nothing. After the war she remarked that she was pleased that as a spy she had never had to tell a lie.

The British, of course, had a small army of spies working for them as well, and they constantly struggled to penetrate Washington's operations. Toward the end of 1779, one of their Philadelphia spies wrote to Maj. John André, the charming, witty, artistically talented director of British intelligence: "Do you wish to have a useful hand in their army and to pay what you find his services worth? The exchange is 44 to 1." The numbers refer to the vertiginous depreciation of the Continental dollar; British spies, too, wanted to be paid in hard money.

The Americans did their best to make trouble for André by spreading around Philadelphia and New York the rumor that he was given to molesting boys. It is not clear whether Washington was involved in these particular smears, and they hardly chime with André's reputation for charming women, notably a Philadelphia belle named Peggy Shippen, who eventually married Gen. Benedict Arnold.

In any event, André was very successful at keeping tabs on the Americans. Surviving letters from his spies show him obtaining good estimates of American army strength in 1779. At one point Gen. Philip Schuyler made a motion in the Continental Congress that it leave Philadelphia because "they could do no business that was not instantly communicated" to the British.

André's most successful agent was a woman named Ann Bates, a former schoolteacher who married a British soldier while the army was in Philadelphia. Disguised as a peddler, she wandered through the American camp, counted the cannon there, overheard conversations at Washington's headquarters, and accurately predicted the American attack on the British base in Newport, Rhode Island, in 1778.

HIS AGENTS WERE so good he had to appeal for the lives of three arrested for communicating with the enemy.

The intelligence war reached a climax, or something very close to one, between 1779 and 1781. American morale was sinking with the Continental currency, and trusting anyone became harder and harder. Washington could never be sure when a spy had been "turned" by British hard money, and the British tried to accelerate the decline of the paper dollar by printing and circulating millions of counterfeit bills.

Soon an astonished American was writing, "An ordinary horse is worth twenty thousand dollars." In despair Congress stopped producing money; this brought the army's commissary department to a halt. The Continental desertion rate rose, with veterans and sergeants among the chief fugitives.

Washington struggled to keep the British at bay with more disinformation about his dwindling strength. His spies had achieved such professionalism that he had to appeal to Gov. William Livingston of New Jersey to spare three men arrested in Elizabethtown for carrying on an illegal correspondence with the enemy. That was exactly what they had been doing—as double agents feeding the British disinformation.

The three spies stood heroically silent. Washington told Livingston they were willing to "bear the suspicion of being thought inimical." But realism could not be carried too far; the Continental Army could not hang its own agents. Would the governor please do something? Livingston allowed the spies to escape, and intelligence documents show that three years later they were still at work.

WITHOUT Washington's warning from a spy, the British might have ended the war at Morristown.

By June 1780 agents had given the British high command accurate reports of the American army's weakness in its Morristown camp. The main force had diminished to four thousand men; because of a shortage of fodder, there were no horses, which meant the artillery was immobilized. The British had just captured Charleston, South Carolina, and its garrison of five thousand, demoralizing the South. They decided a strike at Washington's force could end the war, and they marshaled six thousand troops on Staten Island to deliver the blow.

A few hours before the attack, a furtive figure slipped ashore into New Jersey from Staten Island to warn the Continentals of the enemy buildup. He reached the officer in command in Elizabethtown, Col. Elias Dayton, and Dayton sent a rider off to Morristown with the news. Dayton and other members of the New Jersey Continental line, backed by local militia, were able to slow the British advance for the better part of a day, enabling Washington to get his army in motion and seize the high ground in the Short Hills, aborting the British plan.

It was a very close call. Without the warning from that spy, the British army would certainly have come over the Short Hills, overwhelmed Washington's four thousand men in Morristown, and captured their artillery. This probably would have ended the war.

After the royal army retreated to New York, word reached them that a French expeditionary force was landing in Newport, Rhode Island, to reinforce the struggling Americans. The British commander, Sir Henry Clinton, decided to attack before the French had a chance to recover from the rigors of the voyage and fortify.

This was the Culper network's greatest moment. Robert Townsend, alias Culper Jr., discovered the plan shortly after Clinton put six thousand men aboard transports and sailed them to Huntington Bay on the north shore of Long Island. They waited there while British frigates scouted Newport Harbor to assess the size of the French squadron.

Townsend's warning sent Washington's disinformation machine into overdrive. Within twenty-four hours a double agent was in New York, handing the British top-secret papers, supposedly dropped by a careless courier, detailing a Washington plan to attack the city with every Continental soldier and militiaman in the middle states.

The British sent horsemen racing off to urge Sir Henry Clinton in Huntington Bay to return to New York with his six thousand men. Clinton, already discouraged by the British admiral's lack of enthusiasm for his plan to take Newport, glumly agreed and sailed his soldiers back to their fortifications. There they waited for weeks for an assault that never materialized.

When Clinton was in Huntington Bay, he and two aides were made violently ill by tainted wine they drank with dinner aboard the flagship. He ordered the bottle seized and asked the physician general of the British army to examine the dregs in the glasses. The doctor said the wine was "strongly impregnated with arsenic." During the night the bottle mysteriously disappeared, and Clinton was never able to confirm the assassination attempt or find the perpetrator. This may have been Washington's way of getting even for the Hickey plot.

The main event in the later years of the intelligence war was the treason of Benedict Arnold in 1780. However, the American discovery of Arnold's plot to sell the fortress at West Point to the British for six thousand pounds—about half a million dollars in modern money—was mostly luck. There was little that Benjamin Tallmadge or his agents could claim to their credit except having passed along a hint of a plot involving an American general a few weeks before.

There is no doubt that West Point would have been handed over and Benedict Arnold and John André given knighthoods if three wandering militiamen in Westchester County had not stopped André on his return to New York with the incriminating plans in his boot. The motive of these soldiers was not patriotism but robbery; Westchester was known as "the neutral ground," and Loyalists and rebels alike wandered there in search of plunder.

Hanging John André was one of the most difficult things Washington had to do in the intelligence war. The major was the object of universal affection, and Alexander Hamilton and others on Washington's staff urged him to find a way to commute the sentence. Washington grimly replied that he would do so only if the British handed over Arnold. That of course did not happen, and André died on the gallows. In the next twelve months, Washington made repeated attempts to capture Arnold. He ordered an American sergeant named Champe to desert and volunteer to join an American legion that Arnold was trying to create. To give Champe a convincing sendoff, Washington ordered a half a dozen cavalrymen to pursue him, without telling them he was a fake deserter. Champe arrived in the British lines with bullets chasing him.

WASHINGTON WOULD SEEM TO have liked these little touches of realism. Unusually fearless himself, he had once said as a young man that whistling bullets had "a charming sound." One wonders if spies such as Honeyman and Champe agreed.

Soon Champe was a member of Arnold's staff, living in the former general's house on the Hudson River in New York. Through cooperating agents, Champe communicated a plan to knock Arnold unconscious when he went into his riverside garden to relieve himself one moonless night. A boatload of Americans would be waiting to carry him back to New Jersey and harsh justice.

On the appointed night the boat was there, and Arnold went to the garden as usual, but Champe was on a troopship in New York Harbor. Clinton had ordered two thousand men, including Arnold's American legion, south to raid Virginia. Champe had to watch for an opportunity and deserted back to the American side.

Arnold's defection badly upset American intelligence operations for months. He told the British what he knew of Washington's spies in New York, and they made several arrests. Townsend quit spying for six months, to the great distress of Washington and Tallmadge.

The intelligence war continued during the year remaining until Yorktown. Washington's reluctant decision to march south with the French army to try to trap a British army in that small Vir-ginia tobacco port was accompanied by strenuous disinformation efforts intended to tie the British army to New York for as long as possible. In the line of march as the allied force moved south through New Jersey were some thirty large flatboats. British spies reported that the Americans were constructing large cooking ovens at several points near New York. Both seemed evidence of a plan to attack the city.

HANGING John André was one of the most difficult things he had to do in the intelligence war.

Benedict Arnold, now a British brigadier, begged Sir Henry Clinton to ignore this deception and give him six thousand men to attack the long, vulnerable American line of march. Clinton said no. He wanted to husband every available man in New York. By the time the British commander's Philadelphia spies told him where Washington was actually going, it was too late. The royal army under Charles Lord Cornwallis surrendered after three weeks of pounding by heavy guns, the blow that finally ended the protracted war.

EVEN AFTER THE FIGHTING WOUND down, intelligence activity went on. In the fall of 1782, a year after Yorktown, a French officer stationed in Morristown wrote, "Not a day has passed since we have drawn near the enemy that we have not had some news of them from our spies in New York." For a final irony, the last British commander in America, Sir Guy Carleton, sent Washington a report from a British agent warning about a rebel plot to plunder New York and abuse Loyalists as the British army withdrew, and Washington sent in Major Tallmadge and a column of troops—not only to keep order but also to protect their agents, many of whom had earned enmity for appearing to be loyal to George III.

Among the American spies in New York was a huge Irish-American tailor named Hercules Mulligan who had sent Washington invaluable information. His greatest coup was a warning that the British planned to try to kidnap the American commander in 1780. Mulligan reported directly to Washington's aide Col. Alexander Hamilton.

Another of the deepest agents was James Rivington, editor of the unctuously loyal New York *Royal Gazette*. He is believed to have stolen the top-secret signals of the British fleet, which the Americans passed on to the French in 1781. The knowledge may have helped the latter win the crucial naval battle off the Virginia capes that September, sealing Cornwallis's fate at Yorktown.

The day after the British evacuated New York, Washington had breakfast with Hercules Mulligan—a way of announcing that he had been a patriot. He also paid a visit to James Rivington and apparently gave him a bag of gold coins. When he was composing his final expense account for submission to the Continental Congress with his resignation as Commander in Chief, Washington included from memory the contents of the bag of coins Robert Morris had rushed to him in late December 1776; 410 Spanish dollars, 2 English crowns, 10 shillings, and 2 sixpence. The circumstances under which he received it, Washington remarked, made it impossible for him ever to forget the exact amount of that crucial transfusion of hard money. It is another piece of evidence, barely needed at this point, that intelligence was a centerpiece of the strategy of protracted war—and that George Washington was a master of the game.

Thomas Fleming writes often for American Heritage. *His most recent book is* Duel: Alexander Hamilton, Aaron Burr, and the Future of America (*Basic Books, 1999*).

Founders Chic:
Live From Philadelphia

They cut political deals and stabbed each other in the back on the way to inventing freedom.
Why Jefferson, Adams and their brethren are suddenly hot again.

By Evan Thomas

GOOD THING THE FOUNDERS DIDN'T rely on pollsters. At the time of the Revolution, the American colonists, John Adams recalled, were "about one third Tories"—loyal to the British crown— "and [one] third timid, and one third true blue." Adams was true blue. "Sink or swim, live or die, survive or perish, I am with my country from this day on," he told a friend in 1774. "You may depend on it."

By the summer of '76, as Adams cajoled his fellow delegates to the Second Continental Congress in Philadelphia to declare independence from Great Britain, perishing was a distinct possibility. On the night of July 2, as the delegates were casting their first votes, word reached Philadelphia that a hundred British warships and troop transports had been sighted off New York.

The empire was striking back. The colonists had driven British forces from Boston in March, but now a vast armada—some 400 ships, packed with regiments of crack British redcoats and highly trained Hessian mercenaries— was arriving from the motherland to crush the upstart rebellion. By August there were more British soldiers in New York (32,000) than there were people (30,000) in Philadelphia, the largest Colonial city, a couple of days' march away. Between them stood George Washington's Army of some 7,000 men, mostly untested, ill-equipped farmers.

The Founders were acutely aware that in signing the Declaration of Independence they were committing treason, for which the penalty was death

---

By affixing their signatures to the Declaration of Independence, the Founders were acutely aware that they were committing treason, the penalty for which was death. "We must all hang together, or most assuredly, we will hang separately," darkly joked Benjamin Franklin. On July 4, as the Declaration was being sent to the printers, one signer, Benjamin Harrison of Virginia, said to another, Elbridge Gerry of Massachusetts, "I shall have a great advantage over you, Mr. Gerry, when we are all hung for what we are now doing. From the size and weight of my body, I shall die in a few minutes, but from the lightness of your body you will dance in the air an hour or two before you are dead." Gerry was reported to have smiled, briefly. No one doubted the gravity of their actions. As he signed the document, Stephen Hopkins of Rhode Island, who suffered from palsy, exclaimed, "My hand trembles, but my heart does not."

Two and a quarter centuries later, we have a new appreciation for the courage and the vision of the Founders (no longer called the Founding Fathers, for reasons of political correctness). As soon as this week, Congress is expected to authorize a national memorial to John Adams. David McCullough's new biography of Adams, published last month, went straight to No. 1 on the best-seller list, and historian Joseph Ellis's Pulitzer Prize-winning "Founding Brothers" has been a top seller for more than half a year. Why? "Partly, it's a desire for authenticity," McCullough told NEWS-WEEK. In an age of media-obsessed, poll-driven politicians who cannot, it sometimes seems, make a speech or cast a vote without hiring a consultant, many Americans are nostalgic for an earlier era of genuine statesmen. By humanizing the Founders, McCullough and others have rescued them from the sterility of schoolbooks and, vividly and often movingly, showed them overcoming their fears and flaws.

ADAMS, JEFFERSON, WASHINGTON and all the rest were the real thing, all right. They were an Even Greater Generation. While the World War II veterans deserve honor for preserving freedom in the world, in a real sense the Founders not only won freedom—they created it. The United States may seem inevitable today—a quasi-divine inspiration, schoolchildren were long told—but its genesis was painful and harrowing, and the nation was very nearly stillborn.

Washington's pickup Army could have been annihilated by the British in New York that summer of '76, had it not slipped away in the dead of night under the cover of some providential fog. The Continentals' victories over the course of the next few years were sporadic and small. General Washington was a genius at lifting morale and knowing when to retreat to fight again another day. But independence was not secured until France, Britain's global rival, intervened to bottle up the British Army at Yorktown, Va., in 1781. And America did not become a true nation until the Founders produced a constitution that was a blend of visionary foresight and careful compromise in 1787.

In an age of poll-driven politicians who cannot make a speech without hiring a consultant, Americans are nostalgic for an earlier era of genuine statesmen

---

It is hard to think of the Founders as revolutionaries. They seem too stuffy, too much the proper gentlemen in breeches and powdered wigs. But Jefferson, Adams, Madison et al. were, in fact, extreme radicals. They were far from pure. For all their high-minded rhetoric, the Founders were not above deal-cutting and backstabbing. They would have been right at home on "Hardball," had such a thing existed. It is certainly also true that they ducked the question that later split apart the nation and haunts us still—the moral obligation to free the slaves who made up almost a fifth of the Colonies' population. Yet "to focus, as we are apt to, on what the Revolution did not accomplish—highlighting and la-

menting its failure to abolish slavery and change fundamentally the lot of women—is to miss the great significance of what it did accomplish," wrote Brown University historian Gordon Wood, perhaps the leading scholar of the Revolutionary era, in his 1991 book, "The Radicalism of the American Revolution." "Indeed, the Revolution made possible the anti-slavery and women's movements of the 19th century, and in fact all our current egalitarian thinking."

Two men in particular stand out in the Revolutionary generation. Thomas Jefferson was lean, elegant, remote, spendthrift and a little devious. John Adams was stout, bristly, frugal and perhaps too honest about himself and everyone else. Jefferson had a great faith in improving mankind but "comparatively little interest in human nature," observes McCullough. "Adams," on the other hand, "was not inclined to believe mankind improvable, but believed an understanding of human nature was of utmost importance." Jefferson and Adams were in effect the perfect match for an undertaking that required equal parts dreaminess and hardheadedness, cunning and honor. Their rivalry, falling-out and later renewal of friendship offers a human template for understanding the depth and reach of the Founders' accomplishment, a creation so extraordinary that it surprised—and ultimately frightened—the Founders themselves.

IN HIS DRAFT OF THE DECLARATION OF independence, Thomas Jefferson wrote for all time, "We hold these truths to be self-evident, that all men are created equal…" Yet until that time equality had not been self-evident in the least. Since at least the days of ancient Rome, society had been divided into "the vulgar mob" and their "betters." In many places, an ordinary man had to take off his hat and step out of the street when a gentleman rode by, or risk being trampled with impunity. "Order is Heaven's first law; and this confest, / Some are, and must be, greater than the rest," wrote the 18th-century satirist Alexander Pope.

The Founders were creatures of a new "Enlightenment." They refused to accept that birth dictated place. "Virtue is not

hereditary," wrote Thomas Paine, whose "Common Sense" aroused egalitarian sensibilities in the 13 Colonies. The common man, the Founders believed, was not a beast to be kept tightly leashed; he was a blank slate upon which virtue and goodness could be written. "The mind once enlightened cannot again become dark," wrote Paine.

Jefferson was especially optimistic, even utopian. Heavily influenced by the French *philosophes*, who found benevolence to be man's natural state, Jefferson believed that the "will of the people" was inherently benign. Men (though, not yet, blacks or women) were fully capable of self-governance. Indeed, men behaved best, Jefferson argued, when governed least. From the luxury of his mountaintop farm in Virginia, filled with French furniture and worked by 200 slaves, the Sage of Monticello imagined a nation of honest and free farmers, laboring and living in harmony, lightly led by a natural aristocracy of virtue and talent.

Adams knew better. The Massachusetts lawyer had always been a self-declared student of the "labyrinth of human nature." Happily married, he listened closely to his wise wife, Abigail, who in 1775 wrote him, "I am more and more convinced that man is a dangerous creature, and that power whether vested in the many or few is ever grasping… The great fish swallow up the small fish." Adams replied: "I think you shine as a stateswoman." Adams used self-awareness as a tool of political science. He had only to look at his own vanity, his yearning for praise and distinction, to know that power needed to be checked. Forcefully, and as it turned out wisely, he insisted that the popular will of the legislature be balanced by a strong executive and an independent judiciary.

An irascible contrarian, Adams argued too hotly for his own good. Following George Washington as the nation's second president, he believed the chief executive should be called "His Majesty." His more democratically inclined colleagues in the fledgling republic accused Adams of wishing to restore the monarchy and mocked him as "Your Rotundity." Feeling surrounded and betrayed, Adams foolishly enacted the Alien and Sedition Acts so he could jail his critics, a terrible moment for free expression. Adams was not paranoid in suspecting that even his friends were conspiring against him. Stirring up trouble (though always from behind a veil) was Adams's own vice president, Thomas Jefferson. Using scandal-mongering journalists to spread vicious rumors about his revolutionary comrade, Jefferson helped ensure that Adams served only one term (1797–1801) as president—and was succeeded by Jefferson.

IN HIS MAGISTERIAL AND READABLE biography of Adams, McCullough clearly takes the side of his protagonist. In "John Adams," the hero is honest, if to a fault, and perceptive, while Jefferson is deceitful and naive. McCullough is perhaps too harsh on Jefferson. Great political leaders often need to be a little slippery and even self-delusional to survive factional struggles and balance irreconcilable interests. (In the 20th century Franklin Roosevelt and Ronald Reagan come to mind.) Unlike Adams, Jefferson was elected to a second term and accomplished much as president, most notably the Louisiana Purchase.

Adams sulked over Jefferson's perfidy for more than a decade, but he finally swallowed his pride and reached out to his fellow Founder. From their retirements—Jefferson's at Monticello, Adams's at his more modest farm in Quincy, Mass., which he self-mockingly dubbed "Montezito"—the two old statesmen repaired their friendship through 128 letters between 1812 and 1826. Writing with their eyes firmly fixed on posterity, Adams and Jefferson relived—and on occasion rewrote—the past. "I look back with rapture to those golden days," penned Adams to Jefferson in 1825, "when Virginia and Massachusetts lived and acted together like a band of brothers." In pungent, incisive prose (Adams) or with elegant, sometimes lyrical fluidity (Jefferson), the two men reflected, with growing apprehension, on the present and future of the republic they had helped create.

They bemoaned the rise of faction and interest in the political system, and crime and licentiousness in society. Freedom had brought their countrymen a measure of happiness, perhaps, but not, it seemed, greater virtue. America's capacity for alcohol consumption was staggering: by the 1820s Americans were downing spirits at the rate of five gallons per person per year, nearly triple today's levels and higher than Europe's.

Jefferson was bewildered and disillusioned. He had lived too long, longer than most of the Founders. "All, all dead," he wrote to a friend in 1825, "and ourselves left alone amidst a new generation we know not, and who knows us not." He was sick and, attached to French wines and furnishings as well as French philosophers, too indebted to free his 200 slaves.

Adams, too, was discouraged. He was bothered by the rise of evangelical societies and mob rule, which he linked to a streak of unreason unanticipated by even the most prescient Founders. "Where is now, the progress of the human mind?" he railed. "When? Where? and How? is the present Chaos to be arranged to Order?" he demanded as early as 1813. Yet Adams was also able to see beyond the tumult of the moment to appreciate that the new republic would stand for—he predicted—two centuries.

On July 4, 1826, the 50th anniversary of the Declaration of Independence, both Adams and Jefferson lay dying. Told that it was the Fourth, Adams stirred and said, "It is a great day. It is a good day." At Monticello, as bells celebrating Independence Day could be heard faintly ringing in the valley below, Thomas Jefferson died at around 1 p.m. At his home in Quincy, Adams could hear cannons, then natural thunder. Before he, too, died, he whispered, "Jefferson survives." Both Adams and Jefferson live on, newly remembered and praised. And so, 175 years later, does their legacy, the longest-lasting republic in the history of mankind.

Founding Friendship

WASHINGTON, MADISON AND THE CREATION
OF THE AMERICAN REPUBLIC

Stuart Leibiger looks at one of the most significant relationships behind
the politics that produced the American Constitution.

The friendships and political collaborations among America's founding fathers have long been a source of fascination. In fact, scholars have generated a whole literature about the critical roles these collaborations played in the American Revolution, for example, the John Adams–Thomas Jefferson friendship that produced the Declaration of Independence, and that of James Madison and Alexander Hamilton that yielded the *Federalist Papers*, perhaps the greatest American political commentary ever written. Historians have also studied the James Madison–Thomas Jefferson collaboration that brought about, in the words of the documentary editor Julian Boyd, 'the most extended, the most elevated, the most significant exchange of letters between any two men in the whole sweep of American history'. Yet all this scholarship neglects the most important founding father of all: George Washington (1732–99).

Washington has been called the Revolution's 'Indispensable Man'. If you took him out of the equation, then most likely the American Revolution would have failed. Yet, none of the so-called 'great collaborations' that historians have written about includes Washington, whose friendship with James Madison was the most important association in the founding of the United States.

The American Revolution is unusual among modern world revolutions because it produced not a dictatorship, but a republic. One of the main reasons for this outcome was Washington's careful use of power. By never abusing it, and by giving it away, his power increased: from commander-in-chief of the Continental Army in 1775, he became president of the Constitutional Convention of 1787, and finally President of the United States for two terms in 1789 and 1793. In these roles, he resisted the temptation to use the army as his personal bodyguard and remained true to the ideals of American Republicanism.

When he was commissioned to portray Washington in 1785, the celebrated French sculptor Jean-Antoine Houdon (1741–1828) chose not to depict the General's glorious victories at Trenton or Yorktown, but instead Houdon's statue of 1788 shows Washington in the act of retiring from the army, returning his military cloak and sword to the state and resuming civilian life, represented by a walking stick and ploughshare. Houdon understood that Washington exhibited greatness by returning power to the people, and by going home to Mount Vernon.

Few people today realise that Washington and Madison were close friends. On the surface they had little in common. True, both men came out of the Virginia gentry, and thus shared a distinct political and social culture, but the similarities end there. George Washington was a military officer and a farmer, a large and athletic man of action. He possessed intelligence, but not a university education. Gracious and magnanimous, he was also taciturn, demanding and unforgiving. In contrast, Madison was small and sickly, perhaps even an epileptic. A bookworm, educated at Princeton University, Madison was highly intellectual and philosophical. Though shy and retiring in large social gath-

'The resignation of General Washington, December 23rd, 1783' after a painting by John Trumbull. Madison was not actually present at the resignation, but Trumbull decided to include him in this work. He stands to the right of the left door frame.

erings, he was remarkably sweet-tempered and a wonderful conversationalist.

The relationship flourished because each man shared similar goals and possessed something the other needed. Both were committed to finalising the American Revolution by establishing an extremely republican and energetic federal government. Washington relied on Madison's advice, pen and legislative skill, while Madison manipulated Washington's prestige to achieve his own political goals.

The two first came face to face in August 1781, when Washington marched his army through Philadelphia on his way south to try to capture British troops under General Cornwallis in Virginia. Madison, at the time, was a member of the Confederation Congress. The relationship had actually begun, however, years before in 1777, when Madison became a member of the Virginia council of state under Governor Patrick Henry. In this role, Madison engaged in an extensive correspondence between the Virginia executive and Washington, commander-in-chief of the Continental Army. The correspondence dealt primarily with keeping Washington's troops manned and supplied. Through this communication, Madison developed a tremendous admiration for Washington. He also received a first-hand education in

civilian-military relations from the finest practitioner of that delicate art. As a result, Madison became more continental minded, and supportive of Washington's attempts to turn the American army into a paid, professional force.

By 1780, the calibre of delegates to Congress had declined precipitously, as talented men opted for state over federal service. Alarmed by this trend, Washington appealed to his native state to send men of the highest ability to Philadelphia. Virginia responded by electing four new delegates, including Madison. Thus Washington initiated Madison's advancement from state to federal service. During his years in Congress, Madison's political education continued. While in Philadelphia, he got to know Washington personally and their collaboration began.

The Newburgh Conspiracy exemplifies their association at this stage. In 1783, a faction of Congressmen (including Alexander Hamilton) and several Continental Army officers toyed with the idea of using a military *coup* led by Washington to scare Congress into raising revenue to pay the troops. At this moment the Revolution could have spun out of control. But the plan went nowhere, because Washington refused to have anything to do with it. During the crisis, he co-operated closely with a small group of moderate Congressmen, especially Madison.

While Washington pleaded with the army to have faith in Congress, Madison's forces worked feverishly on a plan to generate revenue, working within the republican ideals of the Revolution, rather than trying to scare Congress into raising money.

James Madison by Charles Willson Peale. The miniature was painted in 1783, the year Madison and Washington became allies over the Newburgh Conspiracy.

At the end of 1783, with the Revolutionary War over, both Washington and Madison retired to Virginia. Here they recognised something that few other Americans could see at this point: that the British Empire had been the glue that had held the thirteen colonies together. When Americans won their independence, the thirteen states started to spin off in separate directions, with new republics going their own ways. Washington and Madison believed that a new glue would have to be found to bind the states together again. They set about pushing for a stronger federal government.

In 1785, the two men launched a project to improve the Potomac River (making it navigable) deep into the Ohio country, then the western frontier. As the project grew beyond the borders of Virginia, more and more states participated—first Maryland, then Pennsylvania, and so on. The movement led to a series of conventions, first at Mount Vernon in 1785, then at Annapolis in 1786, and finally at Philadelphia in 1787, which of course produced the United States Constitution.

Between 1784 and 1787, the relationship between Washington and Madison developed as they became political confidants and intimate friends. The growth of their friendship is echoed in subtle shifts in the way they addressed each other and signed off in their letters. A typical eighteenth-century letter between two gentlemen might have closed with the words, 'your most obedient and humble servant'. At first, Washington's and Madison's letters ended in fairly generic terms. But after Madison made a three-day visit to Mount Vernon in 1785, Washington began adding the word 'affectionately' to the closings of his letters. Madison did not immediately reciprocate—not surprisingly considering he was nineteen years Washington's junior. But Madison visited Mount Vernon again in 1786. After this second visit, he, too, began closing his letters with the word 'affectionately'.

Exactly what went on during Madison's sojourns at Mount Vernon is hard to say. One hopes to find a detailed account in Washington's diary; instead, he writes only, 'home all day with Mr Madison'. Washington's reticence nevertheless speaks volumes. For him to forgo his daily ride to his farms to stay at home with a guest was truly remarkable. Clearly there was not only socialising, but serious business taking place. Madison visited Washington's plantation a total of ten times between 1785 and 1791. During the visits, which lasted up to a week, the two discussed important state affairs, such as Washington's decision to attend the Federal Convention and to accept the presidency.

Washington was reluctant to participate in the Federal Convention of 1787 because he did not want to waste his immense prestige on what could well turn out to be an abortive assembly (as the Annapolis convention had been which he had wisely not attended). Acting on his own, Madison, as a member of the Virginia legislature, nominated Washington as a delegate to the convention. When Washington insisted that his name be removed from the Virginia list, Madison persuaded him to leave it there. Even if Washington planned not to attend, Madison argued, the idea that he would participate would convince other states to send their best men. Madison's tactics worked. Washington's name secured a full turnout, allowing him to attend after all.

The fifty-five delegates to the Federal Convention met from May to September 1787 in Philadelphia's Independence Hall, then known as the Pennsylvania State House because it was the state capitol building. Washington and Madison stood out in their commitment to a government that was both very powerful and extremely republican. They voted alike nearly all of the time. The convention was often frustrating, especially for Madison, who failed to work many favourite details into the Constitution. On days that he suffered bitter defeats, such as the day the convention decided to grant two senators to each state instead of basing Senate representation on population, as Madison had hoped, he and Washington would dine together in the evening, Washington bucking up his dejected friend.

Individually, Washington and Madison played vital roles at Philadelphia, but their collaboration was also crucial in that together they constituted a bulwark within the Virginia delegation. Without Washington and Madison, the Virginia delegation as a whole might have opposed the Constitution. As a pair they offset fellow members George Mason and Edmund Randolph, who opposed the final document. Had the most influential state refused to endorse the Constitution at Philadelphia, ratification could never have been achieved.

During the ratification campaign, Washington—as the nation's inevitable choice for the presidency—maintained a low profile. Nevertheless, he collaborated closely with Madison to win approval of the Constitution. Together Washington at

A page from a 1786 letter from Madison to George Washington, whom he had by now visited three times.

Mount Vernon in the south and Madison at Congress in the north helped co-ordinate the entire Federalist campaign. Madison secretly provided Washington with copies of his essays for the *Federalist Papers* and other propaganda to be reprinted in Richmond. Interestingly, Madison revealed his authorship of the essays to Washington, but not to Thomas Jefferson or even to his own father.

Madison had not planned to attend the Virginia ratifying convention because he thought that the authors of the Constitution should not pass judgement on it. But Washington, knowing that Madison alone could answer the Antifederalist objections of Patrick Henry, convinced him to seek election. At the Virginia Convention in June 1788, Madison delivered perhaps his finest performance, parrying Henry's every thrust until the Constitution won approval by a narrow margin. However, Madison became so stressed by the contest that he became ill. Back at Mount Vernon, Washington, as worried about Madison's health as he was about the Constitution, wrote pleading with him to take a few days vacation at Mount Vernon, where he could regain his strength. In closing, Washington wrote:

> I can assure you that no one will be happier in your company than your sincere & Affecte Servt, Go: Washington.

Not often did so exacting a man as Washington urge someone to take a break, especially with the country's fate at stake. But he could see that Madison's labours might take too heavy a toll on a man whose friendship he cherished and whose abilities he needed.

Washington's election as first president under the new Constitution was a foregone conclusion. However, Madison made sure that his friend did not waver about accepting the presidency. To ghostwrite his inaugural address, Washington turned to his collaborator. Washington provided him with an outline of major points, which Madison worked into a draft. Madison, in short, served much like a modern speechwriter—while Washington deserves credit for the ideas, both men deserve credit for

The Pennsylvanian State House, scene of the 1787 Federal Convention. As a pair, Washington and Madison had a crucial bearing on the convention's outcome.

the language. Not only did Madison ghostwrite Washington's First Inaugural Address, as a member of the House of Representatives he wrote the House's reply to the Address, and, finally, the President's response to the House's reply. This dialogue with himself captures the central role Madison played in launching the federal government in 1789. Even though he held no official position, he acted as something of a prime minister, providing a bridge between the legislature and the executive.

When Washington took office, he and John Adams were virtually the entire executive branch of the federal government because it took months to create the executive departments. For example, Thomas Jefferson did not come aboard as Secretary of State for nearly a year. Not only was Washington initially alone, but virtually everything he did set important precedents that would be followed by his successors. Aware of this responsibility, Washington relied heavily on his right-hand man during these months. Madison provided advice on policy, appointments and presidential etiquette.

He also acted as Washington's 'hidden-hand' in resolving the fiasco over a title for the President. In 1789, the Senate, led by John Adams, voted to bestow on Washington the elaborate title 'His Highness, the President of the United States of America, and Protector of Their Liberties'. Washington, who realised that such a designation sounded too monarchical, was horrified. But he had to be careful not to offend or alienate the Senate. So he briefed Madison that the House must insist on the simpler title 'Mr President'. Madison convinced the House to hold firm, and eventually the Senate backed down.

Treasury Secretary Alexander Hamilton's financial programme is often seen as having driven a wedge between Washington and the emerging Republican Party, including Madison. But more important than the disagreements that arose between them over Hamilton's funding and assumption plan is the fact that all sides supported the Compromise of 1790. This bargain not only settled the national debt, but also permanently located the national capital on the Potomac River (after a ten-year stop in Philadelphia during the 1790s).

After 1790, with the cabinet finally in place, Madison stopped providing day-to-day advice, but he was still called in when precedent-setting situations arose. The best example is Washington's planned retirement in 1792. Concerned not to establish a tradition of dying in office that might allow his successors to serve for life, Washington hoped to retire at the end of one term. He turned to Madison for help in drafting a farewell message. Madison pleaded with the President to serve another term, warning that without Washington's stabilising influence, the emerging political parties might destroy the fledgling nation. Eventually, Washington agreed to serve a second term.

A year into this, Washington's Secretary of State, Thomas Jefferson, unhappy over constantly fighting Hamilton in cabinet meetings, decided to resign. Hoping to replace Jefferson with a Republican strong enough to balance the Federalist Hamilton, Washington invited Madison to succeed Jefferson. But Madison, equally reluctant to become locked in combat with Hamilton, declined. Madison's refusal to join the cabinet was a crucial turning point both in Washington's presidency and in the two men's friendship. Without a strong Republican in the cabinet, Washington's policies inevitably turned Federalist because virtually all his advisers were Federalists.

'View of Congress on the Road to Philadelphia'. Senator Robert Morris of Pennsylvania leads members of Congress to their new abode, temporary seat of the government from 1790 to 1800.

Despite their growing political differences, Washington and Madison remained close friends. Even as late as 1794, Washington and his wife, Martha, played a pivotal role on behalf of Madison in helping to arrange his marriage. Dolley Todd, a young Quaker widow, had lost her husband in the 1793 yellow fever epidemic that ravaged Philadelphia. Many suitors, including James Madison, came to court her. Finding that the forty-three-year-old Madison had been courting the twenty-six-year-old Dolley, Washington's wife Martha summoned Dolley to the President's house. Dolley's grand-niece recorded what happened:

> A report soon got about of their engagement; such un-wonted attentions from Mr Madison excited comment…

> It reached the Presidential mansion, where General and Mrs Washington were much interested; and impatient to hear the truth, sent for Mrs Todd, who all unconscious obeyed the summons at once.

> 'Dolley', said Mrs Washington, 'is it true that you are engaged to James Madison?' The fair widow, taken aback, answered stammeringly, 'No', she 'thought not'. 'If it is so', Mrs Washington continued, 'do not be ashamed to confess it: rather be proud; he will make thee a good husband, and all the better for being so much older. We both approve of it; the esteem and friendship existing between Mr Madison and my husband is very great, and we would wish thee to be happy'.

And so, with a little encouragement from the Washingtons, Dolley married James, or, as she called him 'the great Little Madison'. The ceremony took place on September 15th, 1794, at Harewood, the home of Washington's nephew George Steptoe Washington, near present Charles Town, West Virginia.

On the day he died Washington complained about having been betrayed by Madison.

Sadly, much of the goodwill generated by Madison's marriage was shattered by the Whiskey Rebellion of 1794 (in response to Hamilton's Whiskey Tax of 1791, which excited strong feeling from the backcountry where whiskey was the chief commodity, culminating in open rebellion in the four western counties of Pennsylvania). Unlike many Republicans, Madison supported Washington's decision to put down the Whiskey Rebellion by force. But he could not support his friend's decision to blame the rebellion on the Democratic Societies and political clubs that supported the Republican Party. Madison's act of defiance in this respect infuriated Washington, causing him to question the younger man's loyalty to him personally and to the nation. From this point onwards the friendship between the two men went downhill, as their politics polarised; Washington, increasingly Federalist, wanted to go further in his quest for a strong federal government. While Madison, staunch Republican, worried that the President's policies—political, financial, and industrial—threatened to restore

America's connection to Britain that had been severed during the Revolution.

The controversy over the 1795 Jay Treaty with Britain confirmed Washington's suspicions about Madison. Madison and the Republicans opposed the Jay Treaty because they believed that it neglected American interests, and that it virtually overturned the American Revolution by re-attaching the United States to Britain. When Republicans in the House of Representatives tried to block the appropriations necessary to implement the treaty, a major showdown between Washington and Madison ensued. The issue was whether the treaty power belonged only to the President and Senate, or whether the House could pass judgement on treaties as well by refusing appropriations. Not only did Madison loose this fight over the Jay Treaty, he lost his friendship with Washington as well. Convinced that Madison's behaviour had been virtually treasonous, Washington broke off their association once and for all.

HT Archive
Dolly Payne Todd (1768–1849), who married Madison in September 1794.

After they both retired to Virginia in March 1797, neither man saw or corresponded with the other again. Instead, they drifted further apart ideologically. On the day he died Washington complained about having been betrayed by Madison. On December 13th, 1799, Washington, suffering from a cold, spent the evening reading newspapers with Tobias Lear, his secretary. According to Lear, Washington

> requested me to read to him the debates of the Virginia Assembly… On hearing Mr Madison's observations… he appeared much affected and spoke with some degree of asperity on the subject, which I endeavored to moderate, as I always did on such occasions.

President Washington in evening dress, c. 1793.

The next night, the first president died of complications from an inflamed throat. One can't help wondering whether yelling about Madison had helped initiate his demise.

In many ways Washington and Madison have been misunderstood. Washington has been portrayed as a popular figurehead, a hands-off leader who reigned, but did not rule. His collaboration with Madison casts him in a new light, showing that he possessed a strong constitutional vision and always maintained control of his administration. Indeed, he was the central politician of his age. Conversely, the relationship with Washington shows that Madison richly deserves the attention historians have lavished on him as the Father of the Constitution. He was Washington's ideal collaborator in meeting the challenges posed by American independence: the need to design a government where the majority rules, but the minority is protected.

Why has the greatest partnership of the American founding, also been the most unheralded? Perhaps because Washington and Madison kept it a secret, with one or both partners working behind the scenes. Even at its zenith in 1789 and 1790, only the highest federal officials had an inkling of its existence, and few of them understood its true extent. The main evidence of their collaboration was their private correspondence, which each guarded carefully as long as he lived. Madison never wrote a tell-all book after Washington died, revealing his insider status in the first administration. Not only did Madison avoid enhancing his own reputation at Washington's expense, he (unlike John Adams) never became jealous of Washington's fame. Instead he quietly enjoyed knowing that he had been the Indispensable Man's 'Indispensable Collaborator'.

FOR FURTHER READING

Stuart Leibiger, *Founding Friendship: George Washington, James Madison, and the Creation of the American Republic* (University Press of Virginia, 1999); Lance Banning, *The Sacred Fire of Liberty: James Madison and the Founding of the Federal Republic* (Cornell University Press, 1995); Drew McCoy, *The Last of The Fathers: James Madison and the Republican Legacy* (Cambridge University Press, 1989); John E. Ferling, *The First of Men: A Life of George Washington* (University of Tennessee Press, 1988); Garry Wills, *Cincinnatus: George Washington and the Enlightenment* (Doubleday, 1984); Ralph Ketcham, *James Madison: A Biography* (Macmillan New York, 1971).

www.mountvernon.org

www.virginia.edu/gwpapers

www.virginia.edu/pjm

www.montpelier.org

Stuart Leibiger is Assistant Professor of History at La Salle University, Philadelphia.

This article first appeared in *History Today,* July 2001, pp. 21-27. © 2001 by History Today, Ltd. Reprinted by permission.

Your Constitution Is Killing You

A reconsideration of the right to bear arms

By Daniel Lazare

A well regulated Militia, being necessary to the security of a free State, the right of the people to keep and bear Arms, shall not be infringed.

—Second Amendment to the Constitution of the United States

On June 17, in the aftermath of the massacre at Columbine High School and a similar, if less grisly, incident the following month in Conyers, Georgia, the House of Representatives passed a "juvenile crime bill" steadfast in its refusal to limit the ease with which juveniles can lay their hands on firearms. House Republicans, it was clear, were determined to avoid making any connection between the fact that there are an estimated 240 million guns in the United States, nearly one per person, a number that is increasing by some 5 to 7 million a year, and the increase of violence in our culture. Instead, the problem was that we had forgotten the importance of "family values," that our children had become "spoiled with material things," that we had given in to "liberal relativism." Guns weren't the problem; the problem was

"the abandonment of God" in the public sphere.

Representatives Henry Hyde (R., Ill.) and Tom DeLay (R., Tex.) were particularly enthusiastic in their efforts to look beyond guns for a solution. Hyde put the blame on the entertainment industry and tried to push through an amendment to the crime bill that would have made it a jailable offense to sell overtly violent or sexual material to minors. Even when 127 of his fellow Republicans voted against the measure, Hyde refused to let go. "People were misled," he said, "and disinclined to oppose the powerful entertainment industry." DeLay's approach was even more entertaining. At a "God Not Guns" rally, he read aloud an e-mail he claimed to have received that very morning: "The student writes, 'Dear God, Why didn't you stop the shootings at Columbine?' And God writes, 'Dear student, I would have, but I wasn't allowed in school.'" (So much for divine omnipotence.) An hour later DeLay was on the House floor, telling his colleagues that "our school systems teach the children that they are nothing but glorified apes who are evolutionized out of some primordial soup of mud." Other DeLayisms: "We place our children in daycare centers where they learn their socializa-

tion skills... under the law of the jungle..."; "Our children, who historically have been seen as a blessing from God, are now viewed as either a mistake created when contraception fails or inconveniences that parents try to raise in their spare time." A proposal to allow the display of the Ten Commandments in public schools was subsequently voted into the bill.

Liberals cannot bear to admit the truth about gun control; the right wing is right. The second amendment confers an individual right

---

Among the further futile gestures housed in a second piece of crime legislation that failed the next day was a measure to reduce the Senate's proposed waiting time for purchases at gun shows and to limit the number of gun shows subject to any waiting period whatsoever. All this despite polls showing two-to-one support for stricter gun control even before Columbine. Two centuries ago, the great fear among the men who drew up the United States Constitution was of a popularly elected legislature falling all over itself to do the public's bidding; today we are witness to a popularly elected body falling all over itself not to carry out the democratic will. Why?

The standard liberal response is that the National Rifle Association made them do it. The NRA has used its immense campaign war chest to punish gun-control advocates and stifle dissent. It has twisted and distorted the Constitution. It has cleared a path for troglodytes like Hyde and DeLay. But the real problem is more disconcerting. The reason that Hyde and Co. are able to dominate the gun debate, the reason that the gun lobby is so powerful, is not the NRA but the basis on which the NRA's power rests; i.e., the Second Amendment. The truth about the Second Amendment is something that liberals cannot bear to admit: The right wing is right. The amendment does confer an individual right to bear arms, and its very presence makes effective gun control in this country all but impossible.

For decades liberal constitutional scholars have maintained that, contrary to the NRA, the Second Amendment does not guarantee an individual's right to own guns, merely a right to participate in an official state militia. The key phrase, they have argued, is "[a] well regulated Militia," which the introductory clause describes as nothing less than essential to "the security of a free State." A well-regulated militia is not just a goal, consequently, but *the* goal, the amendment's raison d'être. Everything else is subordinate. The right "to keep and bear Arms" is valid only to the degree that it serves this all-important end. There is therefore no *individual right* to bear arms in and of itself, only a *collective* right on the part of the citizens of the states to do so as members of the various official state militias. The right to own the assault weapon of one's choice exists only in the fevered imagination of the National Rifle Association. Its constitutional basis is nil. The only right that the Second Amendment confers is the right

to emulate Dan Quayle and join the National Guard.

This is the cheerful, anodyne version of the Second Amendment we're used to from the American Civil Liberties Union and other liberal groups. But as the gun issue has heated up since the Sixties and Seventies, constitutional scholars have taken a second look. The result has been both a renaissance in Second Amendment studies and a remarkable about-face in how it is interpreted. The purely "collectivist" interpretation has been rejected across the board by liberals and conservatives as ahistorical and overly pat. The individualist interpretation, the one that holds that Americans have a right to bear arms whether they're serving in an official state militia or not, has been more or less vindicated. In fact, some academics have gone so far as to compare the NRA's long campaign in behalf of an expansive interpretation of the Second Amendment to the ACLU's long campaign in behalf of an expansive reading of the First. As the well-known constitutional scholar William Van Alstyne put it, "The constructive role of the NRA today, like the role of the ACLU in the 1920s,... ought itself not lightly to be dismissed. Indeed, it is largely by the 'unreasonable' persistence of just such organizations in this country that the Bill of Rights has endured." Language like this is what one might expect at some Texas or Colorado gun show, not in the pages of the Duke Law Journal.

With day traders and students shooting citizens, the implications of an individual right to bear arms are profound

---

No less strikingly, the Second Amendment renaissance has also led to a renewed appreciation for the amendment's ideological importance. Previously, scholars were inclined to view the Second Amendment as little more than a historical curiosity, not unlike the Third Amendment, which, as almost no one remembers, prohibits the peacetime quartering of troops in private homes without

the owners' consent. Harvard's Laurence Tribe gave the Second Amendment no more than a footnote in the 1988 edition of his famous textbook *American Constitutional Law,* but a new edition, published this August, treats the subject much more extensively. It is now apparent that the amendment, despite its brevity, encapsulates an entire worldview concerning the nature of political power, the rights and duties of citizenship, and the relationship between the individual and the state. It *is* virtually a constitution-within-the-Constitution, which is undoubtedly why it fuels such fierce passions.

With crazed day traders and resentful adolescents mowing down large numbers of their fellow citizens every few weeks, the implications of this new, toughened-up version of the Second Amendment would seem to be profound. Politically, there's no doubt that it has already had an effect by encouraging the gun lobby to dig in its heels after Littleton, Conyers, the Mark Barton rampage in Atlanta, and the earlier shootings in Kentucky, Arkansas, and elsewhere. When Joyce Lee Malcolm, professor of history at Bentley College in Waltham, Massachusetts, and the author of a path-breaking 1994 study, *To Keep and Bear Arms: The Origins of an Anglo-American Right* (Harvard University Press), told a congressional committee a year later that "[i]t is very hard, sir, to find a historian who now believes that it is only a collective right... [t]here is no one for me to argue against anymore," it was just the sort of thing that pro-gun forces on Capitol Hill wanted to hear. If it wasn't a sign that God was on their side, then it was a sign that the Constitution was, which in American politics is more or less the same thing.

The judicial impact is a bit harder to assess. Although the Supreme Court has not ruled on the Second Amendment since the 1930s, it has repeatedly upheld gun control measures. But there is evidence that judicial sentiment is beginning to take heed of the academic change of heart. Two years ago, Supreme Court Justice Clarence Thomas indicated that he thought it was time to rethink the Second Amendment; Justice Antonin Scalia apparently thinks so as well. Then, just this past April, two weeks before Eric

Harris and Dylan Klebold shot up Columbine High School, a federal judge in a Texas gun case issued a ruling so enthusiastically "individualist" that it was virtually a brief in favor of what is now known in academic circles as the "Standard Model" of the Second Amendment. "The plain language of the amendment," declared Judge Sam R. Cummings, "shows that the function of the subordinate clause [i.e., the portion referring to a well-regulated militia] was not to qualify the right [to keep and bear arms], but instead to show why it must be protected." Rather than mutually exclusive, the collective right to join a state militia and the individual right to own a gun are, according to Cummings, mutually reinforcing. Although anti-gun groups predicted that the decision would soon be overturned, it is clear that a purely collectivist reading is becoming harder and harder to defend; the individualist interpretation, harder and harder to deny.

We have long been in the habit of seeing in the Constitution whatever it is we want to see. Because liberals want a society that is neat and orderly, they tell themselves that this is what the Constitution "wants" as well. This is a little like a nineteenth-century country vicar arguing that the Bible stands for moderation, reform, and other such Victorian virtues when in fact, as anyone who actually reads the text can see, it is filled with murder, mayhem, and the arbitrary vengeance of a savage god. By the same token, the increasingly sophisticated scholarship surrounding the Second Amendment has led to renewed respect for the constitutional text as it is rather than as we would like it to be. The Constitution, it turns out, is not neat and orderly but messy and unruly. It is not modern but pre-modern. It is not the product of a time very much like our own but reflects the unresolved contradictions of a time very different from our own.

Could it be that the Constitution is not the greatest plan on earth, that it contains notions that are repugnant to the modern sensibility? "When we are lost, the best thing for us to do is to look to our Constitution as a beacon of light and a guide to

get us through trying times." So declaimed Representative Zoe Lofgren (D., Calif.) during the House impeachment debate last October. Considering how we've all been taught since childhood to revere this document, probably not one American in a thousand would disagree. But what if Zoe Lofgren is wrong—what if the sacred text is seriously, if not fatally, flawed? Could it be that constitutional faith is not enough to get us through trying times? In a faithbound republic like the United States, this is pretty heretical stuff. Yet one of the nice things about the Second Amendment renaissance is the way it forces us to grapple with such heresy. Instead of allowing us to go on blindly trusting in the wisdom of a group of tribal patriarchs known as the Founding Fathers, it compels us to think for ourselves.

Could it be that the constitution is not the greatest plan, that it contains notions repugnant to the modern sensibility?

The framers, as it turns out, were of two minds where the power of the people was concerned. The Preamble to the Constitution implies a theory of unbounded popular sovereignty in which "we the people" are so powerful that we can "ordain and establish" new constitutions and, in the process, abrogate old ones such as the disastrous Articles of Confederation. The rest of the document implies that "we the people" are so powerless that when it comes to an anachronism such as the Second Amendment, the democratic majority is effectively precluded from changing a Constitution made in the people's name. We the people can move mountains, but we cannot excise one troublesome twenty-seven-word clause. Because we have chained ourselves to a premodern Constitution, we are unable to deal with the modern problem of a runaway gun culture in a modern way. Rather than binding society together, the effort to force society to conform to the dictates of an outmoded

plan of government is tearing it apart. Each new crazed gunman is a symptom of our collective—one might say our constitutional—helplessness. Someday soon, we will have to emancipate ourselves from our eighteenth- century Constitution. The only question is how.

Americans tend to give history short shrift; after all, when your Constitution is a timeless masterpiece, who needs to bother with something as boring as the past? But in order to unlock the meaning of the Second Amendment, it is necessary to know a little about the world in which it was created. The most important thing to understand is the eighteenth century's role as the great transitional period. Capitalism, industrialism, the rise of the great metropolis, the creation of new kinds of politics—these were beginning to make themselves felt, and as they did so they were creating shock waves and counter shock waves from one end of the English-speaking world to the other. Urbanization fueled passionate defenses of the old agrarian way of life. A new system of government centered on a prime minister, a cabinet, and an all-powerful House of Commons provoked endless screeds in favor of the old system of checks and balances among a multitude of coequal governing institutions.

This is the source of the great eighteenth-century polarization between what was known as Court and Country— the powerbrokers, influence-wielders, and political fixers on one side, and all those who felt shut out by the new arrangement on the other. Since the 1960s, historians have made immense strides in reconstructing this Anglo-American ideological world. In essence, we now know that it was dominated by fierce controversy over the nature of political power: whether it was harmful or beneficial, oppressive or liberating, whether it should be concentrated in a single legislative chamber or distributed among many. The Country opposition believed passionately in the latter. As a couple of coffeehouse radicals named John Trenchard and Thomas Gordon put it in their hugely popular *Cato's Letters* in the 1720s, "Power is like fire; it warms, scorches, or destroys according as it is watched, provoked, or increased." The solution was to divide power among so many competitive institutions that politicians' "emulation, envy, fear, or interest, always made them spies and checks upon one another." Since power was growing, oppression was growing also. "Patriots," therefore, were continually fighting a rear-guard action against corruption and tyranny, which were forever on the increase.

Guns were a big part of the eighteenth-century Anglo-American debate, in which the popular militia represented freedom at its most noble

---

We can recognize in eighteenth-century beliefs like these such modern U.S. attitudes as the cult of checks and balances, hostility to "big gummint," and the Zoe Lofgrenesque conviction that everything will turn out well so long as we remain true to the constitutional faith of our forefathers. Guns, as it turns out, were also a big part of the eighteenth-century Anglo-American debate. "Standing armies," the great bugaboo of the day, represented concentrated power at its most brutal; the late-medieval institution of the popular militia represented freedom at its most noble and idealistic. Beginning with the highly influential Niccolò Machiavelli, a long line of political commentators stressed the special importance of the popular militias in the defense of liberty. Since the only ones who could defend popular liberty were the people themselves, a freedom-loving people had to maintain themselves in a high state of republican readiness. They had to be strong and independent, keep themselves well armed, and be well versed in the arts of war. The moment they allowed themselves to surrender to the wiles of luxury, the cause of liberty was lost.

Thus, we have Sir Walter Raleigh warning that the first goal of a would-be tyrant is to "unarm his people of weapons, money, and all means whereby they may resist his power." In the mid-

seventeenth century, we have the political theorist James Harrington stressing the special importance of an armed yeomanry of self-sufficient small farmers, while in the early eighteenth we have Trenchard and Gordon warning that "[t]he Exercise of despotick Power is the unrelenting War of an armed Tyrant upon his unarmed Subjects." In the 1770s, James Burgh, another writer in this long Country tradition, advised that "[n]o kingdom can be secured [against tyranny] otherwise than by arming the people. The possession of arms is the distinction between a freeman and a slave." A pro-American English radical named Richard Price added in 1784 that

[T]he happiest state of man is the middle state between the *savage* and the *refined,* or between the wild and the luxurious state. Such is the state of society in CONNECTICUT, and in some others of the *American* provinces; where the inhabitants consist, if I am rightly informed, of an independent and hardy YEOMANRY, all nearly on a level—trained to arms,—instructed in their rights—cloathed in home-spun—of simple manners—strangers to luxury—drawing plenty from the ground—and that plenty, gathered easily by the hand of industry.

Not only were guns needed for self-defense but their widespread possession confirmed America's self-image as Homeland of Liberty

---

This was the Country myth in all its glory, the image of the roughhewn, liberty-loving "republican" as someone who called no one master, equated freedom and independence, and was not afraid to fight in defense of either or both. Joyce Lee Malcolm points out that where English patriots were content to pay lip service to the importance of arming the people, their cousins across the sea took the notion quite literally. A law

passed by the Plymouth Colony in 1623 required "that every freeman or other inhabitant of this colony provide for himselfe and each under him able to beare arms a sufficient musket and other serviceable peece for war." A 1639 law in Newport ordered that "noe man shall go two miles from the Towne unarmed, eyther with Gunn or Sword; and that none shall come to any public Meeting without his weapon." Measures like these were both practical and symbolic. Not only were guns necessary for self-defense but their widespread possession confirmed America's self-image as a homeland of liberty.

Ideas like these do not seem to have abated the least bit during the colonial period; indeed, by the 1770s they were at full boil. By the time British Redcoats faced off against heavily armed colonial irregulars at the Battle of Lexington and Concord in April 1775, it was as if both sides were actors in a political passion play that had been centuries in the making. It was the standing army versus the people's militia, the metropolis versus the hinterlands, centralized imperial power versus the old balanced constitution. Although the militias performed less than brilliantly in the Revolutionary War—Washington, professional soldier that he was, thought that the ragtag volunteer outfits were more trouble than they were worth—the myth lingered on. Americans needed to believe that amateur citizen-soldiers had won the war because their ideology told them that it was only via a popular militia that republican virtue could be established.

It is worth noting that even among those who were skeptical about the militias' military worth, the concept of a people in arms does not seem to have been at all problematic. Although Alexander Hamilton argued against separate state militias at the Constitutional Convention in 1787, for example, he seemed to have had nothing against popular militias per se. In 1788, he argued in *The Federalist Papers* that in the unlikely event that the proposed new national government used what was known at the time as a "select" militia—i.e., an elite corps—to oppress the population at large, the rest of the militia would be more than enough to fight them off. Such "a large body of citizens," he wrote, "little if at all inferior to them in discipline and the use of arms,... [would] stand ready to defend their own rights and those of their fellow-citizens." This is one reason why the argument that the Second Amendment confers only a collective right to join the National Guard is specious: today's National Guard is far closer to the eighteenth-century concept of a select militia than to the broad, popular militia the Framers clearly had in mind. And if the Second Amendment was nothing more than a guarantee of a right on the part of the states to organize state militias, it would imply that only the federal government was potentially tyrannical. Yet it is clear from James Madison's writings in *The Federalist Papers* that he saw state governments as potential sources of tyranny as well. Madison wrote that "the advantage of being armed" was one of the things that distinguished Americans from all other nations and helped protect them against abuse of power at all levels of government, federal and state. Antifederalists quite agreed. Their only quibble was that they demanded a Bill of Rights; they wanted the right to bear arms put in writing for all to see.

The meaning of what is now the Second Amendment becomes clearer still if we take a look at how its wording evolved. Madison's original version, which he drew up in 1789 as a member of the newly created House of Representatives, was on the wordy side but at least had the merit of clarity:

> The right of the people to keep and bear arms shall not be infringed; a well armed and well regulated militia being the best security of a free country; but no person religiously scrupulous of bearing arms shall be compelled to render military service in person.

By reversing the order between the right to bear arms and a well-regulated militia, Madison reversed the priority. Rather than a precondition, his original version suggested that a well-ordered militia was merely one of the good things that flowed from universal gun owner-

ship. A committee to which the amendment was referred, however, changed the order so that the amendment now read,

> A well regulated militia, composed of the body of the people, being the best security of a free State, the right of the people to keep and bear arms shall not be infringed, but no person religiously scrupulous shall be compelled to bear arms.

This was confusing but at least made plain that a militia was essentially synonymous with the people at large. Unfortunately, that notion, too, was lost when the Senate got hold of the amendment and began chopping out words right and left. The reference to "the body of the people" wound up on the cutting-room floor, as did the final clause. The effect was to deprive later generations of an important clue as to what a well-regulated militia actually meant. Although the final version was leaner and more compact, it was also a good deal less clear.

If the Framers were less than explicit about the nature of a well-regulated militia, it was because they didn't feel they had to be

Nonetheless, a few things seem evident. If the Framers were less than explicit about the nature of a well-regulated militia, it was because they didn't feel they had to be. The idea of a popular militia as something synonymous with the people as a whole was so well understood in the eighteenth century that it went without saying, which is undoubtedly why the Senate felt that the reference to "the body of the people" could be safely eliminated. It is also important to note that the flat-out declaration "[t]he right of the people to keep and bear arms shall not be infringed" remained unchanged throughout the drafting process. As Joyce Lee Malcolm has noted, the Second Amendment is a reworking of a provision contained in the English Bill of Rights of 1689. But whereas the English

Bill of Rights specified that subjects "may have arms for their defense suitable to their conditions, and as allowed by law," the American version avoided any such restrictions. Since all Americans (or, rather, members of the white male minority) were of the same rank, they possessed the same rights. They could bear arms for any purpose. And since the amendment was now part of the Constitution, the right was not limited by ordinary law but was over and above it. It was the source of law rather than the object. In this regard, as in virtually all others, Americans saw their role as taking ancient liberties and strengthening them so as to render tyranny all the more unlikely.

In the search for the meaning of the second amendment, we must recognize that "meaning" is problematic across the span of centuries

Although members of the legal academy assume that this is where the discussion ends, they're wrong: it's where the real questions begin. In attempting to nail down the meaning of the Second Amendment, we are therefore forced to recognize that "meaning" itself is problematic, especially across the span of more than two centuries. Once we have finished dissecting the Second Amendment, we are still left with a certain tension that necessarily exists between a well-regulated militia on the one hand and a right to bear arms on the other. One suggests order and discipline, if not government control; the other suggests voluntarism and a welling up from below. Eighteenth-century Country ideology tried to resolve this contradiction by envisioning the popular militia as a place where liberty and discipline would converge, where a freedom-loving people would enjoy the right to bear arms while proving their republican mettle by voluntarily rising to the defense of liberty. But although this certainly sounded nice, a harrowing eight-year war for independence had demonstrated the limits of such voluntarism. No-nonsense Federalists such as Washington and Hamilton recognized that there was no substitute for a professional army, not to mention a strong, centralized nation-state. But they also recognized that they had to get along with elements for whom such ideas were anathema. As a result, they felt they had no choice but to put aside their scruples and promise effective discipline from above and spontaneous self-organization from below, strong national government and states' rights, as contradictory as those notions might now seem.

The *meaning* of the Second Amendment, therefore, incorporates the contradictions in the Founders' thinking. But what's true for the Second Amendment is true for the Constitution as a whole. In June, William Safire rather naively suggested in his *New York Times* column that the solution to the problem of "the Murky Second" was to use the constitutional amending process to clarify its meaning. Did Americans have an unqualified right to bear arms or merely a right to enlist in the National Guard? Since the Founders had "botched" the wording, the solution was simply to fix it. This is indeed logical, but the problem is that the amending process is entirely useless in this instance. Because Article V stipulates that two thirds of each house, plus three fourths of the states, are required to change so much as a comma, as few as thirteen states—representing, by the way, as little as 4.5 percent of the total U.S. population—would be sufficient to block any change. Since no one would have any trouble coming up with a list of thirteen states in the South or the West for whom repealing the sacred Second Amendment would be akin to repealing the four Gospels, the issue is moot.

Since "we the people" are powerless to change the Second Amendment, we must somehow learn to live within its confines. But since this means standing by helplessly while ordinary people are gunned down by a succession of heavily armed maniacs, it is becoming more and more difficult to do so. As a result, politicians from President Clinton on down are forever coming up with ways of reconciling the irreconcilable, of reining in the gun trade without challenging the Second Amendment-fueled gun culture. The upshot is an endless series of ridiculous proposals to ban some kinds of firearms but not others, to limit handgun purchases to one a month, or to provide for background checks at otherwise unregulated traveling gun bazaars. Instead of cracking down on guns, the administration has found it easier to crack down on video games and theater owners who allow sixteen-year-olds to sneak into adult movies. The moral seems to be that guns don't kill people—fart jokes in the R-rated *South Park: Bigger, Longer & Uncut* do.

Why must we subordinate ourselves to a 208-year-old law that, if the latest scholarship is correct, is contrary to what we want?

This is the flip side of the unbounded faith of a Zoe Lofgren or a Barbara Jordan, who famously declared during Watergate, "My faith in the Constitution is whole, it is complete, it is total...." If one's faith in the Constitution is total, then one's faith in the Second Amendment is total as well, which means that one places obedience to ancient law above the needs of modern society. Once all the back-and-forth over the meaning of the Second Amendment is finished, the question we're left with is: So what? No one is suggesting that the Founders' thinking on the gun issue is irrelevant, but because they settled on a certain balance between freedom and order, are we obliged to follow suit? Or are we free to strike a different balance? Times change. From a string of coastal settlements, the United States has grown into a republic of 270 million people stretching across the entire North American continent. It is a congested, polluted society filled with traffic jams, shopping malls, and anomic suburbs in which an eighteenth-century right to bear arms is as out of place as silk knee britches and tricornered hats. So why must we subordinate ourselves to a 208-year-old law that, if the latest scholarship is correct, is contrary to what the democratic majority believes is in its best interest? Why can't *we* create the kind of society we want as opposed to living with laws meant to create the kind of society *they* wanted? They are dead and buried and will not be around to suffer the consequences. We the living will.

There is simply no solution to the gun problem within the confines of the U.S. Constitution. As the well-known Yale law professor Akhil Reed Amar put it recently, the Constitution serves to "structure the conversation of ordinary Americans as they ponder the most fundamental and sometimes divisive issues in our republic." In other words, the Constitution's hold on our society is so complete that it controls the way we discuss and debate, even the way we think. Americans are unable to conceive of an alternative framework, to think "outside the box," as the corporate strategists put it. Other countries are free to change their constitutions when it becomes necessary. In fact, with the exception of Luxembourg, Norway, and Great Britain, there is not one advanced industrial nation that has not thoroughly revamped its constitution since 1900. If they can do it, why can't we? Why must Americans remain slaves to the past?

Daniel Lazare is the author of The Frozen Republic: How the Constitution Is Paralyzing Democracy, *published by Harcourt Brace. His book about the prospects for re-urbanization in the twenty-first century,* America's Undeclared War, *was published on April 23, 2001.*

Do the People Rule?

Presidents as diverse as William McKinley, Gerald Ford, and Jimmy Carter have
spoken the simple words: "Here the people rule." But the meaning of the words is by
no means as straightforward as it may seem. Who exactly are the people?
The inhabitants of 50 different states, or the inhabitants of a single nation?
One people, or 50 peoples joined by compact? The questions are as old as the nation,
and perhaps best answered today by recognizing validity in each position.

Michael Lind

If American government were a cake, what kind of cake would it be? Political science and law examinations at American universities frequently ask some version of that question. Is the best metaphor for the relationship between the federal and state governments in the U.S. Constitution a layer cake, in which each level retains its own identity? Or does the United States have a "marble cake federalism," in which, according to the political scientist Morton Grodzin, "ingredients of different colors are combined in an inseparable mixture, whose colors intermingle in vertical and horizontal veins and random swirls"? Layer cakes and marble cakes do not exhaust the metaphorical possibilities. The political scientists Aaron Wildavsky and David Walker have suggested, respectively, that a birthday cake and a fruitcake can symbolize American federalism. All the culinary constitutionalism seems appropriate for a nation that some claim was once a melting pot but is now a salad bowl.

This battle of metaphors reflects a deep and enduring disagreement among Americans about the nature of popular sovereignty in the United States. Is the United States a creation of the individual states—or are the states a creation of the Union? Is there a single American people—or are there as many "peoples" as there are states?

The debate began when the ink was hardly dry on the new federal constitution drafted in Philadelphia in the summer of 1787. That fall, delegates from across Pennsylvania convened in Philadelphia to ratify or reject the document. On October 6, 1787, the delegates heard from James Wilson, a Scots-born lawyer who had been one of the leading thinkers at the past summer's constitutional convention (President George Washington would appoint him to the Supreme Court in 1789).

"There necessarily exists in every government," Wilson told the delegates, "a power from which there is no appeal; and which, for that reason, may be termed supreme, absolute and uncontrollable. Where does this power reside?"

Wilson rejected the British idea that the government—in the case of Britain, the crown-in-parliament—was sovereign: "The idea of a constitution limiting and superintending the operations of legislative authority seems not to have been accurately understood in Britain. To control the power and conduct of the legislature by an overruling constitution was an improvement in the science and practice of government reserved to the American states." However, Wilson continued, it would be a mistake to assume that the constitution is sovereign: "This opinion approaches a step nearer to the truth, but does not reach it. The truth is that, in our governments, the supreme, absolute, and uncontrollable power remains in the people. As our constitutions are superior to our legislatures, so the people are superior to our constitutions."

Although the idea of popular sovereignty reached its fullest development in the United States during the War of Independence and the early years of the American republic, it was an ancient concept. The Roman republic and, at least in theory, the subsequent Roman Empire were based on the *imperium populi*, the delegated sovereignty of the people. The idea of popular sovereignty was revived in the late Middle Ages and the Renaissance by Christian and humanist opponents of the divine right of kings.

In 17th-century England, during decades of civil war and other political turmoil, English thinkers worked out the basics of the modern doctrine of popular sovereignty. Drawing on ear-

been a single American people, which has existed in the form of successive "unions." Lincoln summarized this view in his first inaugural address: "[W]e find the proposition that, in legal contemplation, the Union is perpetual confirmed by the history of the Union itself. The Union is much older than the Constitution. It was formed, in fact, by the Articles of Association in 1774. It was matured and continued by the Declaration of Independence in 1776. It was further matured, and the faith of all the then thirteen states expressly plighted and engaged that it should be perpetual, by the Articles of Confederation in 1778. And, finally, in 1787 one of the declared objects for ordaining and establishing the Constitution was 'to form a more perfect union.'"

The paramount debate in American history has not been about the ultimate sovereignty of the people, but rather about the identity of the people.

Lincoln's nationalist interpretation of history drew on the thinking of the Supreme Court justice Joseph Story in his *Commentaries on the Constitution of the United States* (1833). According to Story, the Continental Congress, formed by delegates from the then-British colonies, "exercised de facto and de jure sovereign authority, not as the delegated agents of the governments de facto of the colonies, but in virtue of original powers derived from the people." The Declaration of Independence was "implicitly the act of the whole people of the united colonies," not of separate state peoples that had independently seceded from the British Empire.

© Bettmann/CORBIS

The Tearing Down of the Statue of George III (1857), William Walcutt's painting of a revolutionary crowd in New York City, is a classic celebration of the people's sovereignty.

lier writers, philosopher John Locke argued that every people has a right to change its government whenever the government becomes tyrannical. Although the theory of popular sovereignty remains controversial in Great Britain, all mainstream American constitutional thinkers have accepted the Lockean premise that, in the words of the Declaration of Independence, "to secure these Rights, Governments are instituted among Men, deriving their just Powers from the Consent of the Governed, that whenever any Form of Government becomes destructive of these Ends, it is the Right of the People to alter or to abolish it, and to institute new Government."

The paramount debate in American history has not been about the ultimate sovereignty of the people, but rather about the identity of the people (meaning a single entity, in the sense of *populus*). Is there a single American people? Or is the United States a federation of as many peoples as there are states?

The two rival interpretations of popular sovereignty in America have been the *nationalist theory* and the *compact theory*. The nationalist theory holds that from the beginning there has

Though the compact theory, like its competitor the nationalist theory, comes in several versions, every version holds that the American union is a compact among the states—the state *peoples*, that is, not the state governments. The most familiar version, held by Thomas Jefferson, John C. Calhoun, and the Confederate secessionists, can be described as the *unilateral compact theory*. South Carolina senator John C. Calhoun, its most brilliant proponent, argued in the Senate in 1833 that "the people of the several States composing these United States are united as parties to a constitutional compact, to which the people of each State acceded as a separate sovereign community." Calhoun denied "assertions that the people of these United States, taken collectively as individuals," had ever "formed into one nation or people, or that they have ever been so united in any one stage of their political existence."

According to Calhoun's unilateral version of the compact theory, the people of each state, represented in a constitutional convention, could authorize the secession of the state. They could also "nullify" laws they regarded as unconstitutional, a case that was made in response to President John Adams's unpopular Alien and Sedition Acts by the Virginia and Kentucky

Resolutions of 1798. (Thomas Jefferson was the secret author of the Resolutions.) In the Nullification Crisis of 1832–33, South Carolina claimed a right to nullify a federal tariff law, and backed down only when President Andrew Jackson threatened to use federal force against the state.

© Bettmann/CORBIS

Protective tariffs placed a heavy burden on cotton-growing southerners while aiding manufacturers in the North. The conflict fueled the Nullification Crisis of 1832.

As an interpretation of the federal constitution that went into effect in 1789, the unilateral compact theory is unconvincing. The alleged right of states to declare federal laws unconstitutional is incompatible with the supremacy clause of the Constitution and the role of the Supreme Court in adjudicating conflicts between the state and federal governments. But the claim that there is a constitutional right of unilateral secession is not as easily settled, because the Constitution is silent on whether, or how, states that have ratified it can depart from the Union. The most reasonable inference is that states can leave the United States only by the legal route of a constitutional amendment or by the extralegal route of a new constitutional convention that dissolves the federal constitution and creates a new union with new members. Responding to the possibility that opposition to the War of 1812 would inspire some of the states of New England to secede, Thomas Ritchie, editor of the *Richmond Enquirer*, wrote, "The same formality which forged the links of the Union is necessary to dissolve it. The majority of States which form the Union must consent to the withdrawal of any one branch of it. Until that consent has been obtained, any attempt to dissolve the Union, or obstruct the efficacy of its constitutional laws, is Treason—Treason to all intents and purposes."

The unilateral compact theory, then, is weaker than the nationalist theory of successive unions as an interpretation of the federal constitution of 1787. But as an explanation of American constitutional history right up through the ratification process of the federal constitution, the compact theory is more persuasive than the nationalist theory.

On July 4, 1861, President Lincoln said in a message to Congress, "The Union is older than any of the States, and, in fact it created them as States." Political scientist Samuel H. Beer restated this nationalist argument in *To Make a Nation: The Rediscovery of American Federalism* (1993), when he wrote that "the reallocation of power by the Constitution from state to federal government was simply a further exercise of the constituent sovereignty which the American people had exercised in the past, as when they brought the states themselves into existence."

The argument is flimsy. For one thing, it implies that without permission from the Continental Congress, the colonial populations would not have abolished their colonial governments and created new republican governments. To make matters worse for the nationalist theory, the phrasing of the Declaration of Independence supports the compact theory by referring to the formation of new state governments by the authority of the people of the colonies when it means the people of Massachusetts, the people of Virginia, and so on. And these colonial peoples, which became the peoples of the first states, had come into existence generations earlier—when each colony had been established by royal charter, if not before.

Nationalists also emphasize the description of the United States as "one people" in the Declaration of Independence: "When in the Course of human Events, it becomes necessary for one People to dissolve the Political Bands, which have connected them with another...." But elsewhere the Declaration refers to the colonies in the plural, and concludes that "these United Colonies are, and of Right ought to be, Free and Independent States." The author of the Declaration, Thomas Jefferson, was a fervent champion of the compact theory. Indeed, the Declaration claims that for generations the individual colonies had been separate states in a federal empire held together only by personal allegiance to the British monarch. During the Constitutional Convention, Maryland's Luther Martin summarized the view that was implicit in the Declaration: "At the separation from the British Empire, the people of America preferred the establishment of themselves into thirteen separate sovereignties instead of incorporating themselves into one.

The United States continued to look like a league of sovereign states under its first formal constitution, the Articles of Confederation (1781–89). In his *Defence of the Constitutions of Government of the United States of America* (1787–88), John Adams treated each state as a republic but rejected the applicability of the concept of republicanism to the United States as a whole, on the grounds that, under the Articles, Congress was "not a legislative assembly, nor a representative assembly, only a diplomatic assembly." In April 1787, James Madison observed that under the Articles of Confederation, "the federal system... is in fact nothing more than a treaty of amity of commerce and of alliance, between independent and sovereign states."

The history of the constitutional convention of 1787 and the process of ratification also supports the compact theory. The authors of *The Federalist*—Madison, Alexander Hamilton, and

John Jay—informed their readers that the new federal constitution would replace a league of states with a federal (or as Madison called it, a "compound") republic. If the "Union" under the Articles of Confederation were already a nation-state, albeit a decentralized one, it would have made no sense for Madison, Hamilton, and Jay to warn against disunion if the federal constitution were not adopted.

The method by which the federal constitution was ratified also refutes the arguments of nationalists such as Lincoln and Story that a union based on a single people had existed since 1776 or 1774. Samuel H. Beer writes, "Nationalist theory required that ratification be both popular and national, a procedure which expressed the will of individuals, the ultimate authority in a republic, and which embraced a single nationwide constituency, acting on behalf of the people at large in the United States." During the Constitutional Convention, Pennsylvania's Gouverneur Morris indeed proposed that the Constitution be ratified by "one general Convention, chosen and authorized to consider, amend, and establish the same." His proposal was rejected. The Constitution was ratified not by a national convention or even by the state governments but by the peoples of the states.

One of the peculiarities of the ratification process is that the new constitution went into effect upon being ratified by nine of the 13 states. (A similar rule of nine had earlier been used under the Articles of Confederation to authorize the admission of new states to the United States.) Nationalists argue that the rule of nine meant that the Constitution was ratified by a numerical majority of the American people, considered as a single national community. According to Beer, "Calculated according to the index of representation in the House, as proposed by Madison, any nine states would have had not only a majority of the states but also a majority of the population." Beer himself admits that the rule of nine guaranteed this nationwide numerical majority "without saying so." But the argument that the ratifiers had to be hoodwinked into taking part in a majoritarian procedure that they did not understand weakens rather than strengthens the case for the nationalist interpretation.

If the understanding of the ratifiers of the Constitution and not of the drafters is the one that counts for the purposes of American constitutional law, then one must reject the promising variant of nationalist theory proposed in 1987 by Professor Akhil Amar of Yale Law School. Amar suggested in the *Yale Law Journal* that during the process of ratification of the Constitution, "previously separate state Peoples agreed to 'consolidate' themselves into a single continental people." In contrast with the Story-Lincoln version of nationalist doctrine, Amar's variant would grant that the compact theory is an accurate description of the United States up until 1789, when the United States became a federal republic.

The most interesting part of Amar's theory—the notion that previously distinct state peoples fused during 1787–88 to become a single national people—is contradicted by Madison's statement in *The Federalist* 39 that the federal constitution would be ratified "by the people not as individuals composing one entire nation, but as composing the distinct and independent States to which they respectively belong." Amar's view is also incompatible with the way in which states were later added to the Union. The formation of a state "people" in a territory for only a few months or weeks would be pointless if the "people" were then dissolved into a unitary American people once the new state joined the Union. The compact theory makes more sense. A people in a state formed from a territory delegated a portion of its sovereign power to the federal government on joining the Union, but reserved the rest—and maintained its identity as a distinct population. Texas, the only state that began as an independent republic, would never have joined if its people thought they were dissolving "the people of Texas" and reducing Texas to a mere address.

The Tenth Amendment may be fatal to all versions of the nationalist theory of a single constituent American people: "The powers not delegated to the United States by the Constitution, nor prohibited by it to the States, are reserved to the States respectively, or to the people." Under a nationalist interpretation of the amendment, the single national people divided its sovereign power into three lumps and gave one to the federal government and one to all state governments, while reserving the third lump of sovereignty to itself. Thus, the Tenth Amendment created a zone of reserved popular power upon which neither the states nor the federal government could encroach.

That interpretation is appealing today, when, thanks to the Fourteenth Amendment and the civil rights revolution, the Bill of Rights has been partially held to restrain the state governments as well as the federal government. But it is a way of thinking that was alien to all but a few extreme nationalists during the early Republic. The Supreme Court ruled in *Barron v. City of Baltimore* (1833) that the federal Bill of Rights applied only to the federal government; the peoples of the several states had to limit state governments by passing state bills of rights. The only restraints on the states were a few in the federal constitution, such as the prohibition of bills of attainder and titles of nobility, and the guarantee that every state would have a republican government. Only the Fourteenth and Fifteenth Amendments, which were not ratified until after the Civil War, in 1868 and 1870 respectively, nationalized part or all of the Bill of Rights. (The degree of nationalization is hotly disputed to this day.)

It follows, then, that the compact theory provides the only plausible interpretation of the Tenth Amendment. As odd as it may seem to contemporary Americans, in theory at least there are as many peoples as there are states. Each state people assigns the same portion of its popular sovereignty to the federal government. But each state people—that of Massachusetts or Virginia, for example—is then free to allocate powers to the state government, or reserve them for the people of the state, in different ways, as each sees fit.

It appears, therefore, that Lincoln was mistaken when he argued that "the Union is older than any of the States, and, in fact, created them as States"—and that President Ronald Reagan, in his first inaugural address, was correct: "The Federal government did not create the states; the states created the Federal government." The compact theory of popular sovereignty, which holds that there are as many sovereign peoples as there are states, explains far more of American constitutional history and law than the nationalist theory does with its positing of a single, unitary American people. This conclusion may seem surprising. After all, Americans are highly mobile and rarely feel an intense loyalty to the state in which they happen to live. They define their identities far more commonly by factors such as race, ethnicity, religion, and political ideology than by state patriotism; indeed, the very phrase "state patriotism" seems quaint. Nevertheless, the nationalization of American society has not been accompanied by a nationalization of America's constitutional structure. Even in the 21st century, there is no mechanism such as a national ballot initiative or referendum by which Americans nationwide can express their views. The United States Senate still represents state constituencies, and the only national officer, the president, is chosen by the Electoral College, in accordance with a formula that takes states as well as populations into account. The Electoral College made it possible for George W. Bush to defeat Al Gore, who received more of the popular vote.

Texas. . .would never have joined [the Union] if its people thought they were dissolving "the people of Texas" and reducing Texas to a mere address.

In addition to seeming old-fashioned, the compact theory has long been tainted by its association with the Confederate secessionists and with later southern racists who used "states' rights" theory to defend institutionalized racial segregation. Fortunately, like the nationalist theory, the compact theory comes in more than one version. And even more fortunately, its most plausible variant—that of James Madison—undermines the arguments of both the Confederates and the segregationists and produces a view of the U.S. Constitution that most contemporary liberals as well as most conservatives can accept.

Madison, the "Father of the Constitution," has been accused of inconsistency. It is often said that he was a nationalist when he helped draw up the federal constitution and co-authored *The Federalist*; that he became a states rights theorist when he supported Jefferson's Virginia and Kentucky Resolutions in 1798 and when, as president, he favored limited government; and that he finally returned to his early nationalism late in life when he denounced nullification and the idea of secession. Though Madison, like any public figure, sometimes contradicted himself, he appears more consistent once he is identified as a member of the compact school—but a member with significant differences with other compact theorists, such as John C. Calhoun, his adversary in old age.

On March 15, 1833, the retired Madison wrote a letter to Massachusetts senator Daniel Webster, who, in his famous "Second Reply to Hayne," had defended the authority of the federal government and the desirability of perpetual union. "I return my thanks for the copy of your late very powerful speech in the Senate of the United States," Madison wrote Webster. "It crushes 'nullification' and must hasten the abandonment of 'secession.'" But having agreed with Webster's conclusions, Madison dissented from the logic of the nationalist theory Webster shared with Story (and that would later be taken up by Lincoln):

> It is fortunate when disputed theories can be decided by undisputed facts. And here the undisputed fact is that the Constitution was made by the people, but as embodied into the several states, who were parties to it and therefore made by the States in their highest authoritative capacity. They might, by the same authority and by the same process have converted the Confederacy [the United States under the Articles of Confederation] into a mere league or treaty; or continued it with enlarged or abridged powers; or have embodied the people of their respective states into one people, nation or sovereignty; or as they did by a mixed form make them one people, nation, or sovereignty, for certain purposes, and not so for others.

So far, Madison is merely restating the conventional theory of the Constitution as a compact among different state peoples. But he goes on to say that "whilst the Constitution, therefore, is admitted to be in force, its operation in every respect must be precisely the same"— whether the Constitution is thought to have been authorized by one national people (Webster's view) or by the separate state peoples (Madison's view). The compact can be revised or dissolved, but only with the agreement of all the parties, not just one or a few. In other words, according to Madison, the compact theory, properly understood, leads to the same conclusions as the nationalist theory: Unilateral secession by a state and unilateral nullification of federal laws are unconstitutional. Further, this Madisonian version of the compact theory would not support the later states' rights argument against federal civil rights legislation. After ratification of the Fourteenth Amendment in 1868, the only genuine argument was about what the federal civil rights regime would be—not about whether there would be one.

Madison's subtle version of the compact theory reconciles the actions of Lincoln in preserving the Union with the idea of plural sovereign slates that shaped the logic of the Declaration of Independence as well as the form of the federal constitution and the method by which it was ratified. Madison's mutual compact theory is more convincing than Calhoun's unilateral compact theory (which is incompatible with the federal constitution) and Lincoln's nationalist theory (which does not take accurate account of the War of Independence, the Articles of Confederation, and the ratification process of the Constitution).

Even in Madison's pro-union version of the compact theory, a state people retained the moral right, though not the legal right, to rebel on its own against a tyrannical federal government. In his letter to Webster, he warns against confusing "the claim to secede at will, with the right of seceding from intolerable oppression. The former answers itself, being a violation, without cause, of a faith solemnly pledged. The latter is another name only for revolution, about which there is no theoretic controversy." Madison's theory could establish that unilateral secession was illegal and unconstitutional under the terms of the 1787 constitution, but it could not establish that an illegal secession was an illegitimate act of revolution. But no mere constitutional theory could. The justice or injustice of a revolution is a matter for political and ethical theory, not for constitutional law. Most contemporary Americans would agree that the revolution of the people of South Carolina against the British Empire was justified, but that the later revolution of the same people against the United States was not. In both cases, a majority of the South Carolina population supported the revolution; but the goal of the first was to preserve and increase republican government in North America, while the goal of the second, in fact if not in rhetoric, was to preserve and possibly extend the zone of chattel slavery in North America.

The conclusion must be that popular sovereignty in itself is not a sufficient basis for the moral legitimacy of governments or their acts. In a world in which peoples rather than kings are the sovereigns, the peoples, like kings, may use their sovereign power for evil as well as for good. As James Wilson told the Pennsylvania convention in 1787 when he described the theory of popular sovereignty, "There can be no disorder in the community but may here receive a radical cure. If the error be in the legislature, it maybe corrected by the constitution; if in the constitution, it may be corrected by the people. There is a remedy, therefore, for every distemper in the government, if the people are not wanting to themselves. For a people wanting to themselves, there is no remedy."

MICHAEL LIND, *a senior fellow at the New America Foundation, is the author of* The Next American Nation *(1995) and other books. His new book (with Ted Halstead) is* The Radical Center: The Future of American Politics. *Copyright © 2002 by Michael Lind.*

From *The Wilson Quarterly,* Winter 2002, pp. 40-49. © 2002 by the Woodrow Wilson International Center for Scholars in Washington, DC.

UNIT 3

National Consolidation and Expansion

Unit Selections

Key Points to Consider

- George Washington presided over the formative years of government under the new Constitution. What were his strengths? His weaknesses? In what ways did the election of 1796 mark the beginning of a new era?

- Discuss the importance of Lewis and Clark's expedition west. How did their achievement impact the opening of the west?

- What were the women who attended the Seneca Falls conference trying to accomplish? Why was the question of suffrage so controversial?

- How did President Jackson succeed in removing the Cherokee Indians from Georgia? Why was the Indians' plight called "the trail of tears"?

- Why is John Brown considered the father of American terrorism? Does his legacy still have relevance for American society?

 **Links: www.dushkin.com/online/**
These sites are annotated in the World Wide Web pages.

Consortium for Political and Social Research
http://www.icpsr.umich.edu

Department of State
http://www.state.gov

The Mexican-American War Memorial Homepage
http://sunsite.unam.mx/revistas/1847/

Mystic Seaport
http://amistad.mysticseaport.org/main/welcome.html

Social Influence Website
http://www.workingpsychology.com/intro.html

University of Virginia Library
http://www.lib.virginia.edu/exhibits/lewis_clark/

Women in America
http://xroads.virginia.edu/~HYPER/DETOC/FEM/

Women of the West
http://www.wowmuseum.org/

The government established under the Constitution has, with the exception of the Civil War, endured for more than 200 years. Such stability makes it easy to overlook how fragile the system looked to those who were trying to make it function. The Constitution provided a broad framework only, and even some of its provisions were disputed at the time. Following elections held in 1888, the new goverment got under way the following year. Everyone understood that much of what was done, and the way it was done, would establish precedents for the future. Even such apparently trivial matters as the proper form of addressing the president caused debate. There were more significant issues. What, for instance, was the precise relationship between the president and the Congress? What role would the Supreme Court play? When differences appeared over such matters, which branch would decide? Perhaps most important, should the Constitution be interpreted strictly or loosely? That is, should governmental powers be limited to those expressly granted, or were there "implied" powers that could be exercised as long as they were not expressly prohibited? Various individuals and groups argued on principle, but the truth is that they were largely interested in promoting programs that would benefit the interests they represented.

There were no provisions in the Constitution for political parties. Although President George Washington believed he served the nation as a whole, what he disdainfully referred to as "factions" arose fairly early during his first administration. Secretary of the Treasury Alexander Hamilton usually argued in behalf of measures that would benefit commercial and manufacturing interests located mostly in the Northeast. Secretary of State Thomas Jefferson and his able ally James Madison represented rural and agricultural interests that were concentrated in the West and South. These two groups clashed frequently over what the Constitution did or did not permit, which sources of revenue should be tapped, and a host of other matters. Washington contributed to the development of political parties because he sided with Hamilton most of the time.

The first article in this section, "The Whiskey Rebellion," analyzes the first great crisis of the new nation. At the recommendation of Alexander Hamilton, a federal excise tax was levied on distilled spirits. The burden fell most heavily on back-country farmers who distilled their corn into whiskey. This led to an uprising that had to be put down by force. Author Robert Kyff discusses the class and sectional implications of this conflict. Owing to his tremendous popularity, George Washington was twice elected president without opposition. During his tenure in office, however, "factions" had arisen over controversial policies. These factions developed into a two-party system when Washington refused a third term. "1796: The First Real Election" discusses how this came about.

In the early 1800s, Americans knew little about the vast, uncharted territories that extended from the Mississippi River to the Pacific Ocean. Thomas Jefferson had for years shown an interest in exploring this area, and when he became president he requested funds from Congress to form an expeditionary group that became known as the Corps of Discovery. Headed by Meriwether Lewis and William Clark, in 1804 the Corps embarked on an arduous journey that eventually brought it to the shores of the Pacific. The essay "Lewis and Clark: Trailblazers Who Opened the Continent" describes this expedition from its beginning to its return home and the performance of its two leaders.

"Chief Justice Marshall Takes the Law in Hand" analyzes the role of this fourth chief justice of the Supreme Court. Marshall was responsible for enhancing the power of the Court, and more than anyon else helped ensure that federal law would prevail over states' rights.

There are three articles on women. "Rebecca Lukens: Woman of Iron" tells the story of a woman who took over her late husband's iron mill and turned it into a thriving business. "'All Men & Women Are Created Equal'" treats the first women's rights convention, held in Seneca Falls, New York, in 1848. Within the meeting, most of the resolutions gained wide acceptance—all except the one on suffrage, which caused much controversy. Press coverage of the event often was harsh and sarcastic. The essay "The Lives of Slave Women" is about the conditions under which these women lived and worked, and their efforts to achieve some measure of influence on those conditions.

"Andrew Jackson Versus the Cherokee Nation" describes this president's role in bringing about the removal of the Cherokees from Georgia to west of the Mississippi. This migration became known as "the trail of tears" because of the suffering involved.

The last two articles deal with the growing sectional conflict over slavery. "William W. Brown" details the life of a former slave who escaped. He taught himself how to read and write, and authored several books. He became a popular speaker for the cause of abolitionism. "The Father of American Terrorism" is about John Brown, a fervent abolitionist who committed violent acts in behalf of the cause. His raid on Harpers Ferry in 1859 injected a new furor into the already heated sectional dispute.

The Whiskey Rebellion

*Two hundred years ago a federal tax on distilled spirits
led to our young nation's greatest internal crisis.*

Robert S. Kyff

On August 1, 1794, a motley army assembled at Braddock's Field on the Monongahela River near Pittsburgh. Nearly seven thousand armed militiamen—some dressed in regimental uniforms, others wearing the yellow hunting shirts of Indian fighter—mustered on the plain where, thirty-nine years before, British General William Braddock had been mortally wounded and his forces defeated during the French and Indian War.

To the casual observer the assembly might have appeared to be a celebration, given the holiday atmosphere that prevailed as military drums beat loudly, soldiers marched and countermarched, and riflemen took target practice, filling the air with thick gray smoke. But the purpose of the gathering was deadly serious. These were the "Whiskey Rebels"—backwoods citizens of Pennsylvania's four western counties (Allegheny, Westmoreland, Fayette, and Washington[1]) who had assembled to demonstrate their defiance of the federal government's excise tax on whiskey and to coerce others into joining them in opposition. Many of the rebels advocated outright independence from the United States, and several of the units displayed a six-striped flag representing the six defiant counties of western Pennsylvania and Virginia.

The insurgents' immediate plan was to seize nearby Fort Fayette and then occupy and burn Pittsburgh, which in their eyes exemplified the haughty eastern patricians who had imposed this unfair tax. The rationale at the time, according to an 1859 defense of a key figure in the events, was that "as old Sodom had been burned by fire from heaven, this second Sodom should be burnt by fire from earth!"

The ardent force was led by "Major General" David Bradford, a wealthy lawyer who fancied himself the "George Washington of the West." As the troops assembled, Bradford, dressed in military attire and mounted on a "superb horse in splendid trappings," dashed across the field "with plumes floating in the air and sword drawn." The ostentatious Bradford (prudently deciding to bypass well-defended Fort Fayette) then led his forces eight miles west toward Pittsburgh for what was euphemistically described as a "visit." Relishing the upcoming plunder of Pittsburgh's fancy shops, one upcountry soldier twirled his hat on his rifle barrel and boasted, "I have a bad hat now but I expect to have a better one soon."

The advance of such a lawless, anti-aristocratic mob terrified the citizens of Pittsburgh, even though many sympathized with the rebel cause. The residents' apprehension was heightened by an eerie apparition: a lone horseman riding through the streets holding a tomahawk above his head and warning that revocation of the excise tax would be only the beginning of a larger revolution. "A great deal more is yet to be done," he chanted ominously.

Fearing the worst, Pittsburgh's twelve hundred citizens deployed a shrewd strategy to protect their town. Rather than greeting the insurrectionists with guns, they instead offered the soldiers hams, dried venison, bear meat, and, of course, casks of whiskey. Through these conciliatory actions, and by agreeing to banish known Federalist sympathizers from their limits, the Pittsburgh residents saved their town from destruction. Although the occupying force did burn a few farm buildings and steal some livestock, it soon dispersed, leaving "Sodom" largely undamaged and its populace shaken but unharmed.

The rally at Braddock's Field and the occupation of Pittsburgh marked the high point of what has since become known as the "Whiskey Rebellion." Perhaps because of its bibulous nickname—conjuring up images of a comical, pop-gun skirmish involving moonshining hillbillies—the uprising, regarded by nineteenth-century historians as the most important national cri-

PHOTOGRAPH BY STEVEN P. MASON

The Whiskey Rebellion is the subject of fond annual (and during 1994, bicentennial) commemorations in parts of western Pennsylvania. Re-enactors gather around an authentic rebellion-era still at the Oliver Miller Homestead near Pittsburgh.

sis between the Revolutionary and Civil wars, today is more often remembered as a minor bump on the road to national consolidation.

Such an interpretation, however, overlooks the true significance of the crisis, which, more than any in the nation's formative years, defined the nature of the new federal government and its relationship to its citizens. This single event embodied nearly all of the fundamental issues and conflicts facing the young American republic and its new Constitution: the clash between liberty and order in a democracy; western versus eastern interests; agriculture versus industry; the nature of taxation; the duties and rights of citizens; relations with European powers such as Great Britain and Spain; the influence of the French Revolution; the rise of political parties; and the meaning of the American Revolution itself.

While some historians have dismissed the suppression of the rebellion as "duck soup" for the federal government, the outcome of this Constitutional crisis was, in fact, far from a foregone conclusion. It might well have resulted in the establishment of new states, fully independent of the government in Philadelphia, or perhaps in the alliance of trans-Appalachian counties with British Canada to the north or New Spain to the south. Moreover, the uprising was fraught with fascinating ironies: the requirements of the excise tax that triggered the revolt were relaxed just prior to the largest protest against it; the insurrection itself seemed to be dying out just when the federal government decided to suppress it; and President Washington, who had led the American rebellion against British taxation, now found himself on the opposite side, crushing a revolt against a similar internal tax.

The roots of this complex and intriguing episode lay in the unique character of life on the western frontier during the 1780s and '90s. Separated from the coastal regions by vast stretches of rugged wilderness, westerners lived an isolated and dangerous existence that was characterized by violence, economic uncertainty, and physical hardship. Despite frequent appeals to the federal government for protection, people all along the frontier lived in constant fear of massacre. Between 1783 and 1790 alone, fifteen hundred settlers in the Ohio Valley were killed, wounded, or captured by hostile Native Americans.

Many settlers who had moved west in pursuit of economic opportunity and personal liberty now found themselves living in lice-infested hovels and scratching out a bare subsistence on land owned by absentee landlords. Geography and politics made it difficult for farmers to ship their commodities to larger markets: overland transportation of goods to eastern cities was costly while Spanish control of New Orleans prevented shipment via the Ohio and Mississippi Rivers. The settlers begged the federal government to negotiate with Spain for transportation rights, but by 1791 no agreement had been reached.

Amid such poverty and economic isolation, many backwoodsmen fell into a life of crudity and dissipation. Squalid living conditions, excessive drinking, and random violence were common. Headstrong settlers—many recently arrived from Scotland, Ireland, and Germany—grew increasingly frustrated by the disparity between their expectations of prosperity in America and the harsh realities of frontier life. Increasingly they blamed their troubles on a presumed conspiracy between the federal government, which had proved unable or unwilling to control the Indians or to secure westerners access to Mississippi river trade rights, and the eastern elite.

PHOTOGRAPH BY STEVEN P. MASON

Docents at the restored David Bradford house—the Washington, Pennsylvania, home of the insurrection's most militant firebrand—display a replica of the only surviving Whiskey Rebellion flag. Bradford reportedly jumped from the second-story window at right and disappeared into the night when federal militiamen arrived to arrest him. He fled to Louisiana, where he became a wealthy planter—finally to be pardoned by President John Adams in 1799.

It was against this background of economic impoverishment, political frustration, and social unrest in the trans-Appalachian West that, in March of 1791, the federal government imposed an excise tax on whiskey. Seeking to put the new nation on a sound financial footing, Treasury Secretary Alexander Hamilton convinced Congress and President Washington that the whiskey tax was needed to pay off the debts, now assumed by the federal government, that had been incurred by the former colonies during the Revolutionary War.

The new excise law required that each rural distiller pay either an annual rate of sixty cents for each gallon of his still's capacity or nine cents per gallon produced. Distillers also were expected to keep accurate records of production and to gauge and label each cask before shipment—stipulations that placed a particular burden on part-time, small-scale distillers not accustomed to such strict accounting. Federal excisemen were empowered to inspect stills and search property for contraband goods and illegal distilling operations. And, even more dis-

PHOTOGRAPH BY STEVEN P. MASON

Re-enactors at the Oliver Miller Homestead demonstrate how eighteenth-century Pennsylvania whiskey-makers checked the proof of their product: the persistence and size of bubbles formed by shaking a small sample of the brew were proportional to its alcohol content.

turbing to westerners, the law called for accused tax evaders to be tried in federal courts at Philadelphia, necessitating a costly time-consuming journey that could ruin a distiller financially even if he were found innocent,

The concept of an excise tax—an internal, direct tax on products produced—was especially odious to western Pennsylvanians. Numerous attempts to levy such taxes within the late colony of Pennsylvania had met with failure. Many recent immigrants from the British Isles had experienced first-hand the oppressive practices of the Crown's hated excise collectors, who often confiscated property and employed paid informers. And, of course, it had been an excise tax—the Stamp Tax—that had angered and turned American colonists against Britain, leading to the late war for independence. That the infamous tax of 1765 had been imposed by a government in which they enjoyed no representation, while the tax on whiskey was enacted by their duly elected representatives, mattered little to a populace not yet used to the federal system of government created only a few years before. Finally citizens feared that, once the federal government got its foot in the door with the whiskey tax, it would soon pass internal taxes on other goods. "I plainly perceive," a Georgian predicted, "that the time will come when a shirt shall not be washed without an excise."

Hamilton dismissed many of the objections raised against the whiskey tax. The imposition of the duty he believed, did not unfairly burden whiskey-producing areas because the tax rates— only a few dollars a year for the average small distiller—seemed quite low. And, reasoned Hamilton, if distillers did not want to pay the duty they could simply produce less whiskey. What the Treasury Secretary failed to grasp was the centrality of whiskey to frontier life.

On the nation's western perimeter, whiskey was more than a luxury item or an incidental distraction from the rigors of survival. It was the lifeblood of the backwoods economy and culture. Virtually cut off as they were from eastern markets and the Mississippi River trade, farmers found it more efficient to distill their rye grain into whiskey that could easily be sold or bartered. While the average pack horse, for instance, could carry only four bushels of grain, it could haul the equivalent of twenty-four bushels if that grain were converted into two casks of whiskey. Thus, in this more portable liquid form, "Monongahela Rye" became the "coin of the realm" in western Pennsylvania, used to pay hired workers or to buy everything from salt to nails to gunpowder.

But whisky was much more than just commodity or currency on the frontier; it was a way of life. Whether sweetened with tansy, mint, or maple sugar or swallowed straight, whiskey lubricated nearly every rite of frontier existence. No marriage, baptism, contract signing, brawl, trial, election, meal, or funeral took place without gernous helpings of the local brew. Doctors prescribed it for nearly every ill; ministers sipped it before services, field workers demanded it as refreshment; and the United States Army issued a gill each day to soldiers.

This insatiable thirst for whiskey rendered the still a "necessary appendage of every farm" that could afford it. "In many parts of the country" wrote one observer, you could scarcely get out of sight of the smoke of a still-house." While perhaps only ten to twenty percent of western Pennsylvania farmers actually owned whiskey stills, many neighbors purchased stills together and shared their use. And, even those farmers who performed no distilling had a direct stake in whiskey production because they sold their rye grain to the local distillers.

Given the importance of whiskey on the frontier, it is not surprising that residents of the trans-Appalachian counties violently opposed the federal excise tax. The federal government in far-away Philadelphia—the same government that could not protect them from the Indians and could not secure them trade rights on the Mississippi—was asking westerners to shoulder a disproportionate financial burden by taxing their region's dominant product. Worse yet, in a society based on a barter economy where coin and currency were scarce, the government demanded that its excise be paid not in whiskey or other commodities, but in hard specie.

It soon became clear that, in its search for the sweet honey of revenue, the federal government had stuck its hand into a beehive. Shortly after the whiskey tax went into effect on July 1, 1791, western Pennsylvania responded with protest meetings, petitions, and outright assaults on revenue agents. In September 1791, sixteen Washington County men dressed in women's clothing seized excise collector Robert Johnson, cut off his hair, then tarred and feathered him. When John Connor tried to serve warrants to those accused of the assault, he himself was whipped, tarred and feathered, and tied to a tree.

Mobs burned revenue collectors in effigy and attacked their offices and lodgings. To show that the backwoodsmen equated the excise tax with British colonial oppression, dissidents erected "liberty poles," familiar icons of the Revolutionary War, and set up committees of correspondence similar to those that had kept protestors informed of developments in the struggle against the former mother country.

Inspired by the French Revolution as well as the American, tax resisters formed numerous democratic societies modeled after the Jacobin Clubs, righteously vowing to "erect the temple of LIBERTY on the ruins of palaces and thrones." These extralegal organizations particularly irked President Washington, who, with France's upheavals in mind, viewed them as a direct challenge to Constitutional authority. They masked, he said, "diabolical attempts to destroy the best fabric of human government."

In May 1792, Secretary Hamilton, hoping to defuse the protests that rendered the whiskey revenue virtually uncollectible, persuaded Congress to reduce the tax rates and allow for monthly payments. When this failed to discourage the assemblies and quell the violence, Washington, in September 1792, issued a proclamation ordering the dissolution of any organization or meeting designed to obstruct the enforcement of any federal law. This action, however, also effectively silenced the moderates who sought a peaceful solution to the controversy, thus leaving radical leaders free to pursue their violent tactics.

Sporadic attacks on revenue collectors continued through 1793, completely shutting down the collection of whiskey tax in all frontier regions. Meanwhile, the federal government in Philadelphia—already preoccupied by the Reign of Terror in France, Indian attacks on the frontier, and threats by Spain and Britain—was brought to a near-standstill by a yellow fever ep-

idemic that killed more than four thousand people in that city. Mistaking the federal government's distraction for lack of resolve on excise enforcement, tax protestors pressed their demands for its repeal.

In early 1794, radical leaders took a new tack. Instead of directing violence only against collectors and their offices, they now targeted anyone who complied with the tax or cooperated with its enforcement. Law-abiding distillers were visited by "Tom the Tinker" who "mended" their stills by riddling them with bullets. In Allegheny County for example, mobs destroyed the 120-gallon still of William Cochran and dismantled the grist mill of James Kiddoe simply because both men had registered their stills with authorities as the law required.

Seeking to pacify the insurgents, Congress on June 5, 1794 further amended the excise law to provide accused tax evaders with local trials and small distillers with a special license for temporary operations. But on that same day Congress passed a new revenue act extending excise levies to snuff and sugar—a move that confirmed protestors' fears that the excise on whiskey would inevitably expand to other products.

When federal agents began serving arrest warrants on alleged tax evaders during the summer of 1794, violence erupted anew. At dawn on July 16, forty rebels arrived at Bower Hill, the home of distinguished Revolutionary War officer John Neville, to demand his resignation as Inspector of Revenue for western Pennsylvania. Before his appointment as supervisor of excise collection, Neville—a wealthy whiskey producer whose clapboard mansion boasted such luxuries as mirrors, carpets, and an eight-day clock—had adamantly opposed the whiskey tax, leading rebels to suspect that he had taken a large bribe to assume his federal office. The once-respected Neville now was detested as a turncoat by the insurgents.

When the mob in his front yard ignored an order to disband, Neville fired into their midst, mortally wounding Oliver Miller. The rebels shot back and were closing in on the house when some of Neville's slaves, armed in anticipation of attack, opened fire from the rear, wounding four more militiamen. After a twenty-five minute gun battle, the posse retreated.

The next day an army of five to seven hundred men led by Captain James McFarlane showed up at Bower Hill, which was now defended by ten federal soldiers from Fort Pitt, under the command of Major James Kirkpatrick. After brief negotiations, the rebels set several of the estates' outbuildings on fire and began an exchange of gunfire with the defending troops. During a lull in the fighting, McFarlane, thinking he had heard a call to parley, stepped out from behind a tree and was shot dead by the regulars. Smoke and heat from the burning structures subsequently filled the house, forcing the soldiers to surrender. The insurrectionists pillaged Neville's home and estate, liberating the mirrors and fancy clock. But Neville, who had been secreted in a nearby ravine by the soldiers before the rebels appeared on his property, escaped, as did his family.

With the death of McFarlane—who was a respected Revolutionary War hero—the insurgents now had a martyr. Radical leader David Bradford denounced McFarlane's "murder" and called for the rendezvous of militia forces at Braddock's Field. As it turned out, this dramatic show of force on August 1 marked the rebellion's zenith and helped to provoke its violent suppression.

On learning of the rebels' "visit" to Pittsburgh, President Washington and Secretary Hamilton decided that time for military action had come. The nascent federal government, they believed, could no longer tolerate such blatant defiance of its laws. Although most residents of upcountry Georgia, Kentucky, North Carolina and Virginia also refused to pay the excise tax, the opposition in western Pennsylvania was more visible and violent than in these states, and its suppression would send a strong message to all of the dissidents.

Moreover, it was unthinkable to allow such treason to flourish in the very state that held the nation's capital. Exaggerated rumors of attacks on federal arsenals and invasions of towns by armed mobs swept through eastern cities. With Britain and Spain seeking to bully the young nation and France grappling with its revolution, this was no time for conciliation. At issue, Washington and Hamilton believed, was the very integrity and credibility of the federal government—perhaps even its survival.

Although he had made up his mind to wage war, Washington, hoping to appear conciliatory, in late August went through the motions of sending peace commissioners to seek a non-military solution. Thinking these negotiations legitimate, moderate leaders like Albert Gallatin, who himself later served as Secretary of the Treasury, persuaded many of the dissidents to cease their violence. Ironically, evidence suggests that opposition to the tax was waning just as Washington was preparing for military operations.

By early October, Washington had assembled a 12,950-man army from the state militias of Pennsylvania, New Jersey, Virginia, and Maryland. In many ways these forces were no more disciplined or well-organized than the dissidents they opposed. A curious blend of lower-class and gentlemen volunteers, the impromptu army suffered from high desertion rates, squabbles over chains of command, and persistent rumors that it was really being sent to fight Indians or seasoned British regulars.

But the militiamen's spirit was aroused when rebels derided their fighting prowess. "Brother, you must not think to frighten us," wrote one "Captain Whiskey" in a western Pennsylvania newspaper, "with… your watermelon armies from the Jersey shores; they would cut a much better figure in warring with the crabs and oysters about the Cape of Delaware." A "Jersey Blue" angrily retorted that "the watermelon army of New Jersey [had] ten-inch howitzers for throwing a species of melon very useful for curing a gravel occasioned by whiskey!" From then on this combined federal force would be known, both affectionately and derisively as the "watermelon army."

General Henry "Light Horse Harry" Lee, then governor of Virginia, commanded the force, whose ranks included the governors of Pennsylvania and New Jersey Revolutionary General Dan Morgan, future explorer Meriwether Lewis, five nephews of President Washington, and Alexander Hamilton himself. The

southern wing of the army marched northeastward toward Pennsylvania from Virginia and Maryland, while the right flank proceeded westward from New Jersey and eastern Pennsylvania.

On October 4, President Washington reviewed the northern contingent at Carlisle, Pennsylvania, and his charisma greatly boosted morale. Soldiers and townspeople alike gave the hero of the revolution a royal welcome. One observer noted that "when I saw the President lift his hat to the troops as they passed along, I thought I caught a glimpse of the Revolutionary Scene."

After traveling to Fort Cumberland, Maryland, to review the southern wing of the army, the president returned to Philadelphia. Soon after, the two contingents converged in Bedford, Pennsylvania. Although Lee was left in charge of military operations, Hamilton served as the force's unofficial civilian leader. Officers familiar with Hamilton's ambition noted that the Secretary's tent was bigger than Lee's and that he sometimes gave orders directly to soldiers.

The army's march westward during those brilliant autumn days proved part picnic and part pogrom. As the column crossed the Alleghenies, the Whiskey Rebellion seemed to evaporate ahead of it. Encountering no military opposition, the troops plundered plump chickens, butchered hogs, and imbibed generous portions of the notorious taxable liquid. The officers' diaries and letters read like tourist brochures, noting, for instance, that while Newtown was a poor place for acquiring hay it boasted "mountains of beef and oceans of whiskey."

But the army encountered—and inflicted—hardship as well. Because the huge force constantly out-marched its provisions, rations ran short. The troops' poorly made shoes disintegrated on cold, muddy roads. And the many liberty poles erected along the route served notice of the local citizens' hostility, which often manifested itself in taunts aimed at the soldiers or refusal of food or lodging.

If apprehending suspected leaders of the insurgency for interrogation, the troops could be brutal. On November 13, in what came to be known as the "dreadful night," the New Jersey cavalry dragged 150 suspects from their beds, marched them—some half-clothed and barefooted—through snow and sleet, and incarcerated them in a roofless outdoor pen. General Andrew White, dubbed "Black-beard" for his cruelty, kept his forty captives tied back-to-back in an unheated cellar for two days without food, then herded them like animals through twelve miles of mud and rain.

Because David Bradford[2] and as many as two thousand die-hard rebels fled westward into the wilderness, most of the suspects seized for questioning were not the ringleaders of the uprising. Hamilton and Lee, for instance, interrogated the moderate Hugh Brackenridge intensely for hours before concluding that their prisoner had been trying to temper the rebellion rather than incite it.

In late November, twenty obscure rebels—none of whom had actually been key figures in the uprising—were shipped to Philadelphia for trial. Paraded through the capital's streets on Christmas Day the prisoners looked so wretched that even Presley Neville, son of the besieged excise inspector, felt sorry for them. Ultimately only two suspects were found guilty of treason, and Washington, seeking to appear magnanimous, pardoned both.

Leaving fifteen hundred troops in Pittsburgh to maintain order, the bulk of the watermelon army began its return home in late November. The entire expedition had cost $1,500,000—about one third of the revenues raised by the whiskey tax during its entire life. But cost mattered little given the principles at stake. On January 1, 1795, a "gravely exultant" Washington proclaimed February 19 as a day of thanksgiving for "the reasonable control which has been given to a spirit of disorder in the suppression of the late insurrection."

Indeed, Washington and the Federalists had much to be thankful for. With a relatively painless and largely bloodless military excursion, they had asserted the supremacy of the federal Constitution and ensured that the trans-Appalachian west would remain part of the United States.

The Whiskey Rebellion was a personal triumph for Washington as well. He had placed his political reputation and prestige on the line—and had prevailed. His actions would serve as precedent for John Adams in his handling of the Fries Rebellion in 1799, Andrew Jackson's response to the nullification crisis of the 1830s, and Abraham Lincoln's reaction to secession in 1861.

Ironically the defeat of western Pennsylvanians in the Whiskey Rebellion brought with it the alleviation of many of the region's problems. By spending so much money during its invasion, the watermelon army seeded western Pennsylvania with enough currency to germinate a prosperous commercial economy there. And in the single year following the rebellion, the Jay Treaty reduced Great Britain's Indian agitation and interference on the American western frontier, the Pinckney Treaty secured free trade on the Mississippi from Spain, and the Treaty of Greenville reduced the threat of Indian attack.

Finally by dramatically defining the key political issues of the day—East versus West, agriculture versus commerce, plutocracy versus democracy, order versus liberty—the Whiskey Rebellion fostered the development of a two-party system in American politics. By 1801, with the election of Thomas Jefferson as president, the Republican Party representing many of the principles advocated by insurgents, would gain control of the national government.

Thus, when the Republican Congress in 1802 repealed the hated excise that had started all the fuss, the Whiskey Boys could hoist their first untaxed jugs in ten years and savor sweet victory.

Notes

1. At that time Washington County included what is today Greene County in the southwest corner of the state. Although not playing a central role in the actual insurrection, two other Pennsylvania counties—Bedford and Somerset—are today also associated with the Whiskey Rebellion. Residents of these two counties, which until 1795 comprised Bedford Country, shared their western neighbors' opposition to the excise tax and witnessed the assembling of the army called in to quell the rebellion.

2. After fleeing Pennsylvania, Bradford settled permanently in the Louisiana Territory.

Recommended additional reading: Two excellent book-length narratives of the events described in this article are Thomas P. Slaughter's *The Whiskey Rebellion: Frontier Epilogue to the American Revolution* (Oxford University Press, 1986) and *The Whiskey Rebellion: Southwestern Pennsylvania's Frontier People Test the American Constitution* by Jerry A. Clouse (Pennsylvania Historical and Museum Commission, 1994).

Robert S. Kyff teaches history at Kingswood-Oxford School in West Hartford, Connecticut, and writes a syndicated newspaper column. His article on frontier historian Frederick Jackson Turner appeared in the July/August issues of American History Illustrated.

1796: The First Real Election

BY JOHN FERLING *When George Washington announced that he would retire from office, he set the stage for the nation's first two-party presidential campaign.*

ON THE DAY in April 1789 that he took the oath of office at Federal Hall in New York City as the first president of the United States, George Washington noted in his diary: "I bade adieu to Mount Vernon, to private life, and to domestic felicity and with a mind oppressed with more anxious and painful sensations than I have words to express."

THE BETTMAN ARCHIVE

Throughout the Revolutionary War and the new United States' formative years, John Adams gave tireless service to his country, including eight years as its first vice president. Although he felt entitled to the presidency, Adams, the Federalist candidate, refused to campaign for office.

Washington, who embodied the virtues exalted by his generation, had been given the unanimous vote of the new nation's electors. He had done nothing to promote himself as a candidate for the presidency and had agreed to undertake the mammoth task with the utmost reluctance. Whatever his personal misgivings, Washington's first term in office went smoothly. It was so successful, in fact, that in 1792 he once again received the electors' unanimous endorsement.

Such smooth sailing of the ship of state could not be expected to last, however, and during President's Washington's second term, the United States—and thus its chief executive—began to experience the kinds of problems that plague any government. Relations with the former "mother country" deteriorated until it seemed that another war with Great Britain might be inevitable. And on the domestic front, groups of farmers, especially those in the westernmost counties of Pennsylvania, protested and rebelled against the Washington administration's excise tax on the whiskey that they distilled from their grain, eventually rioting in the summer of 1794.

The hero of America's revolution also suffered personal attacks on his character. Rumors had it that Washington was given to "gambling, reveling, horse-racing and horse whipping" and that he had even taken British bribes while he was commanding American troops.

During the last weeks of 1795, reports spread through Philadelphia—then the national capital—that Washington planned to retire at the conclusion of his second term. It was true that similar rumors had circulated three years before, as the end of his first term drew near, but this time it appeared that he was determined to step down. Nearing his mid-sixties—a normal life span for a man in the eighteenth century—the president longed to retire to the tranquility of Mount Vernon, his beloved home in Virginia.

Although Washington said nothing to John Adams regarding his plans for retirement, his wife Martha hinted to the

THE GRANGER COLLECTION

Republican candidate Aaron Burr of New York, who later gained notoriety by killing political opponent Alexander Hamilton in a duel, ran fourth in the 1796 presidential race.

vice president near Christmas 1795 that her husband would be leaving office. Ten days later, Adams learned that the president had informed his cabinet that he would step down in March 1797.[1] "You know the Consequences of this, to me and to yourself," Adams, aware that he might become the second president of the United States, wrote to his wife Abigail that same evening.

Adam's ascension to the presidency would be neither automatic nor unanimous. Before achieving that high office, he would have to emerge victorious from America's first contested presidential election.

EIGHT YEARS EARLIER, IN SEPTEMber 1787, the delegates to the Constitutional Convention had considered numerous plans for choosing a president. They had rejected direct election by qualified voters because, as Roger Sherman of Connecticut remarked, a scattered population could never "be informed of the characters of the leading candidates." The delegates also ruled out election by Congress. Such a procedure, Gouverneur Morris stated, would inevitably be "the work of intrigue, cabal and of faction."

Finally, the convention agreed to an electoral college scheme, whereby "Each state shall appoint in such manner as the Legislature thereof may direct, a Number of Electors, equal to the whole Number of Senators and Representatives to which the State may be entitled in the Congress." Presidential selection, therefore, would be decided through a state-by-state, rather than a national, referendum.

Each elector chosen by the voters or the legislature of his state would cast votes for two candidates, one of whom had to come from outside his state. The electors' ballots would be opened in the presence of both houses of Congress. If no one received a majority of the votes, or if two or more individuals tied with a majority of the electoral college votes, the members of the House of Representatives would cast ballots to elect the president.[2] Once the president had been decided upon, the candidate from among those remaining who had received the second largest number of electoral votes became the vice president.

The framers of the Constitution believed that most electors would judiciously cast their two ballots for persons of "real merit," as Morris put it. Alexander Hamilton argued in *Federalist 68*—one of a series of essays penned by Hamilton, James Madison, and John Jay to encourage ratification of the Constitution in New York State—that it was a "moral certainty" that the electoral college scheme would result in the election of the most qualified man. Someone skilled in the art of intrigue might win a high state office, he wrote, but only a man nationally known for his "ability and virtue" could gain the support of electors from throughout the United States.

Indeed, the "electoral college" plan worked well during the first two presidential elections in 1788 and 1792, when every elector had cast one of his ballots for Washington. But by 1796, something

unforeseen by the delegates to the Constitutional Convention had occurred; men of different points of view had begun to form themselves into political parties.

The first signs of such factionalism appeared early in Washington's presidency. On one side were the Federalists who yearned for an American society and national government established on the British model. Skeptical of the growing democratization of the new nation, the Federalists desired a centralized national government that would have the strength both to aid merchants and manufacturers and to safeguard America's traditional hierarchical society.

By 1792, Secretary of State Thomas Jefferson and Congressman James Madison—both, like Washington, from Virginia—had taken steps to fashion an opposition party. Jefferson became the acknowledged leader of the new Anti-Federalists, a group soon known as the Democratic-Republican Party because of its empathy for the struggling republic that had emerged from the French Revolution of 1789. This party looked irreverently upon the past, was devoted to republican institutions, sought to give property-owning citizens greater control over their lives, and dreamt of an agrarian nation in which government would be small and weak.

Members of both parties ran candidates in congressional and state races in 1792, but they did not challenge President Washington. Partisanship, however, did surface that year in the contest for the vice presidency. Some Republicans acted behind the scenes in "support… of removing Mr. A," as the clerk of the House noted, mainly because Adams's writings on government included positive statements about the British monarchy. The movement came to naught because it did not have the support of Jefferson, who had known and liked Adams for nearly twenty years. Other Republicans rallied behind George Clinton, the newly elected governor of New York.

The activity of the Republicans threw a scare into the Federalists. Secretary of the Treasury Alexander Hamilton, the acknowledged leader of the Federalists, was so worried that he urged Adams to cut short a vacation and campaign openly against those who were—as he

said—"ill disposed" toward him. Adams, who regarded electioneering with contempt, refused to do so and remained on his farm in Quincy, Massachusetts, until after the electors had cast their ballots.

By March 1796, when Washington finally told his vice president that he would not seek reelection, Adams had decided to run for the office of president. His decision was "no light thing," he said, since he knew that as president he would be subjected to "obloquy, contempt, and insult." He even told Abigail that he believed every chief executive was "almost sure of disgrace and ruin." While she had mixed emotions about his decision, she did not discourage him from running. In fact, she told him that the presidency would be a "flattering and Glorious Reward" for his long years of service. Ultimately Adams decided to seek the office because, he asserted, "I love my country too well to shrink from danger in her service."

As he began his quest, Adams expected formidable opposition, especially from Jefferson. He foresaw three possible outcomes to the election: he might garner the most votes, with Jefferson running second; Jefferson might win and John Jay of New York, long a congressman and diplomat, could finish second; or Jefferson might be elected president, while he was himself reelected vice president. That last scenario was not one Adams was prepared to accept. He decided that he would not serve another term as vice president; if he finished second again, he declared, he would either retire or seek election to the House of Representatives.

Adams considered himself the "heir apparent to President Washington, having languished in the vice presidency—which he described as "the most insignificant office that ever the invention of man contrived or his imagination conceived"—for eight years, awaiting his turn. Furthermore, he believed that no man had made greater sacrifices for the nation during the American Revolution than he. In addition to risking his legal career to protest British policies, he sat as a member of the First Continental Congress for three years and served abroad from 1778–88, making two perilous Atlantic crossings to carry out his

As a South Carolinian, Thomas Pinckney enjoyed southern support. Although he was a Federalist, he suffered from rumors of political maneuvering by Alexander Hamilton, the leader of that party, and failed to get the New England votes that would have enabled him to serve as Adams's vice president.

diplomatic assignments. During that ten years, his public service had forced him to live apart from his wife and five children nearly ninety percent of the time.

Jefferson often proclaimed his disdain for politics, even though he held political office almost continuously for forty years. As 1796 unfolded, he neither made an effort to gain the presidency nor rebuffed the Republican maneuvers to elect him to that office. When he resigned as secretary of state in 1793, Jefferson had said that he did not plan to hold public office again and would happily remain at Monticello, his Virginia estate. But, while he did not seek office in 1796, neither did he say that he would not accept the presidential nomination. Adams—and most Republicans—interpreted Jefferson's behavior as indicating that he wanted to be president.

The Constitution said nothing about how to select presidential nominees. In 1800, the Republican Party would choose its candidates in a congressional nominating caucus; in 1812, the first nominating conventions were held in several states; and the first national nominating convention took place in 1832. But in 1796, the nominees seemed to materialize out of thin air, as if by magic. In

actuality the party leaders decided on the candidates and attempted to herd their followers into line.

The federalists' support centered on Adams and Thomas Pinckney of South Carolina. Pinckney, who had recently negotiated a successful treaty with Spain that established territorial and traffic rights for the United States on the Mississippi River, was chosen for the second slot on the ticket by the party moguls—without consulting Adams—in part because as a Southerner, he might siphon Southern votes from Jefferson.

On the Republican side, Madison confided to James Monroe in February that "Jefferson alone can be started with hope of success, [and we] mean to push him." The Republicans also endorsed Senator Aaron Burr of New York.

All this transpired quietly for Washington did not publicly announce his intention of retiring until the very end of the summer. Not that the parties' plans were a mystery. Before Washington finally informed the nation of his decision on September 19, 1796, in his "Farewell Address"—which was not delivered orally but was printed in Philadelphia's *American Daily Advertiser*—the keenly partisan *Philadelphia Aurora* declared that it "requires no talent at divination to decide who will be candidates.... Thomas Jefferson & John Adams will be the men."

But Washington's address, said congressman Fisher Ames of Massachusetts, was "a signal, like dropping a hat, for the party racers to start." During the next ten weeks, the presidential campaign of 1796 was waged, as Federalists and Republicans—with the exception, for the most part, of the candidates themselves—worked feverishly for victory.

Adams, Jefferson, and Pinckney never left home. While their parties took stands on the major issues of the day these men embraced the classical model of politics, refusing to campaign. They believed that a man should not pursue an office; rather, the office should seek out the man. They agreed that the most talented men—what some called an aristocracy of merit—should govern, but also that ultimate power rested with the people. The qualified voters, or the elected representatives of the people, were capable of selecting the best men

The author of The Declaration of Independence, Thomas Jefferson, became the leader of the Anti-Federalists—otherwise known as the Democratic-Republicans—who opposed ties with Great Britain and admired the ideals of the French Revolution of 1789. He gained the second highest number of electoral votes in 1796, thus becoming the nation's second vice president.

from among the candidates on the basis of what Adams called the "pure Principles of Merit, Virtue, and public Spirit."

Burr alone actively campaigned. Although he did not make any speeches, he visited every New England state and spoke with several presidential electors. Many Federalist and Republican officeholders and supporters spoke at rallies, but most of the electioneering took place through handbills, pamphlets, and newspapers.

The campaign was a rough and tumble affair. The Republicans sought to convince the electorate that their opponents longed to establish a titled nobility in America and that Adams—whom they caricatured as "His Rotundity" because of his small, portly stature—was a pro-British monarchist. President Washington was assailed for supporting Hamilton's aggressive economic program, as well as for the Jay Treaty of 1795, which had settled outstanding differences between the United States and Britain. The *Philadelphia Aurora* went so far as to insist that the president was the "source of all the misfortunes of our country."

The Federalists responded by portraying Jefferson as an atheist and French

Although he was not himself a candidate in the 1796 election, Alexander Hamilton (second from right, above), secretary of the treasury in Washington's first cabinet, played an influential role, supporting John Adams and actively campaigning against Thomas Jefferson.

puppet who would plunge the United States into another war with Great Britain. They also charged that he was indecisive and a visionary. A "philosopher makes the worst politician," one Federalist advised, while another counseled that Jefferson was "fit to be a professor in a college... but certainly not the first magistrate of a great nation." Newspapers such as the *Gazette of the United States* and *Porcupine's Gazette* asserted that Jefferson's election would result in domestic disorder.

Behind-the-scenes maneuvering included a plan by Hamilton, who felt that Pinckney could be more easily manipulated than Adams, to have one or two Federalist electors withhold their votes for Adams. Hearing rumors of the ploy, several New England electors conferred and agreed not to cast a ballot for Pinckney.

Even the French minister to the United States, Pierre Adet, became involved in the election by seeking to convey the impression that a victory for Jefferson would result in improved relations with France. As one historian has noted: "Never before or since has a foreign power acted so openly in an American election."

SIXTEEN STATES TOOK PART IN the balloting. The 138 electors were chosen by popular vote in six states and by the state legislatures of the remaining ten. Seventy votes were required to win a majority.

Adams expected to receive all of New England's 39 votes, but he also had to win all 12 of New York's votes and 19 from the other middle and southern states to win. He concluded that was impossible, especially after learning of Hamilton's machinations. One the eve of the electoral college vote, Adams remarked privately that Hamilton had

"outgeneraled" all the other politicians and stolen the election for Pinckney.

The electors voted in their respective state capitals on the first Wednesday in December, but the law stipulated that the ballots could not be opened and counted until the second Wednesday in February And so for nearly seventy days, every conceivable rumor circulated regarding the outcome of the election. By the third week in December, however, one thing was clear: Jefferson could not get seventy votes. Although 63 electors were Southerners, the South was a two-party region, and it was known that Jefferson had not received a vote from every Southern elector. In addition, because the Federalists controlled the legislatures in New York, New Jersey and Delaware, it was presumed that Jefferson would be shut out in those states.

Beyond that, nothing was certain. Many believed that Pinckney would win, either because of Hamilton's supposed chicanery or because all "the Jeffs," as Ames called the Southern Republican electors, supposedly had cast their second ballot for the South Carolinian in order to ensure that a Southerner succeed Washington. A good number of Americans fully expected that no candidate would get a majority of the votes, thus sending the election to the House of Representatives.

By the end of December, better information arrived in Philadelphia when Ames informed Adams that he had at least 71 electoral votes. On December 28, Jefferson wrote Adams a congratulatory letter and at Washington's final levee in 1796, the First Lady told the vice president of her husband's delight at his victory. Persuaded that he was indeed the victor, an ebullient Adams wrote his wife at year's end that he had "never felt more serene" in his life.

Finally on February 8, 1797, the sealed ballots were opened and counted before a joint session of Congress. Ironically, it was Vice President Adams, in his capacity as president of the Senate, who read aloud the results. The tabulation showed that Adams had indeed garnered 71 votes. Every New England and New York elector had voted for him. The tales about Hamilton's treachery had been untrue; ultimately the former treasury secretary found the prospect of a Jefferson administration too distasteful to risk the subterfuge necessary to defeat Adams, who also got, as expected, all ten votes from New Jersey and Delaware. And in a sense, Adams won the election in the South, having secured nine votes in Maryland, North Carolina, and Virginia.

Jefferson, who finished second with 68 votes, automatically became the new vice president.[3] One Federalist elector in Virginia, the representative of a western district that long had exhibited hostility toward the planter aristocracy voted for Adams and Pinckney as did four electors from commercial, Federalist enclaves in Maryland and North Carolina. Whereas Adams secured enough votes in the South to push him over the top, Jefferson

did not receive a single electoral vote in New England or in New York, New Jersey or Delaware.

Pinckney, not Adams, was the real victim of Hamilton's rumored duplicity. To ensure that the South Carolinian did not obtain more votes than Adams, 18 Federalist electors in New England refused to give him their vote. Had Pinckney received 12 of those votes, the election would have been thrown into the House of Representatives. Instead, he finished third with 59 electoral votes.

Burr polled only thirty votes. Southern Republicans—perhaps sharing the sentiment of the Virginia elector who remarked that there were "traits of character" in Burr which "sooner or later will give us much trouble"—rejected him.

Even among the enfranchised citizens, few bothered to cast ballots in this election. In Pennsylvania, a state in which the electors were popularly chosen, only about one-quarter of the eligible voters went to the polls. But the contest in Pennsylvania was an augury of the political changes soon to come. The Republicans swept 14 of the state's 15 electoral votes, winning in part because they "outpoliticked" their opponents by running better-known candidates for the electoral college and because Minister Adet's intrusive comments helped Jefferson among Quakers and Philadelphia merchants who longed for peace. Many voters had rejected the Federalist Party because they thought of it as a pro-British, pro-aristocratic party committed to an economic program designed to benefit primarily the wealthiest citizens.

And what occurred in Pennsylvania was not unique. Jefferson won more than eighty percent of the electoral college votes in states outside New England that chose their electors by popular vote. In an increasingly democratic United States, the election of 1796 represented the last great hurrah for the Federalist Party.

On March 4, 1797, America's first orderly transferal of power occurred in Philadelphia when George Washington stepped down and John Adams took the oath as the second president of the

United States. Many spectators were moved to tears during this emotional affair, not only because Washington's departure brought an era to a close, but because the ceremony represented a triumph for the republic. Adams remarked that this peaceful event was "the sublimist thing ever exhibited in America." He also noted Washington's joy at surrendering the burdens of the presidency. In fact, Adams believed that Washington's countenance seemed to say: "Ay! I am fairly out and you fairly in! See which of us will be the happiest."

Notes

1. The March 4 date for the beginning of new terms of office went back to tradition begun under the Articles of Confederation and codified by Congressional legislation in 1792. The Twentieth Amendment to the Constitution, ratified in 1933, specified the henceforth Congressional terms would begin on January 3 and that an incoming president and vice president would take their oaths of office at noon on January 20 of the year following their election.

2. Not since 1824 has the winner of a presidential contest been decided by the House of Representatives. In that year, John Quincy Adams gained the presidency when one more than half of the members of the House cast their ballots in his favor, giving him the necessary majority.

3. This first contested presidential election demonstrated a flaw in the Constitution's electoral college scheme since the country now had a Federalist president and a Republican vice president. Four years later, the two Republican candidates, Jefferson and Burr, each received 73 electoral votes. Although it was clear during the election campaign that Jefferson was the presidential candidate and Burr the vice presidential, Burr refused to concede, forcing a vote in the House of Representatives that brought Jefferson into office. To correct these defects the Twelfth Amendment, which provided for separate balloting for president and vice president, was adopted in 1804.

Historian John Ferling is the author of the recently re-released John Adams: A Life *(An Owl Book, Henry Holt and Company, 1996, $17.95 paper).*

Lewis and Clark

Trailblazers Who Opened the Continent

Few Americans better embodied the spirit of adventure and dedication that led 19th-century explorers to brave the perils of an unknown land.

By Gerald F. Kreyche

EVERY SOCIETY has a need for heroes who serve as role models. The U.S. is no exception and has produced its share of them—Pres. Abraham Lincoln, aviator Charles Lindbergh, civil rights leader Martin Luther King, Jr., and the astronauts, to name a few. Heroes belong to the ages, and we can refresh our pride and patriotism by recalling their deeds.

In the early 19th century, two relatively unsung heroes, Meriwether Lewis and William Clark, braved the perils of a vast unknown territory to enlarge knowledge, increase commerce, and establish a relationship with unknown Indians. Their journals produced eight detailed volumes of data ranging from maps, climate, geography, and ethnic observations to the discovery of new species of plants and animals.

In the late 18th century, America's western border was constituted first by the Allegheny Mountains and later the Mississippi River. Little was known of the geography immediately beyond the Father of Waters, and less yet of what lay west of the Missouri River. This was to change, however, for Pres. Thomas Jefferson had an unquenchable yearning for such knowledge and did something about it.

As early as 1784, he conferred with George Rogers Clark about exploring this uncharted area. In 1786 he hired John Ledyard, a former marine associate of British explorer James Cook, to walk from west to east, beginning in Stockholm, Sweden. The intent was to traverse Russia, Alaska, the western Canadian coast, and thence across the Louisiana Territory. Ledyard walked from Stockholm to St. Petersburg, Russia, in two weeks. The Russians stopped him at Irkutsk, Siberia, and Jefferson was disappointed again. Undaunted, Jefferson made plans for Andre Michael to explore the area, but this, too, failed.

After being inaugurated in 1801, Jefferson had the power to make his pet project a reality. He appointed as his private secretary Meriwether Lewis, a well-born young army captain. In January, 1803, in a secret message to Congress, the President asked for funding to realize his exploratory project of what lay between the Missouri River and the Pacific Ocean. The sum of $2,500 was appropriated. (The project eventually was to cost $38,000, an early case of a governmental cost overrun.)

Jefferson asked Lewis to head the project. Lewis had served under William Clark (younger brother of George Rog-

ers Clark) in earlier times and offered him co-leadership of the expedition, designated The Corps of Discovery. Clark accepted Lewis' offer to "participate with him in its fatiegues its dangers and its honors." Clark, no longer on active army status, was told he would receive a regular army captaincy, but Congress refused to grant it. Nevertheless, Lewis designated Clark as captain and co-commander; the expedition's men so regarded him and the journals so record it.

Lewis and Clark were scientist-explorers and singularly complementary. Although both were leaders of men and strict disciplinarians, Lewis was somewhat aloof, with a family background of bouts of despondency; Clark was more the extrovert and father figure. Lewis had great scientific interests in flora, fauna, and minerals, and Clark's surveying and engineering skills fit well with the demands of the expedition. While Lewis tended to view Indians fundamentally as savages, Clark, like Jefferson, saw the Indian as a full member of the human race and child of nature. At all times, the two soldiers were a team, each leading the expedition every other day. No known quarrel between them ever was recorded, although on a few occasions they thought it expedient to separate, probably to cool off and get out of each other's hair.

To prepare for their journey into the unknown, Lewis stayed in the East to study astronomy, plant taxonomy, practical medicine, etc., and to gather equipment from the armory at Harper's Ferry, Va. The supplies would include trading goods such as awls, fishhooks, paints, tobacco twists, Jefferson medals, whiskey, and a generous amount of laudanum (a morphine-like drug). Lewis supervised the building of a 22-foot keelboat needed to take them up the Missouri to a winter quartering place. Additionally, he had his eye out for recruits for the expedition.

Clark went to St. Louis to recruit "robust, helthy, hardy" young, experienced, and versatile backwoodsmen. All were single. The captains needed interpreters, river experts, and hunters able to live under the most demanding conditions. Also sought were men with multiple skills who could do carpentry and blacksmith work and follow orders. With the exception of a hunter-interpreter, George Drouillard, if they were not already in the army, they enrolled in it. Privates received five dollars a month; sergeants, eight dollars. Both leaders and the sergeants kept journals.

On May 14, 1804, the regular group of 29 men, plus a temporary complement of 16 others, set off from the St. Louis area for Mandan, in what is now North Dakota, the site of their winter quarters. With them came Lewis' Newfoundland dog, Scannon, and Clark's body-servant, a black man named York. Clark's journal entry reads, "I set out at 4 o'clock P.M. in the presence of many of the neighboring inhabitants, and proceeded under a jentle brease up the Missourie." Little did they know it would be some 7,200 miles and nearly two and a half years before their return.

The trip upriver was backbreaking, as spring floods pushed the water downstream in torrents. Hunters walked the shores, while the keelboat men alternately rowed, poled, sailed, and rope-pulled the boat against the current. Wind, rain, and hail seemed to meet them at every turn in the serpentine Missouri. Snags and sandbars were everywhere. Bloated, gangrenous buffalo carcasses floated downstream, witnesses to the treachery of thin ice ahead. Often, for security reasons, the expedition party docked at night on small islands, some of which floated away as they embarked in the morning.

Ambassadors of goodwill, they stopped at major Indian villages, counseling peace instead of internecine warfare as well as distributing gifts. At the same time, they questioned the Indians about what lay ahead. Generally, such information was reliable. Tragedy struck at Council Bluffs (now Iowa), where Sgt. Charles Floyd died, probably of a ruptured appendix. He was the only member of the Corps to lose his life. After a proper eulogy, the captains wrote in their journals, as they were to do many times, "We proceeded on." Today, an obelisk marks the general location.

THE MYTH
OF SACAJAWEA

On Nov. 2, 1804, they reached a river confluence about 30 miles north of present-day Bismarck, N.D., and settled in with the Mandan Indians, who welcomed them as security against Sioux attacks. They met Toussaint Charbonneau, a 40-year-old trapper wintering there, who, although ignorant of English, spoke a number of Indian languages. Equally important, he had a teenage wife, Sacajawea, a Shoshone who had been captured and traded by the Hidatsa (Minitari). Her tribe were horse-people and lived near the headwaters of the Missouri, two facts that enticed Lewis and Clark to hire Charbonneau and, as part of the deal, arrange for her to accompany them to the area. It would prove burdensome, though, for she delivered a baby boy, Baptiste, who would go with them. Clark took a liking to him and nicknamed him Pompey, even naming and autographing a river cliff prominence (Pompey's Pillar) after him. Later, Clark was to adopt the boy.

A myth of political correctness tells of Sacajawea being the guide for the expedition. Nothing could be further from the truth, as she was six years removed from her people and, when kidnapped, had been taken on a completely different route than that followed by the explorers. She did know Indian herbs, food, and medicine, though, and her presence and that of her child assured others that this was no war party.

Various factors of luck augured the party's success, such as Clark's flaming red hair and York's black skin and "buffalo hair." These would be items of curiosity to up-river Indians. The Corps also had an acrobat who walked on his hands, a one-eyed fiddler, and an air gun that made no explosion when fired. Some Indians previously thought that sound, not the rifle ball, killed, and could not understand this magic. Lewis' dog always was viewed with larcenous eyes, as Indians used dogs for hauling, camp guards, and eating.

On April 7, 1805, the now seasoned expeditionary force left the village and went northwest for parts unknown. Their vehicles were six small canoes and two large perogues. The extras who accompanied them to the fort returned home with the keelboat. Aboard it were samples of flora and minerals, as well as "barking squirrels" (prairie dogs) and other hides and stuffed animals unknown to the East, such as "beardless goats" (pronghorn antelope). Lewis noted, "I could but esteem this moment of departure as among the most happy of my life."

They entered country that was increasingly wild and where white men had not penetrated. Grizzly bears proved to be a considerable threat, but food was plentiful as buffalo abounded. Frequent entries record that "Musquetoes were troublesum." For a time, they were plagued by the ague, dysentery, and boils. Clark drained a half-pint of fluid from one carbuncle on his ankle. The change of diet from meat to camas bulbs to fish didn't help. They laboriously portaged about 16-miles around Great Falls (now Montana), and reached the three forks of the Missouri River, which they named the Jefferson, Madison, and Gallatin. They were but a short distance northwest of what is now Yellowstone National Park.

Lewis followed the Jefferson fork, as Clark and Sacajawea lingered behind. Seeing some Indians, Lewis tried to entice them with presents to meet him, rolling up his sleeves and pointing to his white skin, calling out, "Tabba-bone." Supposedly, this was Shoshone for "white man," but a mispronunciation could render it as the equivalent of "enemy."

The Shoshone feared this was a trick of their hereditary enemies, the Blackfeet, as they never had seen white men. They scarcely were reassured when Clark, Sacajawea, and the rest of the party caught up with Lewis. However, Sacajawea began to suck furiously on her fingers, indicating she was suckled by these people. She also recognized another woman who had been kidnapped with her, but had escaped. When a council was called, she recognized her brother, Cameawhait, a Shoshone chief. This helped the Corps in trading for needed horses to cross the Continental Divide.

The explorers were disappointed, for they had hoped that, by now, they would be close to the Pacific. This could not be so, though as these Indians knew no white men, and the salmon (a saltwater fish) they had were from trade, not the Indians' own fishing. Staying with the Shoshone for about a week, during which his 31st birthday occurred, Lewis wrote introspectively that he regretted his "many hours . . . of indolence [and now] would live for mankind, as I have hitherto lived for myself."

They hired a Shoshone guide known as "Old Toby" and his sons to cross the treacherous Bitterroot Mountains, the Continental Divide. After doing yeoman's service, the Indians deserted the party without collecting pay near the Clearwater and Snake rivers. The reason was the intention of the explorers to run ferocious rapids that seemed to swallow up everything in their fury. The Corps were able to run them without serious consequence, though. They proceeded on and came upon the Flathead Indians. One Flathead boy knew Shoshone, and a roundabout process of translation was established. Clark spoke English, and an army man translated it to French for Charbonneau. He, in turn, changed it to Minitari, and Sacajawea converted it to Shoshone, which the Flathead boy rendered in his language.

The group pursued the Clearwater River, which met the Snake River. This flowed into the Columbia, which emptied into the Pacific Ocean. Numerous Indian tribes inhabited the Columbia—Clatsop, Chinook, Salish, to name a few. Most were poverty-stricken and a far cry from the healthy Plains Indians. Many were blinded by age 30, as the sun reflecting off the water while they were fishing took its toll. Clark administered ointments and laudanum. Most didn't improve healthwise, but the Indians felt better for the drug and any placebo effects.

Lewis and Clark were overjoyed to find some Columbia River Indians using white men's curse words and wearing metal trinkets. Both only could be from ships' crews that plied the Pacific shores. The Corps were nearing the western end of their journey and, on Nov. 7, 1805, Lewis declared, "Great joy in camp we are in view of the Ocian." They constructed a rude Fort Clatsop (now rebuilt) by the Columbia River estuary near Astoria, in what today is Oregon, and sent parties in all directions to gather information. There was great excitement when reports of a beached whale reached the fort. Sacajawea, who continued with the expedition, insisted on seeing this leviathan, and she was accommodated. The men busied themselves hunting, making salt, and preparing for the journey home. (The salt cairn is reconstructed and preserved not many miles from the fort.)

THE JOURNEY HOME

The Corps entertained the hope that they might make contact with a coastal ship to return them home, and one ship, the *Lydia,* did arrive, but, through a communication failure or lying by the Indians, the captain believed the Corps already had left over land.

On March 23, 1806, after a rainy and miserable winter, the expedition left Fort Clatsop and, along the way, split into three groups hoping to explore more territory. They felt duty-bound to learn as much as they could and agreed to meet at the confluence of the Yellowstone and Missouri rivers. They traded beads and boats for horses and faced the worst kind of pilfering, even Scannon being nearly dog-napped.

Lewis, whose route took him through the territory of the fierce Blackfeet, invited a small party into his camp. One of them tried to steal soldier Reuben Field's gun and was stabbed for his efforts; another stole a horse and, losing all patience, Lewis "at a distance of thirty steps shot him in the belly." Fearing a large war party might be nearby, they traveled the next 60 miles nearly non-stop.

On the way to meet Clark, Lewis and a one-eyed hunter, Peter Cruzatte—both dressed in elkskin—went into the brush to hunt. Lewis was shot in the buttocks by Cruzatte, who apparently mistook him for an elk. The wound was painful, but no vital parts were damaged, although Lewis privately wondered if the shooting was deliberate.

Downriver, Lewis' party met two Illinois trappers searching for beaver. When they learned about the Blackfeet incident, they backtracked and accompanied Lewis to the rendezvous. There, with the captains' permission, they persuaded John Colter, who later discovered Yellowstone, to leave the party and to show them the beaver areas.

Having rendezvoused with the others, all stopped at the Mandan village in which they had spent the previous winter. Here, Toussaint Charbonneau, Sacajawea, and Baptiste (Pompey) parted company. The trapper was paid about $400–500 for his services.

Upon their return home, all the men received double pay and land grants from a grateful Congress. Several of the men went back to trap the area from which they had come, commencing the era of the mountain men. One became a judge and U.S. Senator, and another a district attorney. Others returned to farming. Clark had some sort of fallout with York, and the latter was reduced to a hired-out slave, a considerable fall from the prestigious body-servant status. Eventually, though, he was freed by Clark.

Lewis was appointed governor of the Louisiana Territory, but ran into personal and political problems. He suffered severe bouts of depression, began to drink heavily, and had to dose himself with drugs more frequently. To clear his name, he set off for Washington, but grew increasingly suicidal. He attempted to kill himself several times and finally succeeded on the Natchez Trace, at

Grinder's Stand in Tennessee in 1809. Nevertheless, Meriwether Lewis should be remembered not for the circumstances of his death, but for his life of duty, leadership, and love of country.

Clark was appointed governor and Indian agent of the Missouri Territory. He also was given the rank of brigadier general in the militia—not bad for a bogus captain! He married Julia Hancock, a childhood friend, and named one of their children after Lewis, his comrade-in-arms. After Julia's death, Clark married her cousin, Harriet Kennerly.

Sacajawea died a young woman around 1812 at Ft. Union near the Missouri-Yellowstone confluence. Although she was rumored to die an old lady at Ft. Washakie in Wyoming—indeed, a large gravestone with her name is engraved there on the Shoshone Arapaho Reservation—the evidence for the Ft. Union death is more compelling. Clark adopted young Pompey, who later became a famous linguist and toured Europe in the company of royalty. Eventually, he became a mountain man.

William Clark died in 1838, a good friend of the Indians and, like Meriwether Lewis, a genuine American hero.

Dr. Kreyche, American Thought Editor of USA Today, *is emeritus professor of philosophy, DePaul University, Chicago, Ill.*

Chief Justice Marshall Takes the Law in Hand

Upsetting presidents and setting precedents, he helped forge a nation

By Robert Wernick

If you have been brought up pledging allegiance to the flag and the Republic for which it stands, "one nation under God, indivisible, with liberty and justice for all," there is a certain surprise in reading the Constitution and finding that it nowhere contains the word nation (or, for that matter, the word "God").

The Constitution was ratified—though just barely—in 1788, but it took Americans years to decide what this new political experiment was actually going to be. Would it be a cluster of confederated republics? Or a nation in the traditional sense, like France or England?

Today we know what happened and take the result for granted. Yet in 1804, it was the subject of bitter debate, and no less a personage than Thomas Jefferson, the President of the United States, could write, "whether we remain in one confederacy or form into Atlantic and Mississippi confederations, I believe not very important to the happiness of either part."

The definitive answer binding upon all Americans was written in torrents of blood during the Civil War. Long before that, however, the question began to be answered, and a crucial moment in the gradual shift toward nationhood can be pinpointed to a few months in the year 1803, when two great Americans, who detested each other, took separate and independent actions ensuring that a nation, one and indivisible, would eventually result.

One was Thomas Jefferson, third President. The other was John Marshall, fourth Chief Justice of the United States.

In February of that year Marshall handed down a decision in a case called *Marbury v. Madison*. That was the first time the Supreme Court declared unconstitutional a law that had been duly passed by Congress and signed by the President. A few months after *Marbury v. Madison*, Jefferson deliberately exceeded what he was pretty certain were the powers of the Presidency, as defined by the Constitution, by buying Louisiana from Napoleon Bonaparte for $15 million.

Jefferson, of course, is one of the most famous figures of American history: his face is on the nickel, his memorial stands in white marble splendor across the water from those of Washington and Lincoln. The graces and crotchets of his character are well known to us. John Marshall, on the other hand, remains an austere and shadowy figure, remembered almost exclusively for having written a handful of brilliant and decisive opinions, their details familiar mainly to historians and constitutional scholars. Just lately, however, perhaps because the role and functions of the Supreme Court are under such hot debate, Marshall has reappeared in the public eye. Two books, *John Marshall*, by Jean Edward Smith, and *The Great Chief Justice, by Charles Hobson, have been published*, and they help bring him to life not only as a justice but as a towering, many-talented and very appealing figure.

LIBRARY OF CONGRESS

In a romanticized re-creation, Marshall is characterized as the ill-clad orator; no doubt, he is delivering a persuasive speech to his dapper audience.

Marshall came from the same Virginia stock as Jefferson; they were in fact second cousins once removed. But their political opinions were as far apart as their characters. Unlike Jefferson, a slaveholding aristocrat born to wealth, Marshall, the oldest of 15 children, came from a frontier community and was a self-made man. For various reasons, Jefferson did not fight in the American Revolution. As ambassador to France, he was not at the Constitutional Convention of 1787 (SMITHSONIAN, July 1987). Marshall had played a major role in ratifying the Constitution. He was, moreover, tempered by war, having served with George Washington at Valley Forge, and he had to work hard to establish himself as a successful Virginia lawyer. In 1798 President Washington virtually ordered him to run for a seat in Congress.

Marshall remained something of a frontiersman all his life, tall, rangy, plainspoken, self-reliant. Before being appointed to the Supreme Court by President John Adams, he had not only been a frontline soldier, lawyer and legislator but a land speculator, diplomat, pamphleteer and John Adams' Secretary of State. He briefly became a national hero in 1797 when, as one of three American envoys sent to Paris to negotiate a treaty with the government of revolutionary France, he ran up 3against Citizen, ex-bishop and foreign minister Charles Maurice de Talleyrand. The slippery Talleyrand informed him through three emissaries that America would get the treaty only if it suitably greased Talleyrand's palms. The three emissaries were code-named X, Y and Z. Marshall took the lead in bluntly rebuffing this shakedown as dishonorable and an affront to the United States of America. Marshall's tensely worded message home was later summed up by a memorable sound bite, "Millions for defense, but not one cent for tribute." Americans were so outraged at the French behavior that war was threatened, all of which further stirred Jefferson's ire at Marshall, perhaps because Jefferson had a weakness for all things French. He was angry enough to claim the whole thing was "a dish cooked up by Marshall." The country knew better. On his return Marshall was lavishly honored by enthusiastic crowds in Philadelphia, then the nation's capital.

Jefferson often dealt with him vindictively. He even used to run down what he called Marshall's "lax lounging manners," partly because Marshall was as perfectly at home in a rowdy tavern as in a law court or an elegant Paris salon, and got on with everybody. On election day Marshall was the candidate who offered the best whiskey to the voters. There were no fancy airs about him. He was famous for his slovenly dress. He often did the shopping for his ailing wife, Polly, a rarity for a man of his standing. They liked to tell the story of how a dandified young man came up to him in the Richmond marketplace once and, not knowing him, said, in effect, "Here, my man. Just take this turkey to my house," and flipped him a coin. The Chief Justice of the United States cheerfully pocketed it and delivered the turkey. It was on his way.

Jefferson, by contrast, lived beyond his means and was always in debt. He envisioned himself as the representative of poor farmers and the slave-owning, agrarian South, telling them that moneyed interests and manufacturers in the Northeastern cities were up to no good. The Louisiana Purchase notwithstanding, Jefferson thought—like some extreme conservatives of today—that the government had no right to do anything not spelled out in the Constitution.

Marshall had learned sacredness of contracts and the value of sound money as a self-made lawyer. During the starvation winter at Valley Forge, Marshall watched local farmers selling food to the British in Philadelphia—who had real money to pay for it—rather than accept the worthless paper issued by the Continental Congress, which did not have the right to tax. He had a lifelong conviction that a country needs a central government with power and responsibility enough to override local interests.

This was the view of his political party, the Federalists, who believed that the Constitution had authorized the formation of a federal government able to pay the country's debts and provide for its defense. They cited the Preamble to the Constitution as well as Article 1, Section 8, which both asserted that the document's purpose was to "provide for the common Defense and general Welfare." For Federalists, that seemed to cover all sorts of federal initiatives. Jefferson and his party, the Republicans, hated the very idea.

For Jefferson the states were sovereign. It was thus up to any individual state to determine the extent of its powers in settling disputes between the federal and state governments. Though Marshall was not an extreme Federalist, he saw that as a recipe for anarchy. Such decisions, it followed, could best be made by an independent judiciary. Judges, presumably, had nothing to gain from their actions; they alone could be impartial umpires. The heart of the judiciary was the Supreme Court.

In those early years of the Republic, however, the Supreme Court had none of the authority it enjoys today. It heard cases for a few weeks each year; the judges also had to serve as circuit court judges in various legal districts. When gathered in the raw city of Washington they all lived together in a ramshackle boarding-house. Even when the Capitol eventually went up, the Court's quarters were far from supreme; a first-floor committee room served until 1810, and then the justices found themselves in a dark, cramped space beneath the magisterial halls of Congress.

The justices had a tradition in their conferences; they would have wine only when the weather was bad. If it was sunny out, though, Marshall would sometimes say to his colleagues: "Our jurisdiction extends over so large a territory that the doctrine of chances makes it certain that it must be raining somewhere."

Marshall's charm, his taste in wine and whiskey, along with his formidable intellect and legal learning, won the support of colleagues, many of whom, as the years went by, were expressly appointed to disagree with him. In years on the bench he was obliged to write only one dissenting opinion in a constitutional case.

John Adams appointed him Chief Justice shortly after being defeated by Jefferson in the Presidential election of 1800. Marshall was then Secretary of State, and Adams asked him to stay on till the new Republican administration took over on March 4, 1801. Adams appointed other Federalists at the last minute as well, including one William Marbury, named justice of the peace for the District of Columbia. The nomination was approved by the Senate the day before Jefferson's inauguration. Marbury's commission was duly made out and signed by President Adams at the very end of his term. As Secretary of State, Marshall affixed the great seal of the United States to it. But in the rush of events leading up to the transfer of power, he left it on his desk and didn't send it out.

The Court had a tradition in their conferences; they would have wine only when the weather was bad.

Jefferson was an intensely partisan politician, and he was greatly annoyed by the last-minute appointments of Federalist judges. He regularly accused Federalists of wanting to establish a monarchy and cozy up to Great Britain. He wanted to be rid of all Federalists, Marshall especially.

Jefferson simply ordered that the commissions not be delivered. Marbury was out of the job, and after nine months he turned to the law. He requested that the Court issue a writ of mandamus (in Latin, "we command"), which by law compels a government official to perform a duty. Marbury wanted the new Secretary of State, James Madison, to be forced to deliver to him his duly signed and sealed commission. The result was *Marbury v. Madison*, a case that called forth heated political invective between Federalists and Republicans. It was also a ticklish matter for the new Chief Justice, who handled it with the intellectual grip, clarity of reasoning and political adroitness that would mark his whole career. His method was always to narrow his focus, brushing aside the extraneous, until he got to

the precise point on which a case turned. In Marbury, he managed to find an elegant legal solution that gave something to both sides.

Article 3 of the Constitution had established a Supreme Court but left the organization of other courts to be defined by Congress. An early attempt was the Judiciary Act of 1789, which, in addition to creating some district and circuit courts, in Section 13 took up some of the Supreme Court's jurisdictions, and granted it the power under certain circumstances to issue writs of mandamus "to persons holding office under the authority of the United States."

Marshall found that Marbury clearly had a right to his commission, it having been signed by the President. He had, indeed, been illegally deprived of it by the government. But, Marshall reasoned, in the case at hand the Supreme Court had no power to issue a writ of mandamus, ordering the government to deliver it. Why? Because Section 13 of the Judiciary Act unconstitutionally enlarged the Court's original jurisdiction. The whole of the new nation's laws should depend on the Constitution, so Congress, he reasoned, could not change the jurisdictions and powers of the Court as a matter of political will. Since the power of the Supreme Court to issue a writ of mandamus did not apply, the Court could do nothing for Marbury.

The Republicans at first were delighted. Marshall, after all, had ruled in their favor and Federalist Marbury was out of a job. Moreover, the practical effect of his finding seemed to limit, rather than extend, the Court's power. So the Republicans failed to realize that Marshall's ruling had created a judicial precedent that resounds heavily through our history, especially today. For the first time the Supreme Court had invoked the principle that under the terms of the Constitution it could overturn as unconstitutional a law passed by Congress and signed by a President. It would be 54 years, and long after Marshall's death, before the Supreme Court struck down another law passed by Congress (the Dred Scott Case, argued in 1856–57). The precedent had been set, and in the law precedent counts for almost everything.

Nowadays, though supporters may grouse when the Court refuses to approve some radical reform that they think would render the country far better, everyone takes it for granted that the Supreme Court has the last word. Instead of challenging that right, each side tries to pack the Court with justices who see things their way. The process of matching laws against the Constitution, known as judicial review, is now standard operating procedure. In 1803 it was a defining moment for the Court. The Constitution nowhere expressly states that the Supreme Court has authority to impose its interpretation on the President or Congress.

If Jefferson failed to see what Marshall's decision would mean in the long run, it may have been because the President was involved in a deal with Napoleon that, in May 1803, resulted in the Louisiana Purchase, the acquisition of more than a fourth of what is now the United States.

In effect the agreement guaranteed peace and almost unlimited expansion and prosperity for the American people, at a bargain-basement price. The only trouble was that Jefferson felt sure that the purchase was unconstitutional. After all, a central tenet of his political philosophy was the idea that the federal government could not do a single thing that was not specifically authorized in the Constitution. Jefferson believed the country consisted of sovereign states that retained their sovereignty even after joining the Republic and ratifying the Constitution. He knew that the clause in the Constitution giving the President, with the consent of the Senate, the right to make treaties (Article 2, Section 2) could be stretched to imply that it was legal to annex 828,000 square miles of territory. But if that was so, then other phrases in the Constitution might be made to imply all sorts of things—as they are today. The Constitution would be turned, the President said, into a blank sheet of paper on which one could write anything one wanted.

If he didn't grab Louisiana, however, his career might be ruined, and his party's future as well, for people were overwhelmingly in favor of it. As many Presidents have done since, he found that principles that had been proclaimed rigid and unchangeable when he was out of power became somewhat more supple when he was actually running the country. He and Congress quietly slipped the constitutional issue under the rug.

The trial of Aaron Burr, a former Vice President, set Jefferson and Marshall further at odds with each other

---

Jefferson hoped that the Louisiana precedent would be soon forgotten, but it was not to be. After the War of 1812, Congress had voted to spend 5 million federal dollars on "internal improvements"—building roads and digging canals. Jefferson's successor, James Madison, vetoed the bill. "The power to regulate commerce among the several states," he wrote, "cannot include a power to construct roads and canals, and to improve the navigation of water-courses in order to facilitate, improve, and secure such a commerce.... To refer the power in question to the clause 'to provide for the common defense and general welfare' would be contrary to the established and consistent rules of interpretation."

Madison's veto was sustained, despite a pointed question put by Senator John C. Calhoun, "On what principle can the purchase of Louisiana be justified?" But—except where slavery was concerned—the tide was beginning to run against "strict construction," and states' rights. People wanted those roads and canals, along with all sorts of other services; and in the long run they were willing to defer to the national government to get them. What was needed, it turned out, was a "broad construction" of the kind that Marshall consistently placed on the text of the Constitution and that allowed the United States to grow into the great commercial-industrial nation it became—rather than the collection of rural communities of which Jefferson dreamed.

In case after case Marshall kept whittling away at the theory of states' rights. Jefferson could only look on in horror as the black-robed justice, appointed for life, did his work. In vain, as seats on the Supreme Court became vacant, did Jefferson and his successors appoint good Republicans to the Supreme Court. Under the driving logic of the Chief Justice, the newcomers

duly studied the Constitution and ended by regularly voting on the nationalist side.

Jefferson was often overwhelmed by Marshall's powers of intellectual persuasion. "So great is his sophistry you must never give him an affirmative answer," he said, "or you will be forced to grant his conclusion. Why, if he were to ask me if it were daylight or not, I'd reply, 'Sir, I don't know, I can't tell.'" Through all the last 20 years of his life, Jefferson saw his party—by then they called themselves Democrats—win all the Presidential elections, till it became for a while the only effective political party. Still, Marshall and his court gained in judicial prestige as they established the judicial branch of the government as the umpire of disputes between the conflicting powers of the state and federal governments.

In 1807, Aaron Burr, who uttered the immortal phrase "Great souls care little for small morals," and who had been Vice President in Jefferson's first term, was picked up on the Mississippi River with nine longboats and 60 adventurers and charged with treason. He claimed he was innocent, but Jefferson was convinced it was part of a plot to threaten the union by creating an independent empire in the Mississippi Valley. When Burr went on trial in Richmond with Justice Marshall presiding as a circuit court judge in Virginia, Burr's defense lawyers asked the court to subpoena certain papers in Jefferson's files.

The President was outraged. Using excuses that are all too familiar today, he refused to hand over the papers, saying they contained state secrets; besides, he argued, a President was not bound to be at the beck and call of a mere judge. Marshall issued the subpoena, a decision that still reverberates in today's newspaper headlines. Though he conceded that as President, Jefferson deserved special treatment because he might have more important things to do, he insisted that under the Constitution the President of the United States is a citizen and not above the law. And thus, like anybody else, obliged to comply with a subpoena. In the end, after threatening to get Marshall thrown off the bench, Jefferson sent the papers—saving what face he could by not formally answering the subpoena.

The jury ultimately handed in a verdict of "Not Guilty." But throughout the proceedings, Jefferson raged against Marshall, writing that the case proved the "error in our Constitution, which makes any branch independent of the nation," and that only the "tricks of the judges" had stood between Burr and the gallows. Marshall, for his part, remained impassive, saying the "court feels no inclination to comment."

Case after case followed, most of them routine, but some inaugurating changes in the very nature of the country. In all of them Marshall followed two fundamental principles. The first was that it was up to the courts to protect the rights of the individual in the face of the massed powers of government, notably the right to keep and enjoy one's own property. The three crucial rights were to life, liberty and property, according to John Locke, who influenced the makers of the Constitution, the other two being guaranteed by the right not to have property taken by the state—except, as the Fifth Amendment allows, under certain limited circumstances and with due recompense. Marshall's second principle involved establishing the extent of federal authority over the states.

In 1810 Marshall received the case of *Fletcher v. Peck*, involving litigation that had been dragging on for 15 years about the Yazoo lands—a plot of some 35 million acres, including most of Alabama and Mississippi. The land had been sold by the legislature of Georgia to a syndicate of speculators for $500,000, a price of 1 ½ cents per acre. When it was later learned that all but one of the legislators had profited financially from the deal, angry voters threw them all out and elected new ones. The new legislature repealed the act authorizing the sale and ordered the original copy of it burned in a public square. In the meantime, hundreds of more or less innocent private individuals had bought pieces of the land, and wanted their money back. The Supreme Court decided that the motives of the legislators who had voted the original act were irrelevant. The State of Georgia had made a valid contract with the purchasers, and could not declare ownership of property null and void.

Eventually Congress voted $5 million to pay off the Yazoo claimants and bought the land itself, incidentally making a handsome profit for the federal government. Marshall had established once and for all that when a state makes a contract, it is required, like anyone else, to keep it.

In 1819 he took up another epoch-making case, *Dartmouth College v. Woodward*. The college had been privately owned by a self-perpetuating board of trustees under a charter incorporated in 1769 by the British crown. In 1816 a political squabble caused the state legislature to, in effect, take over the college from its trustees. With Daniel Webster as their attorney, the trustees sued and Marshall agreed with them. The original charter, he held, was a contract, and under Article I, Section 10 of the Constitution, no state had the right to pass any "law impairing the Obligation of Contracts."

Gibbons v. Ogden was once described as the "emancipation proclamation of American Commerce."

The state had no more right to break its contract with a corporation than with an individual; a corporation, in fact, must be seen legally as something like an immortal individual. This decision had the long-range effect of keeping corporations safe from capricious interference by legislators. Corporations were still a relatively new and untested form of social organization. By the end of the 18th century, American states had issued charters for only 310 corporations, and only 8 of them were for commercial purposes (the rest having religious, educational or political aims). After the *Dartmouth College* decision, the number of corporations would rise exponentially till, by the end of the 19th century, they dominated the American economy.

In the same year, Marshall wrote the unanimous decision *McCulloch v. Maryland*, which has been described as the most important case in the history of the Supreme Court because it definitively established the priority of federal law over state law. It involved the Second Bank of the United States, which was chartered by Congress in 1816 and served as the repository

for the public funds. But it was basically a private institution that competed with banks chartered by the various states. Banks in the state of Maryland did not appreciate the competition, and so Maryland decided to levy a heavy stamp tax on all banks "not chartered by the legislature," meaning the Second Bank of the United States.

Maryland argued that the federal government was created by the states, and that state law took precedence over federal law in every matter, such as banking, not specifically cited in the Constitution. Marshall, on the other hand, determined that the Constitution was not made by the states but by the people ("We, the people of the United States,... do ordain and establish..."). Any act of the federal government not directly contrary to the Constitution therefore was the law of the land, whatever a state, or the Supreme Court, might think of its merits. Coining the famous phrase, "The power to tax involves the power to destroy," Marshall declared that the Maryland tax on a bank established by the U.S. Government was void.

In 1824, he struck another devastating blow to states' rights.

It was in the case of *Gibbons v. Ogden*, in a decision once described as the "emancipation proclamation of American commerce," that Marshall's decision nullified a law by which the State of New York granted a monopoly on the use of its waters to the line of steamboats belonging to Robert Fulton and his partner, Robert Livingston. The law had been used to restrain competition by barring a rival line owned by Thomas Gibbons from making the crossing between New Jersey and New York City. This, Marshall held, was in flagrant violation of the constitutional provision giving Congress the power to "regulate Commerce... among the several States." All of the now immense regulatory apparatus of the modern American government had its inception in this judgment.

The effect of all such cases was to prevent the states from ever erecting economic walls around their borders. That America moved so rapidly from an overwhelmingly agricultural society to the highly urbanized industrialized and mobile one it would become is in good part owing to the way the Marshall court cleared away efforts to put obstacles in the way of the free flow of trade and people across state boundaries. No wonder Marshall has been described as a definer of the nation.

There were things that Marshall could not do. Judicial conservative though he was, he held views in advance of his time, believing in the equality of women and detesting slavery. But as a judge bound by the laws of the land, there was not much he could do about either, though in 1829 in *Boyce v. Anderson* he ruled that "a slave has volition, and has feelings.... He cannot be stowed away as a common package. In the nature of things, and in his character, he resembles a passenger, not a package of goods."

He was also indignant about the fate of the Indian nations being dispossessed of their land to make room for the westward movement. The Cherokees in Georgia had done their best to adjust to the new way of life by abandoning hunting for agriculture and writing a constitution for themselves based on that of the United States. The State of Georgia was nevertheless determined to get rid of them. Marshall was powerless to intervene, but he struck a blow in 1832 in *Worcester v. Georgia* when he declared the Georgia statutes relative to the Indians "repugnant to the Constitution, laws, and treaties of the United States." He ordered the release of Samuel Worcester and Elihu Butler, missionaries who had been arrested and detained for interfering with Georgia's Indian policies.

The State of Georgia ignored the order, and President Andrew Jackson is reported to have said, "Well, John Marshall has made his decision, now let him enforce it." The Cherokees lost all their land and had to embark on their long, tragic march a thousand miles to the west.

Jefferson died on July 4, 1826, on the 50th anniversary of the adoption of the Declaration of Independence he had mostly written. In Philadelphia, the great Liberty Bell tolled to mark his passing. Marshall died in Philadelphia two days after the Fourth of July, nine years later, and to mourn his passing they rang the Liberty Bell yet again.

The two men died unreconciled, each fearful of his country's future. Jefferson saw his beloved union of self-reliant states being pressed "at last into one consolidated mass" by the decisions of the Marshall court. Marshall glumly watched the electoral triumphs of the states' rights candidates while yielding "slowly and reluctantly to the conviction that the Constitution cannot last. The Union," he said, "has been prolonged thus far by miracles. I fear they cannot continue."

In his 74 articles for SMITHSONIAN, *on everything from goats to the Spanish Civil War, the author has exercised a lot of judicial restraint.*

From *Smithsonian*, November 1998, pp. 156-160, 162-173. © 1998 by Robert Wernick. Reprinted by permission.

Rebecca Lukens: Woman of Iron

In 1825 Rebecca Lukens took over her late husband's iron mill. The company still thrives—a testament to the managing abilities of this pioneering woman CEO.

By Joseph Gustaitis

In 1810, when she was sixteen, Rebecca Pennock was a dreamy, romantic girl, fond of appreciating nature's picturesque beauty from the back of a horse and bounding "over hill and dale as wild, happy, and joyous as youth could make me." By 1840, however, Rebecca Pennock Lukens had become a business-woman renowned for her shrewdness—an entrepreneur on the cusp of the Industrial Revolution in the United States and the owner of a thriving steel mill on the banks of Pennsylvania's Brandywine River.

Rebecca was born on January 6, 1794, to Martha and Isaac Pennock, whose family had been in Pennsylvania since the days of William Penn. Although Isaac had been deeded three hundred acres of farmland by his father in 1792, he saw opportunity in the iron business and wanted nothing to do with farming. Recognizing that the new United States, free from restrictions that had been imposed during the colonial era, would no longer have to buy industrial wares from Great Britain, he proceeded to establish an iron works known as the Federal Slitting Mill on Bucks Run some four miles from Coatesville.[1]

Another area resident, Jesse Kersey, was inspired by the opening of the Lancaster Turnpike to develop a community on land owned by his father-in-law, Moses Coates, that would attract residents and industry. He formed a partnership with Isaac Pennock in 1810 and together they purchased 110 acres of Coates's land. Pennock converted a saw mill on the property into an iron works,

calling it the Brandywine Iron Works and Nail Factory after the pleasant river that ran alongside it and provided the water power that kept the machinery humming. By 1817 Isaac had become the sole proprietor of the business.

As a child, Rebecca enjoyed considerable freedom, finding special pleasure in the company of three nearby older cousins, a boy and two girls. With them she roved the countryside, and from them she acquired her first taste of the joys of learning. At twelve she was sent to boarding school and then a year later to another institution, where, she later recalled, "life began to open new charms to me."

When she returned home at sixteen, Rebecca, as the oldest child, was called upon to help raise her six younger siblings, especially the baby. She took a liking to the infant, but missed her studies and garnered solace in solitary reading. Soon permitted to return to a school in Wilmington, Delaware, she demonstrated a characteristic mix of practicality and romance by excelling in chemistry and French.

When Rebecca met Dr. Charles Lloyd Lukens, he had a medical practice in Abington, Pennsylvania. At their first meeting, Rebecca wrote, he "bowed with a peculiar grace, and for a moment my eyes rested on his interesting face and his tall and commanding figure." She was smitten and never ceased to regard Dr. Lukens with anything but deep love. They were married in 1813.

Dr. Lukens gave up his medical practice and joined his new father-in-law's iron business. By around 1817—the

same time that Isaac became the sole owner of the works—he leased the operation to Lukens, explaining to Rebecca that she would inherit the business when he died.[2] The former physician set about transforming himself into an iron-maker. The United States was then entering an expansive, optimistic period. Although the country was already feeling the frictions that would later lead to civil war, its mood was progressive and forthright, as states west of the Alleghenies were ushered into the Union. Mills and factories sprouted as the young republic began developing its industrial muscle. An enterprising man could go far, and Lukens was well positioned.

This was the beginning of the Age of Steam. And, steam power requires boilers, which, in turn, require iron plate. In 1818, Lukens's mill became the first in the United States to roll iron boiler plate. Orders came in from steamboat manufacturers, and the Brandywine Iron Works became one of the world's most renowned makers of rolled iron and steel.

In late March 1825, Lukens received his most prestigious commission. John Elgar of York, Pennsylvania, needed iron "of the best quality and sound" in order to build an iron-hulled steamboat to ply the Susquehanna River. Lukens' iron fit the bill. The *Codorus*, the first steamer to operate on the river, was launched in November, but Lukens was not there to see it. That summer, he died at age thirty-nine, leaving Rebecca with two children and one more on the way.

Lukens's love for his wife, it seems, also included a keen appreciation of her talents. For it was his idea—and his dying request—that she carry on the business. For Rebecca, it was not only a time of grief, but a time of peril. The iron works was in debt and in need of repair. As well, her family was not happy about her running the firm. As she later put it, "Necessity is a stern taskmistress; my every want gave me courage." Lukens's brother Solomon took over the supervision of the business's day-to-day affairs, but Rebecca was the sole manager and owner.

So far, most of Brandywine Iron Works' business was in the making of iron plate for ships, but only a year after Rebecca took over the firm, the first railway steam locomotive in the United States was run on a small track in Hoboken, New Jersey. Rebecca had the foresight to see in the new railways—such as the Philadelphia & Columbia Railroad begun in the 1830s—opportunity for her business, and Brandywine started manufacturing iron for locomotives.

During the Panic of 1837—in reality a full-blown depression that plagued the country for six years—Rebecca refused to lay workers off, but instead set them to repairing the mill or working on her farm. When there was no cash, she paid them in produce. "The difficulties of the times throw a gloom on everything," she wrote. "All is paralyzed—business at a stand."

Rebecca survived, and by the mid-1840s she was able to think about stepping down. She had paid off all debts, solved the legal problems caused by her father's ambiguous will, and turned the business into the top boiler-plate company in the United States. Moreover, two of her daughters had married husbands who were well able to shoulder the firm's burdens. As she contemplated her achievements, she said, "I had built a very superior mill, though a plain one, and our character for making boiler iron stood first in the market, hence we had as much business as we could do.... There was difficulty and danger on every side. Now I look back and wonder at my daring."

On December 10, 1854, five years after she retired from managing the firm, Rebecca died. The company that she built—Lukens Steel—still thrives on the banks of the Brandywine River and is renowned for steel plate. Rebecca herself has not been forgotten. January 6, 1994—the bicentennial of her birth—was proclaimed "Rebecca Lukens Day" by the Pennsylvania State Senate. Three months later, she was inducted into the National Business Hall of Fame at a banquet in New York City.

Notes

1. A slitting mill was so named because it produced iron sheets that were then slit into strips to make such items as barrel hoops and wheel rims.

2. Isaac Pennock died in 1824.

This article was told by Joseph Gustaitis and originally published in American History Magazine *in April 1999. New York writer Joseph Gustaitis is a frequent contributor to* American History *magazine.*

Andrew Jackson Versus the Cherokee Nation

"Old Hickory" had been an Indian fighter, and he continued the struggle as president. His new weapon was the Indian Removal Act, which would force Eastern tribes to relocate west of the Mississippi.

By Robert V. Remini

The great Cherokee Nation that had fought the young Andrew Jackson back in 1788 now faced an even more powerful and determined man who was intent on taking their land. But where in the past they had resorted to guns, tomahawks, and scalping knives, now they chose to challenge him in a court of law. They were not called a "civilized nation" for nothing. Many of their leaders were well educated; many more could read and write; they had their own written language, thanks to Sequoyah, a constitution, schools, and their own newspaper. And they had adopted many skills of the white man to improve their living conditions. Why should they be expelled from their lands when they no longer threatened white settlements and could compete with them on many levels? They intended to fight their ouster, and they figured they had many ways to do it. As a last resort they planned to bring suit before the Supreme Court.

Prior to that action, they sent a delegation to Washington to plead their cause. They petitioned Congress to protect them against the unjust laws of Georgia that had decreed that they were subject to its sovereignty and under its complete jurisdiction. They even approached the President, but he curtly informed them that there was nothing he could do in their quarrel with the state, a statement that shocked and amazed them.

So the Cherokees hired William Wirt to take their case to the Supreme Court. In the celebrated *Cherokee Nation v. Georgia* he instituted suit for an injunction that would permit the Cherokees to remain in Georgia without interference by the state. He argued that they constituted an independent nation and had been so regarded by the United States in its many treaties with them.

Speaking for the majority of the court, Chief Justice John Marshall handed down his decision on March 18, 1831. Not sur-

prisingly, as a great American nationalist, he rejected Wirt's argument that the Cherokees were a sovereign nation, but he also rejected Jackson's claim that they were subject to state law. The Indians were "domestic dependent nations," he ruled, subject to the United States as a ward to a guardian. Indian territory was part of the United States but not subject to action by individual states.

When the Cherokees read Marshall's decision they honestly believed that the Nation had won the case, that Georgia lacked authority to control their lives and property, and that the courts would protect them. The Supreme Court, the Principal Chief told his people, decided "in our favor." So they stayed right where they were, and missionaries encouraged them to stand fast.

But they figured without Andrew Jackson—the man the Cherokees called Sharp Knife—and the authorities of Georgia. In late December 1830, the state passed another law prohibiting white men from entering Indian country after March 1, 1831, without a license from the state. This move was obviously intended to keep interfering clergymen from inciting the Indians to disobey Georgia law. Eleven such missionaries were arrested for violating the recent statute, nine of whom accepted pardons from the governor in return for a promise that they would cease violating Georgia law. But Samuel A. Worcester and Dr. Elizur Butler refused the pardon, and Judge Augustin S. J. Clayton sentenced them to the state penitentiary, "there to endure hard labor for the term of four years." They appealed the verdict and their case came before the Supreme Court.

On March 3, 1832, Marshall again ruled in *Worcester v. Georgia,* declaring all the laws of Georgia dealing with the

Cherokees unconstitutional, null, void, and of no effect. In addition he issued a formal mandate two days later ordering the state's superior court to reverse its decision and free the two men.

Jackson was presently involved in a confrontation with South Carolina over the passage of the Tariffs of 1828 and 1832. The state had nullified the acts and threatened to secede from the Union if force were used to make her comply with them. The last thing Jackson needed was a confrontation with another state, so he quietly nudged Georgia into obeying the court order and freeing Butler and Worcester. A number of well-placed officials in both the state and national governments lent a hand and the governor, Wilson Lumpkin, released the two men on January 14, 1833.

With the annoying problem of the two missionaries out of the way, both Georgia and Jackson continued to lean on the Cherokees to get them to remove. "Some of the most vicious and base characters that the adjoining states can produce" squatted on their land and stole "horses and other property" and formed a link with as many "bad citizens" of the Cherokee Nation "as they can associate into their club." Missionaries decried what was happening to the Cherokees. If only "whites would not molest them," wrote Dr. Elizur Butler in *The Missionary Herald.* They have made remarkable progress in the last dozen years and if left alone they can and will complete the process toward a "civilized life."

Ross resolutely resisted any thought of leading his people from their ancient land into a god-forsaken wilderness.

But allowing eastern Indians full control of their eastern lands was virtually impossible in the 1830s. There was not army enough or will enough by the American people to bring it about. As Jackson constantly warned, squatters would continue to invade and occupy the land they wanted; then, if they were attacked, they would turn to the state government for protection that usually ended in violence. All this under the guise of bringing "civilization" to the wilderness.

Even so, the Cherokees had a strong leader who had not yet given up the fight. They were led by the wily, tough, and determined John Ross, a blue-eyed, brown-haired mixed-blood who was only one-eighth Cherokee. Nonetheless he was the Principal Chief, and a most powerful force within the Nation. He was rich, lived in a fine house attended by black slaves, and had influence over the annuities the United States paid to the tribal government for former land cessions. His appearance and lifestyle were distinctly white; in all other respects he was Indian.

From the beginning of Jackson's administration Ross urged his people to stand their ground and remain united. "Friends," he told his people, "I have great hopes in your firmness and that you will hold fast to the place where you were raised. Friends if you all unite together and be of one mind there is no danger."

And the Cherokees cheered his determination. They approved wholeheartedly of his leadership and they took comfort in what he said. So, with the Nation solidly behind him, Ross resolutely resisted any thought of leading his people from their ancient land into a god-forsaken wilderness.

John Ridge, a leader of the Treaty Party, was assassinated by opponents in 1839.

Still the Cherokees held out, even though even they had begun to feel the unrelenting pressure. A so-called Treaty Party emerged within the Nation, made up of chiefs and headmen who understood Jackson's inflexible will and had decided to bow to his wishes and try to get the best treaty possible. They were led by very capable, hard-headed, and pragmatic men, including the Speaker of the Cherokee National Council, Major Ridge; his son, the educated and politically ambitious John Ridge; and the editor of the Cherokee *Phoenix,* Elias Boudinot.

John Ridge took a leading role in the emergence of the Treaty Party, for when the *Worcester* decision was first handed down he instantly recognized that Chief Justice Marshall had rendered an opinion that abandoned the Cherokees to their inevitable fate. So he went to Jackson and asked him point-blank whether the power of the United States would be exerted to force Georgia into respecting Indian rights and property. The President assured him that the government would do nothing. He then advised Ridge "most earnestly" to go home and urge his people to remove. Dejected, the chief left the President "with the melancholy conviction that he had been told the truth.

From that moment he was convinced that the only alternative to save his people from moral and physical death, was to make the best terms they could with the government and remove out of the limits of the states. This conviction he did not fail to make known to his friends, and hence rose the *'Treaty Party.'"*

The members of this Treaty Party certainly risked their lives in pressing for removal, and indeed all of them were subsequently marked for assassination. Not too many years later, Elias Boudinot and John Ridge were slain with knives and tomahawks in the midst of their families, while Major Ridge was ambushed and shot to death.

John Ross, on the other hand, would not yield. As head of the National Party that opposed removal he was shrewd enough to recognize immediately that the President would attempt to play one party off against the other. "The object of the President is unfolded & made too plain to be misunderstood," he told the Nation. "It is to create divisions among ourselves, break down our government, our press & our treasury, that our cries may not be heard abroad; that we may be deprived of the means of sending delegations to Washington City to make known our grievances before Congress…and break down the government which you [Cherokees] have, by your own free will & choice, established for the security of your freedom & common welfare."

Under the circumstance, Ross decided to go to Washington and request a meeting with the President in order to try again to arrange some accommodation that would prevent the mass relocation of his people to what was now the new Indian Territory, which Congress had created in 1834 and which eventually became the state of Oklahoma. He was tormented by the knowledge that his people would be condemned to a "prairie badly watered and only skirted on the margin of water courses and poor ridges with copes of wood." Worse, districts would be laid out for some "fifteen or twenty different tribes, and all speaking different languages, and cherishing a variety of habits and customs, a portion civilized, another half civilized and others uncivilized, and these congregated tribes of Indians to be regulated under the General Government, by no doubt white rulers." The very thought of it sent shivers through Ross's entire body.

Since he had fought with Jackson at the Battle of Horseshoe Bend during the Creek War he reckoned that his service during that battle would provide him with a degree of leverage in speaking with the President. And, as Principal Chief, he could speak with the duly constituted authority of the Cherokee Nation as established under the Cherokee Constitution of 1827.

He had another reason for requesting the interview. He had heard a rumor that Jackson had commissioned the Reverend John F. Schermerhorn, an ambitious cleric who had assisted in the removal of the Seminoles from Florida, to negotiate with Ridge and his associates and see if a deal could be worked out that would result in a treaty. Definitely alarmed, Ross asked to speak with the President at which time he said he would submit his own proposal for a treaty.

Jackson never liked Ross. He called him "a great villain." Unlike Ridge and Boudinot, said Jackson, the Principal Chief headed a mixed-blood elite, and was intent on centralizing power in his own hands and diverting the annuities to those who

LIBRARY OF CONGRESS

Major Ridge, John Ridge's father, was also a member of the Treaty Party. He was killed in an ambush on the same day his son died.

would advance his authority and their economic self-interests. Real Indians were full-blooded Indians, not half-breeds, he declared. They were hunters, they were true warriors who, like Ridge and Boudinot, understood the President's concern for his red children and wished to prevent the calamity of certain annihilation that would ensue if they did not heed his pleas to move west. As for Ross's authority under the Cherokee Constitution, Jackson denied that it existed. He said that this so-called Constitution provided for an election in 1832 and it had not been held. Instead the Principal Chief had simply filled the National Council with his henchmen—another indication, claimed Jackson, of an elitist clique who ruled the Nation and disregarded the interests of the majority of the people.

Despite his feelings about the chief, Jackson decided to grant Ross's request for a meeting. Above all else he wanted Cherokee removal and if that meant seeing this "great villain" and hearing about his proposal for relocating the tribe then he would do it. As a consummate politician, Jackson understood the value of playing one party off against another, so when he granted the interview he directed that Schermerhorn suspend his negotiations with the Treaty Party and wait for the outcome of his interview with the Principal Chief.

Actually Jackson and Ross were much alike. They were both wily, tough, determined, obsessed with protecting the interests of their respective peoples, and markedly dignified and polite when they came together in the White House on Wednesday,

February 5, 1834. It was exactly noon when the Principal Chief arrived, and the Great Father greeted him with the respect due Ross's position. The chief returned the compliment. For a few minutes their conversation touched on pleasantries, then they got down to the question at hand and began playing a political game that involved the lives of thousands, both Native Americans and white settlers.

Unfortunately, despite his many talents and keen intelligence, Ross was no match for the President. He simply lacked the resources of his adversary.

The Principal Chief opened with an impassioned plea. "Your Cherokee children are in deep distress," he said, "… because they are left at the mercy of the white robber and assassin" and receive no redress from the Georgia courts. That state, he declared, has not only "surveyed and lotteried off" Cherokee land to her citizens but legislated as though Cherokees were intruders in their own country.

Jackson just listened. Then the Principal Chief acted imprudently and made impossible demands on the President. To start, he insisted that in any treaty the Nation must retain some of their land along the borders of Tennessee, Alabama, and Georgia, land that had already been occupied by white settlers. He even included a small tract in North Carolina. He then required assurances that the United States government would protect the Cherokees with federal troops in the new and old settlements for a period of five years.

Jackson could scarcely believe what was being demanded of him. Under other circumstances he would have acted up a storm in an attempt to frighten and cower the chief. But, on this occasion he decided against it. Instead, in a calm and quiet but determined voice, he told Ross that nothing short of an entire removal of the Cherokee Nation from all their land east of the Mississippi would be acceptable.

Having run into a stone wall, Ross headed in another direction. In view of the gold that had recently been discovered in Georgia and North Carolina, he wanted $20 million for all their eastern land plus reimbursement for losses sustained by the Nation for violations of former treaties by the United States. He also asked for indemnities for claims under the 1817 and 1819 Cherokee treaties. The total amount almost equaled the national debt.

On hearing this, Jackson also changed direction. His voice hardened, his intense blue eyes flared, and the muscles in his face tightened and registered his growing displeasure. Obviously the Principal Chief had not caught the President's meaning when he rejected the first demand. Jackson snapped at Ross, rejected the proposal as "preposterous" and warned him that the Great Father was not to be trifled with. If these demands were the best the chief could offer then there was no point in continuing the discussion.

That brought Ross up short. Completely surprised by Jackson's reaction he protested his sincerity, and to prove it he offered to accept any award the Senate of the United States might recommend. Apparently the chief was attempting to set up a bidding contest between the upper house and the chief executive. Surprisingly, Jackson accepted the offer and assured Ross that he would "go as far" as the Senate in any award that

might be proposed. And on that conciliatory note the interview ended.

In less than a week Ross received his answer about what the Senate would offer. John P. King of Georgia chaired the Committee on Indian Affairs that considered the question. That was bad enough. Then the committee came up with an offer of $5 million. The figure shocked the Principal Chief. Jackson probably knew beforehand what would happen and therefore agreed to Ross's suggestion. Now the Indian was faced with rejecting the money outright or accepting this paltry sum and thereby losing credibility with his people. Naturally he chose the former course. He claimed he had been misunderstood, that he could not possibly agree to such an amount, and that his reputation among the Cherokees would be shattered if he consented to it. He left Washington an angry and bitter man.

Having disposed of Ross, Jackson turned back to Schermerhorn and instructed him to renew the negotiations with the Treaty Party. With little difficulty the cleric managed to arrange a draft removal treaty signed on March 14, 1835, by Schermerhorn, John Ridge, Elias Boudinot, and a small delegation of Cherokees. After due notice the treaty was submitted to the Cherokee National Council at New Echota, Georgia, for approval and sent to the President for submission to the Senate. The draft stipulated that the Cherokees surrender to the United States all its land east of the Mississippi River for a sum of $5 million, an amount that one modern historian has called "unprecedented generosity." This cession comprised nearly 8 million acres of land in western North Carolina, northern Georgia, northeastern Alabama, and eastern Tennessee. A schedule of removal provided that the Cherokees would be resettled in the west and receive regular payments for subsistence, claims, and spoliations, and would be issued blankets, kettles, and rifles.

At approximately the same time this draft treaty was drawn up and considered at New Echota, a large delegation of Cherokee chiefs—in the desperate hope that their assembled presence would make a difference and prevent the treaty from going forward to the Senate—went to Washington and asked to speak to their Great Father. In contrast to his grudging granting of Ross's request, Jackson was anxious to meet the delegation and give the chiefs one of his celebrated "talks."

The Indians arrived at the White House at the designated hour, and Jackson treated them with marked respect, as though they really were dignitaries of a foreign nation. Yet he did not remotely say or do anything that would indicate an acceptance of their independence or sovereignty. Once the Indians had assembled they faced the President as he began his talk.

"Brothers, I have long viewed your condition with great interest. For many years I have been acquainted with your people, and under all variety of circumstances, in peace and war. Your fathers are well known to me…. Listen to me, therefore, as your fathers have listened…."

Jackson paused. He turned from side to side to look at and take in all the Cherokees standing around him. After a few moments he began again.

"You are now placed in the midst of a white population…. You are now subject to the same laws which govern the citizens of Georgia and Alabama. You are liable to prosecutions for offenses, and to civil actions for a breach of any of your contracts. Most of your people are uneducated, and are liable to be brought into collision at all times with your white neighbors. Your young men are acquiring habits of intoxication. With strong passions… they are frequently driven to excesses which must eventually terminate in their ruin. The game has disappeared among you, and you must depend upon agriculture and the mechanic arts for support. And yet, a large portion of your people have acquired little or no property in the soil itself…. How, under these circumstances, can you live in the country you now occupy? Your condition must become worse and worse, and you will ultimately disappear, as so many tribes have done before you."

They had two years—that is, until May 23, 1838—to cross over the Mississippi and take up their new residence in the Indian Territory.

These were his usual arguments, but he judged them essential for success.

You have not listened to me, he scolded. You went to the courts for relief. You turned away from your Great Father. And what happened? After years of litigation you received little satisfaction from the Supreme Court and succeeded in earning the enmity of many whites. "I have no motive, Brothers, to deceive you," he said. "I am sincerely desirous to promote your welfare. Listen to me, therefore, while I tell you that you cannot remain where you are now…. It [is] impossible that you can flourish in the midst of a civilized community. You have but one remedy within your reach. And that is to remove to the West and join your countrymen, who are already established there." The choice is yours. "May the great spirit teach you how to choose."

Jackson then concluded by reminding them of the fate of the Creeks, that once great and proud Nation. How broken and reduced in circumstances their lives had now become because they resisted. It was a not-so-subtle threat that also struck home. "Think then of these things," he concluded. "Shut your ears to bad counsels. Look at your condition as it now is, and then consider what it will be if you follow the advice I give you."

That ended the talk, and the Indians filed from the room more disappointed and depressed than ever. Jackson would not budge, and they knew their kinsmen were dead set against removal. It was a stalemate that could end only in tragedy.

Meanwhile Schermerhorn called "a council of all the people" to meet him at New Echota in Georgia during the third week of December 1835 to approve the draft treaty, making sure that a large contingent of Treaty Party members attended. Like Jackson, he had the temerity to warn other Cherokees that if they stayed away their absence would be considered a vote of consent for the draft.

Despite the threat and the warning, practically the entire Nation stayed away. As a consequence the treaty was approved on December 28 by the unbelievably low number of 79 to 7. The numbers represented only the merest fraction of the Nation. A vast majority—perhaps fifteen-sixteenths of the entire population—presumably opposed it and showed their opposition by staying away. The entire process was fraudulent, but that hardly mattered. Jackson had the treaty he wanted, and he did not hesitate to so inform the Senate.

The Treaty of New Echota closely, but not completely, resembled the draft treaty in that the Cherokees surrendered all their eastern land and received $4.5 million in return. They would be paid for improvements, removed at government expense, and maintained for two years. Removal was to take place within two years from the date of the treaty's approval by the Senate and President.

A short while later some 12,000 Cherokees signed a resolution denouncing the Treaty of New Echota and forwarded it to the Senate. Even the North Carolina Cherokees, in a separate action, added 3,250 signatures to a petition urging the Senate to reject it. But Jackson was assured by the Treaty Party that "a majority of the people" approved the document "and all are willing peaceable to yield to the treaty and abide by it." Such information convinced the President that the Principal Chief and his "half breed" cohorts had coerced the Cherokees into staying away from New Echota under threat of physical violence.

At New Echota the Treaty Party selected a Committee of Thirteen to carry the treaty to Washington and they were empowered to act on any alteration required by the President or the U. S. Senate. This Committee invited Ross to join the group and either support the treaty or insist on such alterations as to make it acceptable. "But to their appeal [Ross] returned no answer," which further convinced the President that the treaty represented the genuine interests and the will of the majority of Cherokees.

Militiamen charged into the Cherokee country and drove the Cherokees from their cabins and houses.

Although Henry Clay, Daniel Webster, Edward Everett, and other senators spoke fervently against the treaty in the Senate, a two-thirds majority of 31 members voted for it and 15 against. It carried by a single vote on May 18. Jackson added his signature on May 23, 1836, and proclaimed the Treaty of New Echota in force.

And they had two years—that is until May 23, 1838—to cross over the Mississippi and take up their new residence in the Indian Territory. But every day of that two-year period John Ross fought the inevitable. He demanded to see the President and insisted that Jackson recognize the authority of the duly elected National Council, but Sharp Knife would have none of him and turned him away. Back home the Principal Chief advised his people to ignore the treaty and stay put. "We will not recognize the forgery palmed off upon the world as a treaty by a knot of unauthorized individuals," he cried, "nor stir one step with reference to that false paper."

Not everyone listened to him. They knew Andrew Jackson better. Some 2,000 Cherokees resigned themselves to the inevitable, packed their belongings, and headed west. The rest, the vast majority of the tribe, could not bear to leave their homeland and chose to hope that their Principal Chief would somehow work the miracle that would preserve their country to them.

But their fate could not have been worse. When the two-year grace period expired and Jackson had left office, his hand-picked successor, President Martin Van Buren, ordered the removal to begin. Militiamen charged into the Cherokee country and drove the Cherokees from their cabins and houses. With rifles and bayonets they rounded up the Indians and placed them in prison stockades that had been erected "for gathering in and holding the Indians preparatory to removal." These poor, frightened and benighted innocents, while having supper in their homes, "were startled by the sudden gleam of bayonets in the doorway and rose up to be driven with blows and oaths along the weary miles of trail which led to the stockade. Men were seized in the fields, women were taken from their wheels and children from their play." As they turned for one last glimpse of their homes they frequently saw them in flames, set ablaze by the lawless rabble who followed the soldiers, scavenging what they could. These outlaws stole the cattle and other livestock and even desecrated graves in their search for silver pendants and other valuables. They looted and burned. Said one Georgia volunteer who later served in the Confederate army: "I fought through the Civil War and have seen men shot to pieces and slaughtered by thousands, but the Cherokee removal was the cruelest I ever saw."

In a single week some 17,000 Cherokees were rounded up and herded into what was surely a concentration camp. Many sickened and died while they awaited transport to the west. In June the first contingent of about a thousand Indians boarded a steamboat and sailed down the Tennessee River on the first lap of their westward journey. Then they were boxed like animals into railroad cars drawn by two locomotives. Again there were many deaths on account of the oppressive heat and cramped conditions in the cars. For the last leg of the journey the Cherokees walked. Small wonder they came to call this 800-mile nightmare "The Trail of Tears." Of the approximately 18,000 Cherokees who were removed, at least 4,000 died in the stockades along the way, and some say the figure actually reached 8,000. By the middle of June 1838 the general in charge of the Georgia militia proudly reported that not a single Cherokee remained in the state except as prisoners in the stockade.

At every step of their long journey to the Indian Territory the Cherokees were robbed and cheated by contractors, lawyers, agents, speculators, and anyone wielding local police power. Food supplied by the government disappeared or arrived in short supply. The commanding officer, General Winfield Scott, and a few other generals "were concerned about their reputation for humaneness," says one modern historian, "and probably even for the Cherokee. There just wasn't much they could do about it." As a result many died needlessly. "Oh! The misery and wretchedness that presents itself to our view in going among these people," wrote one man. "Sir, I have witnessed entire families prostrated with sickness—not one able to give help to the other, and these poor people were made the instruments of enriching a few unprincipled and wicked contractors."

And this, too, is part of Andrew Jackson's legacy. Although it has been pointed out many times that he was no longer President of the United States when the Trail of Tears occurred and had never intended such a monstrous result of his policy, that hardly excuses him. It was his insistence on the speedy removal of the Cherokees, even after he had left office, that brought about this horror. From his home outside Nashville he regularly badgered Van Buren about enforcing the treaty. He had become obsessed about removal. He warned that Ross would exert every effort and means available to him to get the treaty rescinded or delayed and that, he said, must be blocked. But the new President assured him that nothing would interfere with the exodus of the Cherokees and that no extension of the two-year grace period would be tolerated under any circumstance.

Principal Chief John Ross also shares a portion of blame for this unspeakable tragedy. He continued his defiance even after the deadline for removal had passed. He encouraged his people to keep up their resistance, despite every sign that no appreciable help would be forthcoming from the American people or anyone else; and he watched as they suffered the awful consequences of his intransigence.

Despite the obscene treatment accorded the Cherokees by the government, the tribe not only survived but endured. As Jackson predicted, they escaped the fate of many extinct eastern tribes. Cherokees today have their tribal identity, a living language, and at least three governmental bodies to provide for their needs. Would that the Yemassee, Mohegans, Pequots, Delawares, Narragansetts, and other such tribes could say the same.

Excerpted from *Andrew Jackson and His Indian Wars* by Robert V. Remini. Copyright © Robert V. Remini, 2001. Reprinted by arrangement with Viking Penguin, a division of Penguin Putnam, Inc.

Robert B. Remini is the author of a three-volume biography of Andrew Jackson as well as biographies of Daniel Webster and Henry Clay and many other books about Jacksonian America.

From *American History*, August 2001, pp. 48-53, 55-56. © 2001 by Primedia Enthusiast Publications, Inc. All rights reserved.

One hundred and fifty years ago the people attending the first Women's Rights Convention adopted the radical proposition that

"All men & women are created equal"

By Constance Rynder

THE ANNOUNCEMENT OF an upcoming "Woman's Rights Convention" in the *Seneca County Courier* was small, but it attracted Charlotte Woodward's attention. On the morning of July 19, 1848, the 19-year-old glove maker drove in a horse-drawn wagon to the Wesleyan Methodist Chapel in the upstate New York town of Seneca Falls. To her surprise, Woodward found dozens of other women and a group of men waiting to enter the chapel, all of them as eager as she to learn what a discussion of "the social, civil, and religious rights of women" might produce.

The convention was the brainchild of 32-year-old Elizabeth Cady Stanton, daughter of Margaret and Judge Daniel Cady and wife of Henry Stanton, a noted abolitionist politician. Born in Johnstown, New York, Cady Stanton demonstrated both an intellectual bent and a rebellious spirit from an early age. Exposed to her father's law books as well as his conservative views on women, she objected openly to the legal and educational disadvantages under which women of her day labored. In 1840 she provoked her father by marrying Stanton, a handsome, liberal reformer and further defied convention by deliberately omitting the word "obey" from her wedding vows.

Marriage to Henry Stanton brought Elizabeth Cady Stanton—she insisted on retaining her maiden name—into contact with other independent-minded women. The newlyweds spent their honeymoon at the World Anti-Slavery Convention in London where, much to their chagrin, women delegates were denied their seats and deprived of a voice in the proceedings. Banished to a curtained visitors' gallery, the seven women listened in stunned silence as the London credentials committee charged that they were "constitutionally unfit for public and business meetings." It was an insult Cady Stanton never forgot.

Among the delegates was Lucretia Coffin Mott, a liberal Hicksite Quaker preacher and an accomplished public speaker in the American abolitionist movement, who was also disillusioned by the lack of rights granted women. A mother of six, Mott had grown up on Nantucket Island, "so thoroughly imbued with women's rights," she later admitted, "that it was the most important question of my life from a very early age." In Mott, Cady Stanton found both an ally and a role model. "When I first heard from her lips that I had the same right to think for myself that Luther, Calvin and John Knox had," she recalled, "and the same right to be guided by my own convictions... I felt a new born sense of dignity and freedom." The two women became fast friends and talked about the need for a convention to discuss *women's* emancipation. Eight years passed, however, before they fulfilled their mutual goal.

For the first years of her marriage, Cady Stanton settled happily into middle-class domestic life, first in Johnstown and subsequently in Boston, then the hub of reformist activity. She delighted in being part of her husband's stimulating circle of reformers and intellectuals and gloried in motherhood; over a 17-year period she bore seven children. In 1847, however, the Stantons moved to Seneca Falls, a small, remote farming and manufacturing community in New York's Finger Lakes district. After Boston, life in Seneca Falls with its routine household duties seemed dull to Cady Stanton, and she renewed her protest against the conditions that limited women's lives. "My experience at the World Anti-Slavery Convention, all I had read of the legal status of women, and the oppression I saw everywhere, together swept across my soul, intensified now by many personal experiences." A meeting with Lucretia Mott in July of 1848 provided the opportunity to take action.

On July 13, Cady Stanton received an invitation to a tea party at the home of Jane and Richard Hunt, wealthy Quakers living in Waterloo, New York, just three miles west of Seneca Falls. There she again met Lucretia Mott, Mott's younger sister, Martha Coffin Wright, and Mary

Ann McClintock, wife of the Waterloo Hicksite Quaker minister. At tea, Cady Stanton poured out to the group "the torrent of my long-accumulating discontent." Then and there they decided to schedule a women's "convention" for the following week. Hoping to attract a large audience, they placed an unsigned notice in the *Courier* advertising Lucretia Mott as the featured speaker.

Near panic gripped the five women as they gathered around the McClintocks' parlor table the following Sunday morning. They had only three days to set an agenda and prepare a document "for the inauguration of a rebellion." Supervised by Cady Stanton, they drafted a "Declaration of Sentiments and Resolutions," paraphrasing the Declaration of Independence. The document declared that "all men and women are created equal" and "are endowed by their Creator with certain unalienable rights...." These natural rights belong equally to women and men, it continued, but man "has usurped the prerogative of Jehovah himself, claiming it as his right to assign for her a sphere of action, when that belongs to her conscience and to her God." The result has been "the establishment of an absolute tyranny over her."

There followed a specific catalog of injustices. Women were denied access to higher education, the professions, and the pulpit, as well as equal pay for equal work. If married they had no property rights; even the wages they earned legally belonged to their husbands. Women were subject to a high moral code, yet legally bound to tolerate moral delinquencies in their husbands. Wives could be punished, and if divorced a mother had no child custody rights. In every way, man "has endeavored to destroy [woman's] confidence in her own powers, to lessen her self-esteem, and to make her willing to lead a dependent and abject life." Above all, every woman had been deprived of "her inalienable right to the elective franchise."

Eleven resolutions demanding redress of these and other grievances accompanied the nearly 1,000-word Declaration. When Cady Stanton insisted upon including a resolution favoring voting rights for women, her otherwise supportive husband threatened to boycott the event. Even Lucretia Mott warned her, "Why Lizzie, thee will make us ridiculous!" "Lizzie," however, refused to yield.

Susan B. Anthony and Elizabeth Cady Stanton remained close friends from the time they met in 1851 until Cady Stanton's death in 1902. Both women became leaders in the fight for women's equality. Lucretia Mott was another of the great women of the nineteenth century.

Although the gathering was a convention for and of women, it was regarded as "unseemingly" for a lady to conduct a public meeting, so Lucretia's husband, James Mott, agreed to chair the two-day event. Mary Ann McClintock's husband, Thomas, also participated. Henry Stanton left town.

When the organizers arrived at the Wesleyan Chapel on the morning of Wednesday, July 19, they found the door locked. No one had a key, so Cady Stanton's young nephew scrambled in through an open window and unbarred the front door. As the church filled with spectators, another dilemma presented itself. The first day's sessions had been planned for women exclusively, but almost 40 men showed up. After a hasty council at the altar the leadership decided to let the men stay, since they were already seated and seemed genuinely interested.

Tall and dignified in his Quaker garb, James Mott called the first session to order at 11:00 A.M. and appointed the McClintocks' older daughter (also named Mary Ann) secretary. Cady Stanton, in her first public speech, rose to state the purpose of the convention. "We have met here today to discuss our rights and wrongs, civil and political." She then read the Declaration aloud, paragraph by paragraph, and urged all present to participate freely in the discussions. The Declaration was re-read several times, amended, and adopted unanimously. Both Lucretia Mott and Cady Stanton addressed the afternoon session, as did the McClintock's younger daughter, Elizabeth. To lighten up the proceedings, Mott read a satirical article on "woman's sphere" that her sister Martha had published in local newspapers. Later that evening, Mott spoke to the audience on "The Progress of Reforms."

The second day's sessions were given over to the 11 resolutions. As Mott feared, the most contentious proved to be the ninth—the suffrage resolution. The other 10 passed unanimously. According to Cady Stanton's account, most of those who opposed this resolution did so because they believed it would compromise the others. She, however, remained adamant. "To have drunkards, idiots, horse racing rum-selling rowdies, ignorant foreigners, and silly boys fully recognized, while we ourselves are thrust out from all the rights that belong to citizens, is too grossly insulting to be longer quietly submitted to. The right is ours. We must have it." Even Cady Stanton's eloquence would not have carried the day but for the support she received from ex-slave and abolitionist Frederick Douglass, editor of the antislavery newspaper, *North Star*. "Right is of no sex," he argued; a woman is "justly entitled to all we claim for man." After much heated debate the ninth resolution passed, but by only a small majority.

Thomas McClintock presided over the final session on Thursday evening and read extracts from Sir William Blackstone's *Commentaries on the Laws of England* that described the status of women in English common law. Cady Stanton took questions before short speeches were given by young Mary Ann McClintock and Frederick Douglass. Lucretia Mott closed the meeting with an appeal to action and one additional resolution of her own: "The speedy success of our cause depends upon the zealous and untiring efforts of both men and women, for the overthrow of the monopoly of the pulpit, and for securing to women of equal participation with men in the various trades, professions, and commerce." It, too, passed unanimously.

In all, some 300 people attended the Seneca Falls Convention. The majority were ordinary folk like Charlotte Woodward. Most sat through the 18 hours of speeches, debates, and readings. One hundred of them—68 women (including Woodward) and 32 men—signed the final draft of the Declaration of Sentiments and Resolutions. Women's rights as a separate reform movement had been born.

Press coverage was surprisingly broad and generally venomous, particularly on the subject of female suffrage. Philadelphia's *Public Ledger and Daily Transcript* declared that no lady would want to vote. "A woman is nobody. A wife is everything. The ladies of Philadelphia… are resolved to maintain their rights as Wives, Belles, Virgins and Mothers." According to the Albany *Mechanic's Advocate*, equal rights would "demoralize and degrade [women] from their high sphere and noble destiny… and prove a monstrous injury to all mankind." The *New York Herald* published the entire text of the Seneca Falls Declaration, calling it "amusing" but conceding that Lucretia Mott would "make a better President than some of those who have lately tenanted the White House." The only major paper to treat the event seriously was the liberal *New York Tribune*, edited by Horace Greeley, who found the demand for equal political rights improper, yet "however unwise and mistaken the demand, it is but the assertion of a natural right and as such must be conceded."

Stung by the public outcry, many original signers begged to have their names removed from the Declaration. "Our friends gave us the cold shoulder, and felt themselves disgraced by the whole proceeding," complained Cady Stanton. Many women sympathized with the convention's goals but feared the stigma attached to attending any future meetings. "I am with you thoroughly," said the wife of Senator William Seward, "but I am a born coward. There is nothing I dread more than Mr. Seward's ridicule." Even the McClintocks and the Hunts refrained from active involvement

in women's rights after the Seneca Falls Convention.

But Cady Stanton saw opportunity in public criticism. "Imagine the publicity given our ideas by thus appearing in a widely circulated sheet like the *Herald*!" she wrote to Mott. "It will start women thinking, and men, too." She drafted lengthy responses to every negative newspaper article and editorial, presenting the reformers' side of the issue to the readers. Mott sensed her younger colleague's future role. "Thou art so wedded to this cause," she told Cady Stanton, "that thou must expect to act as pioneer in the work."

News of the Seneca Falls Convention spread rapidly and inspired a spate of regional women's rights meetings. Beginning with a follow-up meeting two weeks later in Rochester, New York, all subsequent women's rights forums featured female chairs. New England abolitionist Lucy Stone organized the first national convention, held in Worcester, Massachusetts, in 1850. Like Cady Stanton, Stone saw the connection between black emancipation and female emancipation. When criticized for including women's rights in her anti-slavery speeches, Stone countered: "I was a woman before I was an abolitionist—I must speak for the women."

As Cady Stanton later put it, "I forged the thunderbolts and she [Susan B. Anthony] fired them."

QUAKER REFORMER Susan B. Anthony joined the women's rights movement in 1852. She had heard about the Seneca Falls Convention, of course, and her parents and sister had attended the 1848 Rochester meeting. Initially, however, she deemed its goals of secondary importance to temperance and abolition. All that changed in 1851 when she met Cady Stanton, with whom she formed a life-long political partnership. Bound to the domestic sphere by her growing family, Cady Stanton wrote articles,

speeches, and letters; Anthony, who never married, traveled the country lecturing and organizing women's rights associations. As Cady Stanton later put it, "I forged the thunderbolts and she fired them." In time, Susan B. Anthony's name became synonymous with women's rights.

Women's rights conventions were held annually until the Civil War, drawing most of their support from the abolitionist and temperance movements. After the war, feminist leaders split over the exclusion of women from legislation enfranchising black men. Abolitionists argued that it was "the Negro's Hour," and that the inclusion of female suffrage would jeopardize passage of the Fifteenth Amendment to the Constitution, which enfranchised all male citizens regardless of race. Feeling betrayed by their old allies, Cady Stanton and Anthony opposed the Fifteenth Amendment. Their protest alienated the more cautious wing of the movement and produced two competing suffrage organizations.

In 1869, Lucy Stone, Julia Ward Howe—well known author of "Battle Hymn of the Republic"—and others formed the moderate American Woman Suffrage Association, while Cady Stanton, Anthony, Martha Wright, and the radical faction founded the National Woman Suffrage Association (NWSA). Lucretia Mott, now an elderly widow, sought in vain to reconcile the two camps.

Both organizations sought political equality for women, but the more radical NWSA actively promoted issues beyond suffrage. Guided by the original Seneca Falls Resolutions, the NWSA demanded an end to all laws and practices that discriminated against women, and called for divorce law reform, equal pay, access to higher education and the professions, reform of organized religion, and a total rethinking of what constituted a "woman's sphere." Cady Stanton spoke about women's sexuality in public and condemned the Victorian double standard that forced wives to endure drunken, brutal, and licentious husbands. Anthony countenanced—and occasionally practiced—civil disobedience; in 1872 she provoked her own arrest by illegally casting a ballot in the presidential election. By the time the two rival organizations merged in 1890 to form the National American Woman Suffrage Association (NAWSA), much had been accomplished. Many states had enacted laws granting married women property rights, equal guardianship over children, and the legal standing to make contracts and bring suit. Nearly one-third of college students were female, and 19 states allowed women to vote in local school board elections. In two western territories—Wyoming and Utah—women voted on an equal basis with men. But full suffrage nationwide remained stubbornly out of reach. NAWSA commenced a long state-by-state battle for the right to vote.

NAWSA's first two presidents were Cady Stanton and Anthony, by then in their seventies. Old age did not mellow either one of them, especially Cady Stanton. Ever the rebel, she criticized NAWSA's narrow-mindedness and viewed with increasing suspicion its newly acquired pious, prohibitionist allies. NAWSA's membership should include all "types of classes, races and creeds," she stated, and resist the evangelical infiltrators who sought to mute the larger agenda of women's emancipation.

Cady Stanton had long advocated reform of organized religion. "The chief obstacle in the way of woman's eleva-tion today," she wrote, "is the degrading position assigned her in the religion of all countries." Whenever women tried to enlarge their "divinely ordained sphere," the all-male clerical establishment condemned them for violating "God's law." Using the Scriptures to justify women's inferior status positively galled her. In 1895, she published *The Woman's Bible*, a critical commentary on the negative image of women in the Old and New Testaments. Even Anthony thought she had gone too far this time and could do little to prevent conservative suffragists from venting their wrath. During the annual convention of NAWSA, both the book and its author were publicly censured. Henceforth, mainstream suffragists downplayed Cady Stanton's historic role, preferring to crown Susan B. Anthony as the stateswoman of the movement.

Elizabeth Cady Stanton died in 1902 at the age of 86, and Susan B. Anthony died four years later, also at 86. By then a new generation of suffrage leaders had emerged—younger, better educated, and less restricted to the domestic sphere. The now-respectable, middle-class leadership of NAWSA adopted a "social feminist" stance, arguing that women were, in fact *different* from men and therefore needed the vote in order to apply their special qualities to the political problems of the nation.

However, more militant suffragists, among them Quaker agitator Alice Paul and Cady Stanton's daughter, Harriot Stanton Blatch, continued to insist upon women's absolute equality. They demanded a federal suffrage amendment as a necessary first step toward achieving equal rights. Paul's National Woman's Party gained the movement valuable publicity by engaging in confrontational tactics, including picketing the White House, being arrested, and going on hunger strikes while in prison.

Voting rights came in the wake of World War I. Impressed by the suffragists' participation in the war effort, Congress passed what came to be known as the "Susan B. Anthony Amendment" in 1919. Following state ratification a year later, it enfranchised American women nationwide in the form of the Nineteenth Amendment to the Constitution.

It had been 72 years since that daring call for female voting rights was issued at the Seneca Falls Convention. On November 2, 1920, 91-year-old Charlotte Woodward Pierce went to the polls in Philadelphia, the only signer of the Seneca Falls Declaration who had lived long enough to legally cast her ballot in a presidential election.

Constance B. Rynder is a professor of history at the University of Tampa, Florida, and specializes in women's history.

The Lives of Slave Women

Deborah Gray White

Slave women have often been characterized as self-reliant and self-sufficient, yet not every black woman was a Sojourner Truth or a Harriet Tubman. Strength had to be cultivated. It came no more naturally to them than to anyone else, slave or free, male or female, black or white. If slave women seemed exceptionally strong it was partly because they often functioned in groups and derived strength from their numbers.

Much of the work slaves did and the regimen they followed served to stratify slave society along sex lines. Consequently slave women had ample opportunity to develop a consciousness grounded in their identity as females. While close contact sometimes gave rise to strife, adult female cooperation and dependence of women on each other was a fact of female slave life. The self-reliance and self-sufficiency of slave women, therefore, must be viewed in the context not only of what the individual slave woman did for herself, but what slave women as a group were able to do for each other.

It is easy to overlook the separate world of female slaves because from colonial times through the Civil War black women often worked with black men at tasks considered by Europeans to be either too difficult or inappropriate for females. All women worked hard, but when white women consistently performed field labor it was considered temporary, irregular, or extraordinary, putting them on a par with slaves. Actress Fredericka Bremer, visiting the ante-bellum South, noted that usually only men and black women did field

work; commenting on what another woman traveler sarcastically claimed to be a noble admission of female equality, Bremer observed that "black (women) are not considered to belong to the weaker sex."[1]

Bremer's comment reflects what former slaves and fugitive male slaves regarded as the defeminization of black women. Bonded women cut down trees to clear lands for cultivation. They hauled logs in leather straps attached to their shoulders. They plowed using mule and ox teams, and hoed, sometimes with the heaviest implements available. They dug ditches, spread manure fertilizer, and piled coarse fodder with their bare hands. They built and cleaned Southern roads, helped construct Southern railroads, and, of course, they picked cotton. In short, what fugitive slave Williamson Pease said regretfully of slave women was borne out in fact: "Women who do outdoor work are used as bad as men."[2] Almost a century later Green Wilbanks spoke less remorsefully than Pease in his remembrances of his Grandma Rose, where he implied that the work had a kind of neutering effect. Grandma Rose, he said, was a woman who could do any kind of job a man could do, a woman who "was some worker, a regular manwoman."[3]

It is hardly likely, though, that slave women, especially those on large plantations with sizable female populations, lost their female identity. Harvesting season on staple crop plantations may have found men and women gathering the crop in sex-integrated gangs, but at other times women often worked in

exclusively or predominantly female gangs.[4] Thus women stayed in each other's company for most of the day. This meant that those they ate meals with, sang work songs with, and commiserated with during the work day were people who by virtue of their sex had the same kind of responsibilities and problems. As a result, slave women appeared to have developed their own female culture, a way of doing things and a way of assigning value that flowed from their perspective as slave women on Southern plantations. Rather than being squelched, their sense of womanhood was probably enhanced and their bonds to each other strengthened.

Since slaveowners and makers seemingly took little note of the slave woman's lesser physical strength, one wonders why they separated men and women at all. One answer appears to be that gender provided a natural and easy way to divide the labor force. Also probable is that despite their limited sensitivity regarding female slave labor, and the double standard they used when evaluating the uses of white and black female labor, slave-owners did, using standards only they could explain, reluctantly acquiesce to female physiology. For instance, depending on their stage of pregnancy, pregnant women were considered half or quarter hands. Healthy nonpregnant women were considered three-quarter hands. Three-quarter hands were not necessarily exempt from some of the herculean tasks performed by men who were full hands, but usually, when labor was being parceled out and barring a shortage of male hands to do the very heavy work or a rush to get that work completed, men did the more physically demanding work. A case in point was the most common differentiation where men plowed and women hoed.[5]

A great deal of both field labor and nonfield labor was structured to promote cooperation among slave women.

Like much of the field labor, nonfield labor was structured to promote cooperation among women. In the Sea Islands, slave women sorted cotton lint according to color and fineness and removed cotton seeds crushed by the gin into the cotton and lint. Fence building often found men splitting rails in one area and women doing the actual construction in another. Men usually shelled corn, threshed peas, cut potatoes for planting, and platted shucks. Grinding corn into meal or hominy was women's work. So too were spinning, weaving, sewing, and washing.[6] On Captain Kinsler's South Carolina plantation, as on countless others, "old women and women bearin' chillun not yet born, did cardin' wid handcards." Some would spin, others would weave, but all would eventually learn from some skilled woman "how to make clothes for the family… knit coarse socks and stockins."[7]

"When the work in the fields was finished women were required to come home and spin one cut a night," reported a Georgian. "Those who were not successful in completing this work were punished the next morning."[8] Women had to work in the evenings partly because slaveowners bought them few ready-made clothes. On one South Carolina plantation each male slave received annually two cotton shirts, three pairs of pants, and one jacket. Slave women, on the other hand, received six yards of woolen cloth, six yards of cotton drilling, and six yards of cotton shirting a year, along with two needles and a dozen buttons.[9]

Perhaps a saving grace to this "double duty" was that women got a chance to interact with each other. On a Sedalia County, Missouri, plantation, women looked forward to Saturday afternoon washing because, as Mary Frances Webb explained, they "would get to talk and spend the day together."[10] Quiltings, referred to by former slaves as female "frolics" and "parties," were especially convivial. Anna Peek recalled that when slaves were allowed to relax, they gathered around a pine wood fire in Aunt Anna's cabin to tell stories. At that time "the old women with pipes in their mouths would sit and gossip for hours."[11] Missourian Alice Sewell noted that sometimes women would slip away and hold their own prayer meetings. They cemented their bonds to each other at the end of every meeting when they walked around shaking hands and singing, "fare you well my sisters, I am going home."[12]

The organization of female slave work and social activities tended not only to separate women and men, but also to generate female cooperation and interdependence. Slave women and their children could depend on midwives and "doctor women" to treat a variety of ailments. Menstrual cramps, for example, were sometimes treated with a tea made from the bark of the gum tree. Midwives and "doctor women" administered various other herb teas to ease the pains of many ailing slaves. Any number of broths—made from the leaves and barks of trees, from the branches and twigs of bushes, from turpentine, catnip, or tobacco—were used to treat whooping cough, diarrhea, toothaches, colds, fevers, headaches, and backaches.[13] According to a Georgia ex-slave, "One had to be mighty sick to have the services of a doctor." On his master's plantation "old women were… responsible for the care of the sick."[14] This was also the case on Rebecca Hooks's former Florida residence. "The doctor," she noted, "was not nearly as popular as the 'granny' or midwife, who brewed medicines for every ailment."[15]

Female cooperation in the realm of medical care helped foster bonding that led to collaboration in the area of resistance to abuses by slaveholders. Frances Kemble could attest to the concerted efforts of the black women on her husband's Sea Island plantations. More than once she was visited by groups of women imploring her to persuade her husband to extend the lying-in period for childbearing women. On one occasion the women had apparently prepared beforehand the approach they would take with the foreign-born and sympathetic Kemble, for their chosen spokeswoman took care to play on Kemble's own maternal sentiments, and pointedly argued that slave women deserved at least some of the care and tenderness that Kemble's own pregnancy had elicited.[16]

Usually, however, slave women could not be so outspoken about their needs, and covert cooperative resistance prevailed. Slaveowners suspected that midwives conspired with their female patients to bring about abortions and infanticides, and on Charles Colcock Jones's Georgia plantation, for example, this seems in fact to have been the case. A woman named Lucy gave birth in secret and then denied that she had ever been pregnant. Although the midwife attended her, she too claimed not to have delivered a child, as did Lucy's mother. Jones had a physician examine Lucy, and the doctor confirmed what Jones had suspected, that Lucy had indeed given birth. Twelve days later the decomposing body of a full-term infant was found, and Lucy, her mother, and the midwife were all hauled off to court. Another woman, a nurse, managed to avoid prosecution but not suspicion. Whether Lucy was guilty of murder, and whether the others were accessories, will never be known because the court could not shatter their collective defense that the child had been stillborn.[17]

The inability to penetrate the private world of female slaves is probably what kept many abortions and infanticides from becoming known to slaveowners. The secrets kept by a midwife named Mollie became too much for her to bear. When she accepted Christianity these were the first things for which she asked forgiveness. She recalled, "I was carried to the gates of hell and the devil pulled out a book showing me the things which I had committed and that they were all true. My life as a midwife was shown to me and I have certainly felt sorry for all the things I did, after I was converted."[18]

Health care is not the only example of how the organization of slave work and slave responsibilities led to female cooperation and bonding; slave women also depended on each other for childcare. Sometimes, especially on small farms or new plantations where there was no extra woman to superintend children, bondswomen took their offspring to the field with them and attended to them during prescheduled breaks. Usually, however, infants and older children were left in the charge of an elderly female or females. Josephine Bristow, for example, spent more time with Mary Novlin, the nursery keeper on Ferdinand Gibson's South Carolina plantation, than she spent with her mother and father, who came in from the fields after she was asleep: "De old lady, she looked after every blessed thing for us all day long en cooked for us right along wid de mindin'."[19] In their complementary role as nurses, they ministered to the hurts and illnesses of infants and children.[20] It was not at all uncommon for the children's weekly rations to be given to the "grannies" as opposed to the children's parents.[21] Neither the slaveowner nor slave society expected the biological mother of a child to fulfill all of her child's needs. Given the circumstances, the responsibilities of motherhood had to be shared, and this required close female cooperation.

Cooperation in this sphere helped slave women overcome one of the most difficult of predicaments—who would provide maternal care for a child whose mother had died or been sold away? Fathers sometimes served as both mother and father, but when slaves, as opposed to the master, determined maternal care, it was usually a woman who became a child's surrogate mother. Usually that woman was an aunt or a sister, but in the absence of female relatives, a non-kin woman assumed the responsibility.[22] In the case of Georgian Mollie Malone, for example, the nursery superintendent became the child's substitute mother.[23] When Julia Malone's mother was killed by another Texas slave, little Julia was raised by the woman with whom her mother had shared a cabin.[24] On Southern plantations the female community made sure that no child was truly motherless.

Because black women on a plantation spent so much time together, they inevitably developed some appreciation of each other's skills and talents. This intimacy enabled them to establish the criteria by which to rank and order themselves. The existence of certain "female jobs" that carried prestige created a yardstick by which bondswomen could measure each other's achievements. Some of these jobs allowed for growth and self-satisfaction, fringe benefits that were usually out of reach for the field laborer. A seamstress, for example, had unusual opportunities for self-expression and creativity. On very large plantations the seamstress usually did no field work, and a particularly good seamstress, or "mantua-maker," might be hired out to others and even allowed to keep a portion of the money she earned.[25] For obvious reasons cooks, midwives, and female folk doctors also commanded the respect of their peers. Midwives in particular often were able to travel to other plantations to practice their art. This gave them an enviable mobility and also enabled them to carry messages from one plantation to the next.

Apart from the seamstresses, cooks, and midwives, a few women were distinguished as work gang-leaders. On most farms and plantations where there were overseers, managers, foremen, and drivers, these positions were held by men, either black or white. Occasionally, however, a woman was given a measure of authority over slave work, or a particular aspect of it. For instance Louis Hughes noted that each plantation he saw had a "forewoman who… had charge of the female slaves and also the boys and girls from twelve to sixteen years of age, and all the old people that were feeble."[26] Similarly, a Mississippi slave remembered that on his master's Osceola plantation there was a "colored woman as foreman."[27]

Clearly, a pecking order existed among bondswomen—one which they themselves helped to create. Because of age, occupation, association with the master class, or personal achievements, certain women were recognized by other women—and also by men—as important people, even as leaders. Laura Towne met an aged woman who commanded such a degree of respect that other slaves bowed to her and lowered their voices in her presence. The old woman, Maum Katie, was according to Towne a "spiritual mother" and a woman of "tremendous influence over her spiritual children."[28]

Sometimes two or three factors combined to distinguish a particular woman. Aunt Charlotte was the aged cook in John M. Booth's Georgia household. When Aunt Charlotte spoke, said Booth, "other colored people hastened to obey her."[29] Frederick Douglass's grandmother wielded influence because of her age and the skills she possessed. She made the best fishnets in Tuckahoe, Maryland, and she knew better than anyone else how to preserve sweet potato seedlings and how to plant them successfully. She enjoyed what Douglass called "high reputation," and accordingly "she was remembered by others."[30] In another example, when Elizabeth Botume went to the Sea Islands after the Civil War, she employed as a house servant a young woman named Amy who performed her tasks slowly and sullenly, until an older woman named Aunt Mary arrived from Beaufort. During slavery Amy and Aunt Mary had both worked in the house but Amy had learned to listen and obey Aunt Mary. After Aunt Mary arrived the once obstreperous Amy became "quiet, orderly, helpful and painstaking."[31]

A slaveowner lamented that Big Lucy, one of his oldest slaves, had more control over his female workers than he did.

The leadership of some women had a disruptive effect on plantation operations. Bennet H. Barrow repeatedly lamented the fact that Big Lucy, one of his oldest slaves, had more control over his female workers than he did: "Anica, Center, Cook Jane, the better you treat them the worse they are. Big Lucy the Leader corrupts every young negro in her power."[32] A self-proclaimed prophetess named Sinda was responsible for a cessation of all slave work for a considerable period on Butler Island in Georgia. According to a notation made by Frances Kemble in 1839, Sinda's prediction that the world would come to an end on a certain day caused the slaves to lay down their hoes and plows in the belief that their final emancipation was imminent. So sure were Sinda's fellow slaves of her prediction that even the lash failed to get them into the fields. When the appointed day of judgment passed uneventfully Sinda was whipped mercilessly. Yet, for a time, she had commanded more authority than either master or overseer.[33]

Bonded women did not have to go to such lengths in order to make a difference in each other's lives. The supportive atmosphere of the female community was considerable buffer against the depersonalizing regimen of plantation work and the general dehumanizing nature of slavery. When we consider that women were much more strictly confined to the plantation than men, that many women had husbands who visited only once or twice a week, and that slave women outlived slave men by an average of two years, we realize just how important the female community was to its members.

If we define a stable relationship as one of long duration, then it was probably easier for slave women to sustain stable emotional relationships with other bondswomen than with bondsmen. This is not to say that male-female relationships were unfulfilling or of no consequence. But they were generally fraught with more uncertainty about the future than female-to-female relationships, especially those existing between female blood kin. In her study of ex-slave interviews, Martha Goodson found that of all the relationships slaveowners disrupted, through either sale or dispersal, they were least likely to separate mothers and daughters.[34] Cody found that when South Carolina cotton planter Peter Gaillard divided his estate among his eight children, slave women in their twenties and thirties were twice as likely to have a sister with them, and women over 40 were four times more likely to have sisters with them than brothers. Similarly, daughters were less likely than sons to be separated from their mother. Over 60 percent of women aged 20 to 24 remained with their mothers when the estate was divided, as did 90 percent of those aged 25 to 29.[35] A slave song reflected the bonds between female siblings by indicating who took responsibility for the motherless female slave child. Interestingly enough, the one designated was neither the father nor the brother:

A motherless chile see a hard time.
Oh Lord, help her on de road.
Er sister will do de bes' she kin,
Dis is a hard world, Lord, fer a
    motherless chile.[36]

If female blood ties did indeed promote the most enduring relationships among slaves, then we should probably assume that like occupation, age, and personal achievement these relationships helped structure the female slave community. This assumption should not, however, obscure the fact that in friendships and dependency relationships women often treated non-relatives as if a consanguineous tie existed. This is why older women were called Aunt and Granny, and why unrelated women sometimes called each other Sister.[37]

While the focus here has been on those aspects of the bondswoman's life that fostered female bonding, female-to-female conflict was not uncommon. It was impossible for harmony always to prevail among women who saw so much of each other and who knew so much about one another. Lifelong friendships were founded in the hoe gangs and sewing groups, but the constant jockeying for occupational and social status created an atmosphere in which jealousies and antipathies smoldered. From Jesse Belflowers, the overseer of the Allston rice plantation in South Carolina, Adele Petigru Allston heard that "mostly amongst the Women" there was a "goodeal of quarling and disputing and telling lies."[38] The terms of a widely circulated overseer's contract advised rigorous punishment for "fighting, particularly amongst the women."[39] Some overseers followed this advice. According to Georgian Isaac Green, "Sometimes de women uster git whuppin's for fightin'."[40]

Occasionally, violence between women could and did get very ugly. Molly, the cook in James Chesnut's household, once took a red hot poker and attacked the woman to whom her husband had given one of her calico dresses.[41] Similarly, when she was a young woman in Arkansas, Lucretia Alexander came to blows with another woman over a pair of stockings that the master had given Lucretia.[42] In another incident on a Louisiana cotton plantation, the day's cotton chopping was interrupted when a feisty field worker named Betty lost her temper in the midst of a dispute with a fellow slave named Molly and struck her in the face with a hoe.[43]

The presence of conflict within interpersonal relationships between female slaves should not detract from the more important cooperation and dependence that prevailed among them. Conflict occurred *because* women were in close daily contact with each other and because the penalties for venting anger on other women were not as severe as those for striking out at men, either black or white. It is not difficult to understand how dependency relationships could become parasitical, how sewing and washing sessions could become "hanging courts," how one party could use knowledge gained in an intimate conversation against another.

Just how sisterhood could co-exist with discord is illustrated by the experience of some black women of the South Carolina and Georgia Sea Islands between 1862 and 1865. On November 7, 1861, Commodore S. F. DuPont sailed into Port Royal Sound, quickly defeated the Confederates, and put Union troops ashore to occupy the islands. Almost before DuPont's guns ceased firing, the entire white population left the islands for the mainland. A few house servants were taken with the fleeing whites but most of the slaves remained on the islands. The following year they and the occupying army were joined by a host of government agents and Northern missionaries. Several interest groups were gathered in the islands and each had priorities. As Treasury agents concerned themselves with the cotton, and army officers recruited and drafted black soldiers, and missionaries went about "preparing" slaves for freedom, the black Sea Islanders' world was turned upside down. This was true for young and middle-aged men who served in the Union army, but also for the women who had to manage their families and do most of the planting and harvesting in the absence of the men.[44]

During the three years of upheaval, black female life conformed in many ways to that outlined here. Missionaries' comments indicate that certain women were perceived as leaders by their peers. Harriet Ware, for instance, identified a woman from Fripp Point on St. Helena Island named Old Peggy as "the leader." This woman was important because she, along with another woman named Binah, oversaw church membership. Ware's housekeeper Flora told her, "Old Peggy and Binah were the two whom all that came into the Church had to come through, and the Church supports them."[45]

On the Coffin's Point Plantation on St. Helena Island, a woman named Grace served her fellow women at least twice by acting as spokeswoman in disputes over wages paid for cotton production. On one occasion the women of the plantation complained to Mr. Philbrick, one of the plantation superintendents, that their wages were not high enough to permit them to purchase cloth at the local store. They were also upset because the molasses they bought from one of the other plantation superintendents was watered down. As Grace spoke in their behalf, the women shouted words of approval. At least part of the reason for Grace's ascendancy stemmed from the fact that she was among the older women of the island. She was also a strong and diligent worker who was able despite her advanced age to plant, hoe, and harvest cotton along with the younger women.[46]

Ample evidence exists of dependency relationships and cooperation among Sea Island women throughout the war years. In slavery sick and "lying-in" women relied on their peers to help them, and the missionaries found this to be the case on the islands during the Union occupation as well. For instance, Philbrick observed that it was quite common for the blacks to hire each other to hoe their tasks when sickness or other inconveniences kept an individual from it. In 1862 some of the Coffin's Point men were recruited by government agents to pick cotton elsewhere in the Sea Islands. This left many of the women at Coffin's Point completely responsible for hoeing the land allotted to each. Women who were sick or pregnant stood to lose their family's allotment since neglected land was reassigned to others. However, the women saw to it, according to Philbrick, that "the tasks of the lying-in women [were] taken care of by sisters or other friends in the absence of their husbands." No doubt these "other friends" were women, since in the same letter Philbrick noted that the only men left on the plantation were those too old to work in the cotton.[47]

Another missionary, Elizabeth Hyde Botume, related similar episodes of female cooperation. Regardless of the circumstances surrounding a pregnancy, it was common for the women of Port Royal to care for, and keep company with, expectant and convalescing mothers. Several times Botume was approached by a spokeswoman seeking provisions for these mothers. Sometimes she gave them reluctantly because many of the women were not married. Usually, however, she was so impressed by the support that the pregnant women received from their peers that she suspended judgment and sent clothes and groceries for the mothers and infants. On one occasion she was approached by several women who sought aid for a woman named Cumber. The women were so willing to assist one of their own that Botume remarked abashedly: "… their readiness to help the poor erring girl made me ashamed."[48] These were not the only instances of cooperation among the black women. Some moved in with each other and shared domestic duties; others looked after the sick together.[49] With so many of the men away, women found ways of surviving together and cooperating. Predictably, however, along with the "togetherness" went conflict.

Many situations held possibilities for discord. Charles P. Ware, a missionary from Boston, wrote that the work in the crops would go more smoothly if only he could get the women to stop fighting. At least some of the fights were caused by disputes over the distribution of the former mistress's wardrobe. According to Ware, when a woman said, "I free, I as much right to ole missus' things as you," a fight was sure to erupt.[50] Harriet Ware witnessed a fight in which the women "fired shells and tore each other's clothes in a most disgraceful way." The cause of the fight was unknown to her but she was sure it was the "tongues of the women." Jealousy, she noted, ran rampant among the women, and to her mind there was "much foundation for it."[51]

The experiences of the Sea Islands women in the early 1860s comprised a special episode in American history, but their behavior conformed to patterns that had been set previously by bonded women on large plantations. Historians have shown that the community of the quarters, the slave family, and slave religion shielded the slave from absolute dependence on the master and that parents, siblings, friends, and relatives served in different capacities as buffers against the internalization of degrading and dependent roles. The female slave network served as a similar buffer for black women, but it also had a larger significance. Treated by Southern whites as if they were anything but self-respecting women, many bonded females helped one another to forge their own independent definitions of womanhood, their own notions about what women should be and how they should act.

Notes

1. Fredericka Bremer, *Homes of the New World*, 2 vols. (New York, 1853), 2: 519; Frances Anne Kemble, *Journal of a Residence on a Georgian Plantation*, ed. John A. Scott (New York, 1961 [1863]), p. 66. See also: Harriet Martineau, *Society in America*, 3 vols. (London, 1837), 2: 243, 311–12.

2. Benjamin Drew, *The Refugees: A North Side View of Slavery*, in *Four Fugitive Slave Narratives* (Boston, 1969), p. 92.

3. George Rawick, ed., *The American Slave, A Complete Autobiography*, 19 vols. (Westport, CT, 1972), Ga., vol. 13, pt. 4: 139.

4. Frederick Olmsted, *A Journey in the Seaboard Slave States* (New York, 1856), pp. 430–32; Olmsted, *The Cotton Kingdom*, ed. David Freeman Hawke (New York, 1971), p. 176; William Howard Russell, *My Diary North and South (Canada, Its Defenses, Condition and Resources)*, 3 vols. (London, 1865),

1: 379–80; Solomon Northrup, *Twelve Years a Slave, Narrative of Solomon Northup* in Gilbert Osofsky, ed., *Puttin' on Ole Massa* (New York, 1969), pp. 308–309; Rawick, *American Slave*, Ark., vol. 10, pt. 5: 54; Ala., vol. 6: 46, 336; Newstead Plantation Diary 1856–58, entry Wednesday, May 6, 1857, Southern Historical Collection (SHC), University of North Carolina at Chapel Hill; Adwon Adams Davis, *Plantation Life in the Florida Parishes of Louisiana 1836–1846 as Reflected in the Diary of Bennet H. Barrow* (New York, 1943), p. 127; Frederick Olmsted, *A Journey in the Back Country* (New York, 1907), p. 152; *Plantation Manual*, SHC, p. 4; Eugene Genovese, *The Political Economy of Slavery: Studies in the Economy and Society of the Slave South* (New York, 1961), p. 133; Stuart Bruchey, ed., *Cotton and the Growth of the American Economy: 1790–1860* (New York, 1967), pp. 176–80.

5. See note 4.

6. J. A. Turner, ed., *The Cotton Planters Manual* (New York, 1865), pp. 97–98; Guion B. Johnson, *A Social History of the Sea Islands* (Chapel Hill, NC, 1930), pp. 28–30; Jenkins Mikell, *Rumbling of the Chariot Wheels* (Columbia, SC, 1923), pp. 19–20; Bruchey, *Cotton and the Growth of the American Economy*, pp. 176–80.

7. Rawick, *American Slave*, S.C., vol. 2, pt. 2: 114.

8. Ibid., Ga., vol. 13, p. 3: 186.

9. *Plantation Manual*, SHC, p. 1.

10. Rawick, *American Slave*, Ok., vol. 7: 315.

11. George P. Rawick, Jan Hillegas, and Ken Lawrence, ed., *The American Slave: A Composite Autobiography, Supplement, Series 1*, 12 vols. (Westport, CT, 1978), Ga., Supp. 1, vol. 4: 479.

12. Rawick, *American Slave*, Mo., vol 11: 307.

13. For examples of cures see: Ibid., Ark., vol. 10, pt. 5: 21, 125; Ala., vol. 6: 256, 318; Ga., vol. 13, pt. 3: 106.

14. Ibid., Ga., vol. 12, pt. 1: 303.

15. Ibid., Fla, vol. 17: 175; see also: Rawick *et al., American Slave, Supplement*, Miss. Supp. 1, vol. 6: 317; Ga. Supp. 1., vol. 4: 444; John Spencer Bassett, *The Southern Plantation Overseer, as Revealed in His Letters* (Northampton, MA, 1923), pp. 28, 31.

16. Kemble, *Journal of a Residence on a Georgian Plantation*, p. 222.

17. Robert Manson Myers, ed., *The Children of Pride: A True Story of Georgia and the Civil War* (New Haven, CT, 1972), pp. 528, 532, 542, 544, 546.

18. Charles S. Johnson, ed., *God Struck Me Dead: Religious Conversion Experiences and Autobiographies of Negro Ex-Slaves* in Rawick, *American Slave*, vol. 19: 74.

19. Rawick, *American Slave*, S.C., vol. 2, pt. 1: 99.

20. Ibid., Ga., vol. 12, pt. 2: 112; S.C., vol 2, pt. 2: 55; Fla., vol. 17: 174; see also Olmsted, *Back Country*, p. 76.

21. See, for instance, *Plantation Manual*, SHC, p. 1.

22. Rawick, *American Slave*, Ala., vol. 6: 73.

23. Rawick *et al., American Slave, Supplement*, Ga. Supp. 1, vol. 4, pt. 3: 103.

24. Rawick, *American Slave*, Tex., vol. 5, pt. 3: 103.

25. Hughes, *Thirty Years a Slave*, p. 39; Rawick, *American Slave*, Fla., vol. 17: 158; S. C., vol. 2, pt. 1: 114; White Hill Plantation Books, SHC, p. 13.

26. Hughes, *Thirty Years a Slave*, p. 22.

27. Ophelia Settle Egypt, J. Masuoha, and Charles S. Johnson, eds., *Unwritten History of Slavery: Autobiographical Accounts of Negro Ex-Slaves* (Washington, 1968 [1945]), p. 41.

28. Laura M. Towne, *Letters and Diary of Laura M. Towne Written from the Sea Islands of South Carolina 1862–1884*, ed. Rupert Sargent Holland (New York, 1969 [1912]), pp. 144–45. See also: Kemble, *Journal of a Residence on a Georgian Plantation*, p. 55.

29. Rawick, *American Slave*, Ga. vol. 13, pt. 3: 190.

30. Frederick Douglass, *My Bondage and My Freedom* (New York, 1968 [1855]), p. 36.

31. Elizabeth Hyde Botume, *First Days Amongst the Contrabands* (Boston, 1893), p. 132.

32. Davis, *Plantation Life in the Florida Parishes*, p. 191. See also pp. 168, 173.

33. Kemble, *Journal of a Residence on a Georgian Plantation*, pp. 118–19.

34. Martha Graham Goodson, "An Introductory Essay and Subject Index to Selected Interviews from the Slave Narrative Collection" (Ph.D. diss., Union Graduate School, 1977), p. 33.

35. Cheryll Ann Cody, "Naming, Kinship, and Estate Dispersal: Notes on Slave Family Life on a South Carolina Plantation, 1786 to 1833," *William and Mary Quarterly* 39 (1982): 207–09.

36. Rawick, *American Slave*, Ala., vol. 7: 73.

37. Herbert G. Gutman, *The Black Family in Slavery and Freedom, 1750–1925* (New York, 1976), pp. 216–22.

38. J. H. Easterby, ed., *The South Carolina Rice Plantations as Revealed in the Papers of Robert W. Allston* (Chicago, 1945), p. 291.

39. Bassett, *The Southern Plantation Overseer*, pp. 19–20, 32.

40. Rawick, *American Slave*, Ga., vol. 12, pt. 2: 57.

41. C. Vann Woodward, Ed., *Mary Chestnut's Civil War* (New Haven, CT, 1981), pp. 33–34.

42. Norman Yetman, *Voices from Slavery* (New York, 1970), p. 13.

43. J. Mason Brewer, *American Negro Folklore* (New York, 1968), p. 233.

44. Willie Lee Rose, *Rehearsal for Reconstruction: The Port Royal Experiment* (New York, 1964), p. 11.

45. Elizabeth Ware Pearson, ed., *Letters from Port Royal: Written at the Time of the Civil War* (New York, 1969 [1906]), p. 44.

46. Ibid., pp. 250, 303–04.

47. Ibid., p. 56.

48. Botume, *First Days Amongst the Contrabands*, p. 125.

49. See for instance: Ibid., pp. 55–56, 58, 80, 212.

50. Pearson, *Letters from Port Royal*, p. 1133.

51. Botume, *First Days Amongst the Contrabands*, pp. 210–11.

Deborah Gray White is associate professor of history and Africana studies at Rutgers University, New Brunswick, New Jersey. This chapter is adapted from her book, *Ar'n't I a Woman? Female Slaves in the Plantation South*, published in 1984 by W. W. Norton.

WILLIAM W. BROWN

After his 1834 escape to freedom, fugitive slave William Wells Brown used
his literary talents for the abolitionist cause and to record
the history of America's blacks.

By Marsh Cassady

AT JUST AFTER 8 P.M. on February 2, 1857, an air of expectancy gripped the crowd assembled in the town hall in the little village of Salem, Ohio. The audience leaned forward in their seats, eager to catch a glimpse of the middle-aged black man who strode confidently onto the stage. William Wells Brown, the object of their curiosity, cleared his throat and began to recite from *Experience, or How to Give a Northern Man a Backbone,* the first play authored by an African American.[1]

For almost a year, Brown had traveled about the Northeast reading his drama, which dealt with the evils of slavery and urged the abolitionists in attendance to do something about the plight of blacks held in bondage. No copies of this 1856 play have survived, but fortunately, his second such work, *The Escape, or A Leap For Freedom,* fared better following its 1858 publication.

These two plays—the only ones known to have been written by Brown—represented only a tiny portion of his literary achievements. Virtually illiterate in his youth, Brown went on to become a historian, an essayist, a journalist, and a lecturer, as well as America's first black novelist, playwright, and travel-book author.

Born near Lexington, Kentucky, sometime between 1813 and 1815, William was the son of Elizabeth, a slave on a farm owned by Dr. John Young. His father was George Higgins, Young's half-brother or cousin.

In 1816, Dr. Young moved to Missouri with his family and slaves, settling in Saint Charles County on the northern shore of the Missouri River. Four years later, Young went off to serve in the state's first legislature, leaving his farm in the hands of overseer Grove Cook, a cruel man who made frequent use of the whip. In his autobiography, William described a beating that his mother received, remembering that "cold chills ran over me, and I wept aloud."

While William was still a boy, the Youngs took an infant nephew into their home. Since his name too was William, they, changed the young slave's name to Sanford. The youth did not take losing his only possession—his name—lightly and endured several beatings for persisting in calling himself William.

Light skinned, William also found himself at the wrong end of the lash when people mistook him for a member of the Young family, a resemblance that was obviously beyond his control. This question of skin color caused William to suffer the scorn of some fellow slaves as well. As he later wrote, "the nearer a slave approaches an Anglo-Saxon in complexion the more he is abused by both owner and fellow-slaves. The owner flogs him to keep him 'in his place,' and the slaves hate him on account of his being whiter than themselves."

When Dr. Young moved to St. Louis in 1827, he hired William out to work in a variety of jobs. In his first book, *Narrative of William Wells Brown, A Fugitive Slave,* William wrote of his treatment at the hands of a tavern keeper named Major Freeland, a drunkard who severely beat the then-teenager. After brief stints working on a steamboat and at the Missouri Hotel in the city, William was hired by Elijah P. Lovejoy, editor of the *St. Louis Times.* There for only a brief time, William was nonetheless able to acquire the rudiments of an education.

In 1832, William was put in the employ of James Walker, a slave trader, for one year and was forced to take part in the transportation of fellow slaves down river for auction. By the time William's distasteful service to Walker had expired, Dr. Young found himself in financial difficulty. To ease his situation, he made plans to sell William, despite an earlier promise to Higgins that he never would sell his son. Regretful that such a move was necessary, Young give William a week to find a new owner. Instead, William talked his mother into trying to flee to Canada. Against her better judgement, Elizabeth agreed.

Eleven days later the pair was captured in Illinois; Elizabeth was sold into the deep South and never saw her son again. William was sold for $500.00 to a St. Louis tailor, Samuel Willi, who hired him out as a servant on a steamboat. Less than a year later, Willi sold William to a merchant and riverboat owner, Enoch Price. When his new owner, acting as captain, took one of his boats to New Orleans and then to Cincinnati, in the free state of Ohio, he took William along.

On January 1, 1834, William carried a passenger's trunk ashore in Cincinnati. Seizing this chance to escape, he kept on walking and quickly made his way out of the city. For six days, he wandered by himself during the night hours, ill-clothed for the winter weather and without food.

Nearly frozen and sick with a fever, he finally approached a man who "had on a broad-brimmed hat and a very long coat, and was obviously walking for exercise. As soon as I saw him, and observed his dress, I thought to myself, 'You are the man that I have been looking for!' Nor was I mistaken. He was the very man!"

Wells Brown, a Quaker, gave the youth shelter and food, and cared for him until he was well. On learning that William had no family name, he offered his own, and the runaway slave became William Wells Brown.

With a new name and a fresh start in a free state, the light-skinned William traveled to Cleveland, where he worked at odd jobs until navigation resumed on the Great Lakes in the spring. When shipping again opened up, William found employment as a steward on a Lake Erie steamer, the *Detroit*.

That same year, he met and married Elizabeth Schooner, whom he called Betsey. The couple's first child died not long after birth, but they had two more daughters, Clarissa and Josephine.[2]

During the nine years he plied the lakes, William taught himself to read and write, and helped other fugitives escape to freedom in Canada. By 1840, Brown and his family had moved to Buffalo, New York, and made their home a stop on the Underground Railway; 69 runaways made good their escape through Brown's efforts during 1842 alone.

Soon after his arrival in Buffalo, Brown organized the Union Total Abstinence Society and began his association with the Western New York Anti-Slavery Society. He lectured for the abolitionist cause, using his speeches to attack America's idea of democracy, which he felt only existed for whites, and the hypocrisy of using religion to ensure the docility of slaves.

Although a speech he delivered before the Female Anti-Slavery Society of Salem, Massachusetts, in 1847 was his first published work, his first book was his "slave narrative," a popular genre of the period, which was released that same year. In the two years following its publication, the biography went through four editions. While this work did show the influence of previously published slave narratives, Brown's was unique in its inclusion of cases other than his own to point up the overwhelming cruelty of slavery.

After seeing a copy of William's slave narrative, Enoch Price, his former owner, wrote in 1848 offering William his freedom for $325.00. Brown refused, firm in his belief that freedom can not be bought or sold but is a divine and moral right. "God," he declared, "made me as free as he did Enoch Price," and therefore, not a penny would be paid for his freedom "with my consent."

A year later, he published *The Anti-Slavery Harp: A Collection of Songs for Anti-Slavery Meetings,* a compilation of 46 pieces to be sung to familiar melodies. He gave a series of anti-slavery presentations throughout New England, illustrating the evils of involuntary servitude by presenting two escaped slaves from Georgia, William and Ellen Craft. And, he traveled to France in August 1849 as the American Peace Society's delegate to the International Peace Congress in Paris.

In 1850, the 1793 Fugitive Slave Law was strengthened, making it dangerous for Brown to return home. William, therefore, chose to remain abroad. With England as his base, he spent the next four years traveling throughout Great Britain and to Europe, giving lectures about the slavery question and completing three more books. The First—*A Description of William Wells Brown's Panoramic Views of the Scenes in the Life of an American Slave, from His Birth in Slavery to His Death or His Escape to His First Home of Freedom on British Soil*—consisted of stories and a series of 24 sketches, which were drawn by artists at his direction.

Three Years in Europe: or, Places I have Seen and People I Have Met, published in 1852, was a compilation of 23 letters Brown had written since his arrival there, comparing the freedom of life in Europe to the tyranny faced by blacks in America. The book was well received, one reviewer noting that Brown wrote "with ease and ability, and his intelligent observations upon the great question to which he has devoted, and is devoting, his life, will command influence and respect."

Brown's novel, *Clotel: or, The President's Daughter: A Narrative of Slave Life in the United States,* was published in London in 1853. The book took its title from allegations that Thomas Jefferson had fathered several mixed-race children, whom he then abandoned to slavery. Published about a year after Harriet Beecher Stowe's *Uncle Tom's Cabin,* however, Brown's work failed to create much of a stir or garner critical acclaim.

"Brown believed that freedom cannot be bought and sold, but is a divine and moral right."

While abroad, Brown also used his time to become versed in the practice of medicine. In a day when formal training still was not required for doctors, he attended lectures and conducted private study, gradually obtaining sufficient knowledge to become a medical practitioner. Instead of pursuing that profession, however, he continued to devote himself to the anti-slavery cause.

In 1854, Brown finally agreed to purchase his freedom so that he might return to the United States and fight more effectively for the abolition of the "most cruel system of oppression that ever blackened the character or hardened the heart of man."

Soon after he arrived in America, Brown published *The American Fugitive in Europe*, an enlarged version of his *Three Years in Europe*. This new edition was the first book written by Brown to be reviewed by a major American newspaper. *The New York Daily Tribune* declared that the work was a "lively and entertaining record of foreign travel" and, due to its origins, a worthy "novelty in literature."

During the Civil War, Brown joined fellow abolitionists Frederick Douglass and T. Morris Chester in recruiting in Massachusetts, New York, Pennsylvania, and New Jersey for the all-black 54th Massachusetts Regiment. The war years also saw publication of Brown's first historical work, *The Black Man: His Antecedents, His Genius, and His Achievements*. An anthology of biographical sketches of blacks with significant accomplishments to their credit, this work went through ten editions in just three years.

Two years after the war, Brown brought out *The Negro in the American Rebellion, His Heroism and His Fidelity*. And in 1874, he published his most complete and important historical undertaking, *The Rising Son; or, The Antecedents and Advancements of the Colored Race*, which traced the roots of America's blacks from Africa. As he had in his previous histories, Brown strongly refuted the era's belief in the inferiority of the black race.

William Wells Brown died in Chelsea, Massachusetts, in 1884. Despite his literacy achievements and his many contributions in the struggle for freedom and equality, he was buried in an unmarked grave in the Cambridge, Massachusetts, cemetery.

He was eulogized in the Boston newspapers as "one of the most intelligent, earnest and active members of the little band of oldtime abolitionists" and as a "prolific writer, commanding a clear intellect and facile pen...." Brown, who spent his last years fighting for improved education for black children, did his utmost throughout his life to combat racial prejudice and its resulting indignities, consistently emphasizing the need for cooperation among people of all races.

Notes

1. Brown may have originally entitled this work *The Dough Face*.
2. William and Elizabeth Brown's marriage lasted only until 1848. In February 1860, he wed Annie Elizabeth Gray; they had two children—Clotelle and William Wells, Junior.

Freelance writer Marsh Cassady of San Diego, California, is the author of 41 books.

From *American History*, January/February 1996. © 1996 by Primedia Enthusiast Publications, Inc. All rights reserved.

The Father of American Terrorism

Two hundred years after his birth, Americans still revere him as a martyr and loathe him as a fanatical murderer. What was he?

By Ken Chowder

ON DECEMBER 2, 1859, A TALL OLD MAN IN A BLACK COAT, black pants, black vest, and black slouch hat climbed into a wagon and sat down on a black walnut box. The pants and coat were stained with blood; the box was his coffin; the old man was going to his execution. He had just handed a last note to his jailer: "I John Brown am now quite *certain* that the crimes of this *guilty, land: will* never be purged *away;* but with Blood. I had… *vainly* flattered myself that without *very much* bloodshed; it might be done."

As he rode on his coffin, John Brown gazed out over the cornfields of Virginia. "This *is* a beautiful country," he said. "I never had the pleasure of seeing it before."

The United States in 1859 was a nation that harbored a ticking time bomb: the issue of slavery. And it was a place where an astonishing number of men were willing to die for their beliefs, certain they were following a higher law. John Brown was one of those God-fearing yet violent men. And he was already more than a man; he was a legend. In fact, there were two competing legends. To slaveholders he was utter evil—fanatic, murderer, liar, and lunatic, and horse thief to boot—while to abolitionists he had become the embodiment of all that was noble and courageous.

After a lifetime of failure John Brown had at last found a kind of success. He was now a symbol that divided the nation, and his story was no longer about one man; it was a prophecy. The United States, like John Brown, was heading toward a gallows—the gallows of war.

A scaffold had been built in a field outside Charlestown, Virginia. There were rumors of a rescue attempt, and fifteen hundred soldiers, commanded by Col. Robert E. Lee, massed in the open field. No civilians were allowed within hearing range, but an actor from Virginia borrowed a uniform so he could watch John Brown die. "I looked at the traitor and terrorizer," said John Wilkes Booth, "with unlimited, undeniable contempt." Prof. Thomas Jackson, who would in three years be known as Stonewall, was also watching: "The sheriff placed the rope

METROPOLITAN MUSEUM OF ART, NEW YORK CITY. ARTHUR HOPPOCK HEARN FUND, 1950.

John Steuart Curry's melodramatic 1939 John Brown, his back to a Kansas tornado, has become the standard image of the man.

around [Brown's] neck, then threw a white cap over his head.… When the rope was cut by a single blow, Brown fell through.… There was very little motion of his person for several moments, and soon the wind blew his lifeless body to and fro."

A Virginia colonel named J. T. L. Preston chanted: "So perish all such enemies of Virginia! All such enemies of the Union! All such foes of the human race!"

B UT HANGING WAS NOT THE END OF JOHN BROWN; IT WAS THE beginning. Northern churches' bells tolled for him, and cannon boomed in salute. In Massachusetts, Henry David Thoreau spoke: "Some eighteen hundred years ago, Christ was crucified; This morning, perchance, Captain Brown was hung… He is not Old Brown any longer; he is an angel of light."

John Brown's soul was already marching on. But the flesh-and-blood John Brown—a tanner, shepherd, and farmer, a simple and innocent man who could kill in cold blood, a mixture of opposite parts who mirrored the paradoxical America of his time—this John Brown had already vanished, and he would rarely appear again. His life instead became the subject for 140 years of spin. John Brown has been used rather than considered by history; even today we are still spinning his story.

> *When his farm was sold*
> *he seemed to snap.*
> *He barricaded himself in,*
> *and the sheriff got up a posse.*

As far as history is concerned, John Brown was genuinely nobody until he was fifty-six years old—that is, until he began to kill people. Not that his life was without incident. He grew up in the wilderness of Ohio (he was born in 1800, when places like Detroit, Chicago, and Cleveland were still frontier stockades). He married at twenty, lost his wife eleven years later, soon married again, and fathered a total of twenty children. Nine of them died before they reached adulthood.

At seventeen Brown left his father's tannery to start a competing one. "I acknowledge no master in human form," he would say, many years later, when he was wounded and in chains at Harpers Ferry. The young man soon mastered the rural arts of farming, tanning, surveying, home building, and animal husbandry, but his most conspicuous talent seemed to be one for profuse and painful failure.

In the 1830s, with a growing network of canals making barren land worth thousands, Brown borrowed deeply to speculate in real estate—just in time for the disastrous Panic of 1837. The historian James Brewer Stewart, author of *Holy Warriors,* says that "Brown was a typical story of someone who invested, as thousands did, and lost thousands, as thousands did as well. Brown was swept along in a current of default and collapse."

He tried breeding sheep, started another tannery, bought and sold cattle—each time a failure. When one venture lost money, Brown quietly appropriated funds from a partner in a new business and used it to pay the earlier loss. But in the end his farm tools, furniture, and sheep went on the auction block.

When his farm was sold, he seemed to snap. He refused to leave. With two sons and some old muskets, he barricaded himself in a cabin on the property. "I was makeing preparation for the commencement and vigorous prosecution of a tedious, distressing, wasteing, and long protracted war," Brown wrote. The sheriff got up a posse and briefly put him in the Akron jail. No shots were fired, but it was an incident people would remember, years later, when the old man barricaded himself at Harpers Ferry.

Brown's misadventures in business have drawn widely varying interpretations. His defenders say he had a large family to support; small wonder he wanted badly to make money. But others have seen his financial dreams as an obsession, a kind of fever that gave him delusions of wealth and made him act dishonestly.

P ERHAPS IT WAS THIS LONG STRING OF FAILURES THAT CREATED the revolutionary who burst upon the American scene in 1856. By that time Brown had long nurtured a vague and protean plan: He imagined a great event in which he—the small-time farmer who had failed in everything he touched—would be God's messenger, a latter-day Moses who would lead his people from the accursed house of slavery. He had already, for years, been active in the Underground Railroad, hiding runaways and guiding them north toward Canada. In 1837 he stood up in the back of a church in Ohio and made his first public statement on human bondage, a single pungent sentence: "Here before God, in the presence of these witnesses, I consecrate my life to the destruction of slavery." For years, however, this vow seemed to mean relatively little; in the early 1850s, as anger over slavery began to boil up all over the North, the frustrated and humiliated Brown was going from courtroom to courtroom embroiled in his own private miseries.

Finally it happened. The John Brown we know was born in the place called Bloody Kansas. Slavery had long been barred from the territories of Kansas and Nebraska, but in 1854 the Kansas-Nebraska Act decreed that the settlers of these territories would decide by vote whether to be free or slave. The act set up a competition between the two systems that would become indistinguishable from war.

> *At Pottawatomie, he watched as*
> *his followers split open*
> *heads and cut off arms.*

Settlers from both sides flooded into Kansas. Five of John Brown's sons made the long journey there from Ohio. But

NATIONAL PORTRAIT GALLERY, SMITHSONIAN INSTITUTION, WASHINGTON, D.C.
Brown with his hand raised as in oath in a daguerreotype made around 1846 by Augustus Washington, an African-American photographer.

Brown himself did not go. He was in his mid-fifties, old by the actuarial tables of his day; he seemed broken.

Then, in March of 1855, five thousand proslavery Missourians—the hard-drinking, heavily armed "Border Ruffians"—rode into Kansas. "We came to vote, and we are going to vote or kill every God-damned abolitionist in the Territory," their leader declared. The Ruffians seized the polling places, voted in their own legislature, and passed their own laws. Prison now awaited anyone who spoke against slavery.

In May, John Junior wrote to his father begging for his help. The free-soilers needed arms, "more than we need bread," he said. "Now we want you to get for us these arms." The very next day, Brown began raising money and gathering weapons and in August the old man left for Kansas, continuing to collect arms as he went.

IN MAY 1856 A PROSLAVERY ARMY SACKED THE FREE-SOIL town of Lawrence; not a single abolitionist dared fire a gun. This infuriated Brown. He called for volunteers to go on "a secret mission." The old man, in his soiled straw hat, stuck a revolver in his belt and led a company of eight men down to-

ward Pottawatomie Creek. Proslavery people lived in the cabins there.

Late on the night of May 23, 1856, one of the group, probably Brown, banged on the door of James Doyle's cabin. He ordered the men of the family outside at gunpoint, and Brown's followers set upon three Doyles with broadswords. They split open heads and cut off arms. John Brown watched his men work. When it was over, he put a single bullet into the head of James Doyle.

After Brown was sentenced, he began comparing himself to Jesus Christ. And he was not alone.

His party went to two more cabins, dragged out and killed two more men. At the end bodies lay in the bushes and floated in the creek; the murderers had made off with horses, saddles, and a bowie knife.

What came to be called the Pottawatomie Massacre ignited all-out war in Kansas. John Brown, the aged outsider, became an abolitionist leader. In August some 250 Border Ruffians attacked the free-soil town of Osawatomie. Brown led thirty men in defending the town. He fought hard, but Osawatomie burned to the ground.

A few days later, when Brown rode into Lawrence on a gray horse, a crowd gathered to cheer "as if the President had come to town," one man said. The spinning of John Brown had already begun. A Scottish reporter named James Redpath had found Brown's men in their secret campsite, and "I left this sacred spot with a far higher respect for the Great Struggle than ever I had felt before." And what of Pottawatomie? Brown had nothing to do with it, Redpath wrote. John Brown himself even prepared an admiring account of the Battle of Osawatomie for Eastern newspapers. Less than two weeks after the fight, a drama called *Ossawattomie Brown* was celebrating him on Broadway.

That autumn, peace finally came to Kansas, but not to John Brown. For the next three years he traveled the East, occasionally returning to Kansas, beseeching abolitionists for guns and money, money and guns. His plan evolved into this: One night he and a small company of men would capture the federal armory and arsenal at Harpers Ferry, Virginia. The invaders would take the guns there and leave. Local slaves would rise up to join them, making an army; together they all would drive south, and the revolution would snowball through the kingdom of slavery.

On the rainy night of October 16, 1859, Brown led a determined little procession down the road to Harpers Ferry. Some twenty men were making a direct attack on the U.S. government; they would liberate four million souls from bondage. At first the raid went like clockwork. The armory was protected by just one man, and he quickly surrendered. The invaders cut telegraph lines and rounded up hostages on the street.

Then Brown's difficulties began. A local doctor rode out screaming, "Insurrection!," and by midmorning men in the heights behind town were taking potshots down at Brown's followers. Meanwhile, John Brown quietly ordered breakfast from a hotel for his hostages. As Dennis Frye, the former chief historian at Harpers Ferry National Historical Park, asks, "The question is, why didn't John Brown attempt to leave? Why did he stay in Harpers Ferry?" Russell Banks, the author of the recent John Brown novel *Cloudsplitter*, has an answer: "He stayed and he stayed, and it seems to me a deliberate, resigned act of martyrdom."

At noon a company of Virginia militia entered town, took the bridge, and closed the only true escape route. By the end of the day, John Brown's revolution was failing. Eight invaders were dead or dying. Five others were cut off from the main group. Two had escaped across the river; two had been captured. Only five raiders were still fit to fight. Brown gathered his men in a small brick building, the enginehouse, for the long, cold night.

THE FIRST LIGHT OF OCTOBER 18 SHOWED BROWN AND HIS tiny band an armory yard lined with U.S. Marines, under the command of Col. Robert E. Lee. A young lieutenant, J. E. B. Stuart, approached beneath a white flag and handed over a note asking the raiders to surrender. Brown refused. At that Stuart jumped aside, waved his cap, and the Marines stormed forward with a heavy ladder. The door gave way. Lt. Israel Green tried to run Brown through, but his blade struck the old man's belt buckle; God, for the moment, had saved John Brown.

A few hours later, as he lay in a small room at the armory, bound and bleeding, Brown's real revolution began. Gov. Henry A. Wise of Virginia arrived with a retinue of reporters. Did Brown want the reporters removed? asked Robert E. Lee. Definitely not. "Brown said he was by no means annoyed," one reporter wrote. For the old man was now beginning a campaign that would win half of America. He told the reporters: "I wish to say… that you had better—all you people of the South—prepare yourselves for a settlement of this question.… You may dispose of me very easily—I am nearly disposed of now; but this question is still to be settled—this negro question I mean; the end of that is not yet."

His crusade for acceptance would not be easy. At first he was no hero. Leaders of the Republican party organized anti-Brown protests; "John Brown was no Republican," Abraham Lincoln said. Even the *Liberator,* published by the staunch abolitionist William Lloyd Garrison, called the raid "misguided, wild, and apparently insane."

In the South the initial reaction was derision—the Richmond *Dispatch* called the foray "miserably weak and contemptible"—but that soon changed to fear. Stuart's soldiers found a carpetbag crammed with letters from Brown's supporters; a number of prominent Northerners had financed the raid. It had been a conspiracy, a wide-ranging one. But how wide?

A reign of terror began in the South. A minister who spoke out against the treatment of slaves was publicly whipped; a man who spoke sympathetically about the raid found himself thrown in jail. Four state legislatures appropriated military funds. Georgia set aside seventy-five thousand dollars; Alabama, almost three times as much.

Brown's trial took just one week. As Virginia hurried toward a verdict, the Reverend Henry Ward Beecher preached, "Let no man pray that Brown be spared! Let Virginia make him a martyr!" John Brown read Beecher's words in his cell. He wrote "Good" beside them.

On November 2 the jury, after deliberating for forty-five minutes, reached its verdict. Guilty. Before he was sentenced, Brown rose to address the court: "I see a book kissed here,… the Bible.… [That] teaches me to 'remember them that are in bonds, as bound with them.' I endeavored to act up to that instruction.… I believe that to have interfered… in behalf of His despised poor was not wrong, but right. Now, if it is deemed necessary that I should forfeit my life…, and mingle my blood further with the blood of my children and with the blood of millions in this slave country whose rights are disregarded… I say let it be done!"

FOR THE NEXT MONTH THE CHARLESTOWN JAIL CELL WAS John Brown's pulpit. All over the North, Brown knew, people were reading his words. He wrote, "You know that Christ once armed Peter. So also in my case I think he put a sword into my hand, and there continued it so long as he saw best, and then kindly took it from me."

The author of the Pottawatomie Massacre was now comparing himself to Jesus Christ. And he was not alone. Even the temperate Ralph Waldo Emerson called him "the new Saint whose fate yet hangs in suspense but whose martyrdom if it shall be perfected, will make the gallows as glorious as the cross." There were rescue plans, but John Brown did not want to escape. "I am worth inconceivably more to hang than for any other purpose," he wrote.

It wasn't until the 1970s
that John Brown the hero re-emerged,
in two excellent studies.

He got that wish on December 2, and the mythologizing of the man began in earnest. Thoreau, Emerson, Victor Hugo, Herman Melville, and Walt Whitman all wrote essays or poems immortalizing him. James Redpath eagerly waited for the moment when "Old B was in heaven"; just a month after the execution, he published the first biography. Forty thousand copies of the book sold in a single month.

Less than a year and a half later, the guns began firing on Fort Sumter. If the country had been a tinder box, it seemed to many that John Brown had been the spark. "Did John Brown fail?" Frederick Douglass wrote. "… John Brown began the war that ended American slavery and made this a free Republic."

His reputation seemed secure, impermeable. The first biographies of the man James Redpath called the "warrior saint" all glorified him. But then, in 1910, Oswald Garrison Villard, grandson of the abolitionist William Lloyd Garrison, wrote a massive and carefully researched book that pictured Brown as a muddled, pugnacious, bumbling, and homicidal madman. Nineteen years later Robert Penn Warren issued a similar (and derivative) study. Perhaps the most influential image of John Brown came, not surprisingly, from Hollywood: In *Santa Fe Trail* Raymond Massey portrayed him as a lunatic, pure and simple.

It wasn't until the 1970s that John Brown the hero re-emerged. Two excellent studies by Stephen B. Oates and Richard Owen Boyer captured the core of the conundrum: Brown was stubborn, monomaniacal, egotistical, self-righteous, and sometimes deceitful; yet he was, at certain times, a great man. Boyer, in particular, clearly admired him: At bottom Brown "was an American who gave his life that millions of other Americans might be free."

Among African-Americans, Brown's heroism has never been in doubt. Frederick Douglass praised him in print; W. E. B. Du Bois published a four-hundred-page celebration of him in 1909; Malcolm X said he wouldn't mind being with white people if they were like John Brown; and Alice Walker, in a poem, even wondered if in an earlier incarnation she herself hadn't once been John Brown.

But, as Russell Banks points out, Brown's "acts mean completely different things to Americans depending upon their skin color." And the image that most white people today have of John Brown is still of the wild-eyed, bloodthirsty madman. After all, he believed that God spoke to him; he killed people at Pottawatomie in cold blood; he launched an attack on the U.S. government at Harpers Ferry with not even two dozen men. How sane could he have been?

Let's look at those charges one by one. First: *He conversed with* God. Brown's religious principles, everyone agrees, were absolutely central to the man. As a child he learned virtually the entire Bible by heart. At sixteen he traveled to New England to study for the ministry. He gave up after a few months but remained deeply serious about his Calvinist beliefs. Brown had a great yearning for justice for all men, yet a rage for bloody revenge. These qualities may seem paradoxical to us, but they were ones that John Brown had in common with his deity. The angry God of the Old Testament punished evil: An eye cost exactly an eye.

If God spoke directly to John Brown, He also spoke to William Lloyd Garrison and to the slave revolutionary Nat Turner. To converse with God, in Brown's day, did not mean that you were eccentric. In fact, God was on everyone's side. John Brown saw the story of Moses setting the Israelites free as a mandate for emancipation, but at the same time, others used the Bible to justify slavery (Noah did, after all, set an everlasting curse on all the dark descendants of Ham). It was all in the Bible, and Americans on both sides went to war certain that they were doing God's bidding. So it is that John Brown believed that God had appointed him "a special agent of death," "an instrument raised up by Providence to break the jaws of the wicked."

Second: *He killed in cold blood.* Brown was a violent man, but he lived in increasingly violent times. Slavery itself was of course a violent practice. In 1831 Nat Turner led seventy slaves to revolt; they killed fifty-seven white men, women, and children. A few years later a clergyman named Elijah Lovejoy was gunned down for speaking out against slavery. By the 1850s another distinguished clergyman, Thomas Wentworth Higginson, could lead a mob to the federal courthouse in Boston and attack the place with axes and guns. "I can only make my life worth living," Higginson vowed, "by becoming a revolutionist." During the struggle in Kansas Henry Ward Beecher's Plymouth Church in Brooklyn was blithely shipping Sharps rifles west; "there are times," the famous preacher said, "when self-defense is a religious duty." By the late fifties, writes the historian James Stewart, even Congress was "a place where fist fights became common… a place where people came armed… a place where people flashed Bowie knives." On February 5, 1858, a brawl broke out between North and South in the House of Representatives; congressmen rolled on the floor, scratching and gouging each other.

Brown's Pottawatomie Massacre was directly connected to this national chaos. On the very day Brown heard about the sacking of Lawrence, another disturbing report reached him from Washington: A Southern congressman had attacked Sen. Charles Sumner, a fierce abolitionist, on the floor of Congress, caning him almost to death for insulting the South. When the news got to Brown's campsite, according to his son Salmon, "the men went crazy—*crazy*. It seemed to be the finishing, decisive touch." Brown ordered his men to sharpen their broadswords and set off toward Pottawatomie, the creek whose name still stains his reputation.

So it is that "Brown is simply part of a very violent world," according to the historian Paul Finkelman. At Pottawatomie, Finkelman says, "Brown was going after particular men who were dangerous to the very survival of the free-state settlers in the area." But Dennis Frye has a less analytical (and less sympathetic) reaction: "Pottawatomie was cold-blooded murder. [It was] killing people up close based on anger and vengeance."

To Bruce Olds, the author of *Raising Holy Hell*, a 1995 novel about Brown, Pottawatomie was an example of conscious political terrorism: "Those killings took place in the middle of the night, in the dark—that was on purpose. In his writings, [Brown] uses the word 'terror' and the word 'shock.' He intended to produce both of those, and he did."

Maybe Pottawatomie was insane, and maybe it was not. But what about that Harpers Ferry plan—a tiny band attacking the U.S. government, hoping to concoct a revolution that would carry across the South? Clearly *that* was crazy.

Yes and no. If it was crazy, it was not unique. Dozens of people, often bearing arms, had gone South to rescue slaves. Secret military societies flourished on both sides, plotting to expand or destroy the system of slavery by force. Far from being the product of a singular cracked mind, the plan was similar to a number of others, including one by a Boston attorney named Lysander Spooner. James Horton, a leading African-American history scholar, offers an interesting scenario. "Was Brown crazy to assume he could encourage slave rebellion?... Think about the possibility of Nat Turner well-armed, well-equipped.... Nat Turner might have done some pretty amazing things," Horton says. "It was perfectly rational and reasonable for John Brown to believe he could encourage slaves to rebel."

Elements on both the far left and the far right are at this moment vitally interested in his story.

B UT THE QUESTION OF BROWN'S SANITY STILL PROVOKES DIS-sension among experts. Was he crazy? "He was obsessed," Bruce Olds says, "he was fanatical, he was monomaniacal, he was a zealot, and... psychologically unbalanced." Paul Finkelman disagrees: Brown "is a bad tactician, he's a bad strategist, he's a bad planner, he's not a very good general—but he's not crazy."

Some believe that there is a very particular reason why Brown's reputation as a madman has clung to him. Russell Banks and James Horton make the same argument. "The reason white people think he was mad," Banks says, "is because he was a white man and he was willing to sacrifice his life in order to liberate black Americans." "We should be very careful," Horton says, "about assuming that a white man who is willing to put his life on the line for black people is, of necessity, crazy."

Perhaps it is reasonable to say this: A society where slavery exists is by nature one where human values are skewed. America before the Civil War was a violent society, twisted by slavery. Even sober and eminent people became firebrands. John Brown had many peculiarities of his own, but he was not outside his society; to a great degree, he represented it, in its many excesses.

The past, as always, continues to change, and the spinning of John Brown's story goes on today. The same events—the raid on Harpers Ferry or the Pottawatomie Massacre—are still seen in totally different ways. What is perhaps most remarkable is that elements at both the left and right ends of American society are at this moment vitally interested in the story of John Brown.

On the left is a group of historical writers and teachers called Allies for Freedom. This group believes that the truth about the Harpers Ferry raid has been buried by the conventions of history. Its informal leader, Jean Libby, author of *John Brown Mysteries,* says, "What we think is that John Brown was a black nationalist. His ultimate goal was the creation of an independent black nation." The Allies for Freedom believes, too, that far from being the folly of a lunatic, Brown's plan was not totally unworkable, that it came much closer to succeeding than historians have pictured. Libby thinks that many slaves and free blacks *did* join the uprising—perhaps as many as fifty. Why would history conceal the fact of active black participation in Harpers Ferry? "The South was anxious to cover up any indication that the raid might have been successful," Libby says, "so slaves would never again be tempted to revolt."

Go a good deal farther to the left, and there has long been admiration for John Brown. In 1975 the Weather Underground put out a journal called *Osawatomie*. In the late 1970s a group calling itself the John Brown Brigade engaged in pitched battles with the Ku Klux Klan; in one confrontation in Greensboro, North Carolina, in 1979, five members of the John Brown Brigade were shot and killed. Writers also continue to draw parallels between John Brown and virtually any leftist who uses political violence, including the Symbionese Liberation Army (the kidnappers of Patty Hearst in the 1970s), the Islamic terrorists who allegedly set off a bomb in the World Trade Center in Manhattan, and Ted Kaczynski, the Unabomber.

A T THE SAME TIME, JOHN BROWN IS FREQUENTLY COMPARED to those at the far opposite end of the political spectrum. Right-to-life extremists have bombed abortion clinics and murdered doctors; they have, in short, killed for a cause they believed in, just as John Brown did. Paul Hill was convicted of murdering a doctor who performed abortions; it was, Hill said, the Lord's bidding: "There's no question in my mind that it was what the Lord wanted me to do, to shoot John Britton to prevent him from killing unborn children." If that sounds quite like John

Brown, it was no accident. From death row Hill wrote to the historian Dan Stowell that Brown's "example has and continues to serve as a source of encouragement to me…. Both of us looked to the scriptures for direction, [and] the providential similarities between the oppressive circumstances we faced and our general understandings of the appropriate means to deliver the oppressed have resulted in my being encouraged to pursue a path which is in many ways similar to his." Shortly before his execution Hill wrote that "the political impact of Brown's actions continues to serve as a powerful paradigm in my understanding of the potential effects the use of defensive force may have for the unborn."

Nor was the murder Hill committed the only right-wing violence that has been compared to Brown's. The Oklahoma City bombing in 1995 was a frontal attack on a U.S. government building, just like the Harpers Ferry raid. Antiabortion murders, government bombings, anarchist bombs in the mail—nearly every time political violence surfaces, it gets described in the press as a part of a long American tradition of terrorism, with John Brown as a precursor and hero, a founding father of principled violence.

He gets compared to anarchists, leftist revolutionaries, and right-wing extremists. The spinning of John Brown, in short, is still going strong. But what does that make *him*? This much, at least, is certain: John Brown is a vital presence for all sorts of people today. In February PBS's *The American Experience* is broadcasting a ninety-minute documentary about him. Russell Banks's novel *Cloudsplitter* was a critical success and a best-seller as well. On the verge of his two hundredth birthday (this May 9), John Brown is oddly present. Perhaps there is one compelling reason for his revival in this new millennium: Perhaps the violent, excessive, morally torn society John Brown represents so aptly was not just his own antebellum America but this land, now.

Ken Chowder wrote "John Brown's Holy War," the documentary that appeared on PBS's The American Experience.

From *American Heritage,* February/March 2000, pp. 81-91. © 2000 by Forbes, Inc. Reprinted by permission of *American Heritage* magazine, a division of Forbes, Inc.

UNIT 4
The Civil War and Reconstruction

Unit Selections

Key Points to Consider

- How and why did the Civil War change from a limited conflict to almost total war? What kept Abraham Lincoln from issuing the Emancipation Proclamation earlier, and why did he finally take the step?

- Discuss the experiences of black Americans during the war, both those who served in the military and those who remained within Southern lines.

- What was Robert E. Lee's historic contribution to peace? Describe the reasoning that led to his decision?

- How has Reconstruction often been portrayed by historians? Even though Reconstruction failed to meet its objectives, does its "animating vision" still have relevance?

 **Links: www.dushkin.com/online/**
These sites are annotated in the World Wide Web pages.

The American Civil War
http://sunsite.utk.edu/civil-war/warweb.html

Anacostia Museum/Smithsonian Institution
http://www.si.edu/archives/historic/anacost.htm

Abraham Lincoln Online
http://www.netins.net/showcase/creative/lincoln.html

Gilder Lehrman Institute of American History
http://vi.uh.edu/pages/mintz/gilder.htm

Secession Era Editorials Project
http://history.furman.edu/benson/docs/

There had been sectional disputes well before the Constitution was framed, and were reflected in some of its provisions. The provision that a two-thirds majority was necessary to pass treaties in the Senate, for instance, represented a sectional compromise. Commercial and manufacturing interests were powerful in the North. These interests favored policies such as high tariffs to protect domestic industries, and federal support for the construction of turnpikes, canals, and railroads to enlarge markets. The agricultural South wanted low tariffs to reduce the prices of the imports that they bought and opposed the taxes necessary for transportation improvements. These issues could be negotiated, however, because they had no moral content and failed to stir much public emotion.

Slavery was another matter. Part of the controversy over the institution involved economics, to be sure. Northerners were afraid that the spread of slavery into newly acquired territories would inhibit the growth of "free" farming. Southerners were equally adamant that their institution of labor be permitted to exist wherever it proved viable. Compromises over this matter were hammered out in 1820 and 1850, but these amounted only to truces that proved unsatisfactory to both sides. As more and more Northerners came to regard slavery as an evil system that had to be abolished, the issue proved impervious to compromise. Southerners stoutly defended the institution, arguing that it was beneficial to both blacks and whites. Incidents such as John Brown's raid, discussed in section three, raised emotions to a fever pitch.

Moderates in both national parties, realizing that the issue had the potential to split the nation, tried to keep it offstage. The Democratic Party managed to stay together until almost the very end, although there were defections. The Whig Party collapsed under the strain. The subsequent emergence of the Republican Party brought things to a head. This party drew almost its entire strength from the North, and Southerners began to regard it as the party of abolitionism. The Republican presidential candidate in 1860, Abraham Lincoln, stated that although he opposed the expansion of slavery he had no intention of trying to move against it where it already existed. Suspicious Southerners believed that prohibiting the spread of slavery merely constituted the first step towards abolishing the institution—and their way of

life—altogether. Lincoln's victory in 1860 caused Southern states to begin seceding from the Union, and his refusal to let them go in peace led to the Civil War.

There are three essays in this section about military aspects of the struggle. "'The Doom of Slavery': Ulysses S. Grant, War Aims, and Emancipation, 1861–1863" describes how the Civil War changed from a limited conflict to a concept of total war against Southern resources and morale. "A Gallant Rush for

Glory" describes the courageous assault by a black regiment against a Confederate stronghold in South Carolina. The attack failed with heavy losses, but showed that blacks could fight as bravely as whites. "Between Honor and Glory" tells of the last weeks of the war. Robert E. Lee's beleaguered Army of Northern Virginia made exhausting marches to avoid being trapped, but to no avail. Others urged Lee to instruct his troops to disband and carry on guerilla warfare. Lee refused to take this advice, which might have prolonged the fighting for years.

Thomas Dyer, in "A Yankee Scarlett O'Hara in Atlanta," tells the fascinating story of an ardent unionist who lived in Atlanta during the war. Cyrena Bailey Stone's recently discovered diary provides an eyewitness account of daily life in Atlanta during the latter months of the conflict. The essay "Bats, Balls, and Bullets" denies the popular myth that the game of baseball was invented in 1839 by Abner Doubleday, who went on to become a general in the Civil War. Author George Kirsch shows that the sport actually had evolved from several bat-and-ball games over decades. A fairly modern version was being widely played during the Civil War, especially by Northerners. After the war, a number of Northern and Southern journalists predicted that exhibition tours of leading teams would help dissipate sectional hatreds. "Coffee, Bibles & Wooden Legs: The YMCA Goes to War" describes how this organization raised funds and sent volunteers to help soldiers. Northern and Southern chapters did so separately, however, and did not get back together until after the war ended.

Abraham Lincoln came in for a great deal of criticism during the war, as did his Southern counterpart, Jefferson Davis. "Jefferson Davis and the Jews" describes how the anti-Semitic Henry S. Foote kept up a constant barrage against Jews in the Davis administration. A number of political commentators and cartoonists savaged Lincoln in the Northern Press, as discussed in "Lincoln Takes the Heat."

A struggle took place after the war ended over how the South should be reintegrated into the union. The most important issue was what status blacks would have in the society. Moderates such as Lincoln wished to make Reconstruction as painless as possible, even though this meant white domination of the Southern states. "Radical" or "advanced" Republicans wished to guarantee freed people the full rights of citizenship, using force if necessary to achieve this goal. Southern whites resisted "radical Reconstruction" any way they could and, when Northern will eroded, ultimately prevailed. Eric Foner's "The New View of Reconstruction" argues that even though radical Reconstruction failed in the short run, it provided an "animating vision" for the future.

"The Doom of Slavery": Ulysses S. Grant, War Aims, and Emancipation, 1861–1863

Brooks D. Simpson

Like many northerners, Ulysses S. Grant went to war in 1861 to save the Union—and nothing more—in what he predicted would be a short conflict. By 1863, after two years of bloody struggle against a stubborn enemy, Grant came to understand that a war to preserve the Union must of necessity transform that Union. Central to that revolutionary transformation was the acceptance of emancipation as a war aim and the enrollment of ex-slaves in the bluecoat ranks. The intensity of Confederate resistance compelled Union commanders to accept this notion, while the influx of black refugees into Yankee camps helped to force a decision. In 1861 Grant believed that the Union should keep hands off slavery if a quick peace and rapid reconciliation was desired. By 1863 circumstances had changed. Notions of a limited conflict gave way to the concept of a total war waged against Southern resources and morale as well as manpower. New means were needed to attain victory. To save the Union one must destroy slavery. Grant's experiences as a field commander are illustrative of this process, suggesting the interaction between the progress of the war effort, the escalation of Southern resistance, and the transformation of war aims to encompass emancipation.

From war's beginning Grant realized that at the core of the dispute was the institution of slavery. His position on the peculiar institution was ambiguous, and he left no detailed explanation of his feelings for historians to examine. Marriage to the daughter of a slaveholder entangled him in slavery: he worked alongside slaves, his wife owned four house servants, and he was a slaveholder for a short period. Yet family slaves heard him speak out against the institution, he did not succumb to the blatant prejudices of his age, and he freed the slave he owned at a time when the money a sale might have brought could have been a great boon. He showed no interest in protecting slavery, let alone perpetuating it.[1]

Moreover, Grant understood that the advent of war in the spring of 1861 would affect slavery, no matter the outcome. Southerners were risking the foundation of their society even as they defended it. "In all this I can but see the doom of Slavery," he told his father-in-law. "The North do not want, nor will they want, to interfere with the institution. But they will refuse for all time to give it protection unless the South shall return soon to their allegiance." The disruption of the Southern economy by war would render it vulnerable to international competition, reducing the worth of slaves "so much that they will never be worth fighting over again." Slavery would be destroyed as a consequence of prolonged conflict, a casualty of events rather than the target of Union policy.[2]

Nevertheless, a quick Northern victory, achieved before hatred could become deep-seated, might minimize the impact of the conflict upon slavery. And Grant believed that such a rapid triumph was possible. Startled by the vigorous reaction of Northerners in Sumter's aftermath, he ventured that if Southerners ever discovered what they had wrought, "they would lay down their arms at once in humble submission." Confidently he predicted a Northern triumph in a conflict "of short duration." With "a few decisive victories" by the North the "howling" Confederates would flee the field. "All the states will then be loyal for a generation to come, negroes will depreciate so rapidly in value that no body will want to own them and their masters will be the loudest in their declamations against the institutions in a political and economic view." If slavery was to suffer, it would be as a byproduct of the conflict, not because of deliberate policy decisions to eradicate it. Indeed, to take such steps might only prolong the conflict by engendering resistance born of bitterness.[3]

In June, Grant was commissioned colonel of the 21st Illinois. Soon his regiment was dispatched to Missouri to hunt down scattered rebel detachments. Grant kept a close eye on his men, making sure that they did not disturb citizens along the line of march. He reasoned that a well-behaved army would contradict rumors of a marauding bunch of Yankees bent upon plunder, eroding fears and enhancing the chances of a quick and easy peace. Such considerations were especially crucial in Missouri, where the population was nearly evenly divided between loyalists and secessionists. With the state still teetering on the edge of secession, it was of utmost importance that Grant maintain discipline among his new recruits. He did so, with good results. While there existed "a terrible state of fear among the people" when his troops arrived, he added that within a few weeks they discovered that the bluecoats "are not the desperate characters they took them for." He was convinced that "if orderly troops could be marched through this country… it would create a very different state of feeling from what exists now."[4]

Efforts to foster good feeling, however, met a serious obstacle in the stubborness of the local citizens. "You can't convince them but that the ultimate object is to extinguish, by force, slavery," he complained to his father. To his wife Julia he revealed concern that the war was getting out of hand. Not only were the citizens "great fools," but they "will never rest until they bring upon themselves all the horrors of war in its worst form. The people are inclined to carry on a guerilla Warfare that must eventuate in retaliation and when it does commence it will be hard to control."[5] Should the war transcend conventional limits, it would embitter both victor and vanquished, making it all the more difficult to achieve a lasting peace. Moreover, to abandon notions of a limited war fought between armies, in favor of a people's struggle, carried with it revolutionary implications. While both sides may have gone to war to preserve something—the North to save the Union, the South to protect a way of life—the resulting conflict, should it spill over its initial boundaries,

promised to transform American society whatever the result.

Signs of Confederate determination caused Grant to reconsider his earlier notions about a short war. "I have changed my mind so much that I don't know what to think," he told his sister. While he still believed that the rebels could be crushed by spring, "they are so dogged that there is no telling when they may be subdued." As resistance stiffened, Grant adopted a tougher policy toward secessionist sympathizers, arresting several to prevent them from relaying information, seizing a prosouthern paper, and warning businessmen not to trade with Confederates. If Southerners wanted to broaden the scope of the war, Grant was willing to respond in kind.[6]

Inevitably such a struggle affected the institution of slavery. While Grant did not go to war to free the slaves, he had maintained that Northerners would not prop up slavery while the South continued to fight. Eventually Union field commanders found themselves confronted with the problem of what to do about slavery in the war zone. Despite Grant's avowed disinclination to become involved in political questions, his actions toward civilians, property, and fugitive slaves inescapably carried with them political overtones. In August, General John C. Frémont ordered Grant to take command of troops concentrating in southeast Missouri. Arriving at Cape Girardeau on August 30, Grant observed "Contrabands, in the shape of negroes," working on the fortifications. "I will make enquiries how they come here and if the fact has not been previously reported ask instructions," he informed Frémont's headquarters at St. Louis. Grant was trying to avoid initiating policies which interfered with slavery.[7]

Unknown to Grant, Frémont, tired of harassment by Confederate sympathizers, struck at slavery the same day. His abolitionism, bolstered by a visit from Owen Lovejoy, and his ambition combined to convince him to issue a proclamation which imposed martial law on Missouri, confiscated the property of active Confederate supporters, and declared their slaves free. Local commanders wired Grant for instructions. "Protect all loyal Citizens in all their right[s]," Grant

replied, "but carry out the proclamation of Genl Fremont upon all subjects known to come under it." Frémont's order was soon countermanded by Lincoln, but it had alerted Grant to the possibility that the war could assume a wider scope and thus involve him in the very political questions he wished to avoid.[8] Lincoln's removal of Frémont several weeks later also reminded the new brigadier of the cost of violating established policy.

Grant's decision to invade Kentucky in September 1861 provided him with an opportunity to issue a proclamation outlining war aims, and the contrast with Frémont's missive was marked. Through August, Kentucky had managed to preserve a precarious neutrality in the sectional conflict. Neither side had set foot in the state, although it was obvious that sooner or later Union troops would have to violate its neutrality if they intended to launch an offensive to recapture Tennessee. Grant had been sent to southeast Missouri to plan for just such an invasion, but Confederate forces conveniently relieved him of the onus of disrupting the status quo first by invading Kentucky on September 3. The Rebel commander, General Leonidias Polk, had made a serious error, one on which Grant seized in moving his troops across the Ohio River into Paducah, Kentucky, on September 6.

Once installed at Paducah, Grant issued his own proclamation. He had invaded Kentucky, "not to injure or annoy,… but to respect the rights, and to defend and enforce the rights of all loyal citizens." It was a purely defensive move. "I have nothing to do with opinions. I shall deal only with armed rebellion and its aiders and abetors." Nothing was said about slavery. Grant issued special instructions "to take special care and precaution that no harm is done to inoffensive citizens."[9]

Grant's proclamation was as much a political statement as that issued by Frémont. Both were issued in states still technically loyal to the Union, and both reflected the lack of a declaration of overall war aims from Washington. Frémont, anxious to make a name for himself, had sought to place the war effort on advanced ground; Grant's announcement reflected his own belief that the war was one for reunion, not revolution. In contrast to Frémont, who saw his handiwork annulled by Lincoln, Grant's statement stood. It still remained for the Lincoln administration to make known its policy in order to guide military commanders in their actions.

Although Lincoln's action in countermanding Frémont's proclamation helped people understand what his policy was not, Grant was unsure of what government policy was, especially as it applied to black refugees. Within two weeks of the occupation of Paducah, blacks began entering Union lines, intent on making good their escape from slavery. Like Grant, Kentucky blacks knew that the presence of Union troops meant the disruption of slavery, regardless of the unwillingness of Union commanders to play abolitionist. And, if the Yankee army would not come to the blacks, they would go to it. The slaveholders followed, demanding the return of their property. They were willing to overlook the irony that they were asking the assistance of a government that many of them were rebelling against to protect their right to own slaves, when many of them had justified secession precisely because they had no faith that the same government would protect that right. Grant wired Washington for instructions. None came.[10]

Left on his own, and aware that fugitive slave legislation was still in force, Grant ordered the return of at least one slave. Some two months later he finally received definite guidelines on what to do. Major General Henry W. Halleck succeeded Frémont in November with orders to convince civilians in his command that the sole purpose of the war was to uphold "the integrity of the Union." The day after he assumed command Halleck issued General Orders No. 3, which closed Union lines to black fugitives.[11]

Grant received the order with mixed feelings. To be sure, he still held fast to his belief that the sole object of the war was to restore the Union. "My inclination is to whip the rebellion into submission, preserving all constitutional rights," he told his father. But Grant was willing to admit the possibility that this might not be possible. "If it cannot be

whipped in any other way than through a war against slavery," he continued, "let it come to that legitimately. If it is necessary that slavery should fall that the Republic may continue its existence, let slavery go." The general was willing to consider the possibility that slavery's demise might be a goal of Union war policy, instead of being merely the consequence of the disruptive impact of military operations. But he was not yet ready to take that step. Aware that many Northern newspapers had seized upon Halleck's order to renew their criticism of the narrow scope of Union war aims, Grant charged that such papers "are as great enemies to their country as if they were open and avowed secessionists." Adopting such broad goals would mean that the prospects for reunion and reconciliation would give way to a bitter struggle requiring the North to conquer the entire South.[12]

Despite his reaction to press criticism of Halleck's order, Grant was ambivalent about it. "I do not want the Army used as negro catchers," he explained in approving the return of a fugitive to a loyal master, "but still less do I want to see it used as a cloak to cover their escape. No matter what our private views may be on this subject there are in this Department positive orders on the subject, and these orders must be obeyed." While he still agreed that the army's mission did not include emancipation, he was not willing to endorse active support of slavery in all instances, especially in the face of growing resistance. Noting that it was not the military's policy "to ignore, or in any manner interfere with the Constitutional rights of loyal citizens," he denied the same protection to secessionist slaveholders when he refused to honor a Confederate master's demand for the return of a fugitive who had sought refuge in Grant's camp. "The slave, who is used to support the Master, who supported the rebellion, is not to be *restored* to the Master by Military Authority." The slaveholder might appeal to the civil authorities, but Grant did not "feel it his duty to feed the foe, or in any manner contribute to their comfort." This position, violating the letter of Halleck's order, went further in the direction of emancipation than existing congres-

sional legislation outlining confiscation policy, which concerned only those slaves actively employed in support of the rebellion.[13]

Grant let slip his growing antislavery convictions on other occasions. During the fall of 1861 his forces sparred with Polk's units, and the two armies met once in a pitched battle at Belmont, Missouri. Inevitably, prisoners were taken at these clashes, and Grant met with Polk several times on a truce boat to arrange exchanges and discuss other issues. At the conclusion of one meeting, drinks were served, and Polk offered a toast: "George Washington!" No sooner had Grant tipped the glass to his lips, however, when Polk added, "the first rebel." Chagrined, Grant protested that such sharp practice was "scarcely fair" and vowed to get even. The opportunity came several weeks later, at another truce boat conference. This time Grant proposed a toast: "Equal rights to all." Heartily assenting, Polk began to down the contents of his glass, when Grant quickly added, "white and black." A sputtering Polk admitted that Grant had achieved his object.[14]

Nor was Grant willing to tolerate actions which exceeded the bounds of conventional warfare. In January 1862, upon receiving reports that several of his pickets had been shot by civilians, he ordered that the surrounding area "should be cleaned out, for six miles around, and word given that all citizens making their appearance in within those areas are liable to be shot," thus establishing the Civil War version of a free-fire zone. These orders restored stability. A week later, he instructed the local commander to release all civilians captured under these orders and to allow all slaves to return to their masters.[15]

During early 1862 Grant remained uncertain about the correct policy to pursue toward fugitives, and his capture of Fort Donelson on February 16 added to the problem. Halleck wanted to consolidate Grant's gains by erecting fortifications to hold Donelson and its twin, Fort Henry, and instructed Grant to use slaves owned by secessionists to do the work. Grant sent division commander John A. McClernand out to capture slaves to increase the available work force. At least one expedition interpreted its orders liberally, seizing "mostly old men, women and children." The commander had violated Halleck's order, and the fugitives had to be returned. Grant finally halted McClernand, explaining, "It leads to constant mistakes and embarassment to have our men running through the country interpreting confiscation acts and only strengthens the enthusiasm against us whilst it has a demoralizing influence upon our own troops."[16]

The incident caused Grant a great deal of embarrassment. He reminded his troops that Halleck's order about returning fugitive slaves was still in force and must be observed. Union lines were flooded with slaveholders seeking to recover their slaves, proving that General Orders No. 3 continued to be a necessity. Halleck had issued a new order, reminding officers that civil courts, not military authorities, were empowered to rule on the status of slaves. Keeping fugitives out of camp would keep Grant out of trouble, or so he thought. But the image of Union soldiers returning "old men, women and children" to their masters was too much for many Northerners, and newspapers attacked Grant's action. "I have studiously tried to prevent the running off of negroes from all outside places," an exasperated Grant explained, "as I have tried to prevent all other marauding and plundering." It was not a matter of personal preference. "So long as I hold a commission in the Army I have no views of my own to carry out. Whatever may be the orders of my superiors, and law, I will execute." If Congress passed legislation "too odious for me to execute," he promised to resign. He enforced a strict observance of Halleck's order to avoid more trouble, including the arrest of any soldiers violating the order.[17]

Even when orders from Washington finally arrived, they did not ease Grant's mind. In March he received notification of new War Department guidelines which instructed soldiers not to return fugitives. One suspects that incidents in Grant's own command had contributed to the new directive. In response Grant pointed out the ramifications of such a policy. He had heard from former U.S. Representative J. M. Quarles that Con-

federate enlistments had risen around Clarksville, Tennessee, in reaction to the use of fugitives by a Union post commander. The post commander told Grant that "the return of those two negroes would do more good, & go further to cultivate a union sentiment in & about Clarksville than any other act." Grant forwarded the case, uncertain how to respond in light of the new directives, but expressed his opinion that the blacks should be returned.[18]

As Grant realized, federal policy toward fugitive slaves was intertwined with efforts at reconciliation. After Fort Donelson, he believed that one more Union victory would end the conflict, an impression made plausible by circumstances in his command. Many Tennesseans were declaring their loyalty to the Union; others were enlisting in Grant's regiments. Confederate deserters reported great discontent in rebel ranks. "With one more great success I do not see how the rebellion is to be sustained," Grant told his wife. He thought that the question of fugitive slaves would simply disrupt the reconciliation process at a time when the end seemed so near. But the bloodbath at Shiloh in April disabused Grant of these hopes. He later claimed that the battle changed his thinking about the conduct of the war. After Shiloh, "I gave up all idea of saving the Union except by complete conquest." Previous policies to "protect the property of the citizens whose territory was invaded, without regard to their sentiments," went out the door, and Grant began to make war not only on Confederate armies but the resources which sustained the war effort.[19]

But Grant's change in attitude was a little slower in coming than he liked to recall later. "This war could be ended at once," he told his wife in June, two months after Shiloh, "if the whole Southern people could express their unbiased feeling untrammeled by leaders. The feeling is kept up however by crying out Abolitionest against us and this is unfortunately sustained by the acts of a very few among us." He detailed instances where Tennesseans "inclined to Union sentiments" watched as soldiers encouraged their slaves to escape. This did little to assist reconciliation. Still, as Grant

took command of the District of West Tennessee in June, he expressed his confidence that as soon as his district was "reduced to working order" its residents would "become loyal, or at least law-abiding." Others were not so sure. Dr. Edward Kittoe, a friend of Grant's patron Congressman Elihu B. Washburne, complained, "We curry favour of these secessionists, and real Union men do not fare as well as they: we are obsequious to them, we feed them, we guard their property, we humble ourselves to gain their favor, and in return we receive insult and injury." Unionists were "disgusted," and both officers and men "feel outraged... and very naturally ask is this the way to crush this rebellion." To Kittoe the answer was obvious: "The iron gauntlet must be used more than the silken glove to crush this serpent."[20]

Grant's early hopes for reconciliation were dashed when he observed the temper of the people. Far from anxiously awaiting reunion, most west Tennesseans remained defiantly loyal to the Confederate cause, chafing under occupied rule. They cheered on the small bands of guerrillas who sought to disrupt and disturb Grant's operations. As Grant struggled to secure his lines from raiders, he began to reassess his beliefs about limited war in the face of escalating Confederate resistance. The intensity of the Southern attack at Shiloh, while alarming, remained within the bounds of conventional warfare: but when resisting citizens and marauding guerrillas expanded the scope of conflict beyond these limits, Grant had to meet the challenge. It was combatting a restive populace in occupied territory, stalking guerrillas, and absorbing black refugees, not merely Shiloh, that persuaded Grant to abandon limited war for total war. He did so with surprising speed. On July 1, he ordered the *Memphis Avalanche* to shut down after the paper had complained about the behavior of Union troops. Within days a Unionist paper, the *Bulletin*, replaced it. Two days later he took steps to halt guerrilla activities by ordering that property losses sustained by his army would be made up by assessments on the property of Confederate sympathizers. All captured guerrillas would not be treated as prisoners of war, leaving open the possibility of execution. The order provoked one Mississippian to protest Grant's "infamous and fiendish proclamation… characteristic of your infernal policy…. Henceforth our motto shall be, Blood for blood, and blood for property."[21]

Grant also tired of dealing with Confederate sympathizers in Memphis. On July 10 he issued a special order directing families of Confederate officers and officeholders to move south. Although the order was later modified to allow such families to remain in Memphis upon taking a pledge not to aid enemy operations, it outraged Confederate General Jeff Thompson, who promised revenge. In contrast, a local Unionist applauded the order: "I would suggest that all persons who *uphold,* and *preach* Secession in our midst be required to 'skedaddle' to the land of *'secession'*."[22]

As Federal units probed southward across the Tennessee-Mississippi border, blacks continued to flood into Union lines. Their sheer numbers negated any further attempts at exclusion. If whites were "sullen" at the sight of the bluecoats, Kittoe told Washburne, "the darkies seemed joyous at our presence." Grant's soldiers realized that their mere presence destroyed slavery, "Where the army of the Union goes, *there slavery ceases forever,"* wrote a Wisconsin captain. "It is astonishing how soon the blacks have learned this, and they are flocking in considerable numbers already in our lines." Another officer noted, "All that came within our lines were received and put to work and supplied with clothing and subsistence. This policy was viewed by the soldiers with very general approbation."[23]

Grant moved slowly at first in responding to these new circumstances. "It is hard to say what would be the most wise policy to pursue towards these people," he wrote Washburne. He put blacks to work fortifying Memphis from Confederate attack, much as he had used blacks at Donelson. But he remained unsure of his responsibilities in other cases, and, rather than invite more criticism by acting on his own, he asked for instructions. After arresting Confederate sympathizer Francis Whitfield on July 17, 1862, Grant had to decide what to do

with Whitfield's slaves, who, since they were women and children, could not be used on fortifications. Whitfield, understandably, wanted the slaves sent south to relatives. Grant, preoccupied with enemy movements, asked Halleck what to do. The general-in-chief responded that if Grant had no use for or reason to detain the slaves, "let them go when they please."[24]

Halleck could have been more helpful to the befuddled Grant. On the day of Whitfield's arrest, Congress passed a second confiscation act which declared that slaves owned by rebels who came in contact with Union forces were free. Certainly Halleck should have been aware of this legislation, but he failed to pass policy directives down to his subordinates. Promulgation of a policy did not necessarily guarantee its immediate implementation and enforcement. Grant was not officially informed of the passage of the act for several weeks. Halleck finally instructed him to "clean out West Tennessee and North Mississippi of all organized enemies," eject civilian sympathizers, and confiscate rebel property. "It is time that they should begin to feel the presence of war on one side."[25]

Grant planned to make the war even more oppressive for Southern whites. He cracked down on the activities of Confederate sympathizers and guerrillas, following Halleck's advice to "handle that class without gloves." As William T. Sherman put it to Secretary of the Treasury Salmon P. Chase, "The Government of the United States may now safely proceed on the proper rule that all in the South are enemies of all in the North, and not only are they unfriendly, but all who can procure arms now bear them as organized regiments or as guerrillas." Grant also took steps to close down trade with the enemy, especially cotton speculators. To Chase he declared that such trade profited only "greedy" speculators and the enemy, failed to "abate [the] rancorous hostility" of Rebels, and hurt the war effort. Doubtless Grant's new toughness was due to his realization that the war had taken on a new character, but he was also frustrated with his present situation, holding territory while hunting down pesky guerrilla bands. If he could not attack the

South in battle, he would find another way to strike back.[26]

Washburne apprised Grant of the new attitudes in Washington. "This matter of guarding rebel property, of protecting secessionists and of enforcing 'order No. 3' is 'played out' in public estimation. Your order in regard to the Secessionists of Memphis taking the oath or leaving, has been accepted as an earnest of vigorous and decided action on your part…. The administration has come up to what the people have long demanded—a vigorous prosecution of the war by all the means known to civilized warfare." Such measures included striking at slavery. "The negroes must now be made our auxiliaries in every possible way they can be, whether by working or fighting." The general "who takes the most decided step in this respect," Washburne hinted, "will be held in the highest estimation by the loyal and true men in the country."[27]

Grant followed Washburne's advice, freed of the responsibilities of playing slave catcher. "I have no hobby of my own with regard to the negro, either to effect his freedom or to continue his bondage," he told his father. "If Congress pass any law and the President approves, I am willing to execute it." His headquarters established guidelines for the enforcement of the new confiscation legislation. Blacks would no longer be turned away: instead, they would be put to work. Manpower needs would be met by impressing the slaves belonging to Confederate masters. Uncertain as to the scope of the legislation, Grant excluded unemployed blacks from the lines, and prohibited soldiers "from enticing Slaves to leave their masters." The order had an immediate impact. "If the niggers come into camp for a week as fast as they have been coming for two days past," a Wisconsin private noted some two days after Grant issued his order, "we will soon have a waiter for every man in the Regt."[28]

The result pleased Grant. "The war is evidently growing oppressive to the Southern people," he told his sister. "Their *institution* are beginning to have ideas of their own and every time an expedition goes out more or less of them follow in the wake of the army and come to camp." The general employed them as teamsters, cooks, and hospital attendants, but there was not enough work for all. "I don't know what is to become of these poor people in the end but it [is] weakening the enemy to take them from them."[29]

With the approach of fall the black refugee problem assumed serious dimensions. Grant's troops, busy repelling Confederate offensives near Corinth, found the flood of fugitives obstructing movements and causing health problems. They described the blacks coming by the hundreds each night, "bearing their bundles on their heads and their pickaninnies under their arms." Chaplain John Eaton of the 27th Ohio recalled that the influx of refugees resembled "the oncoming of cities": once in camp, the bedraggled blacks produced "a veritable moral chaos." Sherman wrote his senator brother that "if we are to take along and feed the negroes who flee to us for refuge" on top of clothing and transportation shortages, military movements would bog down. "A perfect stampede of contrabands" confronted William S. Rosecrans, who was preparing to advance against enemy positions. Rosecrans sent them behind his lines to shield them from guerillas, complaining, "But what a burden what shall be done with them then."[30]

At first Grant tried to make use of the refugees, putting them to work in the Corinth fortifications. He sent the women and children to campsites east of Corinth and asked Secretary of War Edwin M. Stanton what he should do next. Some people in Chicago thought they would make excellent servants, a practice Stanton permitted for nearly a month until an adverse reaction in the Midwest, encouraged by electioneering Democrats, forced him to rescind the order.[31] Grant then decided to establish camps for the blacks and to let them bring in the cotton and corn crops under his supervision. They would live off the land, receive wages for their work, and strive toward providing for themselves. The Union authorities would exercise a form of guardianship over the refugees, for Grant did not believe that blacks fresh from slavery were prepared to take on the responsibilities of freedom immediately. He sought to provide them with

some means of making the transition. His plan would allow him to provide for all blacks entering Union lines, not only the males able to work for the army.

Grant explained his reasoning to Chaplain Eaton, whom he had placed in charge of the project. Racial prejudice, Grant believed, was fundamentally a product of mistaken beliefs about behavior. One of those beliefs held by many whites was that blacks would not work of their own free will. Grant's plan would allow blacks to refute that stereotype. Once blacks assisting the military and working on the plantations had proved that they were responsible, whites would begin to accept the idea of handing a musket to a black man, and blacks could enlist in the Union army. And once blacks had fought for their freedom and demonstrated again that they were responsible and hard-working, whites could begin to entertain the idea of granting citizenship, even the ballot, to blacks. "Never before in those early and bewildering days had I heard the problem of the future of the Negro attacked so vigorously and with such humanity combined with practical good sense," Eaton recalled.[32]

Grant, who had once believed that the military should not interfere with slavery, now was pushing a plan of de facto emancipation, using military supervision to oversee the transition from slavery to freedom. It also reflected his belief that racial prejudice was best countered and conquered by actual demonstrations of its falsehoods. If his plan was paternalistic, at least it held out the prospect of progressive change. Of course, it also provided a solution to the problems of conducting military operations while disposing of a potential disaster by promising relief from the disease-ridden conditions currently confronting the freedmen. Grant took an active interest in Eaton's progress, ordering supplies and assistance whenever needed, and making sure that his subordinates followed suit.[33]

Perhaps the most notable aspects of Grant's solution to the refugee problem was that, for once, he acted without asking his superiors for advice. Not until four days after he had ordered Eaton's appointment did Grant tell Halleck what

he was doing and ask for instructions. Halleck, too busy to be bothered by these problems, approved of Grant's policy, although he had only a vague idea of what his subordinate was doing. In fact, the Lincoln administration seemed more interested in taking steps which would halt Grant's plans in their tracks. On September 22, 1862, Lincoln had made public a preliminary version of the Emancipation Proclamation, promising that he would put it into force on January 1, 1863. He sought to take advantage of those hundred days to encourage Tennesseans to reenter the Union on their own, holding out the prospect that if the Volunteer State returned it could do so with slavery intact, since the proclamation applied only to areas under Confederate control. On October 21, 1862, Lincoln informed both Grant and military governor Andrew Johnson of his plan. He wanted them to hold elections for congressmen wherever they could do so. The President hoped that Tennesseans would rejoin the Union "to avoid the unsatisfactory prospect before them."[34]

Grant, who once had held high hopes for the prospect of a speedy reunion, was skeptical of Lincoln's plan. Months before he had heard reports of Unionist speakers such as Emerson Etheridge being mobbed by Rebels; certainly the actions of Memphis's residents struck a telling blow against stories of latent Unionism. Now guerrilla bands were firing on Union steamers with civilians on board. Sherman suggested various ways to punish the guerrillas; Grant approved the expulsion of secessionist families as adequate retaliation. Other policies suggested an intensification of the war effort. With fall came reports of families suffering from a lack of food and shelter. Grant, convinced that those "not actively engaged in rebellion should not be allowed to suffer" amidst plenty, decided that "the burden of furnishing the necessary relief... should fall on those, who, by act, encouragement or sympathy have caused the want now experienced." Some of the troops agreed. They were tired of guarding secessionist property: one private wrote that it made his regiment "squirm like a Sarpent." He concluded that there were "few if any Union men" in the area. Another veteran later remarked that the troops believed by now that "they did not go South to protect Confederate property."[35]

Nevertheless, Grant was not one to question presidential policy. On December 9, 1862, he issued a proclamation to the people of west Tennessee calling for elections in the 8th, 9th, and 10th Congressional districts. All "legal voters" as of 1860 were permitted to participate in the balloting, which would take place on Christmas Eve. Grant was more impressed with the sentiments displayed by the Mississippians, who "show more signs of being subdued than any we have heretofore come across." A reporter noted that many Mississippians wanted to reenter the Union "at whatever cost" before Lincoln's proclamation came into play.[36]

Confederate forces under Nathan Bedford Forrest and Earl Van Dorn had no intention of allowing the election to proceed. They launched an offensive that not only disrupted an attempt by Grant to take Vicksburg but also made it impossible to hold elections. Grant was too busy conducting military operations to take much notice. Attempts at reestablishing loyal governments were futile until military operations rendered territory secure from guerrillas. As the new year started, Grant instructed Brigadier General Stephen A. Hurlbut, commanding at Memphis, to transfer ten secessionist families to Confederate lines for every guerrilla raid launched by the enemy. The general's patience was wearing thin, and protecting his supply lines against cavalry thrusts and armed bands sapped too much energy, time, and men from offensive operations.[37]

But guerrillas proved to be only one of the problems disrupting Grant's control of his own lines. Despite Eaton's project, the flood of refugees threatened to overwhelm Union camps. As Grant reestablished his position around Corinth and Memphis, he sought help from Halleck. "Contraband question becoming serious one," he telegraphed the general-in-chief. "What will I do with surplus negroes?" He glimpsed one possible solution as he shifted his forces to the west bank of the Mississippi opposite Vicksburg in the aftermath of his failed December offensive. It had long been a

favorite belief of Union commanders that if the course of the river was diverted through the construction of a canal, Vicksburg, stripped of its western water barrier, would be rendered vulnerable. Grant, although somewhat skeptical, was willing to try the idea himself, using blacks to do the work. The project illustrated Grant's priorities. The problem presented by black refugees was first and foremost a military problem. Their presence obstructed military movements, disrupted camps, and promised to increase disease and disorder. Grant spared his soldiers of these risks as well as lessened the burden of digging trenches in the dirty swamps by employing black laborers. Military needs having been met, other concerns took over, as Grant worried about the conditions under which the blacks worked.[38]

But this solution was at best a stopgap measure. Nothing seemed to stop the influx of refugees. On February 12, 1863, Grant decided to issue an order excluding blacks from his lines. Soldiers were instructed to stop "enticing" blacks to enter Union camps; freedmen should remain on their plantations and work out a labor arrangement with the planters. "Humanity dictates this policy," he explained to Halleck. "Planters have mostly deserted their plantations taking with them all their able bodied negroes and leaving the old and very young. Here they could not have shelter nor assurances of transportation when we leave." The army was simply not equipped materially or mentally to take on any more freed men. As Grant told one subordinate, "the question is a troublesome one. I am not permitted to send them out of the department, and such numbers as we have it is hard to keep them in."[39]

Unfortunately for Grant, he was caught once more by a shift in administration policy. Halleck told Grant that reports had reached the War Department "that many of the officers of your command not only discourage the negroes from coming under our protection, but, by ill-treatment, force them to return to their masters." Obviously Grant's exclusion order had not gone over well with the top brass. "This is not only bad policy in itself," Halleck continued, "but is directly opposed to the policy adopted by

the government." In the wake of the Emancipation Proclamation, Washington decided to make war in earnest. Halleck—whose General Orders No. 3 in 1861 had epitomized the conservative attitude toward blacks—justified the new approach. "The character of the war has very much changed within the last year. There is now no possible hope of a reconciliation with the rebels. The union party in the south is virtually destroyed. There can be no peace but that which is enforced by the sword. We must conquer the rebels, or be conquered by them."[40]

With this acceptance of a total war approach against the Confederacy came new attitudes toward the treatment of black slaves by the Union army. It is the policy of the government to withdraw from the enemy as much productive labor as possible," Halleck explained, preaching with the passion of the recently converted. "Every slave withdrawn from the enemy, is equivalent to a white man put *hors de combat.*" Freedmen were to be used "so far as practicable as a military force for the defence of forts, depots, &c.… And it is the opinion of many who have examined the question without passion or prejudice, that they can also be used as a military force." Grant was instructed to assist this process by using his "official and personal influence to remove prejudices on this subject," and to assist General Lorenzo Thomas in efforts to organize black regiments."[41]

War had become revolution, taking the very path which Grant had outlined to Eaton the previous November. To arm ex-slaves was to make real the greatest fear of many a white Southerner by equipping blacks with the means to achieve revenge. Grant, who had grown weary of previous attempts at reconciliation, welcomed the change. "Rebellion has assumed that shape now that it can only terminate by the complete subjugation of the South or the overthrow of the Government," he informed Major General Frederick Steele, instructing him to provide for all the black refugees already in his lines and to "encourage all negroes, particularly middle aged males to come within our lines," obviously with an eye toward recruiting them. Then Grant welcomed Thomas to headquarters and did all he could to facilitate his mission. "At least three of my Army Corps Commanders take hold of the new policy of arming the negroes and using them against the rebels with a will," he told Halleck, adding: "You may rely on my carrying out any policy ordered by proper authority to the best of my ability." When several officers tendered their resignations over the new policy, Grant recommended that they be dismissed from the service instead.[42]

While Thomas proceeded with his mission, Grant embarked on yet another campaign against Vicksburg. Crossing the Mississippi below the city, Grant's army won five battles within three weeks, destroyed several factories at Jackson, and laid seige to Vicksburg itself in one of the most brilliant campaigns of the war. His troops took the war to the Southern people. Grant instructed commanders to make sure that their troops would "live as far as possible off the country through which they pass and destroy corn, wheat crops and everything that can be made use of by the enemy in prolonging the war. Mules and horses can be taken to supply all our wants and where it does not cause too much delay agricultural implements may be destroyed. In other words cripple the rebellion in every way."[43]

During the seige he received news that Thomas's recruits had engaged in their first battle at Milliken's Bend, some twenty miles upriver from Vicksburg. At first giving way, the blacks launched a vicious counterattack, spurred on in part by reports that Confederates were murdering blacks taken prisoner in the initial assault. Milliken's Bend proved blacks could fight, and many whites who were skeptical of black enlistment were won over when they heard accounts of the clash. Grant himself was pleased, endorsing the report of the Union commander at the battle with the comment that while the soldiers "had but little experience in the use of fire arms" they had been "most gallant and I doubt not but with good officers they will make good troops."[44]

But in the aftermath of the battle stories began to surface that the Confederates had executed captured black soldiers. Initially Grant was unsure whether such acts had official Confederate sanction, or if they had been perpetrated by "irresponsible persons"; but additional reports suggested that Confederate General Richard Taylor had approved the measures. Grant told Taylor that if the Confederates were initiating a policy, "I will accept the issue. It may be you propose a different line of policy towards Black troops and Officers commanding them to that practiced towards White troops? If so," Grant added, "I can assure you that these colored troops are regularly mustered into the service of the United States," and all Union authorities "are bound to give the same protection to these troops that they do to any other troops." Such a statement had revolutionary implications, for now Grant was demanding that prisoners in blue uniforms be treated equally, whether their skin was black or white. While Taylor denied the stories, he pointed out that all black prisoners would be turned over to state authorities in accordance with Confederate policy. Grant, accepting Taylor's denial of responsibility, was not so gracious about Confederate policy toward black POWs, commenting that "I cannot see the justice of permitting one treatment for them, and another for the white soldiers." But the exchange proved Grant's willingness to accept the notion that equal treatment followed naturally from emancipation, an idea which promised to transform American society.[45]

By the summer of 1863 Ulysses S. Grant's thoughts on the relationship between slavery, war, and reunion had undergone a drastic change from the ones he voiced during his early weeks of field command. He had always assumed that slavery would be a casualty of the war, but his initial passivity toward "the peculiar institution," fueled by a desire to achieve a quick and painless peace based on reconciliation, had given way in the face of fierce Confederate resistance. Once it had become obvious that the war would be long, Grant grasped that Union military operations would help turn it into a social and economic revolution by disturbing the very foundation of Southern society. Moreover, he now welcomed that challenge. To Lincoln he explained that he was giving "the subject of arming black troops my hearty support." The enlistment of blacks, "with the emancipation of the negro, is the heavyest blow yet given the Confederacy.... By arming the negro we have added a powerful ally. They will make good soldiers and taking them from the enemy weaken him in the same proportion they strengthen us."[46]

Such measures signalled the death of slavery. "The people of the North need not quarrel over the institution of Slavery," Grant reassured Washburne. "What Vice President Stevens [Alexander H. Stephens] acknowledges the corner stone of the Confederacy is already knocked out. Slavery is already dead and cannot be resurrected. It would take a Standing army to maintain slavery in the South" now. Then Grant injected a personal note. "I never was an Abolitionest, [not even what could be called anti slavery," he admitted, "but... it became patent to my mind early in the rebellion that the North & South could never live at peace with each other except as one nation, and that without Slavery." To save the Union, one must first destroy slavery. Any other settlement would be flawed. With that in mind, he argued that no peace should be concluded "until this question is forever settled." War had become revolution, and Ulysses S. Grant had been both witness and participant in the process. As he told a committee of Memphis unionists, he, like they, had come to "acknowledge human liberty as the only true foundation of human government."[47]

Notes

1. On Grant and slavery see Brooks D. Simpson, "Butcher? Racist? An Examination of William S. McFeely's *Grant: A Biography*," *Civil War History* 33 (March 1987), 63–83.

2. Ulysses S. Grant to Frederick Dent, April 19, 1861, in John Y. Simon, ed., The Papers of Ulysses S. Grant, 16 vols. to date (Carbondale, Ill.: Southern Illinois University Press, 1967–88), 2:3–4.

3. Ulysses S. Grant to Mary Grant, April 29, 1861, ibid., 2:13–14; Grant to Jesse Root Grant, May 6, 1861, ibid., 2:21–22. In fact, Grant expressed some concern lest slaves rise up in insurrection against their masters.

4. Ulysses S. Grant to Julia Dent Grant, July 19, 1861, ibid., 2:72–73.

5. Ulysses S. Grant to Julia Dent Grant, August 3, 1861, ibid., 2:82–83; Grant to Jesse Root Grant, August 3, 1861, ibid., 2:80–81.

6. Ulysses S. Grant to Mary Grant, August 12, 1861, ibid., 2:105; Grant to John C. Kelton, August 14, 1861, ibid., 2:111; Grant to William H. Worthington, August 26, 1861, ibid., 2:139–40.

7. Ulysses S. Grant to John C. Kelton, August 30, 1861, ibid., 2:154–55.

8. Dudley Taylor Cornish, *The Sable Arm: Negro Troops in the Union Army, 1861–1865* (New York: Norton, 1966), 12–15; John Cook to Ulysses S. Grant, September 11, 1861, Simon, ed., *Grant Papers,* 2:220, and Grant to Cook, September 12, 1861, ibid., 2:243–44. Frémont issued a new proclamation on September 11 in line with Lincoln's policy.

9. Ulysses S. Grant, "Proclamation," September 6, 1861, and Grant to E. A. Paine, September 6, 1861. ibid., 194–95.

10. Ulysses S. Grant to Lorenzo Thomas, September 21, 1861, ibid., 2:291 and annotation.

11. Kenneth Williams, *Lincoln Finds A General,* 5 vols. (New York: Macmillan, 1949–59), 3:106–12.

12. Ulysses S. Grant to Jesse Root Grant, November 27, 1861, Simon, ed., *Grant Papers,* 3:227.

13. Ulysses S. Grant to John L. Cook, December 25, 1861, ibid., 3:342–43; William S. Hillyer (Grant staff officer) to L. F. Ross, January 5, 1862, ibid., 3:373–74; Charles F. Smith to Grant, January 4, 1862, ibid., 3:431.

14. James Grant Wilson, *Life and Public Services of Ulysses Simpson Grant* (New York: De Witt, 1885), 24.

15. Ulysses S. Grant to E. A. Paine, January 11, 19, 1862, Simon, ed., *Grant Papers,* 4:32, 68–69.

16. Henry W. Halleck to Ulysses S. Grant, February 8, 1862, and Grant to Halleck, February 11, 1862, ibid., 4:193–94; General orders No. 46, Department of the Missouri, February 22, 1862, ibid., 4:291; Grant to McClernand, February 18, 1862, ibid., 4:243; Grant to J. C. Kelton, February 22, 1862, ibid., 4:267–68; Grant to McClernand, February 22, 1862, ibid., 4:470.

17. General Orders No. 14, District of West Tennessee, February 26, 1862, ibid., 4:290–91; Grant to Elihu B. Washburne, March 22, 1862, ibid., 4:408; Grant to Philip B. Fouke, March 16, 1862, ibid., 4:377; Grant to Marcellus M. Crocker, March 17, 1862, ibid., 4:384; Grant to William T. Sherman, March 17, 1862, ibid., 4:382–83.

18. Ulysses S. Grant to Nathaniel H. McLean, March 31, 1862, ibid., 4:454; Philip B. Fouke to Grant, March 30, 1862, ibid., 4:454.

19. Ulysses S. Grant to George W. Cullum, February 23, 25, 1862, ibid., 4:276, 286; Grant to William T. Sherman, February 25, 1862, ibid., 4:289; Grant to Philip B. Fouke, March 16, 1862, ibid., 4:377; Grant to Nathaniel H. McLean, March 15, 30, 1862, ibid., 4:368, 447–48; Grant to Julia Dent Grant, March 18, 1862, ibid., 4:389; Ulysses S. Grant, *Personal Memoirs of U.S. Grant,* 2 vols. (New York: Charles L. Webster and Co., 1885–86), 1:368–69.

20. Ulysses S. Grant to Julia Dent Grant, June 12, 1862, Simon, ed., *Grant Papers,* 5:142–43; Kittoe to Washburne, June 24, 1862, Lloyd Lewis–Bruce Catton Research Notes, Ulysses S. Grant Association, Southern Illinois University.

21. Grant to Elihu B. Washburne, June 19, 1862, Simon, ed., *Grant Papers,* 5:146; Grant to William S. Hillyer, July 1, 1862, ibid., 5:181–82 and annotation; General Orders No. 60, District of West Tennessee, July 3, 1862, ibid., 5:190–91 and annotation.

22. "Union" to Grant, July 12, 1862, William S. Hillyer Papers, University of Virginia; see Simon, ed., *Grant Papers,* 5:192–94.

23. Seymour D. Thompson, *Recollections with the Third Iowa Regiment* (Cincinnati, 1864), 275; William P. Lyon, *Reminiscences of the Civil War* (San Jose, Calif.: Muirson and Wright, 1907), 53; Kittoe to Washburne, June 24, 1862, Lewis-Catton Research Notes, Ulysses S. Grant Association.

24. Ulysses S. Grant to Elihu B. Washburne, June 19, 1862, Simon, ed., *Grant Papers,* 5:146; Grant to Halleck, July 19, 1862, and Halleck to Grant, July 19, 1862, ibid., 5:218–19. See also Grant to Halleck, July 8[7], 1862, ibid., 5:199.

25. Herman Belz, *Emancipation and Equal Rights: Politics and Constitutionalism in the Civil War Era* (New York: Norton, 1978), 36–40; General Orders No. 72, District of West Tennessee, August 11, 1862, Simon, ed., *Grant Papers,* 5:273–74; Halleck to Grant, August 2, 1862, ibid., 5:243–44.

26. Grant to Halleck, July 28, 1862, and Halleck to Grant, August 2, 1862, ibid., 5:243–44; Grant to William W. Rosecrans, August 10, 1862, ibid., 5:282; Grant to Isaac F. Quinby, July 26, 1862, ibid., 5:238–41; Grant to Salmon P. Chase, July 31, 1862, ibid., 5:255–56; Grant to Rosecrans, August 7, 1862, ibid., 5:271; Sherman to Chase, August 11, 1862, quoted in John B. Walters, *Merchant of Terror: General Sherman and Total War* (Indianapolis: Bobbs-Merrill, 1973), 57–58.

27. Washburne to Grant, July 25, 1862, Simon, ed., *Grant Papers,* 5:226.

28. Grant to Jesse Root Grant, August 3, 1862, ibid., 5:264; General Orders No. 72, District of West Tennessee, August 11, 1862, ibid., 5:273–74; Stephen Ambrose, ed., A *Wisconsin Boy in Dixie: The Selected Letters of John K. Newton* (Madison. Wis.: The University of Wisconsin Press, 1961), 27–28.

29. Grant to Mary Grant, August 19, 1862, Simon, ed., *Grant Papers* 5:311.

30. Samuel H. M. Byers, *With Fire and Sword* (New York: Neale, 1911), 45; John Eaton, *Grant, Lincoln, and the Freedmen* (New York: Longmans, Green and Co., 1907), 2; William T. Sherman to John Sherman, September 3, 1862, William T. Sherman Papers, LC; Rosecrans to Grant, September 10, 1862, Simon, ed., *Grant Papers,* 6:32.

31. Grant to Thomas J. McKean, September 16, 1862, ibid., 6:54; James M. Tuttle to Edwin M. Stanton, September 18, 1862, ibid., 6:317; V. Jacque Voegeli, *Free But Not Equal: The Midwest and the Negro During the Civil War* (Chicago: University of Chicago Press, 1967), 60–61.

32. Eaton, *Grant, Lincoln and the Freedmen,* 9–15.

33. Ibid., 18–32. For additional discussion about Grant, Eaton, and the development of this policy at Corinth and at Davis Bend, Mississippi, which Grant hoped would become "a negro paradise," see Cam Walker: "Corinth: The Story of a Contraband Camp," *Civil War History* 20 (March 1974), 5–22; Steven J. Ross, "Freed Soil, Freed Labor, Freed Men: John Eaton and the Davis Bend Experiment," *Journal of Southern History* 44 (May 1978), 213–32; Louis S. Gerteis, *From Contraband to Freedman: Federal Policy Toward Southern Blacks, 1861–1865* (Westport, Conn.: Greenwood Press, 1973); and Janet Sharp Hermann, *The Pursuit of a Dream* (New York: Oxford University Press, 1981), 37–60.

34. Grant to Halleck, November 15, 1862, and Halleck to Grant, November 16, 1862, Simon, ed., *Grant Papers,* 6:315; Lincoln to Johnson and Grant, October 21, 1862, ibid., 7:3.

35. General Orders No. 4, Department of the Tennessee, November 3, 1862, ibid., 6:252–53; William W. Lowe to John A. Rawlins, August 18, 1862, ibid., 5:314; John W. Brinsfield, "The Military Ethics of General William T. Sherman: A Reassessment," *Parameters,* Vol. 12, No. 2 (1980), 42; Fred A. Shannon, ed., *The Civil War Letters of Sergeant Onley Andrus* (Urbana: University of Illinois Press, 1947), 25–26; Bruce Catton, *Grant Moves South* (Boston: Little, Brown, 1960), 336.

36. Ulysses S. Grant, "Proclamation," December 9, 1862, Simon, ed., *Grant Pa-*

pers 7:3–4; Grant to Halleck, December 14, 1862, ibid., 7:31–32; Thomas W. Knox, *Camp-Fire and Cotton-Field* (New York: Blelock and Co., 1865), 233.

37. Grant to Steven A. Hurlbut, January 3, 1863, Simon, ed., *Grant Papers,* 7:167–68.

38. Grant to Halleck, January 6, 1863, ibid., 7:186; Grant to George W. Deitzler, February 2. 1863, ibid., 7:278; Eaton, *Grant, Lincoln and the Freedmen,* 44.

39. Special Field Orders No. 2, Department of the Tennessee, February 12, 1863, ibid., 7:339; Grant to Halleck, February 18, 1863, ibid., 7:338, Catton, *Grant Moves South*, 401–2.

40. Halleck to Grant, March 30, 1863, Simon, ed., *Grant Papers*, 8:93n.

41. Halleck to Grant, March 30, 1863, ibid., 8:93n.

42. Grant to Frederick Steele, April 11, 1863, ibid., 8:49; Grant to Halleck, April 19, 1863, ibid., 91–92.

43. Grant to Stephen A. Hurlbut, May 5, 1863, ibid., 8:159–60.

44. Cornish, *The Sable Arm,* 144–45; Grant to Lorenzo Thomas, June 16, 1863, Simon, ed., *Grant Papers* 8:328.

45. Grant to Richard Taylor, June 22, 1863, ibid., 400–401 and annotation; Grant to Taylor, July 4, 1863, ibid., 468–69 and annotation. [Grant was unaware of Federal policy on the treatment of black prisoners of war, expressed in General Orders No. 100, issued April 24. Lincoln, perhaps because of this incident, issued an executive order on July 30, promising to retaliate in kind if Confederate officials mistreated black prisoners.] Cornish, *The Sable Arm,* 165–68.

46. Grant to Lincoln, August 23, 1863, Simon, ed., *Grant Papers*, 9:196.

47. Grant to Washburne, August 30, 1863, ibid., 9:217–18; Grant to Rue Hough and others, August 26, 1863, ibid., 9:203.

The author wishes to acknowledge the assistance provided by a research grant from Wofford College. He thanks Richard H. Sewell and Allan G. Bogue for their advice and counsel and John Y. Simon and David L. Wilson for their encouragement.

Coffee, Bibles & Wooden Legs: The YMCA Goes To War

Split in two by secession, the YMCA still managed to bring mercy and a moral compass to the camps of North and South.

BY Stephen D. Lutz

Patriotic fervor swept through the divided America in the spring of 1861. Citizens of the North and South were so focused on the gathering clouds of war that they paid little mind to the needs of the young volunteers who were heading off to battle. Most people on either side believed their boys would be home in few months, celebrating a relatively painless victory, so there seemed to be little reason to worry about the soldiers' welfare.

But the war lasted longer than people expected. Supplies ran short. Casualties grew to shocking numbers, and wounded soldiers needed treatment. Prisoners of war languished in bleak confines and were often malnourished and ill. Even a well-fed soldier warming his hands by the fire in a quiet company camp had his troubles. Separated from his family and the support it provided, he had to cope with the anxiety of knowing that at any time he could be ordered to charge to his death.

With these concerns in mind, the United States Christian Commission was founded in November 1861. The first civilian volunteer organization dedicated to serving soldiers, the commission was organized by a 17-year-old international

association known today for providing city youths with constructive alternatives to activities that can get them into trouble. That association is the Young Men's Christian Association, better known as the YMCA or simply the Y.

By the end of the Civil War, YMCA chapters in the North, through the auspices of the U.S. Christian Commission, raised an astounding $6 million to care for Union soldiers. The Southern Ys also participated in wartime volunteer work, though an inherent aversion to centralized authority made it more difficult to plan a coordinated effort. There was little or no cooperation between Northern and Southern chapters.

The once-strong ties between the United States chapters began to fray along the Mason-Dixon Line as Southern states seceded. Southern leaders of the Y believed secession was no reason for the association to split along North-South lines. The Y already had chapters in England, Canada, and the United States, they reasoned, why in not the Confederate States as well? Southerners viewed this acceptance of their new confederation as a normal progression of affairs. They wanted political independence from the North, but still

wanted to maintain non-governmental bonds with their Northern brethren.

Northerners viewed the situation differently. Many of them believed the South had no moral or constitutional right to secede from the Union. They believed that when Southern states made the aggressive political move of declaring independence, Southerners were willingly cutting themselves off from their former countrymen in emotional and spiritual ways, too.

In May 1861, the YMCA chapters in Richmond and New Orleans each sent a letter to Y chapters in the North. Both mentioned the upcoming National Convention in St. Louis, which the Southerners wanted to keep scheduled. They asked for peace and Christian fellowship, though they insisted on the South's right to independence. The Richmond letter blamed the "distorting medium of the press" for many of the misunderstandings between the sides. It insisted that such "misrepresentations" cease, concluding that only through "prayers and efforts for the restoration of peace and goodwill" on both sides could the Y remain united.

The New Orleans letter echoed many of those sentiments. The writers conspicuously avoided debating causes of the war, and concentrated instead on trying to reunify the association. They appealed to "those principles and sentiments in your bosoms, upon which the religion of our Divine Savior is based." They wished that there "should be peace between the two Confederacies." There was no hint, however, that the New Orleans Y was rethinking its support for an independent Southern republic.

Northern chapters responded to the Southern chapters' letters with bitter accusations and vindictiveness. For the New York City chapter, the conflict was not merely a matter of misunderstanding. "Have the Southerns the right to rule the Union until they lose an election and then destroy it?" wrote the chapter's correspondence secretary. "No." It did not matter that the Southern letters avoided the slavery issue. For the New Yorkers, it was slavery that had split the country in half.

Members of the Y in the North and South proved the strength of the convictions highlighted in these letters when it came time to fill the military ranks. Like many of their fellow countrymen, they rushed to enlist. So many members of the Y in Charleston, South Carolina, went off to war that the chapter struggled just to keep its doors open. The piano, furniture, and fixtures had to be sold to maintain operations.

In New York, members of the Y filled the ranks of the 7th, 9th, 12th, 71st, and 176th infantry regiments. The Chicago chapter filled five companies of the 72d Illinois Infantry. There also was a company of dragoons (heavily armed, mounted infantry). The Chicago Y was prepared to present these troops a flag and other donations before they left for war, but the soldiers declined the offer. They instead unanimously voted to hold a prayer meeting.

It was clear that the figurative sense of the time-worn cliché "brother versus brother" held more than a kernel of truth. Members of the Young Men's Christian Association would soon be firing their guns at one another across the battlefield. As the New York letter to the Southern chapters put it, "Your Christians will meet ours in battle."

In the early weeks of the war, soldiers in both armies spent most of the their time sitting in camp, bored perhaps, but relatively comfortable. Food and other supplies were adequate. Battle casualties had not yet begun to amass. It was not until the first major battle of the war— the Battle of Manassas in Virginia on July 21, 1861—that anyone began to think seriously about the care and needs of the troops. Almost 3,000 soldiers were wounded in that fight, and those men required at least some basic medical care.

Soon after the Battle of Manassas, the YMCA chapter in Charleston asked the chapter in Richmond about sending aid for the wounded and sick. Charleston wanted Ys throughout the South to send supplies to the front, and they asked that the Richmond chapter oversee collection and distribution. Richmond agreed, and the building that housed the Richmond Y was turned into a supply depot.

The efforts of the Southern Ys continued for quite some time after the guns went silent at Manassas. In mid-August, three private homes in Richmond were turned into hospitals that could accommodate 50 patients at a time. The attending physicians were YMCA members. The hospitals remained open for more than three months at no cost to the new Confederate government.

The Southern Ys found other ways to help Confederate troops as the war continued. In 1862, the association founded a lodge where food, shelter, and other necessities and comforts would be provided to transient soldiers. By the end of that year, 4,700 soldiers had stopped at the facility. By 1864, the Y chapter in Charlottesville, Virginia, was making wooden legs to distribute free of charge to disabled soldiers.

Religious outreach became the signature of the Y's wartime efforts in the South. Y volunteers there moved from Confederate camp to camp, spreading a hopeful message among a war-weary rank and file. Usually referred to as Christian Associations, the volunteer groups played a key role in what turned into great religious revivals in the Confederate army.

Southern Y chapters did their share of useful work during the war, but their effort was hampered by the Confederates'

natural aversion to central control. Like the Southern Ys, Northern Ys responded to the aftermath of the Battle of Manassas. The situation spawned discussions on how to better coordinate aid activities. One of the more promising suggestions to come from all of this talk came from Vincent Coyler, an influential artist and future president of the Y. Coyler said the Y should hold a conference to organize the association's volunteer efforts. His idea was accepted, and on November 14, 1861, delegates from various Y chapters met in New York City. That day, the United States Christian Commission was founded.

Caring for wounded troops was a need that sparked the Y's involvement in wartime services, but the association had other large-scale efforts, too. One was helping prisoners of war in their dire predicament. The Y tried to give these men hope. The association apparently had some success at Johnson's Island Prison off Sandusky, Ohio. Wrote the Rev. R.W. Cridlin:

A Confederate captive arrived following the Gettysburg battles. He found no organized spiritual activities. "Rampant profanity, gambling, slacking" and other "unchristian habits" were in wide practice. Initially met with indifference, the new arrival began prayer meetings and Bible classes. Groups grew in number and frequency.

Shortly after that, Captain W.B. Haygood, a prisoner from Company C of the 44th Georgia, wrote: "We have a Y.M.C.A., Masonic meetings, etc. I attend all of these and fill out the rest of my time by reading the Bible."

On October 31, 1863, a letter signed by 48 Rebel officers on the island was sent to the Confederate government in Richmond, Virginia. The YMCA-U.S. Christian Commission "make no difference or discrimination between Confederate or Federal...," the letter read. "We trust, that the authorities at Richmond and elsewhere will treat any said delegates...with kindness justly due them and grant them speedy return to their Christian work."

By war's end, the amount of service and supplies the YMCA had given to soldiers was staggering, especially in the North. Members of the Washington, D.C., chapter traveled a total of 5,240 miles, making 181 visits, holding 1,498 services, and registering 587 converts. Boston formed an Army Committee on December 2, 1861, to organize similar efforts. St. Louis formed one on December 10 and became a major supply distribution point along the Mississippi River. The Y in Louisville, Kentucky, accounted for 170 sermons, 273 letters written for soldiers, and 66,495 sheets of writing paper and envelopes distributed.

After the war, as feelings of sectional animosity faded, the Northern and Southern chapters of the Y began to reestablish their bonds. As the New Yorkers wrote in their 1861 letter to the Southern chapters: "We affirm, it is not that we love you less, but that we love our country, our whole country, more." That letter went on to say, "by the help of God," the United States will be reunited.

The nation had been battered, ripped, and torn in two, but now it was reunited. So was the association that had helped the North and South survive the harrowing four-year ordeal that was the Civil War—the YMCA.

Stephen D. Lutz writes from Portage, Michigan.

A Gallant Rush for Glory

For the men of the 54th Massachusetts, the assault on a Confederate fort outside Charleston was much more than just another battle. It was their chance to show the world that black troops could fight—and die—for the Union.

by William C. Kashatus

BEFORE UNION FORCES could capture Charleston, South Carolina, they first had to take Fort Wagner, a Confederate stronghold guarding the harbor's entrance. So shortly after 6:30 p.m. on July 18, 1863, Union Colonel Robert Gould Shaw readied 600 men of the 54th Massachusetts Regiment for an assault on the fort. Shaw, the 25-year-old son of Boston abolitionists, was white, as were all his officers. The regiment's men were black.

MASSACHUSETTS HISTORICAL SOCIETY

A recruiting poster from February 1863 was part of the effort to attract black men to the Union Army.

The 54 would spearhead a three-pronged attack aimed at capturing the necklace of heavily fortified islands that dotted Charleston harbor. If they could take Fort Wagner, the Federals would launch a major assault on nearby Fort Sumter. From there, it would only be a matter of time before Charleston fell. But capturing Fort Wagner would be no easy task.

At first glance, the fort appeared to be little more than a series of irregular, low sand hills. In fact, it was much more formidable than that. A timber and sandbag foundation beneath the sand-covered hills allowed the structure to absorb artillery fire without any significant damage. The fort had 11 heavy guns mounted in fixed positions behind the parapets, while smaller wheeled cannon could be quickly repositioned where needed. Defending it were 1,300 men from the 51st and 31st North Carolina Regiments as well as several companies of South Carolina artillerymen.

Fort Wagner sat in the middle of Morris Island's northern sandy peninsula. Four batteries at the island's northern tip guarded the entrance to Charleston harbor. The largest of these batteries was Battery Gregg, whose guns faced the ocean and covered the harbor mouth. South of the batteries, a deep moat with a sluice gate and three guns bounded Fort Wagner along its northern sea face. To the east lay the Atlantic Ocean, and on its western boundary were the impassable marshes of Vincent's Creek. On its

southern side the fort had guns and mortars for direct and flanking fire on any advancing troops. The only possible assault approach was east of the fort, along a slim stretch of sand, narrow even at low tide. Shaw and his troops would have to launch their attack on the seemingly impregnable fort from there.

Colonel Shaw readied his men on the beach. Tightly wedged together, elbow to elbow, the soldiers of the 54th began their gallant rush, determined to disprove the popular belief among whites that Negroes were an inferior race, lacking the courage and intelligence of combat-ready soldiers.

THE ONSET OF THE Civil War set off a rush by free black men to enlist in the U.S. military, but a 1792 law barred "persons of color from serving in the militia." Also, strong opposition in the North as well as a widespread prejudice that blacks were intellectually and socially inferior limited their involvement in the war to driving supply wagons, burying the battle dead, and building railroads.

Yet public opinion slowly began changing. Northern morale faltered after Union forces suffered a series of military defeats, and fewer white men were willing to join the army. Pressured by this turn of events, on July 17, 1862, Congress passed a Confiscation Act that declared all slaves of rebel masters free as soon as they came into Union lines, and a Militia Act that empowered the president to "employ as many persons of African descent" in "any military or naval service for which they may be found competent." Congress also repealed the 1792 law.

Shaw came from a prominent New England anti-slavery family, but he was initially hesitant about accepting command of the 54th. Once in command of the black regiment, he encountered considerable scorn from other white officers.

On August 25, 1862, the War Department authorized Brigadier General Rufus Saxton, military governor of the Union-controlled South Carolina Sea Islands, to raise five regiments of black troops for Federal service, with white men as officers. Volunteers came forward slowly at first, but by November 7 the regiment had reached its quota and was mustered in as the 1st South Carolina Volunteer Regiment under the command of Massachusetts abolitionist Colonel Thomas Wentworth Higginson. A second regiment followed, led by Colonel James Montgomery.

Still, President Abraham Lincoln refused to raise a large black army on political grounds. "To arm the Negroes would turn 50,000 bayonets from the loyal Border States against us that were for us," he told his abolitionist critics. Black leaders continued to urge the necessity of enlisting black troops, realizing that if the black man proved his patriotism and courage on the battlefield, the nation would be morally obligated to grant him first-class citizenship. No one expressed those sentiments more eloquently than Frederick Douglass, a former slave and the nation's most prominent black abolitionist. He insisted that "once the black man gets upon his person the brass letters 'U.S.', a musket on his shoulder and bullets in his pocket, there is no power on earth which can deny that he has earned the right to citizenship in the United States."

Debate continued within the Union command until January 1, 1863, when President Lincoln signed the Emancipation Proclamation. Having freed, by executive order, those slaves in the South, Lincoln could no longer deny the black man the opportunity to fight. Now the Civil War was being fought not only to preserve the Union, but for the freedom of all the American people, white and black. The success of the 1st and 2nd Carolina Colored Troops only reinforced that position. Higginson and Montgomery had already led their black troops on several successful raids into the interior of Georgia and Florida, and in March 1863 they captured and occupied Jacksonville.

On February 13, 1863, Senator Charles Sumner of Massachusetts introduced a bill proposing the "enlistment of 300,000 colored troops." Although the bill was defeated, abolitionist governor John A. Andrew of Massachusetts requested and received authorization from Secretary of War Edwin M. Stanton to organize a colored regiment of volunteers to serve for three years.

Massachusetts had a small black population, and only 100 men volunteered during the first six weeks of recruitment. Disillusioned by the turnout, Andrew organized a committee of prominent citizens and Negro leaders to supervise the recruitment effort. Within two months

the committee collected $5,000 and established a line of recruiting posts from Boston to St. Louis, resulting in the recruitment of 1,000 black men from throughout the Union who became part of the 54th Regiment Massachusetts Volunteer Infantry, Colored, the first black regiment raised in the free states. Toward the end of the second recruiting month, volunteers arrived at the rate of 30 to 40 each day, and Andrew soon had enough men to form a second black regiment, the 55th Massachusetts.

Sergeant Major Lewis Douglass (above) and Private Charles Douglass (next page) were the sons of abolitionist Frederick Douglass. Lewis became the 54th's first sergeant major and took part in the assault on Fort Wagner. Illness prevented Charles from participating in the battle.

For the 54th's commander, Governor Andrew turned to Robert Gould Shaw, captain of the Massachusetts 2nd Infantry. Charming and handsome, Shaw came from a wealthy and socially prominent Boston abolitionist family. His parents Francis and Sarah had joined the American Anti-Slavery Society in 1838, and by 1842 Francis was working with the Boston Vigilance Committee to help runaway slaves gain their freedom. Robert entered Harvard University in 1856 but abandoned his studies during his third year and moved to New York to work in his uncle's mercantile office. Shaw joined an exclusive militia regiment, the 7th New York National Guard, where he talked about what he would do if the South made trouble. Shaw did not possess the strong anti-slavery calling of his parents, but he was fiercely patriotic. When the Civil War began, he was primed to take revenge on the South. To Shaw, the South was the transgressor, and if it took the end of slavery to redeem the honor of America, then he was willing to fight for that. When the 7th disbanded, Shaw accepted a commission in the 2nd Massachusetts Infantry. During his 20 months there, Captain Shaw received a minor wound at Antietam, during the single bloodiest day of the war.

MOORLAND-SPINGARN RESEARCH CENTER, HOWARD UNIVERSITY

When Governor Andrew asked the young captain to lead a black volunteer infantry, Shaw was hesitant. The prospect of heading a regiment of armed blacks would not be popular among the white ranks. Nor did he want to abandon the men of the 2nd Infantry. Shaw initially refused the position but changed his mind after much discussion with his parents. In a February 1863 letter to his future wife, Annie Haggerty, Shaw wrote, "You know how many eminent men consider a negro army of the greatest importance to our country at this time. If it turns out to be so, how fully repaid the pioneers in the movement will be, for what they may have to go through.... I feel convinced I shall never regret having taken this step, as far as I myself am concerned; for while I was undecided I felt ashamed of myself, as if I were cowardly." Shaw received a promotion to major on April 11, 1863, and attained the rank of colonel the following month. Colonel Shaw would now have to navigate the turbulent forces of discrimination that existed within the Union Army.

The men of the 54th trained near Boston at Readville, under the constant scrutiny of white soldiers, many of whom believed black soldiers lacked the stomach for combat. Yet the negative perceptions seemed only to inspire a sense of unity within the ranks of the regiment and their white officers.

Contrary to recruitment promises, the soldiers of the 54th were paid only $10.00 per month, $3.00 less than the white troops. Shaw had become so committed to his men that he wrote to Governor Andrew, insisting that his entire regiment, including white officers, would refuse pay until his soldiers were "given the same payment as all the other Massachusetts troops." Yet Congress did not enact legislation granting equal pay to black soldiers until June 15, 1864.

Shortly after the 54th was mustered into service, the Confederate Congress passed an act stating its intention to "put to death" if captured, "any Negro" as well as "white commissioned officer [who] shall command, prepare or aid Negroes in arms against the Confederate States." The directive only served to strengthen the resolve of the black soldiers.

On May 18 Governor Andrew traveled to the camp to present Shaw with the regimental flags. He made the trip with 3,000 other visitors, including such prominent abolitionists as Frederick Douglass, William Lloyd Garrison, and Wendell Phillips. Douglass had a strong personal link with the 54th—two of his sons, Lewis and Charles, had joined the unit. Andrew presented the flags to Shaw. "I know not, Mr. Commander, in all human history, to any given thousand men in arms, has there been committed a work at once so proud, so precious, so full of hope and glory as the work committed to you," the governor said.

USAMHI

Massachusetts Governor John A. Andrew advocated the enlistment of black men into the Union Army. After President Lincoln issued the Emancipation Proclamation on January 1, 1863, Andrew approached Secretary of War Edwin Stanton and obtained authorization to raise a black Massachusetts regiment.

Ten days later the 54th Regiment of Massachusetts Volunteer Infantry marched through the streets of downtown Boston, greeted by the cheers of thousands who assembled to see them off at Battery Wharf. It was an impressive spectacle. Shaw, atop his chestnut brown horse, led the way. Close behind marched the color bearers, followed by young black soldiers, handsomely clad in their sharp, new uniforms.

The dress parade gradually made its way to the wharf and boarded the *De Molay* bound for Port Royal Island, South Carolina. There the regiment reported to the Department of the South. Once the men arrived, however, reality set in when they were relegated to man-

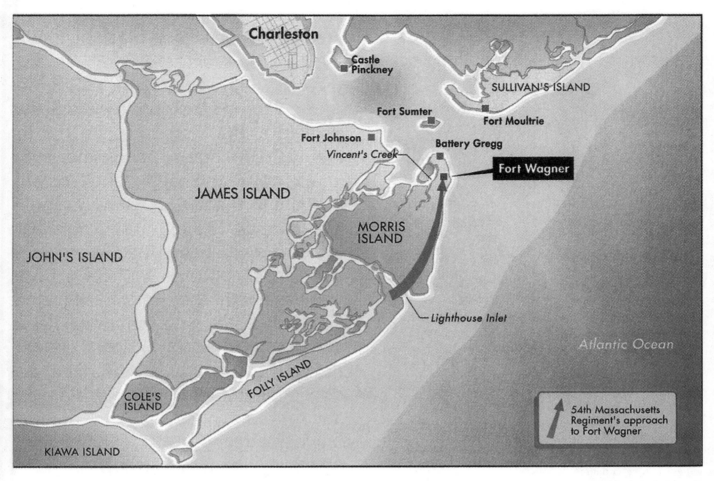

MAP BY RICK BROWNLEE

The 54th Regiment approached Fort Wagner along a narrow stretch of beach by the Atlantic Ocean.

ual labor. Not until June 8, when Shaw and his men joined Colonel James Montgomery and the black troops of his 2nd South Carolina Colored Volunteers on an "expedition" to Georgia, did they see any action, and that was during a pointless raid on the small town of Darien. After plundering the 100 or so residences, three churches, the market-house, courthouse, and an academy, Montgomery ordered Darien set afire. Begrudgingly, Shaw directed one of his companies to torch the town. Fanned by a high wind, the flames eventually destroyed everything but a church and a few houses.

Afterward, Shaw wrote to lieutenant Colonel Charles G. Halpine, the acting adjutant general of the department, to condemn this "barbarous sort of warfare." Shaw knew his complaint could result in his arrest or even court-martial, but he felt compelled to express his feelings. He later learned that Montgomery

had acted in accordance with the orders of his superior officer, General David Hunter. Soon after the Darien raid, President Lincoln relieved Hunter of his command.

The sacking of Darien and the manual labor his troops were compelled to do disheartened Shaw. "Our whole experience, so far, has been in loading and discharging vessels," he wrote to Brigadier General George C. Strong, commander of Montgomery's brigade. "Colored soldiers should be associated as much as possible with the white troops, in order that they may have other witnesses beside their own officers to what they are capable of doing." That opportunity finally arrived on the morning of July 16, 1863. Fighting alongside white troops on James Island, Shaw's men acquitted themselves well in a sharp skirmish. That same night they ferried to Morris Island, where battle lines had already been

drawn for the anticipated attack on Fort Wagner. Despite their exhaustion, hunger, and wet clothes, the men of the 54th were determined to fight on.

WHEN GENERAL STRONG, now Shaw's brigade commander, heard of the of the 54th on James Island, he asked the colonel if he and his regiment would lead the attack on Fort Wagner. Shaw and his men readily agreed and prepared to lead the charge across a narrow beach obstructed by felled branches, crisscrossed wire, and a deep moat—all of which were constructed to slow the attackers, making them vulnerable to enemy fire. Eight all-white units were to follow. All day long, Union artillery bombarded Fort Wagner in an effort to soften the Confederate defense and minimize the bloodshed that would inevitably follow. Late in the day Shaw arranged the 600 able-bodied men of his regiment into two

A Currier & Ives lithograph issued in 1863 depicts the 54th storming the fort.

wings of five companies each and moved them slowly up the beach. He assigned Company B to the right flank, using the surf as its guide. The other companies lined up on its left.

At dusk, General Strong addressed Shaw and his men. Pointing to the flag bearer, he said: "If this man should fall, who will pick up the flag?" Shaw stepped forward. "I will," he said. Addressing his troops with final words of inspiration, Shaw reminded them: "The eyes of thousands will look on what you do tonight." Then, drawing his sword, the young Boston Brahmin barked: "Move in quick time until within a hundred yards of the fort, then, double-quick and charge!" Quickstep became double-quick, and then a full run, as Confederate riflemen on the ramparts of the fort let loose a torrent of fire upon the Union soldiers. Men fell on all sides, but those who were able continued the charge with Shaw in the lead.

Company B passed through the moat to the base of the fort where canister, grenades, and small arms fire rained down

Sergeant William Carney was awarded the Medal of Honor for bravery during the battle.

on them. Surrounded by bloodshed, the 54th commander realized that he could not retreat, and he ordered the final assault on the fort. Shaw somehow managed to reach the parapet before a Confederate bullet pierced his heart.

"Men fell all around me," Lewis Douglass later wrote. "A shell would explode and clear a space of twenty feet, our men would close up again, but it was no use we had to retreat, which was a very hazardous undertaking. How I got out of that fight alive I cannot tell, but I am here."

The intense fire mowed down the color bearers. Sergeant William Carney, a barrel-chested 23-year-old, seized the national flag and planted it upon the fort's parapet. The men of the 54th fought gallantly for about an hour until Confederate guns forced them to abandon their position. Before retreating, Carney once again grasped the flag, and despite bullets in the head, chest, right arm, and leg, he returned it to Union lines. His heroism earned him the distinction of being the first of 21 black men during the war to earn the Medal of Honor.

Subsequent waves of Federal troops tried for two hours to take the fort but failed, and casualties mounted by the hundreds. At the end of the assault, the Union had lost 1,515 killed, wounded or missing. Of that number, 256 were black soldiers from the 54th Massachusetts.

The following morning revealed a grisly scene. The dead lay in contorted positions along the beach, their fingers and legs stiffened from rigor mortis. The soft but painful cries and moans of the dying could be heard, begging for help.

A few days after the siege, a Union party under a flag of truce requested the return of Shaw's body. Brigadier General Johnson Hagood, Fort Wagner's new commander, reportedly answered, "We buried him in the trench with his niggers." Learning of Hagood's reply, Colonel Shaw's father declared, "I can imagine no holier place than that in which he is, among his brave and devoted followers, nor wish for him better company."

From a military standpoint, the assault on Fort Wagner proved to be a costly failure. The blame rested on the shoulders of commanding general Quincy A. Gillmore and his commander in the field, Brigadier General Truman Seymour, who had not ordered the usual preparations for such an assault—no one sent out guides to check the terrain in advance or dispatched lines of skirmishers to soften the enemy. Nor had the 54th ever practiced storming a fort. Nevertheless, the assault proved to be a turning point for black soldiers, serving to dismiss any lingering skepticism among whites about the combat readiness of African Americans. "I have given the subject of arming the Negro my hearty support," General Ulysses S. Grant wrote to President Lincoln in August. "They will make good soldiers and taking them from the enemy weakens him in the same proportion they strengthen us."

When other Union generals remained recalcitrant, Lincoln responded swiftly. "You say you will not fight to free Negroes," he said. "Some of them seem to be willing to fight for you. When victory is won, there will be some black men who can remember that, with silent tongue and clenched teeth, and steady eye and well-poised bayonet, they have helped mankind on to this great consummation. I fear, however, that there will also be some white ones, unable to forget that with malignant heart and deceitful speech, they strove to hinder it."

William C. Kashatus is a professional historian at Chester County Historical Society, West Chester, Pennsylvania.

From *American Heritage,* October 2000, pp. 22-28. © 2000 by Forbes, Inc. Reprinted by permission of *American Heritage* magazine, a division of Forbes, Inc.

A Yankee Scarlett O'Hara in Atlanta

Thomas G. Dyer discovers the secret diary of a Unionist in the heart of the Confederacy who saw the American Civil War at uncomfortably close quarters.

SCARLETT O'HARA dominates the world's image of the American Civil War. But recent research has uncovered a real-life woman, Cyrena Bailey Stone, whose experiences offer a completely new perspective on wartime Atlanta.

Scarlett was a Confederate. Cyrena was a Unionist. Tempestuous, headstrong Scarlett had a conditional attachment to the Confederacy. Steady, courageous Cyrena possessed a principled allegiance to the Union. Scarlett fled Atlanta during the harrowing days of battle and siege. Cyrena stayed. 'This is my home', she wrote on the eve of the great battle for the city in July 1864, '& I wish to protect it if possible.'

We know about Cyrena Stone because of the recent appearance of a diary, anonymously kept during the seven months leading up to the Battle of Atlanta. The document reflects the experience of Cyrena, who recorded the tumult that marked the beginning of the Confederacy's death agony. Aware of the danger of keeping such a journal, she carefully protected her identity, and artfully obscured the identities of fellow members of a secret 'Union Circle' living in the rebel city.

An intensive research effort eventually identified Cyrena Stone, a native Vermonter who had lived in Atlanta for ten years, as the author of the diary. She and her husband, Amherst Stone, an ambitious lawyer, were at the heart of the Unionist community in Atlanta. By early 1864, however, Amherst had fled Atlanta on a blockade-running errand, and had been imprisoned in the North. Cyrena remained in the couple's home on the outskirts of the city. Under conditions of constant stress and danger, she kept her diary and in doing so made a record of a hitherto unknown part of the Civil War.

Throughout the war, Cyrena led a life governed by a passionate commitment to the Union. Although she coped with the challenges of everyday life in the Confederate city, she had difficulty in dealing with the suffocating political atmosphere of a region she believed had steeped itself in treason. For Cyrena Stone, the Confederacy was a confining, stifling sarcophagus. She and the other Atlanta Unionists longed for the coming of

Cyrena Stone

CYRENA ANN BAILEY STONE was born in 1830 in East Berkshire, Vermont, the daughter of a Congregationalist minister and Yankee tinkerer, Phinehas Bailey. Although the details of her childhood are sketchy, she apparently attended common schools in East Berkshire and in a series of villages in Vermont and eastern New York where she and the rest of the extensive Bailey brood lived as her father moved from pastorate to pastorate. The Bailey family was quite poor, but Cyrena's childhood was more or less typical, although marked by death of her mother and several siblings.

In 1850, she married Amherst Willoughby Stone, the son of a prosperous Vermont farmer. Young Stone became a lawyer. He was exceedingly ambitious and sought his fortune in the American South. After their marriage, the two settled in Georgia and eventually in Atlanta where Stone became a prominent businessman-lawyer. With prominence came prosperity, and the two settled into a comfortable existence in a large house on the outskirts of Atlanta, a mile from the centre of the city with its population in 1860 of about 10,000 persons.

As the secession crisis neared, Cyrena and Amherst felt the tugs of patriotism that pulled at transplanted northerners living in the South. Although tested by the defection of Amherst's brother to the southern cause and by her husband's ambivalent loyalties, Cyrena retained a remarkably consistent and courageous loyalty to the Union. During the war, she was reviled, threatened, and arrested, but she managed to escape imprisonment and continued to work with other Unionists in Atlanta to subvert the Confederate cause. When Amherst left for the North on a blockade-running mission in 1863, she remained in their home, persisting in her loyalist activities and awaiting the arrival of William T. Sherman and the Union army.

After the war, she and Amherst returned to Georgia where he became a federal official. She died in 1868 in her native Vermont at the age of 38.

the Union army to 'roll away the stone from the tomb into which Secession has consigned us—without any embalming'.

Relationships with other Unionists did much to sustain Cyrena throughout the war but took on a slightly different character in 1864. Many of the men had escaped through the lines, and her Unionist contacts were almost always with the women who remained. The symbols of national loyalty took on greater importance as the Union army approached. Throughout the conflict, Cyrena kept a small American flag, secreting it in a variety of hiding places, at one time in a jar of preserved fruit, at another in her sugar canister. Atlantans with Union sympathies would regularly visit the Stone household to see the flag, which it was illegal to possess in the Confederacy. One woman came furtively as she did not want her husband to know of her interest 'in the advance of the Federals'. When Cyrena retrieved the hidden banner the tearful woman kissed it 'reverently'.

Cyrena had altered her behaviour in order to cope with the constant probings and tauntings by Confederates who hoped to entrap her in a seditious act that could be interpreted as treason. She learned to control herself in these settings just as she hid her emotions from those who lived in her household. In social situations—and contact did continue with loyal Confederates—war news would invariably be interpreted in the best possible light for the rebel cause. Confederate loyalists would, of course, show enthusiasm. Downcast Unionists, sometimes shocked by Confederate claims, would try to react in ways that would minimise suspicion. At times, Cyrena would fight against normal reactions to wartime news, biting her lips to keep the colour in them, fighting back a blush: 'The face must keep its colour— white or red—though the heart stops beating or flames up in scorching pain' she wrote. When Unionists met unexpectedly on the street, they greeted each other correctly, without seeming overly friendly, in order not to arouse suspicion. After receiving some good news about the progress of the war, Cyrena encountered a Unionist man ('staunch & true') walking with a Confederate officer. 'Very slightly and sedately,' the Unionist bowed toward her, but after he had passed, 'something, which often impels us to look back, made me turn my head; at that instant, his head turned too, & his face was covered with smiles'. Intuition, Cyrena concluded, 'schooled as it has been these years— tells us where to laugh & when not to'.

Rumours of the movements of both Confederate and Union armies dominated many of Cyrena's conversations and preyed constantly on her mind. Sorting out fact from fiction proved difficult, and Cyrena and the other Unionists had their spirits lifted by reports of Yankee advances. Just as often, however, those spirits would be dashed by Confederate propaganda that glossed over setbacks and inflated advantages. Cyrena learned to read between the lines of reports and to weigh them carefully.

'Sherman defeated, & Johnston pursuing!' read one propaganda-filled report in early May. 'I like such defeats & such pursuits as these prove to be,' Cyrena wrote, for she had learned that the day before the Union general George Thomas had taken Tunnel Hill, and that Dalton had been evacuated by the Confederates, that place which was so impregnable'. Confederate General Joseph E. Johnston fell back toward Atlanta for strategic advantage, the reports ran, 'so that when he does make a

Inside the captured city. A view down Marietta Street in the heart of Atlanta just after the Union forces occupied the Confederate stronghold.

stand—dead Yankees will be piled higher than Stone Mountain'. Cyrena saw through the hyperbole. 'The battles are usually reported in this style,' she observed. 'The vandals were mowed down without number. No loss on our side. One man killed, and three slightly wounded.' Retreats became orderly re-positionings with no straggling and no loss of armaments. 'History will probably show the truthfulness of these so-called– "official reports" ' Cyrena concluded cynically.

Early in the war, Atlantans had become accustomed to battles fought several hundred miles away. As Margaret Mitchell later speculated, perhaps they had developed a wishful habit of believing that a great distance would always separate Atlanta from the real war. By the late spring of 1864, however, the Union army was only eighty-five miles to the north, having marched and fought through the rugged, mountainous north Georgia terrain. The city stood in imminent peril, and every day the threat increased. The Unionists dreamed of having Yankees in the streets of Atlanta. They talked incessantly about it among themselves, but it would have been foolhardy to suggest the probability, much less the desirability, of it in any other quarter. If the Confederates had developed their capacity for self-delusion over nearly four years of war, Cyrena had carefully kept her grip on reality, and though she had dreamed of the coming of the Yankees, she tried not to be too emotional; a tall order for a Unionist caught behind the Confederate lines for more than three years.

The closer the Yankee army drew to Atlanta, the more changes Cyrena and the other Unionists began to see in the behaviour and attitudes of Confederate Atlantans. Fear cooled Confederate loyalty, and cold reality warmed attachment to the Union. One Unionist commented to Cyrena that 'it was getting to be a fine thing to be a Union man. Hats are lifted when I meet some who would not speak to me a year ago. It is now "Why, how do you do Mr. Roberts?—very glad to see you" '. Cyrena also reported a conversation between two Atlanta Confederate 'ladies' and another Union friend. 'I know you can protect me when the Yankees come', one woman said. 'You have friends among them & I am coming right to your house to stay, & I shall be all right.' On May 24th, Cyrena recorded the transformation of the city. 'This has been a wild day of excitement,' she wrote.

'From early morning until now—engines have screamed—trains thundered along; wagons laden with government stores, refugees, Negroes and household stuff have rattled out of town. Every possible conveyance is bought, borrowed, begged or stolen'.

She exulted at the sudden transformation of the most ardent Confederate citizens into refugees from the city, noting with unrestrained pleasure the 'packing up & leaving' of those who had boasted about the impregnability of Atlanta. It was, she said, 'perfectly marvellous to behold'.

For Cyrena, the cannon thunder was grand and wonderful music... 'our redemption anthem.'

A 'delirium of fear and excitement' seized the city. There was a 'wild up-heaving' as military camps and fortifications multiplied. At night, she could see campfires in the nearby woods. During the day she could hear the sound of bugles and see large groups of soldiers moving about the city and in the open country near her house. For a few days, the Stones' slaves had claimed to hear the sound of cannon at night and in the early morning (like many Unionists, the Stones owned slaves). Cyrena was dubious; they had imagined the sounds, she told them. But on the morning of May 27th, they coaxed her outside to hear for herself what had been more audible since early morning. Once in the yard, Cyrena caught 'the faintest echo of booming guns'. The sound 'awakened the wildest joy I have ever known,' she wrote. For Cyrena, the muffled cannon thunder was grand and wonderful music, 'the first notes of our redemption anthem'. The cannon could not yet be heard in the city, and when Cyrena told a friend who lived inside Atlanta that the guns could be heard from her house, the woman hurried out to hear for herself. 'Mrs. M_____ a Southern lady... clapped her hands for joy and beckoned "Come boys!—come on!— we're waiting for you!" '

On June 2nd, militia companies arrived and crowded into the area around the Stone residence. Those who had mounts helped themselves to the ripened oats in the field on Cyrena's property. 'It makes no difference,' she wrote, 'the fences are fast disappearing—let it all go.' Four days later, on June 6th, the militia vacated the woods and departed for the front. Many of the men were 'in tears,' protesting that they had no interest in fighting the Yankees, and affirming that they would 'much rather fight the people who brought this war upon our country, and forced us to leave our homes to murder and be murdered'.

In addition to calling up the militia to defend Atlanta, the Confederates impressed large numbers of slaves to shore up the city's defences. Some resisted. Four such resisters escaped and made their way to the Stone house, where they pleaded with Cyrena to hide them. Cyrena took them in, hiding them in the cotton house between the stored bales. There they were fed and hidden for several days until, presumably, they made their escape.

On July 5th, the sounds of distant guns suddenly diminished, and an eerie calm settled on Atlanta. Cyrena feared that the latest rumours of a great defeat of the Yankees could be true, although she knew the Confederates would continue to paint a false picture of military successes in order to boost what little remained of civilian and military morale. The position of the main Union armies was unknown while General Johnston, it was said, had retreated to the Chattahoochee during the night. The uncertainty stretched nerves to snapping point.

Waiting for liberation became excruciatingly difficult. Every tidbit of news, every sound of battle, yielded multiple, often conflicting interpretations. The roar of the cannon resumed and sounded much closer, but the accuracy and significance of that, too, could be debated. On the night of July 18th, the noise of the guns seemed so close that it made Cyrena believe that surely the Union Army would march into Atlanta by morning.

In the sixteen months since her husband had left, Cyrena had grown lonely. The slaves remained and so did her white servants, Tom and Mary Lewis, but Cyrena felt isolated. The exodus of refugees since mid-May had gradually emptied the neighbourhood. 'All of my neighbours have gone—am alone on the hill,' Cyrena wrote on the morning of July 19th, 1864. A friend pleaded that she come into the city and stay with her, but Cyrena decided to remain in the house that she and Amherst had built.

By the morning of July 19th, Joseph F. Johnston had been removed from the Confederate command and replaced by General John Bell Hood. The evening before, Union forces had advanced to within two miles of Peachtree Creek, approximately three miles northwest of the Stones' house. On the morning of July 20th, fighting at Peachtree Creek began, and after a day of bitter, bloody battle, the Confederates were defeated. The next day, July 21st, was stupefyingly hot, as Union and Confederate forces prepared for another engagement that night that might decide the contest for Atlanta. Federal troops sought control of Bald (or Leggett's) Hill, which stood less than two miles from Cyrena's house. A bitter struggle for the hill continued throughout the day.

Cyrena remained at home in the midst of frantic Confederate activity. Her house was just inside the fortified ring of the Confederate city defences, with the troops of General Benjamin Cheatham's corps encircling it. Early in the morning, her yard 'swarmed' with hungry soldiers, who climbed onto the porch with dozens of requests for biscuits, milk, and utensils. 'Yes—yes yes—to every one,' was Cyrena's reply, 'thinking their wants would come to an end sometime, but they only increased'.

An injured Confederate colonel came to the house and asked if he could have a room. She said that he might. But would he

Map of the battle for Atlanta: the fall of the strategic Southern stronghold cut the Confederacy in two and helped seal its fate, to the delight of the secret Unionist sympathisers in the besieged city.

protect them? 'Certainly madam, as long as we remain here,' he replied. A kindly man, he spoke tearfully of his own family. Then suddenly, 'a horrid whizzing screaming thing,' came flying through the air and burst with a loud explosion above the house. Cyrena was shaken. Although she had become accustomed to the 'roaring of cannon & rattle of musketry,' this was her first exposure to artillery fire. She ran to the colonel. He told her the Yankees were 'trying the range of their guns.' Another shell fell but without exploding. Cyrena had been reassured by the colonel's presence, but orders soon came for his unit to move out. She understood the reasons for the departure. 'I can see there is no feeling of security in the positions held by these forces', she wrote. 'They are on the move continually'.

Within the previous few days, other visitors had become temporary members of Cyrena's household. Robert Webster, a black barber who had aided Union prisoners, and his wife, Bess, had taken refuge there. A few nights before, Confederate soldiers had suddenly burst into their home, 'pretending to search for runaway Negroes', and while holding guns against the couple's throats had stolen all of their valuables: 'silk dresses — jewellry watches & spoons were carried off'. The couple were now hiding in Cyrena's barn, protected by a 'kind officer', who was also staying there.

Throughout the day, the sounds of battle increased, 'becoming fiercer each hour.' By the end of the afternoon, a 'horrible pall of battlesmoke' hung over the entire area, darkening the sky. In the dusk, Tom Lewis breathlessly ran into the house. 'I tell you,' he said, 'We've got to git away from here now, for the men are falling back to the breastworks, & they're going to fight right away.' No sooner had Tom spoken

when an army of cannon came pouring onto the grove & yard. An officer came up quickly & said —"They are falling back & will soon fight at the breastworks. It will not be safe for you to remain here madam"… A dark night fell suddenly upon the earth, and how dark the night that shut down upon my heart! Not a star il-

lumined it; hope, courage all gone—no husband or brother near, and an army of men around our home; cannons belching forth a murderous fire not far away, & these silent ones in the yard, look so black & vengeful, as if impatient of a moment's quiet.

Nearly distraught, Cyrena went quickly from room to room —'not knowing what to do, or where to go; what to save—if anything could be saved, or what to leave.' The soldiers who accompanied the officer took charge, rolled up the carpets, and quickly packed many of the Stones' household items. The troops belonged to the Washington artillery from New Orleans. A young lieutenant told Cyrena that they were gentlemen. 'My heart thanked them for their sympathy', Cyrena wrote that night in her diary, 'but I thought they little knew upon what "traitor" they were bestowing it.'

A soldier, 'Mr Y', suddenly appeared. He had come to see if Cyrena was safe. Mr. Y and the Louisiana lieutenant then went to Hood's headquarters, where they learned that there would be no significant fighting that night. The soldiers anticipated early orders to fall back on Atlanta, and thought that the city would probably be abandoned by the Confederate army. Cyrena's first trip as a refugee was put off until morning.

Cyrena Stone's house lay inside strong defences like these, which held up the northern advance for months. Unionists within longed for their liberation.

At midnight, seated in the parlour of her 'dismantled home', with the rolled carpets standing in the corners, she had the presence of mind to write up the day's events and remembered pleasant times past spent in the parlour on 'sabbath twilights', singing old hymns with friends and family. Outside, she saw 'lurid light from the fires dotting the yard & grove.' They shone 'fitfully in the darkness, revealing groups of soldiers here & there—some asleep on the earth, & some leaning against trees in a listless way as if life had no longer any gladness for them'. Now she felt completely alone and nearly despondent 'as the red waves of War rush madly by—sweeping away our pleasant Home'.

Early in the morning, Cyrena said good-bye to the members of the Washington Artillery, who had been ordered to move on. She thanked them, promising always to 'remember their kindness and sympathy'. Before leaving, she packed away most of her books in a large closet, abandoned the piano because there was 'no earthly way of removing it', and left gallons of preserved pickles and 'nice blackberry wine'. She also had to leave behind most of her menagerie—chickens, pigs, and cats. Later that day, almost unbelievably, the kindly Mr Y went back to the house and with the aid of 'some army negroes who were not afraid of shells' brought the piano and a favourite cat to Cyrena.

By nine o'clock on the morning of July 22nd, 1864, Cyrena had left the home she loved:

> A strong feeling came over me as I passed down the shaded walk, where I had so often sauntered the peaceful summer evenings; but I looked not back, for I felt as if leaving those pleasant scenes forever. If such upheavings—such sunderings & losses, were to be the entrance gate into the larger life of liberty for which I had sighed—if this dark narrow way full of thorns & briers that so pierce & lacerate, led out into the broad shining land of my Country—I would go fearless, casting back no look of regret & longing for what I left behind.

Cyrena walked the mile to her friend's house, in the company of Mr Y who brought several small wagonloads of her possessions. After the migration, in the midst of the fury of the battle for Atlanta, her diary abruptly ceases in mid-sentence.

Cyrena survived the battle and siege and remained in Atlanta for some weeks after the Federal occupation. She was among the sizable number of the citizens who chose to go to the North during the forced evacuation of the city. Prior to leaving, she had a reunion with a Vermont cousin, a Union officer who sought her out in the wrecked city. Cyrena was, he said, 'the noblest woman he ever saw' and 'had remained true to the flag all this time'. She had been, he reported, 'shunned and excluded from society' but had 'endured all for righteousness sake'. Cyrena and her husband were reunited in the North in late 1864 and returned to their native Vermont. Eventually, she went back to Georgia, but never to Atlanta where she had composed her dramatic record of Unionist life in the South—an account completely at odds with the stereotype and fiction that surround the Civil War contest for Atlanta.

FOR FURTHER READING

Albert Castel, *Decision in the West: The Atlanta Campaign of 1864* (Lawrence: University Press of Kansas, 1992) Daniel W. Crafts, *Reluctant Confederates: Upper South Unionists in the Secession Crisis* (Chapel Hill: University of North Carolina Press, 1989) Carl N. Degler, *The Other South: Southern Dissenters in the Nineteenth Century* (New York: Harper and Row, 1974) Drew Gilpin Faust, *Mothers of Invention: Women of the Slaveholding South in the American Civil War* (Chapel Hill: University of North Carolina Press, 1996) Frank Klingberg, *The Southern Claims Commission* (Berkeley: University of California Press, 1955) James Michael Russell, *Atlanta, 1847–1890: City Building in the Old South and the New* (Baton Rouge: Louisiana State University Press, 1988)

Thomas G. Dyer is University Professor of Higher Education and History at the University of Georgia. He is the author of Secret Yankees: The Union Circle in Confederate Atlanta *(Johns Hopkins University Press, 1999).*

Between Honor and Glory

By Jay Winik

...**To grasp the full horror** of the march it is necessary to make it yourself. The landscape constantly changes: open fields are exasperatingly punctuated by high hedges and dense windbreaks that are impossible to see through or over or around. On the other side, they seamlessly merge into swamps, or dense, claustrophobic woods, or undergrowth so thick as to be a second forest; or, conversely, they run into long, muddy tracts, known euphemistically as Virginia quicksand.

Once more, Lee pushed his men to the outer limits of human endurance. "I know that the men and animals are exhausted," he bluntly told one of his generals, "but it is necessary to tax their strength." And remarkably, once more, they complied. Damp from the day's rain, their senses numbed from too little nourishment, they stumbled along with scarcely a word of complaint. But by now they were fighting a second struggle, this one from within. The dreadful consequences were inevitable: without food and deprived of sleep, the body begins to feed on itself, consuming vital muscle, raping invaluable tissue, robbing itself of what little energy is left. Thoughts become woozy; some experience a light-headedness, others even hallucinate. And with each hour, the situation worsens: initiative is deadened, and judgment becomes impaired, giving many the mental capacity of a small child. The elements, too—the sun, the wind, and the rain—become merciless. So does thirst. Limbs struggle to obey the simplest motor commands. Yet somehow, Lee's men inched forward...

Davis had called on the Confederacy to shift to a guerrilla war to wear down the North under interminable sacrifice. Militarily the plan had merit.

To the contemporary mind, it is as difficult to contemplate the westward march of the Army of Northern Virginia as it is to step outside all the history that has come after. To us, an extended troop march appears an anachronism. Today, great military machines race across terrain in high-speed tanks and armored personnel carriers. Unless they are poorly equipped, or the battlefield has collapsed around them, they do not march on foot, and, if they do, they certainly do not expect grand victory. It is no accident that one of the most famous military marches of the twentieth century was neither a strategic retreat nor a tactical feint, both of which were part of Robert E. Lee's stock-in-trade, but a journey into captivity known as the Bataan Death March, made over ten days and seventy-five miles by 36,000 defeated American servicemen in the Philippines. Even now, Bataan, where upward of 10,000 men died of thirst, exhaustion, beatings, torture, or beheadings, is a march that skews the modern military imagination.

But Robert E. Lee was not of a twentieth-century mind. The marches he knew were not Bataan, but heroic efforts by Hannibal, Alexander the Great, and Napoleon, for whom the distinction between genius and insanity was often measured by the razor-thin line of success. People must have thought Hannibal especially crazy, setting out from Spain with 40,000 men and an ungodly number of elephants to traverse two hazardous mountain ranges—the Pyrenees and the Alps—and a deep, rushing river, the Rhône, and to endure landslides, blinding snowstorms, and attacks by hostile mountain tribes; they thought him crazy, that is, until he did it in fifteen days and swept down upon the unsuspecting Romans. Now Lee and his veterans, some 35,000 men, had a roughly 140-mile march to make and a solid twelve- to twenty-four-hour lead. Lee understood the odds, but ever the gambler, hadn't he bested them before? Hadn't he gotten to Cold Harbor first? To leave Grant behind now would enshrine him among history's great commanders and tacticians.

With little sleep and even less respite, the men continued to march under the cover of darkness. On and on, hour after hour, from hilltop to hilltop, for the better part of two solid nights and one continuous day, they struggled to keep their lead. By April 4, they were dirty, unwashed, mud-splattered, exhausted, and, most of all, desperately hungry. Still, after months of languishing in the trenches, their morale and élan were surprisingly strong; and at the thought of food in Amelia, so were their spirits. Once replenished, their lead over Grant solidified, they would complete their dash to safety. So what mattered now was each new stride, each new landmark, bringing them closer to the 350,000 rations they expected at Amelia Court House, and taking them a step farther away from Grant's huge force, eagerly trailing behind.

Lee's plans had called for his vast columns of men and material to cross over three separate bridges; but one of them, Bevil's Bridge, was washed out; at another, Genito Bridge, the materials to shore it up had never arrived. Lee improvised: in the first case, three separate corps—Gordon's, Longstreet's, and Mahone's—were densely wedged onto a single bridge; for the second, the Confederates found a nearby railway pass that they neatly planked over. But these delays, costing the Confederates in manpower, in stamina, and, most precious of all, in ticks of the clock, held up the completion of the crossing until the following evening.

The stoic Lee himself made it across the Appomattox River only on the morning of April 4, at 7:30 a.m. Like his men, he had scarcely slept since leaving Petersburg and Richmond. But this morning, his hopes—and theirs—rose at the stirring thought of the relief waiting for them in Confederate boxcars on the Danville line at Amelia. Several hours later, around midday, Amelia itself came into view—a sleepy village of unpaved streets, with houses neatly tucked behind tumbled roses and weathered fences, and a few small shops converging around a grassy square. Lee raced ahead. Upon locating the boxcars, he ordered them to be opened.

This is what he found: 96 loaded caissons, 200 crates of ammunition, 164 boxes of artillery harnesses. But no bread, no beef, no bacon, no flour, no meal, no hardtack, no pork, no ham, no fruit, no cornmeal. And no milk, no coffee, no tea, no sugar. Not one single ration. Lee was stunned.

His men had left Richmond and Petersburg with only one day of rations. That day had come and gone, and much more hard marching lay ahead of them. Already, weakened men and animals were slowly dropping in their tracks. But to eat now meant halting the march to find food—which meant squandering his priceless lead over Grant. And in either case, there was no guarantee that he would secure food—that day, the next, or the next after that.

The general wasted little time, quickly giving the bad news to his division commanders and then writing out an appeal to "the Citizens of Amelia County" in which he called on their "generosity and charity" and asked them "to supply as far as each is able the wants of the brave soldiers who have battled for your liberty for four years."

Then he waited.

As dawn broke on April 5, he received his answer.

The citizens of Amelia County had already been cleaned out by Confederate impressment crews and the exigencies of war. Lee's forage wagons came back virtually empty: there were no pigs, no sheep, no hogs, no cattle, no provender. And there would be no breakfast that morning for the men. His only option now was a hard, forced march toward Danville—where a million and a half rations were stored. It was 104 miles by railroad; four grueling days by foot. But this time could be whittled down to only one day if rations were rushed forward by train to Burkeville, a mere eighteen miles down the line. Lee dispatched an order by wire. Would it work? Just as he could no longer wait in Amelia for rations, no longer could he wait for an answer. With the buffer of the Appomattox River gone and crucial hours lost, Grant's men were closing in. There was no time to waste.

Lee hastily mounted his horse, Traveller, and immediately ordered his men to move toward Burkeville. But it was worse than Lee realized.

Just outside Jetersville, itself a ragtag town consisting of little more than a collection of weathered wooden houses scattered alongside the rail line, Union cavalry had beaten the rebels to the punch; earthworks were blocking the retreat path like a dam; battle flags had been raised; and well-fed bluecoats were peering over the lines. Dug in, "thick and high," the Federals were waiting.

Longstreet had already sought to dislodge them; convinced that it was only cavalry in the way, he briskly attacked. But Sheridan's horsemen were now backed by two Federal corps strung out between Lee and North Carolina. The road of escape—through Burkeville—had been cut off.

Riding down the retreat line, Lee cast a sidelong glance, lifted his field glasses, and gazed out at the freshly dug Union fortifications. For several tense moments, he considered one last massive and final assault. But the Union troops were too well entrenched, and his army was in no condition for an all-out battle. Instead, Lee set his men back in motion, again. This time due west, for Lynchburg.

Thus was delivered what many regimental commanders considered to be "the most cruel marching order" that they had ever given.

In every direction, the dead—men, mules, and horses—began to litter the roadside. Dense columns of smoke rose from exploding vehicles, and shells burst after being touched by flames. Following alongside, Lee learned from two captured Federal spies that the Union was gaining ground. He pushed his men that much harder.

Nighttime fell. It didn't matter. Morning now seamlessly intermingled with evening, darkness with sunset, the fifth of April with the sixth, two hours with eight hours, eight hours with sixteen hours, and eventually, twenty-four hours with forty hours. Hungry, with barely one night of rest in three days, many of the men wandered forward in a giddy, phantasmagoric state, slipping in and out of sleep and confusion as they walked. The evening was little better: as the long, black night wore on, more troops fell by the wayside; they would halt for a few moments' rest, and fail to rise, their dazed eyes gazing haplessly at Lee's line, still lumbering west.

Still outwardly calm, Lee's face nonetheless looked "sunken," "haggard." But there was suddenly the prospect of food to spur his men on. That afternoon, he had learned that more than 80,000 rations of meal and bread—and even such delicacies as French soup packaged in tinfoil along with whole hams—were definitively waiting in Farmville. Nineteen miles away.

So it was in that direction that the Confederates picked up their step and began again, in one long, snaking line, to move.

Grant wasted no time. This was the opportunity that he had hoped for. Sheridan's cavalry and three infantry corps continued to race alongside the retreating rebels, bludgeoning them with sledgehammer blows and quick, in-and-out lightning attacks that heightened panic and fatigue. Fueled by the prospect of victory, the Federals had at long last begun to show a fighting spirit that had been sorely lacking since the Grant-Lee slugfest began almost a year before: gone were the shock and dread of another Wilderness or Cold Harbor; no longer did they fear seeing "the elephant" of battle. It showed in their very stamina: Union men, despite their own obvious exhaustion, now seemed incapable of straggling, some handily marching upward of thirty-five miles per day.

The fighting would outdo much of the war in its savagery. After the methodical rebel order of "Fire!" the line of advancing bluecoats wavered and broke. Then the killing began.

"Lee's surely in a bad fix," he announced. "But if I were in his place, I think I could get away with part of the army." Then he added tantalizingly, "I suppose Lee will."

So meeting with Sheridan and Major General George Meade, he reiterated his central plan. He did not want to follow Lee; he wanted to get ahead of him. Playing for keeps, this time Grant refined his stratagem. At dawn the next day, April 6, he dispatched Sheridan on a northwest swing—no longer aimed at Lee's rear but intended to move ahead of him, directly positioning the hot breath of Union armies against Lee's face. For good measure, he ordered another infantry corps to join the push in the rear…

The skirmishing at Sayler's Creek, across three separate battle sites that would eventually merge into one, began early on April 6 and mounted as the sun climbed. The battle itself began in earnest by the first brush of afternoon, when two dangerous gaps appeared in Lee's lines. Deadly Federal horsemen, swinging sabers and led by the dashing, yellow-haired general, George Armstrong Custer, rushed in through the holes. Soon, three Union corps had cut off a quarter of Lee's army; their guns shattering the unearthly silence of the rolling hills. A row of artillery batteries followed, decking Confederates who had been lingering in the dank and muddy swale. "I had seldom seen a fire more accurate nor one that had been more deadly," one rebel noted. Off-balance from lack of food, dazed by lack of sleep, the rebels were at first stunned, then, as one Confederate put it, they "blanched," and finally, they were "awe-struck."

Sheridan wasted no time in capitalizing on their diminished state. "Go through them!" he shouted angrily. "They're demoralized as hell."

Not completely. At the sight of the Yankees, they rallied. Rebel batteries swung into position, anchored their lines, and trained their barrels on the advancing Federals, while infantry crouched and pointed muskets at the enemy. It was only a prelude to fighting that would outdo much of the rest of the war in its savagery. After the methodical rebel order of "Fire!" the line of advancing bluecoats wavered and broke. The first crisis was apparently over. But then, without warning, the conflict degenerated, and the insensate killing began. The hollow-eyed Confederates sprang to

their feet with empty muskets, starting after the retreating Yankees. Catching up to the Federals, they became entangled in vicious hand-to-hand combat. Men struck one another with bayonets, flogged one another with the butts of guns, and flailed at one another with their feet. "I well remember the yell of demonic triumph with which that simple country lad clubbed his musket and whirled savagely upon another victim," observed one commander. Grabbing one another with dirt-sodden fingers, callused, sweaty hands, and sharp fingernails, they rolled on the ground like wild beasts, biting one another's throats and ears and noses with their teeth. Officers dispensed with their guns, fighting with swords and, when they no longer worked, with fists. Astoundingly, in this jumble of conflict, they were no longer battling one another over territory or vital military advantage or even tactical gain, but out of sheer impulse: they were killing one another over battalion colors.

The Yankees kept coming, and the battered rebels, their assaults increasingly uncoordinated and disjointed, could not keep up the ferocity. By day's end, they were overwhelmed; the dead lay so close and dense that bodies had to be dragged away to let a single horse pass. It was the South's worst defeat of the entire campaign. All told, Grant's army had captured an astonishing 6,000 rebels—Lee's son Custis and the one-legged General Richard Ewell among them—and destroyed much of their wagon train. Adding up the killed and wounded, Lee had lost up to 8,000. Lee himself felt the sting of defeat sharply. Late in the afternoon, he rode out to a high ridge overlooking the battlefield. Sitting on Traveller, on this small rise, the general found the sight astonishing. Lee was a badly shaken man.

"My God!" he cried out. "Has the army been dissolved?"

Bill Mahone, the tall, bearded general, was there, riding at his side. Deeply touched, he took a moment to steady his voice, then quickly offered words of encouragement. "No general, here are troops ready to do their duty."

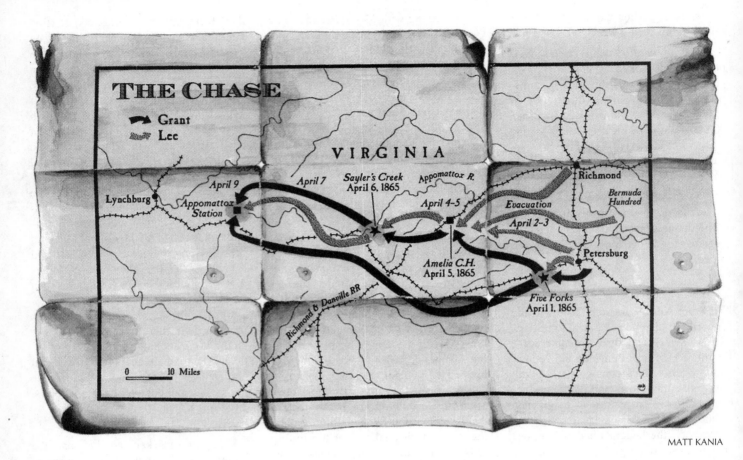

THE CHASE

➤ Grant
➤ Lee

VIRGINIA

Lynchburg

April 9
Appomattox
Station

April 7

Sayler's Creek
April 6, 1865

Appomattox R.

April 4–5

Amelia C.H.
April 5, 1865

Richmond & Danville RR

Richmond

Bermuda
Hundred

Evacuation
April 2–3

Petersburg

Five Forks
April 1, 1865

0   10 Miles

MATT KANIA

As Mahone and his men drew into a line to hold back the Federals, Lee's temper again flared; he, too, was drawn to the fight. Leaning forward in his saddle, he snatched a single battle flag, to rally fresh troops as well as retreating men. On this day, it was no idle gesture. Earlier in the fighting, one flag bearer had been brought down by an artillery shell, only to have his brother grab the standard and promptly be shot through the head. Another Confederate quickly reached for the colors and also fell. So did a fourth. And so did a fifth, until the flag was firmly planted by a sixth in a low bush. Now it was Lee who sought to cheat fate. Riding past Mahone's assembled troops, he held the flag staff high in one hand. At the top of the rise, he stopped and waited. The wind caught the flag, and it snapped and curled around his silver mane, flapping about him and draping his body in Confederate red. Mahone's men fell deathly silent, and then this collective hush was punctuated by a scattered,

spontaneous cry emanating from the frenzied survivors stumbling back: "Where's the man who won't follow Uncle Robert!"…

After Sayler's Creek, Phil Sheridan tersely wired Grant: "If the thing is pressed, I think that Lee will surrender." When Lincoln read this, his melancholy spirits soared.

Lincoln bluntly telegraphed to Grant: "Let the thing be pressed."

It was now April 7.

Lee's remaining forces had again crossed the Appomattox to arrive in Farmville, where the first rations of the march awaited them. While the food was dispensed, campfires were hastily built; bacon sizzled; and corn bread was devoured. His troops, at last able to eat and rest, still had two options: try again to turn south toward Danville, or set out for

Lynchburg and the sheltering protection of the Blue Ridge mountains. But inexplicably, one of Lee's generals had neglected to blast High Bridge—a massive steel and brick structure spanning a floodplain half a mile wide, at a spectacular height of 126 feet. Frantically riding back, an officer finally torched it, but the delay was fatal; a hard-marching Federal column reached the accompanying wagon bridge in time to stomp out the flames. Now there was no river between Lee and Grant's lead troops; indeed, the distance separating them was barely four miles. With Union soldiers approaching, Lee's army stood nearly naked to assault.

Lee was forced to quickly withdraw his men from Farmville and recross the Appomattox to escape the threat, even as Union cavalry drew so close that fighting broke out in the town's streets. The priceless supply train quickly rolled away, while thousands of starving soldiers, who had not yet drawn their rations, watched in agony. Bedlam followed; haversacks still open, muskets in hand, men turned and raced across bridges that were already burning.

Once more, Federal and Confederate soldiers clashed. But now, the shards of Lee's army successfully fended off the Union, smashing the bluecoats along both their front and their flank, even taking some 300 prisoners, including a Union general—all under the direct eye of Lee himself. This time, the rebels inflicted more casualties than they suffered—in fact, the Union had lost some 8,000 men in just the last week alone—and by moonlight, the road west to Lynchburg now beckoned.

"Keep your command together and in good spirits," Lee reassured his son Rooney. "Don't let them think of surrender."

And he concluded: "I will get you out of this."

Shortly before dusk on April 8, as he dismounted to make camp for the night, Lee received a letter from Grant offering generous terms for the surrender of Lee's army and the only condition that he demanded was that the officers and men "be disqualified from taking up arms" until exchanged. Unknown to Lee, Grant had labored more than six hours to compose this letter. In a tactful combination of diplomacy and insight, he suggested that Lee could be spared the humiliation of surrendering in person.

Six straight days of the relentless march had not dimmed Lee's audacity, or his desire for victory.

Lee responded. Of all the sentiments it reflects, despair and surrender are not among them:

Genl
I received at a late hour your note of today. In mine of yesterday I did not intend to propose the surrender of the Army of N. Va.—but to ask the terms of your proposition. To be frank, I do not think the emer-

gency has arisen to call for the surrender of this Army, but as the restoration of peace should be the sole object of all, I desire to know whether your proposals would lead to that and I cannot therefore meet you with a view to surrender… but as far as your proposal may affect the C.S. forces under my command & tend to the restoration of peace, I shall be pleased to meet you at 10 a.m. tomorrow on the old state road to Richmond between the picket lines of the two armies.

The letter was sealed, and the courier dispatched. Under a soft midnight sky, with a bright, nearly full moon overhead, Grant scanned Lee's letter, then handed it to his chief of staff to read aloud. The aide was furious at Lee's brash response, but Grant just coolly shook his head. "It looks as if Lee still means to fight."

With enemy artillery roaring in the background, that night Lee and his weary lieutenants gathered around a campfire in the woods near Appomattox Court House. The Confederates were almost entirely surrounded, outnumbered nearly six to one, with little food, little hope of resupply, little prospect for immediate reinforcement. But there was still the distinct prospect of escape. And before the opportunity slipped away, Lee hoped to turn the momentary lull to his advantage. Six straight days of Lee's relentless march westward had not dimmed his audacity, or his desire to avoid surrender and somehow salvage victory. He devised another plan for breaking through the enemy lines: his men would attack as soon as possible, attempting to slice a hole through Grant's slumbering army, and if successful, they would resume the march southward. General John Gordon, one of Lee's most daring officers, was chosen to lead the breakout. And, if necessary, there remained a fallback position: they could make their way to the Blue Ridge mountains, where, Lee had once said, he could hold out "for twenty years."

Before dawn on April 9, in the pitch black, the advance was to begin. It was Palm Sunday, the day that marked the

start of the Holy Week and Jesus' arrival in Jerusalem. Neither the day nor its significance would have been lost on Lee or his men.

At 5 a.m., just beyond Appomattox Court House, a fog hovered over the landscape like a thick, sprawling ghost; the rolling hills soon echoed with the staccato rattle of artillery; and the Sunday stillness was again shattered by the piercing cry of the rebel yell. Gordon's men fought with a special fury. They drove Federal cavalry from their positions, captured several guns, duly cleared the road of bluecoats, and then swept forward to the crest of a hill. Suddenly, below them, concealed in the woodlands, lay the inexorable logic of the mathematics of war: a solid wall of blue, some two miles wide, was advancing—two Yankee infantry corps, with two other Union corps closing in on Lee's rear. Quipped one soldier at glimpsing this awesome sight: "Lee couldn't go forward, he couldn't go backward, and he couldn't go sideways."

Three hours later, around 8 a.m., a courier from Gordon hastily carried the apocalyptic message to Lee. "I have fought my corps to a frazzle," he wrote. "And I fear I can do nothing…"

Thus the ominous choice was finally set before Lee: surrender or throw his life on one last murderous fight—Lincoln's feared Armageddon. Lee summoned General Longstreet, who brought Mahone and Lee's chief of artillery, the twenty-nine-year-old brigadier general, E. Porter Alexander. All were expecting a council of war. Instead, the discussion turned to surrender. When a moment of vacillation came and an opening occurred, Alexander, one of the most talented and innovative men in Lee's command, took it. Pleading with his chief not to give up, Alexander saw another recourse: a third option.

"You don't care for military glory or fame," he protested, "but we are proud of your name and the record of this army. We want to leave it to our children… a little more blood more or less now makes no difference." Instead, Alexander suggested a Confederate trump card, in fact, the specter most dreaded by Lincoln,

Grant, and Sherman: that the men take to the woods, evaporate into the hills, and become guerrillas. "Two thirds" would get away, Alexander contended. "We would be like rabbits or partridges in the bushes," he said, "and they could not scatter to follow us."

A veteran of Fredericksburg and Gettysburg, Cold Harbor and Petersburg, Alexander was so valued by Lee that Jefferson Davis once noted, he is "one of a very few whom Gen Lee would not give to anybody." And Alexander was already prepared to take to the bush rather than surrender—and so, he later indicated, were countless other men. There were no more miracles to be performed, but there were indeed certainly still options. And this option—guerrilla warfare—was not one to be lightly ignored. During the Revolutionary War, Lee's own father had fought the British as a partisan. Moreover, on April 4, a fleeing President Jefferson Davis had issued his own call for a guerrilla struggle. Yet it was Lee's judgment—and not Davis's—that would be most decisive. ("Country be damned," roared former Virginia Governor Henry Wise to Lee. "There is no country. You are the country to these men!")

Lee paused, weighing his answer. No less than for Davis, surrender was anathema to him. Here, surely, was seduction. And in this fateful moment the aging general would affect the course of the nation's history for all time.

Throughout the years variously referred to as "guerrillaism," or "guerrilleros," or "partisans," or "Partheyganger," or "bushwhackers," guerrilla warfare is and always has been the very essence of how the weak make war against the strong. Insurrectionist, subversive, chaotic, its methods are often chosen instinctively, but throughout time, they have worked with astonishing regularity. Its application is classic and surprisingly simple: shock the enemy by concentrating strength against weakness. Countering numerical superiority, guerrillas have always employed secrecy, deception, and terror as their ultimate tools. They move quickly, attack fast, and just as quickly scatter. They strike at night—

or in the day; they hit hard in the rain, or just as hard in the sunshine; they rain terror when troops are eating or when they have just concluded an exhausting march; they assault military targets, or, just as often, hunt down random civilians. They may hit at the rear of the enemy, or at its infrastructure, or, most devastating of all, at its psyche; the only constant is that they move when least expected, and invariably in a way to maximize impact.

And as military men have often learned the hard way, guerrilla warfare does the job. By luring their adversaries into endless, futile pursuit, guerrillas erode not just the enemy's strength, but, far more importantly, the enemy's morale.

Grant's strategy of exhaustion would be turned on its head. Confronted with a guerrilla phase, the Union would not be able to demobilize its armies. Conscription would continue.

Before the coming of Christ the lightning strikes of the nomadic Scythians blunted the efforts of Darius I to subdue them; Judas Maccabeus waged successful guerrilla operations against the Syrians; the Romans in Spain required several long centuries to subdue the Lusitanians and Celtiberians. The actual word "guerrilla" came from the Spanish insurgency against France in the early 1800s, a conflict Jefferson Davis frequently referred to and which at one point was largely responsible for containing three of Napoleon's armies. Equally familiar to nineteenth-century Americans were the Thirty Years War and the French Religious Wars; the experience of Frederick the Great in Bohemia; of Wellington in Portugal; the partisan war against Revolutionary France; the Netherlands against Philip II; Switzerland against the Hapsburg Empire. And then there were the most honorable examples of all: The Swamp Fox, Francis Marion, Sumter, Pickens, Green, the Liberty Boys in Georgia... West Point

graduate and former U.S. Secretary of War Jefferson Davis knew all this.

The day after Richmond fell, Davis had called on the Confederacy to shift from a static conventional war in defense of territory and population centers to a dynamic guerrilla war of attrition, designed to wear down the North and force it to conclude that keeping the South in the Union would not be worth the interminable pain and ongoing sacrifice. "We have now entered upon a new phase of a struggle the memory of which is to endure for all ages," he declared. "... Relieved from the necessity of guarding cities and particular points, important but not vital to our defense, with an army free to move from point to point and strike in detail detachments and garrisons of the enemy, operating on the interior of our own country, where supplies are more accessible, and where the foe will be far removed from his own base and cut off from all succor in case of reverse, nothing is now needed to render our triumph certain but the exhibition of our own unquenchable resolve." He concluded thus: "Let us but will it, and we are free."

In effect, Davis was proposing that Lee disperse his army before it was finally cornered. From a military point of view, the plan had considerable merit. The Confederacy was well supplied with long mountain ranges, endless swamps, and dark forests to offer sanctuary for a host of determined partisans. Its people knew the countryside intimately and instinctively and had all the talents necessary for adroit bushwhacking, everything from the shooting and the riding, the tracking and the foraging, the versatility and the cunning, right down to the sort of dash necessary for this way of life. Moreover, given that most of them would be battle-hardened and well-trained veterans, arguably an organized Confederate guerrilla army could be among the most effective partisan groups in all of history. The Union army would then be forced to undertake the onerous task of occupying the entire Confederacy—an unwieldy occupation at best, which would entail Federal forces having to subdue and patrol and police an area as large as all of today's France, Spain, Italy, Switzerland, Germany, and Poland combined. Even in early April 1865, the Union had actually conquered only a relatively small part of the South—to be sure, crucial areas for a conventional conflict, like Nashville, New Orleans, Memphis, and, of course, the crown jewel of Richmond—but that would be largely meaningless in a bitter, protracted guerrilla war. As the Romans had found out 2,000 years earlier, cities could become useless baggage weighing down the military forces, what the ancient commanders memorably called "impedimenta."

In moving to occupy vast stretches of land defended only by small, dispersed forces, Grant's strategy of exhaustion would be turned on its head. Consider the nearly insuperable difficulties that he would face: up to that point, no more than roughly a million Union men had been in arms at any one given time. But confronted with a guerrilla phase, the Union would not be able to demobilize its armies, always problematic for a democracy. Wartime conscription would have to continue, with all its attendant political difficulties and war-weariness. Even granting the North's theoretical ability to put more than 2 million men under arms, it would be unlikely that the Federals could ever pacify, let alone manage and oversee, more than fragmented sections of the South against a willful guerrilla onslaught. Rather than having a restored United States, the country could come to resemble a Swiss cheese, with Union cities here, pockets of Confederate resistance lurking there, ambiguous areas of no-man's-land in between. Even the North would not be safe. In 1864, a ragtag group of twelve Confederates, without horses, plus ten lookouts, and financed by a mere $400 in cash from the Confederate secretary of war, had crossed the Canadian border, plundered three Vermont banks, stolen $210,000, and turned the entire state into chaos. From New York to Philadelphia, and Washington to Boston, targets would abound: banks, businesses, local army outposts, and even newspapers and statehouses. All were vulnerable. Month after grinding month, year after year, who would be under siege: the victorious Union or the hardened guerrillas?

Across most of the South, the situation would be even more daunting. In Charles Adams's famous warning, "The Confederacy would have been reduced to smoldering wilderness." As in guerrilla wars throughout history, the Union would have to station outposts in every county and every sizable town; they would be forced to put a blockhouse on every railroad bridge and at every major communications center; they would be reduced to combing every sizable valley and every significant mountain range with frequent patrols. With Lee's army and other loyal Confederates—by some historians' estimates, there were still up to 175,000 men under arms who could be called upon—dispersed into smaller, more mobile units, they could make lightning hit-and-run attacks on the invading forces from safe havens in the rugged countryside and then invisibly slip back into the population. Their molestations need not be constant, or even kill many people; they need only be incessant.

Riding past Mahone's troops, at the top of the rise Lee stopped and waited. The wind caught the flag, draping his body in Confederate red. Then a spontaneous cry from the frenzied survivors. . .

The military balance would be almost meaningless. In truth, more frightening to the Union than the actual casualties it might suffer would be the psychological toll as prolonged occupiers, the profound exhaustion, the constant demoralization. Where would the stamina come from? There would be no real rest, no real respite, no true amity, nor any real sense of victory. Prospects for Northern victory had seemed dim as recently as August 1864, largely because Northerners had grown weary of the war. The Northern home front had nearly crumbled first—and was saved only by the captures of Mobile and, more importantly, of Atlanta, which paved the way for a presidential reelection victory that Lincoln

himself had, just weeks earlier, judged to be an impossibility. Only the heartening prospects of sure and relatively sudden victory had sustained the Federals to this time. In a guerrilla war, all bets would be off. How much longer would the country countenance sending its men into war? How long could it tolerate the necessary mass executions, the sweeping confiscations, the collective expulsions, and all the other agonies and cruelties of a full-scale guerrilla war, which would inevitably pervert its identity as a republic? We know what the French once said of a comparable experience. As its columns sought to put down the guerrilla resistance of Abdelkader in North Africa in 1833, one urgent dispatch to King Louis-Philippe stated sadly: "We have surpassed in barbarity the barbarians we came to civilize." It is hard to imagine Americans willing to pay this price for Union.

Could the South carry it out? Grant and Sherman certainly had no doubt about the Confederacy's ability to wage protracted guerrilla war—it was their greatest fear. At one point, Grant himself ruminated, "To overcome a truly popular, national resistance in a vast territory without the employment of truly overwhelming force is probably impossible." The Union never had any systematic plans to cope with such an eventuality—all of Grant's efforts were principally designed to break up the Confederacy's main armies and to occupy the main cities. The army had failed dismally even in the more limited guerrilla war in Missouri. As General John D. Sanborn, who served under Grant's command, would later admit: "No policy worked; every effort poured fuel on the fire."

Lincoln, too, was equally concerned, and he, as much as anyone else, understood the toll guerrilla war could take on the country. On the Missouri guerrilla conflict he lamented, "Each man feels an impulse to kill his neighbors, lest he first be killed by him. Revenge and retaliation follow. And all this among honest men. But this is not all. Every foul bird comes along, and every dirty reptile rises up." Some of Lincoln's aides put it even more fearfully. Said one, guerrilla warfare is "the external visitation of evil."

Before the Civil War even began, guerrilla activity had already made its mark on the North-South conflict. On May 24, 1856, John Brown and five other abolitionists brutally murdered and mutilated five Southern settlers at Pottawatomie Creek in Kansas. Day after day for over two years, dueling bands of Free-Soil abolitionists and pro-slavery marauders burned, robbed, and killed in an effort to drive the other from "Bleeding Kansas," a grim dress rehearsal for the Civil War to follow. By the time war erupted in 1861, many on the blood-stained Kansas-Missouri border were already veterans of irregular warfare.

And once the war started, across the Confederacy, Southerners quickly took to guerrilla tactics. Sam Hildebrand roamed the woods of southern Missouri slaying scores of Unionists; Champ Ferguson tormented the Cumberland in Tennessee, knifing, mangling, and bludgeoning luckless Federals whenever he encountered them. Before he was eventually captured—and summarily hanged—Ferguson personally extinguished over a hundred lives. In the swamps of Florida, John Jackson Dickison outmaneuvered, outfought, and outfoxed the bluecoats; and anarchy reigned in Unionist Kentucky, where brutal guerrilla bands led by Ike Berry, Marcellus Clark, and scores of others sprang up across the state. At one point, Jesse McNeill and his partisans slipped into Cumberland, Maryland, and in a daring raid captured two Union generals. Whatever draconian measures the Union instituted, including confiscation of property and executions of five guerrillas for every loyalist killed, accomplished little.

Some of the Confederate's guerrillas became legendary, feared not simply in the North, but known internationally on both sides of the Atlantic. Of these, John Mosby was among the most dashing and prominent. Pint-sized, plucky, and daring, he was a bit of a Renaissance man. He read Shakespeare, Plutarch, Washington Irving, and Hazlitt's *Life of Napoleon*, and his words and writings were frequently sprinkled with passages from the classics. The twenty-nine-year-old had been expelled from the University of Virginia—he shot a fellow student—yet he later finagled a pardon from the gov-

ernor, and then, of all things, took up the law. At the outset of the war, he was actually opposed to secession and was an "indifferent soldier" at best; though after joining Jeb Stuart's cavalry, he proved himself to be a fearless courier and cavalry scout and, when he raised a company of his own under the Partisan Ranger Act of April 1862, a remarkable guerrilla leader. His fame rapidly spread with such exploits as the capture of a Northern general, Edwin H. Stoughton, in bed with a hangover—a mere ten miles from Washington, D.C., in March 1863. "Do you know who I am?" bellowed the general, upon being so indiscreetly interrupted. Mosby shot back: "Do you know Mosby, General?" Stoughton harrumphed: "Yes! Have you got the rascal?" Mosby: "No, but he has got you!" (Mosby completed the humiliation by brazenly retreating with his prisoner in full view of Federal fortifications.) Operating on horseback at night, with stealth, surprise, and swiftness, he soon earned the sobriquet of the "Grey Ghost," and the romance surrounding his exploits brought recruit after recruit to his doorstep. In turn, he was sheltered and fed by a large and sympathetic population in northern Virginia, which served as his early warning network—and his refuge. Never amounting to more than a thousand men, Mosby's partisans were confined to small platoons of several dozen. But they mauled Union outposts with such effectiveness and a whirlwind fury that the regions stretching from the Blue Ridge to the Bull Run mountains were quickly dubbed, by friends and foes alike, "Mosby's confederacy." Union supplies could not move through his territory unless well protected, and even then they were likely prey.

The destruction Mosby inflicted upon Union lines was considerable, and he was detested accordingly. Various strategies were employed—without success—to subdue him. One plan called for an elite team of sharpshooters to shadow Mosby until he was either caught or destroyed. It failed. Another promised massive arrests of local civilians in Mosby's confederacy and a wholesale destruction of their mills, barns, and crops. This also failed. While Mosby still

roamed freely, a frustrated General Sheridan, whom Mosby relentlessly foiled in the Shenandoah Valley, once thundered about the restless guerrilla: "Let [him] know there is a God in Israel!" Finally, Grant ordered that any of Mosby's men who were captured should be promptly shot. And in autumn of 1864, General George Custer obliged, capturing six men and executing them all. Three were shot, two were hanged, and a seventeen-year-old boy was dragged bleeding and dying through the streets by two men on horses until a pistol was finally emptied into his face—while his grief-stricken mother hysterically begged for his life. But the Union's hard-line tactics collapsed when Mosby began (albeit reluctantly) hanging prisoners in retaliation. Yet fearsome as he was, Mosby, like his spiritual predecessors Marion, Pickens, and Sumter, represented the civilized face of "little war." And then there was Missouri.

Missouri produced the most bloodthirsty guerrillas of the war. Topping the list was William Clarke Quantrill, a handsome, blue-eyed, twenty-four-year-old former Ohio schoolteacher. A close second was Bloody Bill Anderson, whose father was murdered by Unionists and whose sister was killed in a Kansas City Union prison disaster. Among their disciples were young men destined for later notoriety: Frank and Jesse James, and Coleman Younger.

In early 1862, Quantrill and his band of bushwhackers launched a series of strikes into Kansas that all but paralyzed the state. Then, in 1863, the revenge-minded Quantrill set his sights on a new target: Lawrence, Kansas. One would be hard-pressed to find a place more thoroughly despised by Quantrill and his comrades than Lawrence. It functioned as a Free-Soil citadel during the 1850s, then as a haven for runaway slaves, and, during the war, as a headquarters to the Redlegs, a band of hated Unionist guerrillas. Early in the morning of August 21, Quantrill and his 400 bushwhackers—including Frank James and Coleman Younger—struck. At 5 a.m., Quantrill and his men silently made their way into town. Then the killing began. With a triumphant yell, Quantrill began shouting, "Kill! Kill! Lawrence must be thoroughly cleansed… Kill! Kill!" For the next few hours, his fierce and sweaty long-haired men, unshaven and unwashed, rumbled up and down the streets of Lawrence, looting stores, shops, saloons, and houses. They systematically rounded up every man they encountered and then torched the town. By day's end, the deed was done. The city lay in ashes; 200 homes were burned to the ground. Over 150 innocent civilians, all men and young boys, had been murdered in cold blood.

The event shocked the entire country and captured the attention of the world. Thousands of Federal troopers and Kansas militiamen quickly pursued the bushwhackers, but by the next day, they were safely nestled in the woodlands of Missouri. The Federals swiftly retaliated, issuing the harshest order of the war by either side against civilians, known as General Orders Number 11. Almost as ruthless as the Lawrence raid itself, it was designed to strike at the heart of the guerrillas' power—the support given them by the civilian population. As one officer put it, the order was carried out "to the letter." Four whole counties were quickly depopulated; virtually every citizen was deported; their crops and their forage were destroyed. So were their homes, which were burned. There is no final list of how many innocent people died in the process—although some estimates suggest it surpassed the carnage in Lawrence. Nor is the list of total refugees in this mass exodus fully complete. In one town, the population dwindled from 10,000 to a mere 600. Few of these refugees returned before the war's end. Many never did. When it was all over, these Midwestern counties lay like a silent wasteland, dotted by chimneys rising above the charred debris of blackened farmhouses.

Thus escalated the vicious cycle of retaliation and revenge. For the next six weeks, Quantrill and the partisans skirmished. Yet despite a massive sweep through the woodlands of western Missouri by Federal cavalrymen, Quantrill escaped. He and his men knew the countryside personally, and friends and relatives provided them with shelter, fresh horses, and timely warning in case of pursuit. In a telling instance of the rela-

tive ease with which guerrillas operated, Quantrill himself spent much of the time in comfort, neatly residing at a house near Blue Springs with his mistress, Kate King. On October 6, his gang again struck with considerable fury, overcoming a Federal wagon train at Baxter Springs. They mauled and killed eighty-five men, including the band musicians and James O'Neal, an artist for *Frank Leslie's Illustrated Newspaper*. So great was the wave of disgust over this bloodletting that news of the guerrilla war in the West actually supplanted—temporarily at least—the clash of armies in the East. Even Confederate generals were dismayed at the wanton carnage. Noted one high-ranking military man in Richmond, "they recognize the life of a man less than you would that of a dog killing a sheep."

The Union soldiers hunted the guerrillas like animals, and in return, eventually degenerated into little more than savage beasts, driven by a viciousness unimaginable just two years earlier. By 1864, the guerrilla war had reached new peaks of savagery. Now it was no longer enough to ambush and gun down the enemy. They had to be mutilated and, just as often, scalped. When that was no longer enough, the dead were stripped and castrated. Soon, Quantrill and his men were riding about wearing scalps dangling from their bridles, as well as an assortment of other body parts—ears, noses, teeth, even fingers—vivid trophies of their latest victims.

All order broke down. Groups of revenge-minded Federals, militia and even soldiers became guerrillas themselves, stalking tormenting, torturing, and slaying Southern sympathizers. Ruthless reprisals and random terror became the norm; Missouri was dragged into a whirlpool of vengeance. New and no less bloodthirsty gangs of bushwhackers rose up, led by George Todd, John Thrailkill, and others who roved virtually unchecked, baiting and murdering Federal patrols, and bringing all affairs in Missouri to a halt. Trains were attacked. So were stage lines. Steamboats were not safe, coming under repeated sniper fire. To run the gauntlet on the Missouri, pilots started to request—and received—a thousand dollars for a single trip to Kan-

sas. Petrified, Unionists ran, abandoning their houses and their farms, and converging on fortified towns—actually, by now they were garrisoned—which were reduced to nothing more than isolated enclaves in a sea of death. Soldiers were pinned down at their posts in a countryside dominated by guerrillas, their men as much hunted as hunters.

Missouri was something that had never been witnessed before on American soil. And the Union was utterly unable to cope with the ongoing terror. Federal policies were at once muddled, incoherent, and ineffective. A collective sociopathy reigned in Missouri, civil society was torn apart; all morals disintegrated. Both sides snapped. In a war without fronts, boundaries, and formal organization, the distinction between civilians and soldiers/partisans almost totally evaporated. Both those who sheltered the guerrillas and those who collaborated with the Unionists placed their lives in peril.

A favorite torture tactic was repetitive hanging. One father, as his family watched helplessly, was strung up three times—and only on the last try was the deed done. Another's son was walked to the noose some seven times before he met his fate. Toenails would be pulled off, one by one. Knives would be thrust into bellies—but only partially. To survive, people cheated, lied, and bore false witness against their neighbors—anything to appease the other side. Neutrality became impossible. In the words of historian Michael Fellman, life in Missouri became a "life of secret impeachments, divided loyalties, and whispered confidences."

Townsfolk couldn't trust their own neighbors, not even those they had known for years. The smallest tic in speech came to mean something ominous; the slightest arched eyebrow would be feared. Union troops fared little better. In most instances their deaths came at the hands of some unseen sniper. So all civilians were seen as enemies.

By 1864, most rural Missourians had become refugees, inside or outside the state. "We hear of some outrage every day," blithely confessed one Missourian. Wrote the *Kansas City Journal of Commerce* in 1864, even before the worst of it: "East of us, west of us, north of us, south of us, comes the same harrowing story. Pandemonium itself seems to have broken loose, and robbery, murder and rapine, and death run riot over the country." One Union general said it perhaps most poignantly: "there was something in the hearts of good and typical Christian[s]… which had exploded."

Early in the war, in an attempt to tap the growing discontent behind enemy lines, the Confederate government had legitimized guerrilla organizations with the Partisan Ranger Act of April 1862. Yet, as time went by, and even as the roaming guerrillas tied down Union troops and Union energy, a number of Confederate authorities found the guerrillas' methods distasteful. To the chivalric Southerners, war was about noble sacrifice; it was to be gentlemanly and Christian, and there was an aristocratic code of honor to be adhered to. Typically, when most rebel generals thought of guerrillas, they thought of Mosby. Missouri was another matter.

If Lee were somehow to succeed with guerilla warfare, his place in history would be assured. The temptation must have been vast.

By 1864, because of the atrocities committed by bushwhackers in the West, as well as the penchant for plunder that virtually all guerrilla bands displayed, powerful Southern voices eventually called for repeal of the Partisan Ranger Act. Finally, in early 1865, the Confederate Congress did revoke the act and the government ended its sanction of all partisan groups, with two notable exceptions: Mosby's rangers in the north, and Jesse McNeill's partisans in western Virginia. Lee himself was instrumental in the Congress's decision.

Thus on that morning of April 9, 1865, Lee had two very different faces of guerrilla war to consider: the first was the face of a Mosby. Beyond that, there was the shining example of his own

Carolina ancestors against the British Lord Cornwallis. Or, alternatively, there was the anarchic, scarlet-stained face of Missouri. In all likelihood, a guerrilla war countrywide would be a combination of the two, and, even at this late date, it could likely have an awesome impact: total conquest could be resisted, until, perhaps, attrition and exhaustion would lead the North to sue the South for peace.

The drum of history rarely beats for the men on the losing side in wars. Few are venerated in civic halls and history lessons. Lee was confronted with one last chance, one last opportunity for vindication. If he were somehow to succeed with guerrilla warfare, his place in history would be assured. The temptation must have been vast; no one should think otherwise.

So a sleep-deprived Robert E. Lee—now unable to move west, or south, or east, only north, the very last direction he wanted to go—listened to one of his most trusted advisers in the cool early morning hours of April 9. Hearing Porter Alexander out, he was doing some quick calculations in his head about the effect that generations of bushwhacking—guerrilla warfare—would have on the country. Lee, however, principled to the bitter end, was thinking not about personal glory, but along quite different lines. What is honorable? What is proper? What is right? Likely recalling Missouri, he quickly reasoned that a guerrilla war would make a wasteland of all that he loved. Brother would be set against brother, not just for four years, but for generations. Such a war would surely destroy Virginia, and just as surely destroy the country as well. Even if it worked, and perhaps especially if it worked. For Lee, that was too high a price to pay. No matter how much he believed in the Cause—his daring attempts over the last nine days were vivid testimony to that—there were limits to Southern independence. As he had once said, "it [is] better to do right, even if we suffer in so doing, than to incur the reproach of our consciences & posterity."

But Lee, more so than most other generals, also shunned making political de-

cisions. He was uncompromising about the unique American ethos of respecting the primacy of civilian leadership to make judgments about affairs of state. Yet this was surely a political decision. If he were to surrender his troops, it would be against the advice of Jefferson Davis, against the advice of his civilian authority. But on that Palm Sunday morning of April 9, he forged ahead.

Suppose, he told Porter Alexander, that "I should take your suggestion. The men would be without rations and under no control of officers… They would be compelled to rob and steal in order to live. They would become… bands of marauders, and the enemy's cavalry would… overrun many sections they may never have occasion to visit…

"We would bring on a state of affairs it would take the country years to recover from."

He continued his counsel to Alexander: "Then, General, you and I as Christian men have no right to consider only how this would affect us." We must, he stressed, "consider its effect on the country as a whole." Finally, Lee said, "And as for myself, you young fellows might go bushwhacking, but the only dignified course for me would be to go to General Grant and surrender myself and take the consequences of my acts."

Thus did Robert E. Lee, revered for his leadership in war, make his most historic contribution—to peace. By this one momentous decision, he spared the country the guerrilla war that surely would have followed, a vile and poisonous conflict that would not only have delayed any true national reconciliation for many years to come, but in all probability would have fractured the country for decades into warring military pockets. Nor is it idle to speculate that at such a late date such a mode of warfare might well have accomplished what four years of conventional war had failed to do: cleave North from South.

Just that morning, gloomily staring off into the distance, into the lifting mist, he had cried out, "How easily I could be rid of all this and be at rest! I have only to ride along the line and all will be over." But Lee weighed honor and glory against duty and will. He had already told his immediate staff with a heavy heart: "Then there is nothing left for me to do but to go and see General Grant, and I would rather die a thousand deaths." Poignantly, while tears and grief enveloped his men, he would add, "it is our duty to live."

Though Lee remained unaware, the fall of Richmond just six days before had already brought a spate of stinging calls for revenge, a grisly, thundering, roaring refrain, chanted and chanted again in an ever-rising crescendo, coming from New York, Boston, Philadelphia, Chicago, and, of course, Washington ("Burn it! BURN IT! LET HER BURN!" they cried about Richmond. On treason: "Treason is the highest crime known in the catalogue of crimes, and for him that is guilty of it… I would say death is too easy a punishment!" On Jefferson Davis: "HANG him! HANG him! Yes, I say *HANG* him twenty times!" On the Confederates who had graduated from West Point: "Those who have been fed, clothed, and taught at the public expense ought to stretch the first rope!" On those who had lifted their hands against the North: "Treason must be made odious; traitors must be punished and impoverished!… I would arrest them, I would try them, I would convict them, and I would hang them!" On pardons: "Never! Never!" And on Lee himself, a chorus cried: "*HANG LEE!* HANG LEE! HANG LEE!").

Indeed, the *Chicago Tribune* had recommended just that.

From *The American Spectator,* March 2001, pp. 69-81. © 2001 by The American Spectator.

Jefferson Davis and the Jews

Who Was to Blame for the South's Hard Times and High Prices?
Jews in the Government, Said One Confederate Senator—'Davis's Jews.'

By Peggy Robbins

THE SETTING WAS THE CONFEDER-ATE House of Representatives in 1863, but from the tone of the rhetoric, it could have been 1930s Berlin. A slight, bespectacled man was twisting the stomachs of his fellow legislators with hateful words that seemed incongruous with his grandfatherly appearance. Jews, he snarled, had seized control of the South's economy and of Confederate President Jefferson Davis, and were destroying everything. These Jews— "Davis's Jews"—had to be removed from power. And the first to go should be Davis's right-hand man, Secretary of State Judah Benjamin.

The poison words of Congressman Henry S. Foote appealed to people who wanted to believe there was a conspiracy behind the South's military and economic downturns. But no matter what Foote said, and no matter who believed it, Davis was not about to cave in—especially not on the issue of Benjamin, the Confederacy's highest-placed Jewish citizen and Davis's most trusted cabinet member. Instead, for the first three years of his presidency, Davis would take a merciless verbal thrashing

from Foote over Benjamin and the Jewish "conspiracy" he supposedly represented.

Fighting with Henry Foote was nothing new for Davis. Sixteen years before he became the Confederate president, Davis served with Foote in Washington, D.C., where the two men represented Mississippi in the U.S. Senate. They disagreed at every turn, chiefly over the issue of where federal authority stopped and state authority began. Davis's insistence on greater state authority infuriated Foote, and he exercised no restraint in voicing his opposition. The bad blood between the two men quickly exploded into hatred, then smoldered for years through restraint and separation, only to burst back into flames in the early days of the Confederate nation.

Foote had been making enemies all his life. Leaving his native Virginia for Tuscumbia, Alabama, at the age of 22, he had started a family and begun practicing law. For a lawyer, though, Foote was remarkably prone to getting into trouble. In 1826, Alabama barred him from practicing law for three years after he fought a duel with future governor

John A. Winston. Foote moved on to Mississippi, where he worked as a lawyer or editor in Jackson, Natchez, and several other towns. Foote's real love, though, was politics. Easy to dislike, he was nonetheless a talented, fiery speaker, a wily politician, and a stalwart defender of the Union. He was elected to Mississippi's legislature in 1837 and became one of the state's leading Democrats. Ten years later, he was elected to the U.S. Senate.

DAVIS WAS THREE YEARS YOUNGER than Foote. Tall and austere, he was widely regarded as cold and withdrawn; one reporter said "you mistake him for an icicle." An 1828 graduate of West Point, Davis had fought Indians in the West. In 1835, when his wife Sarah died, he resigned from the army to concentrate on managing his Mississippi plantation, Brierfield. In 1845, he married again, this time to a woman nearly 20 years his junior, Varina Howell. When the Mexican war broke out the following year, Davis rejoined the army and fought in several major battles. Hailed as a hero when he returned home in 1847, he was chosen by the Mississippi legislature to fill the unexpired Senate seat of Jesse Spreight, who had just died.

Foote found the seeming arrogance of his reserved new Senate colleague unbearable. In turn, Foote's abrasive manner made Davis's blood boil. The tension between the two men came to a head on Christmas Day, 1847. Davis was having a drink and talking with several other politicians in Gadsby's Hotel, not far from the White House. Across the room, Foote, was antagonizing him. Finally, Davis had had enough. Pushing through the crowed, he charged Foote and tore into him with his fists. Shocked onlookers separated the two. Davis turned away, and Foote struck him from behind. Davis whirled, knocked his foe to the floor and resumed beating him. Hotel patrons struggled to rescue Foote from the bigger Davis, who was out of control with rage. Cooler heads finally prevailed, and it was decided that "the matter should be dropped as a Christmas frolic."

The senators agreed to keep the matter of the brawl quiet. Both men were new to the Senate, and with the nation's sectional crisis heating up there was much work to be done. Still, they continued to butt heads. A Union Democrat, Foote helped draft the Compromise of 1850, an act designed to appease both North and South on the slavery issue and prevent the threat of civil war. The bill passed, despite bitter opposition from Davis and other Southern Democrats.

In 1851, Mississippi Governor John A. Quitman dropped his bid for reelection, and Davis's supporters convinced the senator to seek the post. Davis resigned his Senate seat to square off against Foote, who represented the state's Union Democrats. Foote wanted the position badly and campaigned all over the state. Meanwhile, a severe fever and inflamed left eye kept Davis at home. Rumors circulated that Davis was dead. He managed to get out and stump during the last two weeks of the campaign, but on November 4, 1851, Foote edged him by just 999 votes.

Davis returned to Brierfield, where he contemplated his humiliating loss at the hands of his old enemy. Through the

newspapers, he and Foote blasted each other over the results of their recent campaign. Foote maligned Davis's military record; Davis labeled Foote a slanderer and a liar. Eventually even the newspaper publishers got tired of the whole affair. One editor for the *Natchez Mississippi Free Trader* insisted the men put an end to their squabbling, otherwise, "we will select others under whose guidance we can secure more harmony and good feeling."

In defeat, ironically, Davis had gained legions of new supporters. Reuben Davis (no relation), a Union Democrat who later served in both the U.S. and Confederate congresses, thought Davis's defeat had left him "the head and front of the Democracy in this State and the whole South." Conversely, Foote, alienated by the growing anti-Federal, states' rights sentiment in Mississippi, resigned the governorship in 1853 and moved to California.

Davis was content to live the life of a private citizen for a while. When Governor James Whitfield, Forte's replacement, offered to reappoint Davis to his still-vacant Senate seat, he declined. But Davis's break from public life did not last long. Old friend Franklin Pierce was elected president in 1852, and wanted Davis to join his cabinet. With some reluctance, Davis accepted and was sworn in as secretary of war on March 7, 1853.

Davis did his job exceptionally well. The U.S. Army of 1853 was something of a mess, with roughly 10,000 men scattered across the continent. During his four years as secretary, Davis slowly expanded the ranks by one-third. He upgraded the soldiers' weapons from outmoded flintlocks to rifled percussion models. He tested new gun carriages, pressed for a new pension system for soldiers' widows, and authorized the construction of new Federal arsenals. He even sent a delegation of officers, including future Union general George B. McClellan, overseas to study military advances being implemented in the Crimean War.

D AVIS FOLLOWED PIERCE OUT OF OF-fice in March 1857, but Mississippi had

elected him to the U.S. Senate the previous November, and he was glad to return to his old post. He remained there until January 21, 1861, when he resigned in the wake of Mississippi's withdrawal from the Union. When the Confederate government was organized in February, Davis was elected president.

The birth of the Confederacy also meant a return to the public eye for Davis's old rival Foote. After moving to California, he had hoped for a cabinet post from Pierce, but Davis's appointment as secretary had thwarted that possibility. Returning to Mississippi to seek a seat in Congress in 1859, he had received little support. Frustrated, Foote had then moved to Nashville, Tennessee, to resume practicing law. There, the coming of war revived his political fortunes. In the fall of 1861, Tennessee elected him to the Confederate States Congress.

Foote was a political chameleon, changing his views to suit his own agenda. Arthur S. Colyar, who practiced law with Foote after the war, acknowledged his associates's skill as a lawyer, but called him "the most changeable of men." He was consistent only in his hatred for Davis. In the new Confederate government, Foote quickly established himself as the president's primary adversary. He consistently voted against all war measures that Davis backed, including conscription and a defensive military strategy. In some of his hottest speeches, he railed against "the continuance of Davis's war"—yet he also criticized Davis for failing to pursue a vigorous war in the Western theater. Meanwhile, he made as many enemies in Richmond as he had made in Washington. When he called Alabama Congressman E. S. Dargan a "damned rascal," Dargan threatened him with a Bowie knife. On another occasion, Foote provoked congressman William G. Swan into stabbing him with an umbrella.

Foote soon found a new target in Davis's administration—Judah P. Benjamin. The 49-year-old Benjamin was a native of the British West Indies whose family had moved to the United States early in his life. Benjamin was Jewish, and his family eventually settled in New Orleans, then home to one of the largest Jewish communities in America. Highly intelligent and an outstanding orator, Benjamin had great success as a lawyer, planter, and politician. In 1852, he became the first Jew to be elected to the U.S. Senate; he was reelected in 1858.

Davis and Benjamin had been acquainted since 1853, but they had become friends in 1858—strangely enough, through an altercation. During a brief exchange on the Senate floor, Davis, who was ill at the time, snapped at a question Benjamin had posed and dismissed it as "the arguments of a paid attorney." Insulted, Benjamin sent Davis a formal challenge to a duel that very afternoon. Davis knew he had been "wholly wrong," and apologized to Benjamin in the Senate the next morning. From this rough beginning came mutual respect and an enduring friendship.

When Davis assumed the Confederate presidency, Benjamin quickly became his most trusted advisor. Tactful and diplomatic, he deftly handled office-seekers and other petitioners—a task for which the stern Davis was poorly suited. After Davis's first cabinet meeting, Secretary of War Leroy P. Walker noted that "there was only one man there who had any sense, and that man was Benjamin."

> To Foote, Judah Benjamin was "the unprincipled minister of an unprincipled tyrant!"

Outside the government, Benjamin had his share of critics. In September 1861, when poor health forced Walker to resign, Davis replaced him with Benjamin. The new secretary of war was not a military man, and quickly ran into problems with Confederate generals such as P. G. T. Beauregard and Thomas J. "Stonewall" Jackson. In February 1862, Roanoke Island, North Carolina, fell to Union forces after Benjamin declined to send reinforcements and more guns to the garrison. In reality, Benjamin had not sent the support because there was none to send. But rather than reveal the new nation's desperate position pub-

licly, Benjamin stoically accepted the public's censures. Davis, who had been behind virtually all of Benjamin's moves as secretary of war, heeded calls for his friend's replacement. He then confounded Foote and other critics by immediately making Benjamin his new secretary of state.

The irascible Foote assailed what he called the "tight and terrible President Davis–Jew Benjamin alliance" at every opportunity. He hurled repeated slurs at "Judas Iscariot Benjamin," who, hand-in-hand with "the President who retains the Jew at his table despite the protest of the Southern people," was leading the South to certain destruction. Foote declared that he would "never consent to the establishment of a Supreme Court of the Confederate States so long as Judah P. Benjamin shall continue to pollute the ears of majestic Davis with his insidious councils." To Foote, Benjamin was "the unprincipled minister of an unprincipled tyrant!"

Benjamin was no stranger to religious intolerance. He usually endured it with the strange smile that seemed a permanent feature of his face. Foote's invective was often designed simply to irk Davis, and Benjamin saw no need to make things harder for the president by caving in to it. Still, Foote took his unending abuse to new heights. Varina Davis wrote of her husband's "personal and aggrieved sense" of the unjust criticism Benjamin received from Davis's enemy.

Davis stood by his "right hand" throughout the war. This maddened Foote. Lamenting his inability to discredit Benjamin and force a wedge "between President Davis and the descendant of those who crucified the Saviour," Foote extended his attacks to include all Jews. During heated congressional debate on January 14, 1863, he declared that Jews had flooded the country, that they traded illegally with the enemy, and that they already controlled nine-tenths of the business in the South. "If the present state of things were to continue," he stated, "the end of the war would probably find nearly *all* the property of the Confederacy in the hands of Jewish Shylocks!" Leveling another shot at Davis, he concluded that Jews had gained their

position because top government officials had "invited" them into the Confederacy.

ACCORDING TO FOOTE, "DAVIS'S Jews" were gaining control of the cotton and tobacco industries and putting the South's economy at risk of collapse. He repeatedly threatened to expose "the Jewish conspiracy," but never produced evidence to back up his accusations. On January 7, 1864, the Richmond *Examiner* reported that a Confederate congressman had accepted a bribe of $3,000 to obtain passports for three Jews, allowing them to leave the Confederacy and enter Union territory. Foote was outraged and insisted on an investigation of the matter. After a thorough probe, a congressional committee reported that "nothing to sustain the charge" had been found.

By January 1865, Foote believed the Confederacy was doomed. His ceaseless abuse of Davis's administration had accomplished little, and many of his colleagues had tired of him. Still a Unionist at heart, he proposed peace talks between the Confederate and Union governments. Davis and his generals had no such inclination.

Foote decided to contact President Abraham Lincoln himself. On January 10, 1863, he and his wife hurried toward the Potomac River and Federal lines, only to be captured by Confederate troops. Foote was sent back to Richmond. Two weeks later, as the Confederate Congress debated his fate, he fled again, and this time he reached Union territory. Imprisoned in New York, he wrote letters to Lincoln, Northern newspapers, and other Federal politicians, trying to gain an audience. He got nowhere. Foote remained in confinement until after Lincoln's assassination in mid-April, when new President Andrew Johnson banished him from the country.

From Canada, Foote pleaded with Johnson to let him return to the United States. He took the Federal oath of allegiance, and in August Johnson relented. An opportunist to the last, Foote later supported the Republican administrations of Ulysses S. Grant and Rutherford B. Hayes. In 1878, Hayes appointed the aging Virginian superintendent of the U.S. Mint in—of all places—New Orleans, where Benjamin had grown up and where many Jews lived. Foote died two years later in Nashville; at the time, noted a reporter, he was "a decrepit old gentleman with a fiery red head, almost entirely bald." Foote never expressed any regret for his abuse of Davis, Benjamin, or Jews in general.

When the Confederacy crumbled in April 1865, Benjamin burned his private papers and fled the country. He never returned. He established himself in England, where he became a prominent and wealthy lawyer and, later, a Queen's counsel. Davis, who had retired to Mississippi, occasionally visited him, but Foote wasted no time dwelling on the past. He refused to discuss the war. In his last years Benjamin rejoined his long-estranged family in Paris, France, where he died in May 1884. "He was," Davis said, "a master of law, and the most accomplished statesman I have ever known." He was also a friend, whom Davis had been more than willing to defend from a bitter and unrelenting anti-Semite.

PEGGY ROBBINS *is a long-time contributor to* Civil War Times.

From *Civil War Times Illustrated,* March 2000. © 2000 by Civil War Times Illustrated.

Lincoln Takes the Heat

Cartoonists & commentators, politicians & publishers, Southerners & Northerners—everyone seemed to feel free to lampoon Lincoln. How the president responded revealed his greatness.

BY Harold Holzer

It now seems a distant memory, but in October 1998 a situation comedy set in the Civil War White House premiered on national television and promptly ignited a firestorm of outrage. *The Secret Life of Desmond Pfeiffer* offended just about everyone: critics, for what one called "jaw dropping" witlessness; African Americans, for making a joke of slavery; feminists, for portraying Hillary Clinton as a sexual predator; and supporters of her husband, for transparently satirizing his problems with affairs, apologies, and grand juries.

Most of all—before it died a quiet death, the victim of anemic ratings—*Desmond Pfeiffer* offended admirers of Abraham Lincoln. The show reduced the Great Emancipator of legend to an inept, insensitive, sex-starved dolt. One scene actually depicted Lincoln fantasizing lasciviously about the brawny young male soldiers in the Union army.

The irreverence was enough to inspire an attendee at a Lincoln Family symposium at Robert Todd Lincoln's Hildene estate in Manchester, Vermont, to circulate an irate petition demanding the show's cancellation. "The nature of this will dishonor the name and character of the man who has been rightly acclaimed our greatest national leader," the petition argued. "We, the undersigned are highly indignant that television wishes to degrade Lincoln in any way." Irreverently portraying the 16th president, it maintained, constituted the desecration of an American saint, an insult to history, and a threat to national memory.

But was it? Forgotten by these and other angry viewers was a contrary historical truth: Abraham Lincoln had been dragged through the mud before, and often. He was mercilessly lampooned, viciously libeled, and relentlessly satirized in his own time—and his reputation not only survived but flourished. In fact, his stoic and good-natured response in the face of such stabs from the stiletto of malicious verbal and visual abuse made him seem nobler at the time, and greater in retrospect.

The national humor mill of the era made *Lincoln* its favorite grist. American humorists portrayed the Civil War, to paraphrase Lincoln, "with malice toward *one*." And that *one* was Lincoln himself. His ungainly form, homely face, and awkward Western manner—not to mention his controversial policies—formed a combustible mixture that inflamed professional and political humorists.

This frequent butt of ridicule was comically maligned in the press, in books, and in cartoons published in the North as well as the South, in Europe as well as America. *Desmond Pfeiffer* was no exception; it was a return to the rule.

The mockery began as soon as Lincoln emerged as a national figure, following his unexpected nomination to the presidency in May 1860. Engravers and lithographers rushed to publish flattering portraits introducing the reputedly ugly candidate to a wary public. But as much as the Republicans sought to make virtues of Lincoln's humble origins and miraculous rise, Democrats encouraged lampoons that mocked those very qualities. Often the same publishers who met the consumer demand for Lincoln portraits also made a lot of money churning out caricature sheets.

Such cartoons usually depicted Lincoln as a country bumpkin with a wild thatch of uncombed hair, clad in ill-fitting pantaloons and open-necked shirts, and wielding a log rail to ward off serious inquiries into his supposedly dangerous views on racial equality. Currier & Ives of New York may have crafted the quintessential 1860 campaign cartoon when they portrayed *The Rail Candidate* astride a log rail labeled "Republican National Platform," being carried to the White House by supporters. "It is true I have Split Rails," the uncomfortable nominee declares, "but I begin to feel as if *this* Rail would split me, it's the hardest stick I ever straddled." Coarser variations on the theme depicted him erecting log-rail camouflage to conceal "niggers in the woodpile"—metaphorically minimizing attention on the stormy slavery issue by focusing voters instead on his inspiring ascent from a log cabin to the White House.

Lincoln had only himself to blame for inspiring the next wave of ridicule early the next year en route to his inauguration in Washington. By donning what security advisor Allen Pinkerton described as "a soft low-crowned hat" and a "bobtailed overcoat" to avoid recognition in hostile Baltimore while changing trains in Baltimore, Lincoln invited charges that he was a coward. Exaggerating his disguise into "a Scotch plaid Cap and a very long military Cloak," cartoonists at *Harper's Weekly* issued a hilarious pictorial paraody under the headline, "The Flight of Abraham." One panel showed him quaking in fear so violently that Henry Seward, incoming secretary of state, explains to President James Buchanan that his successor is suffering "only a little attack of ague." Assailing the sec-

tional hostility that inspired the drastic evasive tactic in Baltimore, the pro-Republican New York *Tribune* was nonetheless forced to admit: "It is the only instance recorded in our history in which the recognized head of a nation…has been compelled, for fear of his life, to enter the capital in disguise." More blunt was the denunciation by the Baltimore *Sun*:

Had we any respect for Mr. Lincoln, official or personal, as a man, or as President elect of the

United States…the final escapade by which he reached the capital would have utterly demolished it…. He might have entered Willard's Hotel with a "head spring" and a "summersault," and the clown's merry greeting to Gen. Scott, "Here we are!" and we should care nothing about it, personally. We do not believe the Presidency can ever be more degraded by any of his successors than it has by him, even before his inauguration.

From *Civil War Times Illustrated*, February 2001. © 2001 by Civil War Times Illustrated.

Bats, Balls, and Bullets

Baseball and the Civil War

George B. Kirsch

A TERRIBLE TENSION CLOUDED THE early months of 1861. All over a partially divided America, people went about their lives with one eye fixed on the horizon of national life, looking for signs of what was to be: the breakup of the Union? peace? war? But life went on, and soon one of the newest but most dependable signs of spring appeared. In dozens of American cities and towns, baseball players set to work preparing their minds, bodies, and—in those days before stadiums, artificial turf, and professional groundskeepers—their grass and dirt playing fields for another season of play.

Then, in mid-April, just as the ball teams were getting warmed up, news of the firing on Fort Sumter in South Carolina sent shock waves through North and South alike. It was war, time to take up swords and muskets and lay aside bats and balls—or so it seemed at first. Instead, baseball went to war with the men in blue and gray, changed as they changed, and emerged stronger than ever to help reunite them in their own national game.

Legend assigns a Civil War connection of sorts to the very origins of baseball itself. Abner Doubleday, the Civil War general who some say aimed the first cannon in defense of Fort Sumter and who distinguished himself in the Battle of Gettysburg in 1863, is the central character in the myth of baseball's creation promulgated by the present-day professional baseball league, Major League Baseball, and the National Baseball Hall of Fame in Cooperstown, New

York. According to a historical commission headed in 1907 by Abraham Mills, president of professional baseball's National League, Doubleday invented the modern rules of the game in 1839 at Cooperstown. The tale rests entirely on the testimony of one Abner Graves, who recalled playing ball with Doubleday as a boy in that bucolic town in upstate New York. Albert G. Spalding, the noted baseball luminary and sporting goods magnate, fully endorsed Graves's story at the time, but later admitted: "It certainly appeals to an American's pride to have had the great national game of Base Ball created and named by a Major General in the United States Army."

Though the Doubleday-Cooperstown myth remains powerful in the American imagination, scholars have long since proven it false. Research has revealed that Doubleday enrolled as a cadet at West Point in the fall of 1838 and possibly never even visited Cooperstown. Although he may have played ball with Graves during his boyhood, in his published writings he never mentioned anything about a role in the creation of baseball. The Mills Commission's conclusion rested entirely on an elderly man's recollection of an event that had occurred 68 year earlier. And Graves's mental capacity at the time of his testimony is suspect; a few years later, he shot his wife and was committed to an institution. Furthermore, Mills had known Doubleday ever since the men served together in the Civil War, but his friend apparently had never said any-

thing about his supposed brainstorm in Cooperstown.

If Abner Doubleday did not invent baseball, then who did? The answer is that no one person created the sport; rather, it evolved in stages from earlier bat-and-ball games, especially rounders, an English game often called "townball" in the United States. New England varieties of townball were called "roundball" or "base." The version of the sport that became widely known as the "Massachusetts game" matched sides of 8 to 15 men on a square field with bases or tall stakes (up to five feet high) at each corner. The batter stood midway between first and fourth (home) base and tried to hit a ball made of yarn tightly wound around a lump of cork or rubber and covered with smooth calfskin. The cylindrical bat varied in length from three to three and a half feet and was often a portion of a rake or pitchfork handle. It normally was held in one hand. The pitcher threw the ball swiftly overhand, and the batter could strike the ball in any direction, there being no foul territory. After hitting the ball, the striker ran around the bases until he was put out or remained safely on a base. He could be retired if the catcher caught three balls he missed, if a fielder caught a ball he hit before it hit the ground, or if a fielder struck him with a thrown ball while he ran the bases (called "soaking" or "burning" the runner). Usually one out ended the inning, and the first team to score a previously agreed upon number of runs won the game.

Voices from the Stands...

In our February issue, we asked readers to send us their thoughts on baseball and its connection to the Civil War. Here is a sampling of what we received.

All men have a hidden desire to compete and win. Baseball is a sport played for the fun of it, and the final score is soon forgotten. War is fought on an extremely serious level, and the outcome is etched in our souls forever.

Victor M. Wein, Pittsburgh, Pennsylvania

You pick up a bat and your back yard becomes the site of the final game of the World Series. It's the bottom of the ninth, the game is tied, and you are the batter, the pitcher, and the announcer all at once. You throw the ball in the air, swing, and drive it past the spot of dirt that is second base. You round that spot with your arms held high and celebrate the possibility of knowing such joy.

Now, you're at Gettysburg. You stand on Seminary Ridge and look out across those fields and wonder, Would I have climbed the fence along the Emmitsburg Road and kept going? Those who did were average people, and perhaps you, too, could have risen to such heroic heights. You walk toward the copse of trees and quietly celebrate the possibility of that kind of commitment.

Austin E. Gisriel, Williamsport, Maryland

I see the hitter at the plate, all alone, facing nine opponents. Yet he remains part of a team. In the Civil War, the Rebs and the Yanks stood in lines, firing away at the other side. Each was a part of a team—a company, regiment, or brigade—but they faced the enemy as individuals, each with his own doubts and fears.

C.J. Calenti, Poughkeepsie, New York

In baseball and in war, two distinct teams compete on a field with a set of rules that are fairly static, but open to interpretation. Strategies are employed to win that often evolve during the course of the conflict. The two teams could be from opposite ends of town, the country, or even the world. But, cultural, ethnic, and racial differences aside, they react the same way: from both we learn about ourselves.

James Dossey, Baker, Louisiana

Soldiers on both sides, at least those who survived the war, stood in later years and cheered baseball's early legends and told their sons about the game. Baseball was played near battlefields grown still by the passage of time, and baseball, like those veterans, will always be remembered.

Bo Bourisseau, Mountville, Ohio

Though the Massachusetts version of baseball thrived during the late 1850s, it faced a formidable rival in New York City's version of the game, which boomed in popularity after 1857. Modern baseball derives most immediately from the latter, specifically, from the game created by the New York Knickerbocker Base Ball Club during the mid-1840s. Some baseball historians believe that a man named Alexander J. Cartwright first suggested that the Knickerbockers try aligning the bases along a diamond instead of a square and placing the batter at home plate. At the very least, Cartwright was the chief organizer of the club and the man responsible for codifying its first rules—namely, that the ball had to be pitched underhand, not overhand; that a ball knocked outside the area bounded by first and third bases was foul; and that a player was out if a ball he hit was caught on the fly or on the first bounce, or if a fielder touched him with the ball as he ran between bases. "Soaking" the runner was prohibited, three outs retired a side from the field, and 21 runs (called "aces") decided the game, provided each side had had an opportunity to make an equal number of outs. The Knickerbockers played their first intraclub games in the Murray Hill section of Manhattan, then moved to the Elysian Fields of Hoboken, New Jersey, in 1846. Their pastime spread very slowly until the late 1850s, when baseball mania swept across the greater New York City region.

At the time hostilities between North and South broke out in 1861, no one knew which form of the game would come to enjoy the greatest popularity, but it was already clear that there were striking parallels between team sports and war. During the late 1850s and early 1860s, the sporting press frequently pointed out the similarities. In wrapping up its review of the 1857 season, a journal called the *New York Clipper* remarked that the players "will be compelled to lay by their weapons of war, enter into winter quarters, there to discuss and lay plans for the proper conducting of next season's campaign." Yet sportswriters were acutely aware of the crucial differences between play and mortal struggle. "God forbid that any balls but those of the Cricket and Baseball field may be caught either on the fly or bound," read a March 1861 *Clipper* article, "and we trust that no arms but those of the flesh may be used to impel them, or stumps, but those of the wickets, injured by them."

After the struggle began, a Rochester reporter noted that "many of our first class players are now engaged in the 'grand match' against the rebellious 'side,' and have already made a 'score'

... Voices from the Stands

After the Civil War, the veterans returned to Hendricks County, Indiana, just west of Indianapolis, taking with them a new game they called townball. My great-grandfather, Jesse Thompson, had had five sons born before he left for the war. Upon his return, a sixth son was born—my grandfather, William. These six boys became the nucleus of Danville's team, the Browns. In 1884, a scout from Detroit visited the area to see one of these boys, Cyrus, play ball. The scout, however, became enamored with the ability of Cyrus's brother, Sam, who was only playing that day because the team agreed to pay him $2.50, the same amount he would have made building a roof.

The scout enlisted Sam as a player for Evansville in the Western League, and his professional career began. The next year he was playing in Indianapolis, and by July 1885, he was a member of the Detroit Wolverines. That was just the start. By the time he ended his career as a member of the Philadelphia Phillies in 1898, he had amassed hitting records that took decades to break. Sam Thompson, who died in 1922, was elected to the National Baseball Hall of Fame in 1974.

Don A. Thompson, Mesa, Arizona

The Battle of Gettysburg was like a game in the World Series. In order to win the championship, the undefeated Rebels once again had to defeat the Yankees. The Rebels were confident, even though the Yankees had home-field advantage this time. The game ended in a tie, but the Yankees viewed it as a victory, and the Rebels could no longer be considered unbeatable. But it is not who wins or loses that matters. It is how the game—or the war—is played, and the Rebels played very well against all odds.

Laura Race, Penn Yan, New York

Born in the decades before the Civil War, baseball spread like wildfire during the war. Union boys in the Midwest learned it from the boys of the East, and Yankees from the North taught it to their Confederate captors. Enthusiasm for the game reached all regions, all classes. What had once been the province of city merchants and professionals, the gentlemen of the day, became a game for the people. The Civil War democratized American society, including baseball, our national pastime.

Tom William Odom, Lake Worth, Florida

Not so much a metaphor of shared experience, the connection between baseball and the Civil War seems more deeply rooted in a return to that which once was. The need to get on with things may be eclipsed by a yearning to reconnect with patterns of life that disappeared on a thousand battlefields. Baseball may have enabled former soldiers to regain a portion of their lost innocence. They would agree that the game of baseball, with its simple message of competition, fair play, and male bonding, is as much a quest for innocence as it is a celebration of the strength of America—South and North—and a lasting epitaph to the courageous energy of that era.

Rich Hill, Metuchen, New Jersey

which, in after years, they will be proud to look upon." Another remarked, "Cricket and Baseball clubs... are now enlisted in a different sort of exercise, the rifle or gun taking the place of the bat, while the play ball gives place to the leaden messenger of death.... Men who have heretofore made their mark in friendly strife for superiority in various games, are now beating off the rebels who would dismember the glorious 'Union of States.'" In April, a Union soldier encamped with his regiment at Culpeper Court House, Virginia, reported, "If General Grant does not send them to have a match with Gen. Lee, they are willing to have another friendly match, but if he does, the blue coats think that the leaden balls will be much harder to stop than if thrown by friendly hands on the club grounds."

Soldier-athletes also believed that baseball was useful in preparing them for the more deadly contests of the battlefield. The Rochester *Express* noted that with "the serious matter of war... upon our hands..., physical education and the development of muscle should be engendered by indulgence in baseball."

Thousands of Northern baseball club members enlisted in the Union army, and a few volunteered for the Confederate cause. The sportsmen who marched off to war took with them their love of play—and sometimes their bats and balls. Military authorities permitted recreation for soldiers at appropriate times and places because it provided useful diversion. The U.S. Sanitary Commission recommended that to preserve the health of soldiers, "when practicable, amusements, sports, and gymnastic exercises should be favored amongst the men." Baseball was listed among the approved pastimes. Officers encouraged sport to relieve the boredom of camp life. Organized games also helped to motivate men during training, to foster group cohesion and loyalty, and to improve recruits' physical fitness.

The *Clipper* praised the practice of athletic games in camp, noting the "beneficial effect they have on the spirits and health, and how they tend to alleviate the monotony of camp life." The journal also remarked that sports had helped create "a wholesome rivalry between companies

... Voices from the Stands

In baseball, you don't have to hate your opponent while the action plays out, and after the contest is over, the camaraderie becomes part of the game. Though death was often the outcome in battle, there was little hatred involved; they were just trying to win. Abner Doubleday would probably have been happier throwing a baseball than lobbing a cannonball from Fort Sumter, but he no doubt noted the similarities.

Roy E. Triebel, Wantagh, New York

Americans are passionate about both the Civil War and baseball because there are not any two things that are more American. The mythical feats of the great generals and players stimulate the passions and imaginations of both the historian and the fan. Robert E. Lee's boldness in dividing his army at Chancellorsville and Babe Ruth's in calling his shot in the 1932 World Series are the stories of legend. While their triumphs are out of reach of the normal man, we can all envision ourselves as bit players.

David F. Nolan, Richmond Hill, Georgia

Baseball played a vital role for the soldiers in camp, relieving them of the horrors of war. After the war they took the game home and created a baseball boom, truly nationalizing the game. But the real story is the game itself. Were it not so much fun to play and watch, baseball would have gone the way of its parents, rounders and cricket, and become just a footnote in American history.

William Gump, Kent, Ohio

Both the war and the game evoke feelings of pride and serve as a testament to the indomitable spirit of man. Americans rally to protect battlefields such as Gettysburg and Antietam to remember forever the heroic deeds of a bygone era. The same sense of maintaining continuity with the past surrounds the desire of many to preserve the pristine nature of the nation's ballparks. So long as the country relishes its past, there will always be someone willing to learn about the great war or relive the epic game seven.

Keith M. Finley, Hammond, Louisiana

Baseball and the Civil War share a common core. In the war, both sides felt that blacks were incapable of independence without support of their white "fathers." In 1863 Abraham Lincoln freed the slaves. Some of them became soldiers, but they were led by white officers. Later, in baseball, blacks were prevented from playing the game with whites until 1947, when Branch Rickey, owner of the Brooklyn Dodgers, enlisted Jackie Robinson for his team. It is now 51 years later, and the game's leadership remains white. Blacks still hold no real power.

Milton Pascaner Decatur, Georgia

and regiments, and augment the *esprit de corps* of the same, to an extent that to those who have not witnessed it would appear marvelous." Baseball was even allowed in certain prison camps. A prominent Southern nine, for example, originated at Johnson's Island, Ohio, where inmates learned the New York game while being held by Union forces.

Baseball-playing soldiers improvised makeshift grounds for their games, constructed rudimentary equipment, and arranged contests both in camp and ever perilously close to enemy positions. One enthusiast sent the *Clipper* the score of a match played on the parade ground of the "Mozart Regiment, now in Secessia" in October 1861. He wanted to report the sports news to civilians on the home-front, "lest you imagine that the 'sacred soil' yields only to the tramp of the soldier; that its hills echo only to the booming gun, and the dying shriek." The game, he wrote, totally "erased from their minds the all absorbing topic of the day."

Soldiers played both the Massachusetts and New York versions of the game, arranging pickup games within their own regiments or challenging rival units. According to an often-repeated story, on Christmas 1862 more than 40,000 Union soldiers witnessed an encounter between the 165th New York Infantry and an all-star squad that included future National League president A.G. Mills. While it is possible that the game actually occurred, the size of the crowd has undoubtedly been exaggerated.

Generally, the men sported within the relative security of their encampments, though sometimes they violated army regulations and competed outside their fortifications and beyond their picket lines. George H. Putnam remembered a contest among Union troops in Texas that was aborted by a surprise enemy assault. "Suddenly there came a scattering fire of which the three fielders caught the brunt," he wrote; "the center field was hit and was captured, the left and right field managed to get into our lines." The Northern soldiers repulsed the Confederate attack, "but we had lost not only our center field but... the only baseball in Alexandria."

While baseball enthusiasts enjoyed their favorite sport in army camps, the game suffered some understandable setbacks on the home front. With so many sportsmen off at war, and with civilian anxieties focused on battlefield news, interest in playful contests naturally waned. Yet the sport persisted, and even progressed, under the trying conditions. In a review of the 1861 season in the New York City area, the *Clipper* reported, "The game has too strong a foot-hold in popularity to be frowned out of favor by the lowering brow of 'grim-vis-aged war.'"

The New York form of the game gained momentum in New England when a tour by the Brooklyn Excelsiors excited Boston's sporting fraternity. In Philadelphia, baseball overtook cricket in popularity during the early 1860s. Near the end of the war, the Federal capital experienced a baseball revival, thanks in part to resident New Yorkers who worked in the U.S. Treasury Department and played for the National and Union clubs on the grounds behind the White House. In the South, the Union conquest of New Orleans took baseball back deep into Dixie, where the war had virtually snuffed out the sport before it could become firmly established. And in the West, a contingent of "Rocky Mountain Boys" played the New York game in Denver in 1862.

As it was before the war, the Middle Atlantic region was at the core of base-ball fever. New York, New Jersey, and Pennsylvania inaugurated the sport's first championship system as well as several intercity all-star contests and club tours. The early 1860s also ushered in an era of commercialism and professionalism, as William H. Cammeyer of Brooklyn and other entrepreneurs enclosed fields and charged admission fees. Before and during the Civil War, amateur clubs offered various forms of compensation—direct payments, jobs, or gifts—to premier players such as James Creighton and Al Reach. The National Association of Base Ball Players, founded in 1857, continued to supervise interclub play and experiment with the sport's rules, endorsing the New York rules even as the New England game remained popular among soldiers. In 1863, a national sporting weekly edited by a George Wilkes, *Wilkes' Spirit of the Times*, grandly proclaimed, "The National Association game has won for itself the almost unanimous approval of all who take any interest in the sport; and the clubs who adopt any other style of playing are every day, becoming 'small by degrees, and beautifully less.'"

The most striking evidence of base-ball's capacity to flourish amid the ad-versity of war was the first invasion of Philadelphia players into the New York City area, in 1862. When a select "nine" competed before about 15,000 spectators in a series of games against Newark, New York, and Brooklyn teams, *Wilkes' Spirit* reported that the Philadelphia challenges awakened in New York "the old *furore* for the game that marked the years 1857–8 and 9." The paper noted that the victory of the guests over a New York team at Hoboken did more to create interest in the game in that city than five ordinary seasons' play would have done. Teams from Brooklyn and New York re-turned the visit later in the summer, gen-erating excitement in their contests with the local teams: the Olympics, Adriatics, Athletics, and Keystones. The following year the Athletics won two of six games against tough opponents and established themselves as contenders for baseball's championship. By the end of the war, trips by Brooklyn, New York, and New Jersey clubs to Philadelphia were com-monplace. Some of the matches were ar-ranged to benefit the U.S. Sanitary Commission.

The tours succeeded despite the atmo-sphere of crisis that pervaded the entire region so near to the seat of war. In most cases, the war did not detract from the excitement of the contests, and there is little evidence that citizens disapproved of men who played ball instead of serv-ing in the army. Understandably, though, military news sometimes completely overshadowed baseball. When Brook-lyn's crack Atlantics swept a series in Philadelphia in August 1864, few fans attended, and there was little additional interest. The *Clipper* explained that the local citizens "were absorbed in the im-portant subject of resisting the rebel in-vasion of the State, and this and the preparations to respond to the Gover-nor's call for 30,000 militia, materially interfered with the sensation their visit would otherwise have created." Most of the Philadelphia clubs could not play many of their best men, the journal re-ported, because they had responded "to the call of duty."

The return of peace to the United States in 1865 ignited a new baseball boom, prompting the *Newark Daily Ad-vertiser* to announce that the sport "is

rightfully called the National Game of America." Veterans played a key role in spreading the sport around the nation af-ter the war. "When soldiers were off duty," declared the *Clipper* in 1865, "base ball was naturalized in nearly ev-ery state in the Union, and thus extended in popularity."

Regional rivalries, tours by prominent clubs, and intersectional matches helped smooth relations between North and South immediately after the Civil War. "Maryland [was] fast being recon-structed on this base-is," punned the *Clipper* in 1865. The game was even tak-ing hold in Richmond, Virginia, the former capital of the Confederacy. "Base ball fever," the *Clipper* reported, "is rap-idly assuming the form of an epidemic among the constructed and reconstructed denizens of the former stronghold of the extinct Davisocracy." But the journal followed up this news with a rebuke of the Richmond club for refusing the chal-lenge of that city's Union team, made up mostly of businessmen and federal offi-cials. "We regret to learn of such petty feeling and sectional animosity being evinced by any party of Southern gentle-men calling themselves ball players," the journal opined. "Our national game is in-tended to be national in every sense of the word, and, until this example was set by the 'Richmond club,' nothing of a sectional character has emanated from a single club in the country."

Northern and Southern journalists believed the tours of the great Eastern ball clubs would help heal the bitter wounds of war. When the Nationals of Washington, D.C., visited Brooklyn in July 1866, the Excelsiors treated them to a lavish dinner, even though a National Association of Base Ball Players rule prohibited expensive entertainment. The *Clipper* argued that the Brooklynites' extravagance showed Southerners that "the ball players' 'policy of reconstruc-tion' is one marked by true fraternal re-gard, irrespective of all political opinions or sectional feelings, the Na-tional Association knowing… 'no North, no South, no East, no West,' but simply the interest and welfare of the game itself, and the cultivation of kindly feelings between the different clubs." When the Nationals stopped at Louisville in 1867, however, *Wilkes' Spirit* reported, "a crowd of the most unruly partisan boors and rowdy boys" extended the so-called invading Yankees a greeting "not at all in accordance with the reputation for chivalric sentiments which the Southern cities have hitherto claimed." The journal singled out the women spectators for special criticism and urged that sectional feelings be kept out of the game. "The Nationals... though from the shores of the Potomac, had too much of the North about them apparently to merit the favor of Southern women," the journal remarked.

During the summer of 1868, the Philadelphia Athletics received a warmer reception in Louisville. For Philadelphia's part, the Pennsylvania city's *Sunday Mercury* defended the Louisville players' gray uniforms, which "had been help up to scorn, and those who wear it denounced as rebels." The paper reported that the choice of uniform color did not

necessarily indicate the players had sided with the South in the war, and even if it did, it "has got nothing to do with our National Game." The article's author concluded, "If Jefferson Davis... was to meet me on the ball field, and salute me as a gentleman, I would endeavor to prove to him that I was one." When a New Orleans newspaper announced the upcoming trip of its Southern Club to Memphis and St. Louis with players who had organized while prisoners of war at Johnson's Island, its editor wondered, along with his Northern counterparts, "would it not be pleasant to see the hatchet buried in the great national game, 'spite of the efforts of politicians to keep up ill feeling between the sections?" *Wilkes' Spirit*, reporting on the New York Mutual Club's December 1869 excursion to New Orleans, observed: "This National Game seems destined to close the National Wounds opened by the late war. It is no idle pastime which draws

young men, separated by two thousand miles, together to contest in friendship, upon fields but lately crimsoned with their brothers' blood in mortal combat."

Of course baseball alone could not heal the wounds of the Civil War, but it did help reunite the nation, establishing itself as a popular institution in the social and cultural worlds of the American people. Publicists relished the sport's success and promoted it as a democratic game that offered all classes and ethnic groups an opportunity to play, if not in a stadium, then at least on a sandlot. Baseball had become the national pastime, and the stage was set for the game's glory years—and the glory years of the nation itself.

George B. Kirsch, a professor of history at Manhattan College, adapted this article from portions of his book The Creation of American Team Sports: Baseball and Cricket, 1838–72 (*University of Illinois Press, 1989*).

America's Rites of Passage

The Author of Play for a Kingdom *discovers America— and himself—in our war and our game*

Thomas Dyja

ON A SUMMER'S DAY SIX YEARS AGO now, I came across a story that would change my life. It was in sports patriarch Albert G. Spalding's 1911 book *Base Ball: America's National Game*, and though it was only a rumor, it deserved to be true. "It is said," the passage read, "that in Virginia, in the long campaign before Richmond, at periods when active hostilities were in abeyance, a series of games was played between picked nines from Federal and Confederate forces." What a rumor—a sort of North-South baseball tournament in the climactic period of the Civil War! Having resolved many years earlier that my first novel would be something different from all the coming-of-age tales I'd read (and written) over the years, I fell on Spalding's story and began work on what would eventually become *Play for a*

Kingdom, a historical novel that I was determined would be anything but autobiographical.

The god of first novels, though, had the last laugh. Wanting to approach the war fresh, I tried to put away all my preconceptions when I began, all the things I believed I knew. But one morning, as I was writing the bloody battle scene of the first day of the Wilderness, my mind flashed back more than 20 years to my childhood in Chicago and the days I had spent re-creating the Battle of Lookout Mountain on my dresser top using scores of Britain's soldiers, and an illustrated edition of Bruce Catton's *This Hallowed Ground* as a guide. I suddenly remembered all my visits to the Grand Army of the Republic museum in the Chicago Public Library, a drive out to Grant's home in Galena, summer vacation trips

to Springfield and "Lincolnland." Bound to my boyhood memories of Wrigley Field, White Sox owner Bill Veeck, and striking out with a regularity usually associated in that place and time with Mayor Daley's garbage crews, *Play for a Kingdom* became a very personal book, a way of revisiting who I once was, who I was becoming, and who I wanted to be. The internal struggles of my characters as they learned to be husbands, fathers, friends, and Americans were all born of the questions I was asking myself as I came of age during those years of writing. And so, despite my best efforts, my first novel ended up a novel of identity.

But it is not just a novel of *my* identity; *Play for a Kingdom* was always meant to be an imagined moment from the creation of the American identity. The Civil War marked this nation's coming of age, and baseball, as promoted by men such as sportswriter Henry Chadwick, took hold as our American game at the same time. Since those pivotal years when America became truly one and baseball beat out cricket for the hearts of American sportsmen, the Civil War and baseball have been linked. That the two are so linked is not coincidence or confluence, but a case of a nation and an organized sport forged together in one furnace by a certain people and their time. The citizens of Grant's and Lincoln's new industrial democracy were the first to pay to watch baseball, and were the first to be paid to play it. What seemed to be a meritocracy of sport developed in the 1860s: the talented, no matter where they came from, would be paid to do their best. The quality of the game improved, and baseball's days as the pastime of a Jeffersonian citizen elite were sacrificed to a greater good, to a form of play for all Americans.

Or so it seemed. There was, for a while, a Freedman's Bureau, and the gifted black catcher Fleet Walker played on the same teams with white men. But the bureau's promised "40 acres and a mule" and all they stood for never showed up, and when Chicago's towering slugger Cap Anson refused to step onto a field with Walker in the 1880s, organized baseball lined right up behind him. The tolerant curiosity of Reconstruction yielded to a sense of threat, and as victory in the Civil War was awarded to those who'd originally lost, a new and very white elite took hold again of baseball with a grip that we've only recently begun to loosen.

And so the dance continues. The all-American sport is still a monopoly, still a boy's club, yet with all the worst excesses of a free market gone mad. Baseball today exists in a business atmosphere where second-best seems fine as long as the money's right. We find ourselves tangled up in debates about designated hitter rules that let pitchers delegate their turn at bat to men who don't play in the field, and playoffs that can send a "wild card" team to the World Series even if it didn't win its division title. Bigger baseball is better baseball, right? Why not Super Size it? Have a monster home run off a third-rate pitcher who made it into the majors only because of overexpansion. These changes in the game, these debates and dissatisfactions, express the nature of America today and the continual, small vibrations in the tension between the individual and the group which both baseball and the Civil War embody.

Baseball and the Civil War have other things in common, things that make them of eternal interest to us. Both are feasts of details, full of the minutiae that make for wonderful hobbies. There's always something more to learn, some statistic or oddity that reconfirms and justifies our fascination. For many of us, our interests become passions, even escapes. Indeed, arcane battle plans and batting averages are much easier to master than everyday life, but hobbies and courses of interest do release some better part of ourselves that we believe has no place in our offices and stations. The challenge to those of us who split our time between office, home, and either battlefield park or ballpark is to bring that better—and, we hope, happier—part back with us, to turn the facts we uncover into explanations for why we are who we are today and how we can be better as a nation.

Baseball and the Civil War are also both very much about community. Even in these days of free agency and of team owners begging and threatening their cities for bigger and better stadiums, our baseball teams still represent our communities, like it or not, just as most Civil War regiments were made up of citizen-soldiers and represented their communities of origin. After the war, following the fortunes of our regiments blurred easily into following the fortunes of our teams, and even now millions of us use baseball and the Civil War as ways to define our communities, and to define ourselves within them. It's important to move past the scores and troop movements and remember these communities, to reenact not just a soldier, but a man from a place. Imagine his place, his time, and learn to see your own place and time from where he stands. Don't just examine baseball and watch baseball, but play baseball with your neighbors and your kids.

The Civil War and baseball are not essential to understanding America; they *are* America, and every journey into the game or the war is a journey of identity for any American. Instead of building battle dioramas and picking over statistical bones, let's use our passions for the Civil War and baseball as ways to learn about ourselves. That is the very information we need for the daily necessity of recreating our nation.

Thomas Dyja is the author of the novel Play for a Kingdom, *published by Harcourt Brace. The book recently won the Casey Award for Best Baseball Book. Dyja lives with his wife and two children in New York City.*

The New View of Reconstruction

Whatever you were taught or thought you knew about the post–Civil War
era is probably wrong in the light of recent study

Eric Foner

In the past twenty years, no period of American history has been the subject of a more thoroughgoing reevaluation than Reconstruction—the violent, dramatic, and still controversial era following the Civil War. Race relations, politics, social life, and economic change during Reconstruction have all been reinterpreted in the light of changed attitudes toward the place of blacks within American society. If historians have not yet forged a fully satisfying portrait of Reconstruction as a whole, the traditional interpretation that dominated historical writing for much of this century has irrevocably been laid to rest.

Anyone who attended high school before 1960 learned that Reconstruction was a era of unrelieved sordidness in American political and social life. The martyred Lincoln, according to this view, had planned a quick and painless readmission of the Southern states as equal members of the national family. President Andrew Johnson, his successor, attempted to carry out Lincoln's policies but was foiled by the Radical Republicans (also known as Vindictives or Jacobins). Motivated by an irrational hatred of Rebels or by ties with Northern capitalists out to plunder the South, the Radicals swept aside Johnson's lenient program and fastened black supremacy upon the defeated Confederacy. An orgy of corruption followed, presided over by unscrupulous carpetbaggers (Northerners who ventured south to reap the spoils of office), traitorous scalawags (Southern whites who cooperated with the new gov-

ernments for personal gain), and the ignorant and childlike freedmen, who were incapable of properly exercising the political power that had been thrust upon them. After much needless suffering, the white community of the South banded together to overthrow these "black" governments and restore home rule (their euphemism for white supremacy). All told, Reconstruction was just about the darkest page in the American saga.

Originating in anti-Reconstruction propaganda of Southern Democrats during the 1870s, this traditional interpretation achieved scholarly legitimacy around the turn of the century through the work of William Dunning and his students at Columbia University. It reached the larger public through films like *Birth of a Nation* and *Gone With the Wind* and that best-selling work of myth-making masquerading as history, *The Tragic Era* by Claude G. Bowers. In language as exaggerated as it was colorful, Bowers told how Andrew Johnson "fought the bravest battle for constitutional liberty and for the preservation of our institutions ever waged by an Executive" but was overwhelmed by the "poisonous propaganda" of the Radicals. Southern whites, as a result, "literally were put to the torture" by "emissaries of hate" who manipulated the "simple-minded" freedmen, inflaming the negroes' "egotism" and even inspiring "lustful assaults" by blacks upon white womanhood.

In a discipline that sometimes seems to pride itself on the rapid rise and fall of his-

torical interpretations, this traditional portrait of Reconstruction enjoyed remarkable staying power. The long reign of the old interpretation is not difficult to explain. It presented a set of easily identifiable heroes and villains. It enjoyed the imprimatur of the nation's leading scholars. And it accorded with the political and social realities of the first half of this century. This image of Reconstruction helped freeze the mind of the white South in unalterable opposition to any movement for breaching the ascendancy of the Democratic party, eliminating segregation, or readmitting disfranchised blacks to the vote.

Nevertheless, the demise of the traditional interpretation was inevitable, for it ignored the testimony of the central participant in the drama of Reconstruction—the black freedman. Furthermore, it was grounded in the conviction that blacks were unfit to share in political power. As Dunning's Columbia colleague John W. Burgess put it, "A black skin means membership in a race of men which has never of itself succeeded in subjecting passion to reason, has never, therefore, created any civilization of any kind." Once objective scholarship and modern experience rendered that assumption untenable, the entire edifice was bound to fall.

The work of "revising" the history of Reconstruction began with the writings of a handful of survivors of the era, such as John R. Lynch, who had served as a black congressman from Mississippi after the Civil War. In the 1930s white scholars like Francis Simkins and Robert Woody carried the task forward. Then, in 1935, the black historian and activist W. E. B. Du Bois produced *Black Reconstruction in America,* a monumental revaluation that closed with an irrefutable indictment of a historical profession that had sacrificed scholarly objectivity on the altar of racial bias. "One fact and one alone," he wrote, "explains the attitude of most recent writers toward Reconstruction; they cannot conceive of Negroes as men." Du Bois's work, however, was ignored by most historians.

Black initiative established as many schools as did Northern religious societies and the Freedmen's Bureau. The right to vote was not simply thrust upon them by meddling outsiders, since blacks began agitating for the suffrage as soon as they were freed.

It was not until the 1960s that the full force of the revisionist wave broke over the field. Then, in rapid succession, virtually every assumption of the traditional viewpoint was systematically dismantled. A drastically different portrait emerged to take its place. President Lincoln did not have a coherent "plan" for Reconstruction, but at the time of his assassination he had been cautiously contemplating black suffrage. Andrew Johnson was a stubborn, racist politician who lacked the ability to compromise. By isolating himself from the broad currents of public opinion that had nourished Lincoln's career, Johnson created an impasse with Congress that Lincoln would certainly have avoided, thus throwing away his political power and destroying his own plans for reconstructing the South.

The Radicals in Congress were acquitted of both vindictive motives and the charge of serving as the stalking-horses of Northern capitalism. They emerged instead as idealists in the best nineteenth-century reform tradition. Radical leaders like Charles Sumner and Thaddeus Stevens had worked for the rights of blacks long before any conceivable political ad-

NEW YORK PUBLIC LIBRARY, PRINT ROOM

Until recently, Thaddeus Stevens had been viewed as motivated by irrational hatred of the Rebels (above). Now he has emerged as an idealist in the best reform tradition.

LIBRARY OF CONGRESS

vantage flowed from such a commitment. Stevens refused to sign the Pennsylvania Constitution of 1838 because it disfranchised the state's black citizens; Sumner led a fight in the 1850s to integrate Boston's public schools. Their Reconstruction policies were based on principle, not petty

political advantage, for the central issue dividing Johnson and these Radical Republicans was the civil rights of freedmen. Studies of congressional policy-making, such as Eric L. McKitrick's *Andrew Johnson and Reconstruction,* also revealed that Reconstruction legislation, ranging from the Civil Rights Act of 1866 to the Fourteenth and Fifteenth Amendments, enjoyed broad support from moderate and conservative Republicans. It was not simply the work of a narrow radical faction.

Even more startling was the revised portrait of Reconstruction in the South itself. Imbued with the spirit of the civil rights movement and rejecting entirely the racial assumptions that had underpinned the traditional interpretation, these historians evaluated Reconstruction from the black point of view. Works like Joel Williamson's *After Slavery* portrayed the period as a time of extraordinary political, social, and economic progress for blacks. The establishment of public school systems, the granting of equal citizenship to blacks, the effort to restore the devastated Southern economy, the attempt to construct an interracial political democracy from the ashes of slavery, all these were commendable achievements, not the elements of Bowers's "tragic era."

Unlike earlier writers, the revisionists stressed the active role of the freedmen in shaping Reconstruction. Black initiative established as many schools as did Northern religious societies and the Freedmen's Bureau. The right to vote was not simply thrust upon them by meddling outsiders, since blacks began agitating for the suffrage as soon as they were freed. In 1865 black conventions throughout the South issued eloquent, though unheeded, appeals for equal civil and political rights.

With the advent of Radical Reconstruction in 1867, the freedmen did enjoy a real measure of political power. But black supremacy never existed. In most states blacks held only a small fraction of political offices, and even in South Carolina, where they comprised a majority of the state legislature's lower house, effective power remained in white hands. As for corruption, moral standards in both government and private enterprise were at low ebb throughout the nation in the postwar years—the era of Boss Tweed, the Credit Mobilier scandal, and the Whiskey Ring. Southern corruption could hardly be blamed on former slaves.

Reconstruction governments were portrayed as disastrous failures because elected blacks were ignorant or corrupt.
In fact, postwar corruption cannot be blamed on former slaves.

Other actors in the Reconstruction drama also came in for reevaluation. Most carpetbaggers were former Union soldiers seeking economic opportunity in the post-war South, not unscrupulous adventurers. Their motives, a typically American amalgam of humanitarianism and the pursuit of profit, were no more insidious than those of Western pioneers. Scalawags, previously seen as traitors to the white race, now emerged as "Old Line" Whig Unionists who had opposed secession in the first place or as poor whites who had long resented planters' domination of Southern life and who saw in Reconstruction a chance to recast Southern society along more democratic lines. Strongholds of Southern white Republicanism like east Tennessee and western North Carolina had been the scene of resistance to Confederate rule throughout the Civil War; now, as one scalawag newspaper put it, the choice was "between salvation at the hand of the Negro or destruction at the hand of the rebels."

At the same time, the Ku Klux Klan and kindred groups, whose campaign of violence against black and white Republicans had been minimized or excused in older writings, were portrayed as they really were. Earlier scholars had conveyed the impression that the Klan intimidated blacks mainly by dressing as ghosts and playing on the freedmen's superstitions. In fact, black fears were all too real: the Klan was a terrorist organization that beat and killed its political opponents to deprive blacks of their newly won rights. The complicity of the Democratic party and the silence of prominent whites in the face of such outrages stood as an indictment of the moral code the South had inherited from the days of slavery.

> *Under slavery most blacks had lived in nuclear family units, although they faced the constant threat of separation from loved ones by sale. Reconstruction provided the opportunity for blacks to solidify their preexisting family ties.*

By the end of the 1960s, then, the old interpretation had been completely reversed. Southern freedmen were the heroes, the "Redeemers" who overthrew Reconstruction were the villains, and if the era was "tragic," it was because change did not go far enough. Reconstruction had been a time of real progress and its failure a lost opportunity for the South and the nation. But the legacy of Reconstruction—the Fourteenth and Fifteenth Amendments—endured to inspire future efforts for civil rights. As Kenneth Stampp wrote in *The Era of Reconstruction,* a superb summary of revisionist findings published in 1965, "if it was worth four years of civil war to save the Union, it was worth a few years of radical reconstruction to give the American Negro the ultimate promise of equal civil and political rights."

As Stampp's statement suggests, the reevaluation of the first Reconstruction was inspired in large measure by the impact of the second—the modern civil rights movement. And with the waning of that movement in recent years, writing on Reconstruction has undergone still another transformation. Instead of seeing the Civil War and its aftermath as a second American Revolution (as Charles Beard had), a regression into barbarism (as Bowers argued), or a golden opportunity squandered (as the revisionists saw it), recent writers argue that Radical Reconstruction was not really very radical. Since land was not distributed to the former slaves, the remained economically dependent upon their former owners. The planter class survived both the war and Reconstruction with its property (apart from slaves) and prestige more or less intact.

Not only changing times but also the changing concerns of historians have contributed to this latest reassessment of Reconstruction. The hallmark of the past decade's historical writing has been an emphasis upon "social history"—the evocation of the past lives of ordinary Americans—and the downplaying of strictly political events. When applied to Reconstruction, this concern with the "social" suggested that black suffrage and officeholding, once seen as the most radical departures of the Reconstruction era, were relatively insignificant.

The Civil War raised the decisive questions of American's national existence: the relations between local and national authority, the definition of citizenship, the balance between force and consent in generating obedience to authority.

Recent historians have focused their investigations not upon the politics of Reconstruction but upon the social and economic aspects of the transition from slavery to freedom. Herbert Gutman's influential study of the black family during and after slavery found little change in family structure or relations between men and women resulting from emancipation. Under slavery most blacks had lived in nuclear family units, although they faced the constant threat of separation from loved ones by sale. Reconstruction provided the opportunity for blacks to solidify their preexisting family ties. Conflicts over whether black women should work in the cotton fields (planters said yes, many black families said no) and over white attempts to "apprentice" black children revealed that the autonomy of family life was a major preoccupation of the freedmen. Indeed, whether manifested in their withdrawal from churches controlled by whites, in the blossoming of black fraternal, benevolent, and self-improvement organizations, or in the demise of the slave quarters and their replacement by small tenant farms occupied by individual families, the quest for independence from white authority and control over their own day-to-day lives shaped the black response to emancipation.

In the post–Civil War South the surest guarantee of economic autonomy, blacks believed, was land. To the freedmen the justice of a claim to land based on their years of unrequited labor appeared self-evident. As an Alabama black convention put it, "The property which they [the planters] hold was nearly all earned by the sweat of *our* brows." As Leon Litwack showed in *Been in the Storm So Long,* a Pulitzer Prize–winning account of the black response to emancipation, many freedmen in 1865 and 1866 refused to sign labor contracts, expecting the federal government to give them land. In some localities, as one Alabama overseer reported, they "set up claims to the plantation and all on it."

In the end, of course, the vast majority of Southern blacks remained propertyless and poor. But exactly why the South, and especially its black population, suffered from dire poverty and economic retardation in the decades following the Civil War is a matter of much dispute. In *One Kind of Freedom* economists Roger Ransom and Richard Sutch indicted country merchants for monopolizing credit and charging usurious interest rates, forcing black tenants into debt and locking the South into a dependence on cotton production that impoverished the entire region. But Jonathan Wiener, in his study of postwar Alabama, argued that planters used their political power to compel blacks to remain on the plantations. Planters succeeded in stabilizing the plantation system, but only by blocking the growth of alternative enterprises, like factories, that might draw off black laborers, thus locking the region into a pattern of economic backwardness.

If the thrust of recent writing has emphasized the social and economic aspects of Reconstruction, politics has not been entirely neglected. But political studies have also reflected the postrevisionist mood summarized by C. Vann Woodward when he observed "how essentially nonrevolutionary and conservative Reconstruction really was." Recent writers, unlike their revisionist predecessors, have found little to praise in federal policy toward the emancipated blacks.

A new sensitivity to the strength of prejudice and laissez-faire ideas in the nineteenth-century North has led many historians to doubt whether the Republican party ever made a genuine commitment to racial justice in the South. The granting of black suffrage was an alternative to a long-term federal responsibility for protecting the rights of the former slaves. Once enfranchised, blacks could be left to fend for themselves. With the exception of a few Radicals like Thaddeus Stevens, nearly all Northern policy-makers and educators are criticized today for assuming that, so long as the unfettered operations of the market-place afforded blacks the opportunity to advance through diligent labor, federal efforts to assist them in acquiring land were unnecessary.

Probably the most innovative recent writing on Reconstruction politics has centered on a broad reassessment of black Republicanism, largely undertaken by a new generation of black historians. Scholars like Thomas Holt and Nell Painter insist that Reconstruction was not simply a matter of black and white. Conflicts within the black community, no less than divisions among whites, shaped Reconstruction politics. Where revisionist scholars, both black and white, had celebrated the accomplishments of black political leaders, Holt, Painter, and others charge that they failed to address the economic plight of the black masses. Painter criticized "representative colored men," as national black leaders were called, for failing to provide ordinary freedmen with effective political leadership. Holt found that black officeholders in South Carolina most emerged from the old free mulatto class of Charleston, which shared many assumptions with prominent whites. "Basically bourgeois in their origins and orientation," he wrote, they "failed to act in the interest of black peasants."

In emphasizing the persistence from slavery of divisions between free blacks and slaves, these writers reflect the increasing concern with continuity and conservatism in Reconstruction. Their work reflects a startling extension of revisionist premises. If, as has been argued for the past twenty years, blacks were active agents rather than mere victims of manipulation, then they could not be absolved of blame for the ultimate failure of Reconstruction.

Despite the excellence of recent writings and the continual expansion of our knowledge of the period, historians of Reconstruction today face a unique dilemma. An old interpretation has been overthrown, but a coherent new synthesis has yet to take its place. The revisionists of the 1960s effectively established a series of negative points: the Reconstruction governments were not as bad as had been portrayed, black supremacy was a myth, the Radicals were not cynical manipulators of the freedmen. Yet no convincing overall portrait of the quality of political and social life emerged from their writings. More recent historians have rightly pointed to elements of continuity that spanned the nineteenth-century Southern experience, especially the survival, in modified form, of the plantation system. Nevertheless, by denying the real changes that did occur, they have failed to provide a convincing portrait of an era characterized above all by drama, turmoil, and social change.

COURTESY OF THE ATLANTA *Constitution*

Some scholars exalted the motives of the Ku Klux Klan (above). Actually, its members were part of a terrorist organization that beat and killed its political opponents to deprive blacks of their rights.

RUTHERFORD B. HAYES LIBRARY, FREMONT, OHIO

Building upon the findings of the past twenty years of scholarship, a new portrait of Reconstruction ought to begin by viewing it not as a specific time period, bounded by the years 1865 and 1877, but as an episode in a prolonged historical process—American society's adjustment to the consequences of the Civil War and emancipation. The Civil War, of course, raised the decisive questions of America's national existence: the relations between local and national authority, the definition of citizenship, the balance between force and consent in generating obedience to authority. The war and Reconstruction, as Allan Nevins observed over fifty years ago, marked the "emergence of modern America." This was the era of the completion of the national railroad network, the creation of the modern steel industry, the conquest of the West and final subduing of the Indians, and the expansion of the mining frontier. Lincoln's America—the world of the small farm and artisan shop—gave way to a rapidly industrializing economy. The issues that galvanized postwar Northern politics—from the question of the greenback currency to the mode of paying holders of the national debt—arose from the economic changes unleased by the Civil War.

Above all, the war irrevocably abolished slavery. Since 1619, when "twenty negars" disembarked from a Dutch ship in Virginia, racial injustice had haunted American life, mocking its professed ideals even as tobacco and cotton, the products of slave labor, helped finance the nation's economic development. Now the implications of the black presence could no longer be ignored. The Civil War resolved the problem of slavery but, as the Philadelphia diarist Sydney George Fisher observed in June 1865, it opened an even more intractable problem: "What shall we do with the Negro?" Indeed, he went on, this was a problem "*incapable* of any solution that will satisfy both North and South."

As Fisher realized, the focal point of Reconstruction was the social revolution known as emancipation. Plantation slavery was simultaneously a system of labor, a form of racial domination, and the foundation upon which arose a distinctive ruling class within the South. Its demise threw open the most fundamental questions of economy, society, and politics. A new system of labor, social, racial, and political relations had to be created to replace slavery.

The United States was not the only nation to experience emancipation in the nineteenth century. Neither plantation sla-

very nor abolition were unique to the United States. But Reconstruction was. In a comparative perspective Radical Reconstruction stands as a remarkable experiment, the only effort of a society experiencing abolition to bring the former slaves within the umbrella of equal citizenship. Because the Radicals did not achieve everything they wanted, historians have lately tended to play down the stunning departure represented by black suffrage and officeholding. Former slaves, most fewer than two years removed from bondage, debated the fundamental questions of the polity: what is a republican form of government? Should the state provide equal education for all? How could political equality be reconciled with a society in which property was so unequally distributed? There was something inspiring in the way such men met the challenge of Reconstruction. "I knew nothing more than to obey my master," James K. Greene, an Alabama black politician later recalled. "But the tocsin of freedom sounded and knocked at the door and we walked out like free men and we met the exigencies as they grew up, and shouldered the responsibilities."

You never saw a people more excited on the subject of politics than are the negroes of the south," one planter observed in 1867. And there were more than a few Southern whites as well who in these years shook off the prejudices of the past to embrace the revision of a new South dedicated to the principles of equal citizenship and social justice. One ordinary South Carolinian expressed the new sense of possibility in 1868 to the Republican governor of the state: "I am sorry that I cannot write an elegant stiled letter to your excellency. But I rejoice to think that God almighty has given to the poor of S.C. a Gov. to hear to feel to protect the humble poor without distinction to race or color.... I am a native borned S.C. a poor man never owned a Negro in my life nor my father before me.... Remember the true and loyal are the poor of the whites and blacks, outside of these you can find none loyal."

Few modern scholars believe the Reconstruction governments established in the South in 1867 and 1868 fulfilled the aspirations of their humble constituents. While their achievements in such realms as education, civil rights, and the economic rebuilding of the South are now widely appreciated, historians today believe they failed to affect either the economic plight of the emancipated slave or the ongoing transformation of independent white farmers into cotton tenants. Yet their opponents did perceive the Reconstruction governments in precisely this way—as representatives of a revolution that had put the bottom rail, both racial and economic, on top. This perception helps explain the ferocity of the attacks leveled against them and the pervasiveness of violence in the post-emancipation South.

> *In the end neither the abolition of slavery nor Reconstruction succeeded in resolving the debate over the meaning of freedom in American life.*

The spectacle of black men voting and holding office was anathema to large numbers of Southern whites. Even more disturbing, at least in the view of those who still controlled the plantation regions of the South, was the emergence of local officials, black and white, who sympathized with the plight of the black laborer. Alabama's vagrancy law was a "dead letter" in 1870, "because those who are charged with its enforcement are indebted to the vagrant vote for their offices and emoluments." Political debates over the level and incidence of taxation, the control of crops, and the resolution of contract disputes revealed that a primary issue of Reconstruction was the role of government in a plantation society. During presidential Reconstruction, and after "Redemption," with planters and their allies in control of politics, the law emerged as a means of stabilizing and promoting the plantation system. If Radical Reconstruction failed to redistribute the land of the South, the ouster of the planter class from control of politics at least ensured that the sanctions of the criminal law would not be employed to discipline the black labor force.

An understanding of this fundamental conflict over the relation between government and society helps explain the pervasive complaints concerning corruption and "extravagance" during Radical Reconstruction. Corruption there was aplenty; tax rates did rise sharply. More significant than the rate of taxation, however, was the change in its incidence. For the first time, planters and white farmers had to pay a significant portion of their income to the government, while propertyless blacks often escaped scot-free. Several states, moreover, enacted heavy taxes on uncultivated land to discourage land speculation and force land onto the market, benefiting, it was hoped, the freedmen.

As time passed, complaints about the "extravagance" and corruption of Southern governments found a sympathetic audience among influential Northerners. The Democratic charge that universal suffrage in the South was responsible for high taxes and governmental extravagance coincided with a rising conviction among the urban middle classes of the North that city government had to be taken out of the hands of the immigrant poor and returned to the "best men"—the educated, professional, financially independent citizens unable to exert much political influence at a time of mass parties and machine politics. Increasingly the "respectable" middle classes began to retreat from the very notion of universal suffrage. The poor were not longer perceived as honest producers, the backbone of the social order; now they became the "dangerous classes," the "mob." As the historian Francis Parkman put it, too much power rested with "masses of imported ignorance and hereditary ineptitude." To Parkman the Irish of the Northern cities and the blacks of the South were equally incapable of utilizing the ballot: "Witness the municipal corruptions of New York, and the monstrosities of negro rule in South Carolina." Such attitudes helped to justify Northern inaction as, one by one, the Reconstruction regimes of the South were overthrown by political violence.

In the end, then, neither the abolition of slavery nor Reconstruction succeeded in resolving the debate over the meaning of freedom in American life. Twenty years before the American Civil War, writing about the prospect of abolition in France's colonies, Alexis de Tocqueville had written, "If the Negroes have the right to become free, the [planters] have the incontestable right not to be ruined by the Negroes' freedom." And in the United States, as in nearly every plantation society that experienced the end of slavery, a rigid social and political dichotomy between former master and former slave, an ideology of racism, and a dependent labor force with limited economic opportunities all survived abolition. Unless one means by freedom the simple fact of not being a slave, emancipation thrust blacks into a kind of no-man's land, a partial freedom that made a mockery of the American ideal of equal citizenship.

Yet by the same token the ultimate outcome underscores the uniqueness of Reconstruction itself. Alone among the societies that abolished slavery in the nineteenth century, the United States, for a moment, offered the freedmen a measure of political control over their own destinies. However brief its sway, Reconstruction allowed scope for a remarkable political and social mobilization of the black community. It opened doors of opportunity that could never be completely closed. Reconstruction transformed the lives of Southern blacks in ways unmeasurable by statistics and unreachable by law. It raised their expectations and aspirations, redefined their status in relation to the larger society, and allowed space for the creation of institutions that enabled them to survive the repression that followed. And it established constitutional principles of civil and political equality that, while flagrantly violated after Redemption, planted the seeds of future struggle.

Certainly, in terms of the sense of possibility with which it opened, Reconstruction failed. But as Du Bois observed, it was a "splendid failure." For its animating vision—a society in which social advancement would be open to all on the basis of individual merit, not inherited caste distinctions—is as old as America itself and remains relevant to a nation still grappling with the unresolved legacy of emancipation.

Eric Foner is Professor of History at Columbia University and author of Nothing but Freedom: Emancipation and Its Legacy.

Index

Index

Test Your Knowledge Form

We encourage you to photocopy and use this page as a tool to assess how the articles in *Annual Editions* expand on the information in your textbook. By reflecting on the articles you will gain enhanced text information. You can also access this useful form on a product's book support Web site at *http://www.dushkin.com/online/*.

NAME: _____   DATE: _____

TITLE AND NUMBER OF ARTICLE: _____

BRIEFLY STATE THE MAIN IDEA OF THIS ARTICLE: _____

_____

LIST THREE IMPORTANT FACTS THAT THE AUTHOR USES TO SUPPORT THE MAIN IDEA:

_____

WHAT INFORMATION OR IDEAS DISCUSSED IN THIS ARTICLE ARE ALSO DISCUSSED IN YOUR TEXTBOOK OR OTHER READINGS THAT YOU HAVE DONE? LIST THE TEXTBOOK CHAPTERS AND PAGE NUMBERS:

_____

LIST ANY EXAMPLES OF BIAS OR FAULTY REASONING THAT YOU FOUND IN THE ARTICLE:

_____

LIST ANY NEW TERMS/CONCEPTS THAT WERE DISCUSSED IN THE ARTICLE, AND WRITE A SHORT DEFINITION:

We Want Your Advice

ANNUAL EDITIONS revisions depend on two major opinion sources: one is our Advisory Board, listed in the front of this volume, which works with us in scanning the thousands of articles published in the public press each year; the other is you—the person actually using the book. Please help us and the users of the next edition by completing the prepaid article rating form on this page and returning it to us. Thank you for your help!

ANNUAL EDITIONS: American History, Volume I, 17th Edition

ARTICLE RATING FORM

Here is an opportunity for you to have direct input into the next revision of this volume.
We would like you to rate each of the articles listed below, using the following scale:

1. **Excellent: should definitely be retained**
2. **Above average: should probably be retained**
3. **Below average: should probably be deleted**
4. **Poor: should definitely be deleted**

Your ratings will play a vital part in the next revision.
Please mail this prepaid form to us as soon as possible.
Thanks for your help!

RATING	ARTICLE	RATING	ARTICLE
	1. 1491		36. The New View of Reconstruction
	2. A "Newfounde Lande"		
	3. Laboring in the Fields of the Lord		
	4. Pocahontas		
	5. The Pueblo Revolt		
	6. Bearing the Burden? Puritan Wives		
	7. Penning a Legacy		
	8. The Right to Marry: *Loving v. Virginia*		
	9. Baptism of Fire		
	10. Flora MacDonald		
	11. Jefferson's Secret Life		
	12. Making Sense of the Fourth of July		
	13. George Washington, Spymaster		
	14. Founders Chic: Live From Philadelphia		
	15. Founding Friendship: Washington, Madison and the Creation of the American Republic		
	16. Your Constitution Is Killing You		
	17. Do the People Rule?		
	18. The Whiskey Rebellion		
	19. 1796: The First Real Election		
	20. Lewis and Clark: Trailblazers Who Opened the Continent		
	21. Chief Justice Marshall Takes the Law in Hand		
	22. Rebecca Lukens: Woman of Iron		
	23. Andrew Jackson Versus the Cherokee Nation		
	24. "All Men & Women Are Created Equal"		
	25. The Lives of Slave Women		
	26. William W. Brown		
	27. The Father of American Terrorism		
	28. "The Doom of Slavery": Ulysses S. Grant, War Aims, and Emancipation, 1861–1863		
	29. Coffee, Bibles & Wooden Legs: The YMCA Goes to War		
	30. A Gallant Rush for Glory		
	31. A Yankee Scarlett O'Hara in Atlanta		
	32. Between Honor and Glory		
	33. Jefferson Davis and the Jews		
	34. Lincoln Takes the Heat		
	35. Bats, Balls, and Bullets		

(Continued on next page)

NO POSTAGE
NECESSARY
IF MAILED
IN THE
UNITED STATES

BUSINESS REPLY MAIL
FIRST-CLASS MAIL PERMIT NO. 84 GUILFORD CT

POSTAGE WILL BE PAID BY ADDRESSEE

McGraw-Hill/Dushkin
530 Old Whitfield Street
Guilford, Ct 06437-9989

ABOUT YOU

Name   Date
_____   _____

Are you a teacher? ❑   A student? ❑
Your school's name
_____

Department
_____

Address   City   State   Zip
_____

School telephone #
_____

YOUR COMMENTS ARE IMPORTANT TO US!

Please fill in the following information:
For which course did you use this book?
_____

Did you use a text with this ANNUAL EDITION? ❑ yes ❑ no
What was the title of the text?
_____

What are your general reactions to the *Annual Editions* concept?
_____

Have you read any pertinent articles recently that you think should be included in the next edition? Explain.
_____

Are there any articles that you feel should be replaced in the next edition? Why?
_____

Are there any World Wide Web sites that you feel should be included in the next edition? Please annotate.
_____

May we contact you for editorial input? ❑ yes ❑ no
May we quote your comments? ❑ yes ❑ no